Understanding Minority-Serving Institutions

Understanding Minority-Serving Institutions

Edited by

Marybeth Gasman
Benjamin Baez
Caroline Sotello Viernes Turner

With a Foreword by

Walter R. Allen

STATE UNIVERSITY OF NEW YORK PRESS

Cover images:
"Brown Hall" (at Tougaloo), courtesy of Mr. Bruce Thomas.
"White Earth Community College," courtesy of
White Earth Community College.
"Fond Du Lac Tribal and Community College," courtesy of
Tom Urbanski, Director of Public Information.

"Dillard University" courtesy of Dillard University.

Published by
State University of New York Press, Albany

Published in the United States of America

For information, contact State University of New York Press, Albany, NY
www.sunypress.edu

Production by Judith Block and Marilyn Semerad
Marketing by Michael Campochiaro

Library of Congress Cataloging-in-Publication Data

Understanding minority-serving institutions / edited by Marybeth Gasman, Benjamin Baez, Caroline Sotello Viernes Turner ; foreword by Walter R. Allen.
p. cm.
Includes bibliographical references and index.
ISBN 978-0-7914-7359-7 (hardcover : alk. paper) —
ISBN 978-0-7914- 7360-3 (pbk. : alk. paper)
1. minorities—Education (Higher)—United States.
I. Gasman, Marybeth.
II. Baez, Benjamin.
III. Turner, Caroline Sotello Viernes.
LC3731.U526 2008
378.7308900973—dc22 2007035449

10 9 8 7 6 5 4 3 2 1

For Berta Vigil Laden

1943–2006

Contents

Part II
Context-Specific Trends and Challenges

ILLUSTRATIONS

Figures

Tables

FOREWORD

Walter R. Allen

Minority-Serving Institutions (MSIs) of higher education are a uniquely American creation. These institutions are best understood in the context formed by the racial-ethnic milieu revealed in the United States past and present. The United States is unique in the world's history, representing the only democracy founded on racial slavery. Students of the U.S. Constitution, our founding document, celebrate the soaring *Enlightenment Age* language which privileged individual rights and freedoms, granting the common man previously denied human dignity. However, in the ultimate contradiction, this landmark document also, at one and the same time, ensconced protections for legalized traffic in human slaves. Black people were defined as three-fifths human; stripped of all legal, constitutional, and human rights protections; and condemned to lives of unremitting humiliation and brutality as chattel slaves. In other aspects, the Constitution also stripped away or strictly limited the rights of women, non-propertied White males, Native Americans, Latinos and Asians. Written into the U.S. Constitution and/or interpreted as law were provisions that denied women the vote; stole the property of Native Americans and Japanese Americans; and denied native-born Mexican Americans citizenship rights. So it was this remarkable document, the U.S. Constitution and the magnificent national experiment it created, The United States of America, that would come to embody and be haunted by contradictions inherent in the conflicting ideals of the Enlightenment and of White Racial Superiority.

Minority-Serving Institutions of higher learning exist at the intersection where the American Dream of unbridled possibilities meets the American

Nightmare of persistent racial-ethnic subordination. In a society that claimed to grant all the rights of liberty and the pursuit of happiness, which promised that Big Dreams could be achieved by simple people through ability, vision, and hard work, it stands to reason education would become a critical vehicle for social mobility. Moreover, at its founding, this nation self-consciously declared its break with the past order of superstition and inherent privilege to embrace a new world founded on human reason and earned status. Not surprisingly, this new nation experienced a literal explosion of educational institutions—from elementary to secondary schools, from colleges to universities. Churches, state, and federal government, private foundations, and independent organizations linked national progress and the realization of the American Dream to expansion of opportunities for education at all levels. Over the country's history, the proliferation of colleges and universities reflects in simplest terms our national belief in the transformative power of education, especially higher education. We have committed to the ideal that education would set us free, overcoming barriers of prejudice, discrimination, and inequality.

Racial mores and structures shaped the evolution of U.S. higher education. The greatest expansion in opportunities for higher education consistently privileged Whites, particularly White males, since they were the dominant group in terms of power, prestige, and privilege. At various historical points, colleges or universities were founded to specifically serve excluded populations such as Native Americans, women or Blacks. Interestingly, over time colleges and universities were also founded to bring higher education within the reach of poor Whites, Whites in rural areas, and Whites who were ethno-nationally identified. Nevertheless, from the earliest days of the Republic to the present, Whites have been the major benefactors of a national higher educational system which has come to be the envy of the world.

Colleges and universities with significant enrollments of students from racial-ethnic minority backgrounds have not received sufficient attention from scholars and policy makers. As a result, our knowledge about the purposes, organization, outcomes, and future of Minority-Serving Institutions of higher education continues to be somewhat limited. The changing face of American society has implications for participation in higher education generally, but this is especially so for higher education institutions serving more students from racial-ethnic minority backgrounds. What we do know is that Minority-Serving Institutions have played critical roles in the expansion of access to higher education for underrepresented racial ethnic minorities such as Blacks, Latinos, Native Americans, and some Asian Pacific Islander groups. It is also clear these institutions make substantial contributions to the enrollment of other Asian American groups who are not necessarily underrepresented in higher education.

This groundbreaking volume expands our knowledge and understanding of Minority-Serving Institutions of higher education. Part I examines the historical, social, and cultural foundations of these institutions. We discover how shared experiences (e.g., patterns of discrimination against racial-ethnic minorities) combined with distinctive, unique elements (e.g., treaties between Native American nations and the U.S. government) to create MSIs. A detailed summary overviews selected historical, institutional, and student characteristics from research about MSIs. Equally revealing is the thoughtful examination of the asymmetrical power exercised by majority, mainstream institutions of higher learning in naming and subordinating MSIs.

The complex set of factors that contributed to the formation and evolution of MSIs provide an important backdrop for part II of the volume, which examines the broad range of MSIs across multiple, specific contexts. Attention is given to MSIs commonly ignored in research and discourse, such as Deaf-Serving Institutions, Tribal Colleges and Universities (TCUs), and Asian American and Pacific Islander (AAPI) serving institutions. We are also introduced to topics as varied as Faculty Development and Governance in Historically Black Colleges and Universities (HBCUs); the effects of race neutral policy on Latino enrollment in Public Higher Education; and predictors of academic success for Latino males in Community Colleges.

The final section of the volume offers rich comparative analyses across and within MSIs. The social justice orientation of Hispanic-Serving and historically Black institutions as revealed in mission statements and administrative statements is examined. In the next instance, faculty attitudes and practices toward teaching Latino, Black and American Indian undergraduates are explored. Other chapters study coalition formation among Minority-Serving Institutions; aspects of student engagement and academic success; and the challenges faced by MSIs in securing and maintaining accreditation from regional associations.

In sum, this volume introduces readers to various aspects of Minority-Serving Institutions. The task before the authors is to reframe the discourse on MSIs. In the process, they challenge how we think about U.S. higher and postsecondary education as an enterprise. Minority-Serving Institutions serve constituencies who are mostly first-generation college goers; who are poor; who have weaker academic backgrounds; and who are members of discriminated racial-ethnic minority groups. At the same time, we see the definition and reality of MSIs morphing and changing, driven by changes in American immigration and demographic patterns. The diversity of MSIs defies simple categorization, including small colleges and large, state universities; HBCUs and TCUs; first-generation, new immigrant students; and students from families with five generations of college degree holders. We are also challenged to see beyond empty rhetoric that applauds individual, institutional, and social diversity even as combined social, historical, and cultural factors continue to ensure extreme serious underrepresentation of the students served by MSIs.

This volume raises important questions and offers thoughtful answers. As such, the volume is a must read for scholars, policy makers, and practitioners who are interested in expanding college access and success for underrepresented racial-ethnic minorities. It has been said the truest measure of a society is to be found in how it treats those on the periphery, who live in the shadows, and who are disadvantaged. Similarly, the circumstances of MSIs and the students they serve reveal much about the true nature of higher education in America. Rhetoric aside, will this society commit to expanded opportunities that will make the American Dream more reality than illusion? Or will the society continue to embrace attitudes and practices that deny these opportunities to all but a select few? How our nation answers these questions is a prelude to the future which awaits. If we are wise, that future will emphasize investments in education, knowing the returns will be magnified many times over.

Acknowledgments

The idea for this book sprung from Committee L of the American Association of University Professors (AAUP). Committee L is dedicated to issues pertaining to Historically Black Colleges and Universities and Faculty of Color. We are grateful to AAUP for bringing the three of us together during an annual meeting to hash out ideas for this book. Ann Springer, in particular, was encouraging and helpful during the early brainstorming sessions related to this book. More recently, we are grateful to Julie Schmid for her assistance to Committee L. The authors in this book deserve credit for their innovative work and adherence to deadlines. We are thankful to each of the authors for their pleasant response to feedback and for their thoroughness. Likewise, the anonymous reviewers, editors, and production staff at State University of New York Press have been supportive, encouraging us to move forward with this book. Those Minority-Serving Institutions that participated in the various research studies in this book deserve thanks for their efforts. The work that they do on a daily basis to educate our nation's next generation of scholars and leaders is highly commendable. We are honored and humbled that Walter R. Allen agreed to write the foreword for this book. Each of us has admired Professor Allen for years, and we are thrilled to have his support for this endeavor. This edited volume would not have come together without the assistance of research assistants at the University of Pennsylvania, including: Noah D. Drezner, Julie Vultaggio, Christopher Tudico, Katherine V. Sedgwick and Pamela Felder Thompson. We would also each like to thank our family, colleagues, and friends for their support and encouragement over the years. Lastly, we dedicate this book to Berta Vigil Laden who dedicated her scholarly career to studying issues of race, equity, and social justice. We are proud to have her as an author in this edited volume.

PART I

The Foundations of Minority-Serving Institutions

CHAPTER 1

On Minority-Serving Institutions

Benjamin Baez, Marybeth Gasman, and Caroline Sotello Viernes Turner

To say that African American, Hispanic or Latino/a, and Native American students participate (and succeed) in higher education in disproportionately lower numbers than White or Asian-American students is to offer what can only be called a "truism." We know this to be the case, and we have pretty good ideas about why this is so. We know most of these students are first-generation college attendees; they often come from poor and low-income households; they can barely afford postsecondary education; they attend poor, segregated public schools; and they experience hostility and unsupportive environments at many historically (HWIs) and predominantly White institutions (PWIs). We also know, almost as well, that racial and ethnic minorities are disproportionately represented in the small number of institutions denoted by the term "Minority-Serving Institutions" (MSIs). MSIs traditionally include historically Black colleges and universities (HBCUs), Hispanic-Serving Institutions (HSIs), Tribal colleges and universities (TCUs) and more recently Asian American and Pacific Islander Serving Institutions (AAPIs). Indeed, one may say that but for MSIs, many students of color would have a significantly lower chance of attaining postsecondary education. The importance of MSIs to higher education, nay, to society, therefore, cannot be underestimated by anyone.

The importance and strengths of MSIs derive primarily from their collective missions to educate and graduate students from underrepresented groups, the culturally sensitive programs they provide those students, and the public service they perform for their racial and ethnic communities. MSIs, perhaps more than PWIs, may see social justice as their raison d'etre. Yet, after having said this, we can say that we know very little about MSIs. Currently much has been written about HBCUs. Given the history of race in this country, many studies of HBCUs are thus historical. The problem is that such histories tend to give general overviews of HBCUs as a collective category and thus tend to treat these institutions monolithically. There have been few attempts to systematically review research on MSIs to determine the state of the field. But, much of the current research is only marginally enlightening, amounting to what we call "catalogue-type" information such as descriptive statistics and narratives about "heroes." Other than histories of particular institutions, few empirical studies of HBCUs exist in the literature, and there is almost no scholarship on HSIs, TCUs, and the even more invisible Asian American and Pacific Islander Serving Institutions. We offer in this book empirical studies of college students, staff, and faculty at MSIs, and thus contribute to a growing literature on these institutions.

Furthermore, most scholars have tended to treat each institutional-type independently of one other, without seeking to explain how these institutions both compete with and support each other. We think little has been done to provide valuable knowledge about MSIs in a way that highlights the relationships between MSIs. Economic and political forces have an impact on different types of MSIs differently, of course, but do such forces also have an impact on MSIs in similar but as yet not fully understood ways? Only with such significant research about MSIs, and their interconnections with each other and with PWIs, can one effectively advocate for their continued support. One primary goal of this book, therefore, is to promote such advocacy by offering research and scholarship that has been sorely missing in the literature on higher education. We think such advocacy cannot take place without also pointing to the interconnectedness of MSIs, as the authors in the last section of the book do. Our hope in advocating this interconnectedness is to dispel the idea that funding must take place as the "competitive" zero-sum game that currently shapes how many of these institutions interact with each other.

Highlighting the interconnectedness of MSIs is important not only because it can help MSIs form coalitions that can press state and federal governments for more funding, but also because this interconnectedness exposes a cultural/political phenomenon common to all. The right-wing backlash against affirmative action will make MSIs even more critical to the success of minority students. In addition to successful litigation against the Universities of Texas, Georgia, and Michigan, and public-policy initiatives prohibiting the use of race in admissions and employment in California, Michigan, and Washington, conservatives have also felt empowered to challenge not only college-admissions policies, but also all kinds of race-conscious practices that seek to narrow the gap between underrepresented and overrepresented ethnic and racial groups. For example, conservative groups, such as the Center for Equal Opportunity, with the help of the conservative regime in the federal government and its allies in state attorneys offices, have challenged programs such as summer sessions for minority students, minority scholarships, fellowships, and internships. PWIs, fearing legal action, have eliminated or opened up these programs to all students. Without the full benefit of these programs at PWIs, underrepresented racial and ethnic minorities may have little recourse but to seek admission at an MSI. These institutions, therefore, have a key, and perhaps contradictory, role to play in this "politics of color-blindness": they must not simply "pick up" the students that PWIs will lose, but also must work simultaneously to challenge the practices and ideologies that lead to this loss in the first place. These practices and ideologies benefit MSIs in the sense that their enrollments will increase, but they also set race relations in this country back 40 years.

We also advocate for MSIs not only, or not simply, because of their value to racial and ethnic minorities, but because they are part of what makes the system of American higher education the envy of the world: In theory, students have in this country an incredible array of postsecondary options. For such institutional diversity alone, MSIs must be supported. And yet, the idea of institutional diversity is just that, an idea, for if we really did value institutional diversity in this country—indeed, if we really did care about racial and ethnic diversity more generally—then we must find perplexing why MSIs continue to struggle to maintain their existence. And, thus, another primary goal of this book is to expose the sociopolitical forces that ensure that MSIs continue to struggle, a struggle that should be deemed paradoxical, at best, since it takes place despite an almost universally uncontested rhetoric that places value in individual, institutional, and social diversity.

Except for a few wealthy private HBCUs and some large HSIs, Minority-Serving Institutions have little financial resources, and many MSIs are on the brink of closure. We can account for part of this by attending to funding patterns. Decreases in state funding to higher education and in federal financial aid to their students seriously undermine the stability of MSIs and, consequently, the successes of the students they serve. Moreover, governmental aid given directly to MSIs seems based on a "competitive" scheme, in which more aid to one type of institution means less aid to another. But while funding patterns are important, they do not completely explain why MSIs are struggling. We must look to other kinds of forces. For example, measures to ensure accountability as a basis for institutional aid affect MSIs disproportionately because these colleges and universities lack the resources by which to maintain the so-called high standards such measures require. And so accreditation agencies, for example, cannot be deemed innocent here, as they tend to punish MSIs more stringently than they do

PWIs, intentionally or not. We might think as possible also that such accreditation and accountability measures seek to "normalize" MSIs and to punish those that resist.

The financial and political obstacles we have pointed to cannot be simply thought of as easily resolved by more funding, for funding is greatly determined by our perceptions of merit, but it is not quite as clear that the reverse is true. In other words, the financial obstacles faced by MSIs, and also their missions to serve underserved populations, give the perception to others that they are of low quality, which in turn leads to poor finances. Giving MSIs more funding, however, will not necessarily mean that they automatically will be deemed meritorious, as many will think that such giving amounts to nothing more than an act of charity. Merit (or, in its institutional form, "quality") is often defined narrowly in terms of scores on standardized admissions tests, and thus MSIs, which enroll a large number of economically and academically "at risk" students, often have difficulty with perceptions about the quality of their academic programs. Furthermore, given their meager financial resources, these institutions often cannot pay their faculty and staff competitive salaries, so they find it hard to attract faculty and staff. And, given their mission to ensure a supportive environment for students, MSIs are more likely to emphasize teaching and public service over scholarship and research, resulting further in the perception that they are of low quality.

We hope that exposure to the research in this book will influence students, researchers, practitioners, and policy makers to question how particular constructions of worth in higher education ensure that MSIs, and by extension racial and ethnic minorities, continue to be devalued in the United States. In other words, we seek to change the discourse on MSIs, from one that simply describes their positions in the hierarchy of education to one that also questions the mechanisms that ensure a hierarchy in the first place. Indeed, does the very term "minority-serving" actually lead to the kind of devaluing that we seek to reverse? Such a label may carry a particular stigma that some MSIs would rather avoid. All "racialized" labels may carry particular meanings of value and worth, and so we should stop and reconsider our labels, as they are always embedded in power relations that value some things over others. The labels we use to signify race are especially troublesome, for they are parts of long-standing racial stratifications in this country, even when they seek to counter the effects of those stratifications. This point should not be taken to mean that "racialized" labels must be discarded—indeed, we wonder whether that is even possible—but it does require us to think about how the labels we use both support and contest racial meanings.

This discussion about the critical use of labels leads to our third primary goal for this book, which is not all that different from our goals of advocating for MSIs and of exposing the forces that ensure their continuing struggle: We hope this book provides a teaching tool for thinking critically about MSIs, higher education, and social justice more generally. We ask students (and future researchers) to think of this book not just as an invitation for reading about aspects of higher education that are just now beginning to gain visibility, but also for reading this information critically. We hope that readers consider how each chapter critically analyzes the research on MSIs, not only with regard to the questions it specifically addresses, but also with regard to the new questions it proposes, explicitly and implicitly, as avenues of research and practice.

For example, some of the authors here define MSIs in terms of the percentages of minority students in the student body (we will, although our authors do not, call this concept a "percentage scheme"). A "percentage scheme" is what defines the HSI—indeed, the HSI does not exist, in a significant sense, outside of such scheme—but, more important, is such a scheme *more* or *less* telling about what actually takes place in a particular institution? Such a percentage scheme can also lead to what may soon count as a new category of institutions: The predominantly Black institution (as opposed to the HBCUs, which does not derive its status from a percentage scheme, and why now a few HBCUs are actually predominantly White). An implicit question here, therefore, is whether this "percentage scheme" means that the "historically" Black institution will (or should) become obsolete. More interesting, do percentage schemes of classification (or, conversely, does the legal classification for HBCU and TCUs) actually define what an institution *is,* that is, what it is culturally, politically, socially?

Reading critically requires, therefore, more than simply asking whether the authors did a good job in asking, answering, and posing questions. Reading critically requires *reading against the text,* so to speak, and asking how the chapters address the political assumptions, beliefs, values, and practices that dictate how we live and work. The studies in this book, therefore, should not be judged simply for the accuracy of the social realities they espouse (or assume), or for the rigor of the methods they use, but for the questions they ask and the critiques they offer. Karl Marx (1959) still seems correct when he stated that the "philosophers have only *interpreted* the world, in various ways; the point, however, is to *change* it" (p. 243; emphasis in original). This means for us that we cannot just simply provide research about MSIs and let that be the end of it; we must also ask how the world in which such research is introduced could be changed as a result. The world can be transformed only when it is seen differently than before. It is in this way that we offer this book to readers as a license to critique, which is the most practical thing we can offer to anyone studying higher education.

So far we have sought to explain our three primary goals for the book (advocacy, exposure, and critique), and we have only alluded to its chapters. We should now provide a more specific introduction to the book's contents. Before we provide such an introduction, we should explain what we hoped to accomplish in our selection of chapters for the book. We selected chapters that reflected interdisciplinary work addressing one or more of three sets of questions, questions which we encourage readers to keep in mind as they read this book. The first set of questions involves the nature of the research. What do we know about these institutions, the students who attend them, and the faculty and staff who work in them? Why do they exist, and should they exist? What benefits do these institutions provide to students, to higher education, and to society at large? What problems are prevalent in these institutions? This first set of questions also deals with the nature of the information about MSIs—is it catalogue-like information, research-based, anecdotal, comparative, or interpretive?

The second set of questions relates to the discourse on MSIs. Who "speaks" for and about these institutions? How are these institutions spoken about? What is the nature of the information circulated about them? What information is missing? Much of the discourse on these institutions focuses on inputs and outputs, which emphasizes the "economic" benefits associated with these institutions (e.g., the number of graduates who attend graduate school; the earnings of these graduates, etc.). Yet, is this economically based language sufficient for appreciating the value of such schools? Is not such language premised on a "negative" idea about these institutions, that is, that they need to justify their existence and dispel claims of academic inferiority by their comparisons with PWIs? What other forms of justification are available? What other discourses might be available for rethinking MSIs?

The third set of questions relates to the interconnections among MSIs. How might we better classify institutions? Do current classification patterns hinder or promote social justice? How are MSIs understood in relation to each other? Are funding patterns creating obstacles to effective collaboration among these institutions? What might be done to counteract the factors that force competition among MSIs? How might MSIs best collaborate and support each other?

We hope these sets of questions reframe the scholarship on MSIs, which, as we explained, is lacking good research and fails to address the interconnections among MSIs. We refused the current logic of dealing only with each institutional type in isolation and organized our book in accordance with three large areas of study: The foundations of MSIs, institution-specific concerns, and common issues across institutions, each constituting the three major sections of this book. The foundations part of this book introduces readers to MSIs and offers studies from various interpretive analyses. The part on institution-specific issues offers quantitative and qualitative empirical studies on students and faculty living and working at MSIs. The last part on common issues offers empirical analyses of practices across MSIs. We now turn to each chapter, in the order they appear in our book, and we offer readers a sample of critical questions that authors more or less explicitly raise in their analyses.

In addition to this introductory chapter, part I of the book, "The Foundations of Minority-Serving Institutions," also contains an historical overview written by Marybeth Gasman. This chapter provides the reader with a backdrop through which to understand and contextualize the other chapters. Likewise, Charmaine Jackson Mercer and James B. Stedman's chapter entitled "Minority-Serving Higher Education Institutions: Selected Institutional and Student Characteristics" provides a contemporary overview. Mercer and Stedman illustrate the importance of MSIs for racial and ethnic minorities. Readers who are unfamiliar with MSIs should find this chapter helpful for thinking about the contributions of the subsequent chapters. In reviewing previously existing research, however, Mercer and Stedman's piece implicitly illustrates how inadequate and "catalogue-like" the current state of research is on MSIs. Much of the research reviewed by Mercer and Stedman is itself not only based on databases, which illustrates the importance of such databases to our understanding of higher education, but also requires that we ask ourselves whether the reliance on databases in our conceptualization of higher education undermines other, more contextual, individualistic, and interpretive studies that might shed different, if not greater, light on what is actually taking place in higher education.

Philo A. Hutcheson, in "Shall I Compare Thee? Reflections on Naming and Power," illustrates through historical and rhetorical analyses, how problematic it is to label a college as "historically Black" and by extension "minority-serving." Hutcheson illustrates how the terms "historically Black colleges and universities" and "predominantly White institutions" produce invidious distinctions binding the former to particular, limited, and undervalued race work, while freeing the latter from having to deal with such *messiness* (our term). Labels, therefore, do things other than simply designate: They carry negative connotations with them. Despite Hutcheson's critique, we really cannot dispense with these classifications, as they allow us to initiate a political identity for MSIs that gives them legitimacy in the political arena, and, indirectly, gives voice to the students they educate. But we read Hutcheson's argument as suggesting not necessarily the elimination of these categories but a greater understanding of how they work, and how they are put to work, to maintain particular power relations. So we must ask ourselves critically, "what's in a name?" For names reflect power. In intending a political identity worthy of respect and support through the labels "MSIs," or "HBCU," or "HSI," or, "TCUs," and so on, are we also reinscribing the oppressive power relations associated with racial stratifications in this country?

Part II of our book, "Context-Specific Trends and Challenges," begins with two chapters that we think are in conversation with Hutcheson's. Chapter 5, Noah D. Drezner's "Arguing for a Different View: Deaf-Serving Institutions as Minority-Serving," makes a compelling argument for treating deaf-serving institutions (DSIs) as MSIs. Again the question of "what's in a name" comes into play. Drezner's reason for treating DSIs as "minority-serving" is so that they can compete for funding, but this is not an unproblematic reason, since funding takes place in a zero-sum game. Will the inclusion of DSIs in this game also result in less funding for MSIs? As Drezner grapples with this question, we might also think of the more fundamental questioning that Drezner requires of us, for in asking us to rethink what "minority-serving" means, we must also ask who gets, in this case, the "privilege" of the term; which institutional politics get the upper hand; and who gets left out as a result? What are the consequences, economically or socially, intended or unintended, associated with expanding the term "minority" to any group that can claim discrimination, now or in the past? If we accept Drezner's argument for why DSIs should be MSIs, which we might add is a very compelling argument, does that put us in the uncomfortable position of having to consider extending the category of MSIs to Catholic institutions, Jewish institutions, or women's colleges? And does expanding the label "minority-serving" beyond race make the term meaningless?

Similarly, in the interesting study by Frances E. Contreras, Lindsey E. Malcom, and Estela Mara Bensimon, we are forced again to ask the question, "what's in a name?" Their chapter, "Hispanic-Serving Institutions: Closeted Identity and the Production of Equitable Outcomes for Latino/a Students," illustrates the excellent use of mission statements in a study. Contreras, Malcom, and Bensimon found, surprisingly, that in their sample of HSIs, the institutions did not explicitly confirm their status as HSIs in their mission statements, and one had to dig more carefully into their institutional statements to discover such confirmation. What accounts for the absence of such confirmation? Is the label "Hispanic-serving" perceived as negative, and if so, can we locate and condemn the social conditions that make this so? Contreras, Malcom, and Bensimon also use an "equity index" to compare student-outcomes data, and they found that Latino/a students may be experiencing unequal outcomes compared to Whites even at HSIs. These findings, then, put into question what the authors sought to uncover in their study of mission statements: The discernment of a "Latino/a agenda" at HSIs. If HSIs do not express their status explicitly, and if Latinos/as cannot match the performance of Whites at HSIs, when can we say honestly that such an agenda exists? Should such an agenda exist, and if so, what should it look like?

The question of what such agendas should look like is central to the following chapters on TCUs and AAPIs. In chapter 7, "Tribal Colleges and Universities: Identity, Invisibility, and Current Issues," Justin P. Guillory and Kelly Ward provide one of the few studies of TCUs available. While highlighting the poor financial conditions, and consequent poor performances of TCUs, Guillory and Ward come down in favor of TCUs. They point out how crucial TCUs are for Native Americans, which are the most underrepresented of all racial and ethnic minorities in higher education. Not only are TCUs often in the remote areas where reservations exist, but they provide the kind of culturally sensitive instruction that Native Americans require and do not get at PWIs. Indeed, given the disrespect Native American culture gets at many PWIs, it is no wonder that many Native American students refuse to attend them. Still, the deplorable conditions at TCUs cannot be denied, as Guillory and Ward explain, but they require us to ask critically why this is so. We must ask after reading their chapter, why do funding and accrediting agencies continue to devalue what TCUs offer their students culturally and to require that they behave like mainstream institutions, or even like HSIs and HBCUs? Is the actual problem, as it is with individuals, that we require conformity in institutional behavior, judging everyone and everything by prevailing standards of normativity, such that the failure of individuals and institutions to conform is deemed pathological?

As with TCUs, there are few studies of institutions serving predominantly Asian populations. In "Asian American and Pacific Islander Serving Institutions: Historical Perspectives and Future Prospects," Julie J. Park and Robert T. Teranishi provide one such study and challenge what they call a "stubborn and persistent" divide between Asian Americans and Pacific Islanders and other people of color. The authors examine the current efforts by some Asian American groups to create a government designation to represent Asian American and Pacific Islander Serving Institutions. Moreover, Park and Teranishi see this effort as part of a larger attempt to bring Asian American issues together with the issues of other people of color. Their chapter challenges us to consider our stereotypes of Asian Americans, asking us to rethink the model minority myth. Their chapter also, however, requires us to consider the issue of whether expanding the category of Minority-Serving Institution furthers or hinders intergroup race relations.

Chapter 9 returns us to the HSI and the empirical study. Berta Vigil Laden, Linda Serra Hagedorn, and Athena Perrakis' chapter, "¿Dónde Están Los Hombres?: Examining Success of Latino Males at Hispanic-Serving Community Colleges," provides a blend of empirical and critical analyses. The authors point out that even two-year HSIs, which do a good job of educating Latino/a students and in promoting their social mobility, still struggle with helping Latino men. Perhaps, whatever successes we may attribute to Latinos in general are really an effect of the successes of Latinas. The authors argue that two-year HSIs must do better at educating Latino men. This is an important argument, of course, but we also know that community-college attendance has a significant and negative relationship with the attainment of a bachelor's degree. Is this the case for two-year HSIs? If so, will greater success in enrolling and retaining Latino males by Hispanic-Serving community colleges actually ensure that these men will not attain a bachelor's degree? In looking into this question, how might we also look critically into the larger social structures that ensure that community-college attendance hinders the attainment of a bachelor's degree?

Stella M. Flores and Otoniel Jiménez Morfin provide a compelling argument about "cascading" in chapter 10, "Another Side of the Percent Plan Story: Latino Enrollment in the Hispanic-Serving Institutions Sector in California and Texas." "Cascading" is a process by which minority students end up in lower-tier institutions as a result of restrictive admissions practices. Their study of enrollment patterns in California and Texas proves their point about cascading, but it also uncovers an interesting, perhaps unintended, consequence of the percentage plans implemented to counter legal policies restricting affirmative action: The percentage plans have moved many Whites and Asians into second-tier institutions, further pushing racial and ethnic minorities into the lower-tier institutions. It appears as well that HSIs are increasing their enrollments of not only Latino/a students, but also of students from other racial and ethnic groups. Other than reraising the questions posed by others, "what's in a name," and "what is the Latino/a agenda," we can ask, is this a good thing for HSIs? Is it good for society as a whole? What is gained and lost as a result?

Andrea L. Beach, Phyllis Worthy Dawkins, Stephen L. Rozman and Jessie L. Grant, in "Faculty Development at Historically Black Colleges and Universities (HBCUs): Current Priorities and Future Directions," moves away from student concerns and addresses faculty life. They use a survey of individuals involved in "faculty-development" activities at HBCUs. They found, as one would expect, that these individuals are very committed to the idea of empowering faculty to ensure effective teaching practices at HBCUs. We might ask, however, whether what counts as faculty development is situated within Western notions of faculty success. For example, attempts to improve "teaching excellence" may be focused around "banking" notions of education, where faculty are trained to convey effectively subject matter but fail to help students think critically of the structures that work against social justice. We think studies of faculty development, and indeed any study of faculty (or administrator, or student) attitudes, must be situated within larger cultural norms about what counts as an "education," and thus, an "educated person."

James T. Minor's "Groundwork for Studying Governance at Historically Black Colleges and Universities" addresses faculty life. In chapter 12, Minor seeks to uncover whether, and to what extent, shared governance takes place at HBCUs. He shows that shared governance is considered important by administrators and faculty at these institutions, but each group differs in how they perceive it, with administrators feeling that there is more shared governance than faculty. He also finds that participants in HBCUs had less confidence in shared governance than those at PWIs. Minor reads his data, which was collected from a larger study of shared governance in higher education, via critical race theory and a "culturally sensitive approach." He concludes, for example, that a "culturally sensitive" approach to understanding HBCUs would explain why there is lower confidence in shared governance than at PWIs. Conventional thinking on shared governance focuses on formal practices, such as senates, but individuals at HBCUs may be focusing less on senates than on more "tribunal or communicative" approaches to faculty involvement. Minor's study alerts us to how race might influence what we "see" (or, with respect to shared governance at HBCUs, "don't see") in higher education, but one should not stop here. One must also seek to explain not just differences associated with race, but how those differences are created, and which individuals and institutions are privileged as a result.

In their chapter, "HBCUs Institutional Advantages: Returns to Teacher Education," Brooks B. Robinson and Angela R. Albert use the Baccalaureate and Beyond Longitudinal Study database to determine that despite beliefs to the contrary, HBCU graduates in teacher education do not make much more money than graduates of other institutions. Theirs is an economic analysis of HBCUs, which reflects a significant trend in higher education: The reduction of higher education, and its worth, to economic considerations, or, more specifically, to "rates of return." Does the reduction of higher education to economic considerations obscure other considerations, other determinants of worth, and, in the long run, prevent us from reimagining social justice in more dynamic ways? More fundamentally, we think econometrics is becoming a dominant framework for determining "truth" in higher education, and we wonder who (or what) gains and loses as a result of such logic.

The last part of the book, "Interconnections and Common Issues," focuses on issues touching upon two or more institution types. Terrell L. Strayhorn and Joan B. Hirt, in "Social Justice at Historically Black and Hispanic-Serving Institutions: Mission Statements and Administrative Voices," provide a mixed-method study of the perceptions of administrators at HBCUs and HSIs. Strayhorn and Hirt ask whether mission statements and administrators' perceptions actually reflect social-justice values. The conventional wisdom suggests that those who work at MSIs would be motivated toward social justice, but can this be verified in mission statements? And even if so, as the authors correctly point out, does this reflect actual beliefs? Is a belief in social justice a significant part of how administrators at MSIs understand their work? Strayhorn and Hirt found that indeed one can see this social-justice focus in mission statements and in administrators' construction of themselves as professionals. Still, after reading this chapter, we may ask whether current economic and political trends tend to work against social justice—in other words, what are these administrators up against?

Chapter 15 by Brian K. Bridges, Jillian Kinzie, Thomas F. Nelson Laird, and George D. Kuh, "Student Engagement and Student Success at Historically Black and Hispanic-Serving Institutions," uses data from national databases to inquire into the extent to which MSIs engage in effective practices seeking to promote the learning and personal development of their students; they also compare these data on MSIs with those for PWIs. They find that generally there are positive institutional effects for minority students attending MSIs. This study goes a long way toward justifying the need for MSIs. One of the critical questions this kind of study implicitly raises, however, is whether the constant need to compare MSIs with PWIs ultimately normalizes MSIs to be like their counterparts, which will be a disservice to MSIs in the long run, since (1) they may not have the same amount of resources; and (2) their missions may be different.

Frances K. Stage and Steven Hubbard, in their chapter entitled "Teaching Latino, African American and Native American Undergraduates: Faculty Attitudes, Conditions, and Practices," move us into the questions surrounding "percentage schemes," as we defined the term previously. As with a number of other chapters in this book, Stage and Hubbard also use a national database (the National Study of Postsecondary Faculty), but this time to compare the attitudes of faculty at MSIs and PWIs (across Carnegie classifications) toward their careers, students, and institutions. Stage and Hubbard's study found little differences among faculty across minority or Carnegie status, except when comparing predominantly Black institutions with PWIs. What we find even more interesting is the way they conceptualized their study; they used a "percentage scheme" to compare institutions, using specifically the 25 percent scheme that characterizes HSIs to determine what qualifies as a "Black" institution. The theme of "percentage schemes" is salient throughout many studies in this book, and it is taken on more directly by Michelle M. Espino and John J. Cheslock in the following chapter, but Stage and Hubbard's study requires that we ask whether classifying institutions by the percentage of their minority enrollments really makes them culturally "minority-serving," and does not an institution's "culture" affect its faculty's attitudes? Should it? This chapter raises the specter of the question that Contreras, Malcom, and Bensimon suggest in their study: What counts as, say, a "Latino/a agenda"? Or, given the studies in this book, what counts as a "Black agenda," a "Native American agenda," an "Asian Agenda," or, perhaps even more broadly, a "minority-serving agenda" in higher education? To what extent can such an agenda be assumed simply by looking at percentages of the student population? To what extent can it be assumed otherwise?

Michelle M. Espino and John J. Cheslock's chapter, "Considering the Federal Classifications of Hispanic-Serving Institutions and Historically Black Colleges and Universities," provides an analysis of how restructuring federal classifications of what counts as an MSI restructures who wins and loses in the zero-sum game that characterizes funding decisions in this country. Using data from another national database, the 2003 Integrated Postsecondary Education Data System, Espino and Cheslock provide scenarios for how the numbers of institutions receiving federal funds would change if various "percentage schemes" were in place. As we have alluded to before, the use of national databases in many of the studies in this book should raise questions about the transformation of knowledge in higher education—how it has been reduced to that which can be collected in a database. What gets lost when the database becomes the central figure in our conceptions of higher education? Nevertheless, we ask readers to take seriously Espino and Cheslock's arguments for who wins and loses in the politics of classification. What should HSIs or HBCUs (and other MSIs for that matter) argue for in the federal classifications? Is it in their best interest to argue for a lower percentage scheme, and thus each institution is eligible for a smaller share of what is constructed as a small pie? Or is it better for students in the long run to have fewer institutions qualify as MSIs, but the ones that do will actually get substantially more money to accomplish their goals?

Deirdre Martinez's "Coalition Formation Among Minority-Serving Institutions" provides a study of why and how MSIs form coalitions with each other, even when the percentage scheme can provide such an obstacle to such coalitions. Using the political-science literature, Martinez addresses how the Alliance for Equity in Higher Education, a coalition of major associations concerned with HBCUs, HSIs, and TCUs, formed despite initial resistance. This study illustrates that while other reasons are important to the formation of such coalitions, "money talks"; that is, MSIs are more likely to join forces to better their funding positions. Coalition-building is important for economic reasons, but might it be understood as attempts by MSIs to resist the "competitive scheme" that characterizes funding decisions. In other words, is it possible that MSIs realize that they are forced to compete with each other and thwart this by forming such coalitions?

Saran Donahoo and Wynetta Y. Lee's "The Adversity of Diversity: Regional Associations and the Accreditation of Minority-Serving Institutions" closes the book with a provocative analysis of accreditation. They propose that MSIs are treated very differently by accrediting agencies. Using *Chronicle of Higher Education* articles, Donahoo and Lee compared MSIs with PWIs with regard to the actions taken by accrediting agencies and found that MSIs are considerably more likely to receive adverse actions by accrediting agencies, at least as reported in the *Chronicle*. Donahoo and Lee's study, more fundamentally, illustrates how cultural beliefs and stigmas get expressed even in seemingly neutral accrediting practices, and, we would argue, perhaps even in purportedly neutral journalistic practices. Does, say, the *Chronicle* disproportionately report adverse actions against MSIs versus PWIs? We may ask, how does race determine what we can "see" in this society?

In conclusion, we hope these studies not only reframe the scholarship on MSIs, but also alter the discourse on race more generally. We think the discourse on race currently assumes that it reflects something essential and material about individuals or institutions. While this certainly is often the case, we propose that one also consider that the "problem" of race is discursive, that is, bound up in systems of knowledge. MSIs "speak" race when they act, and the effect of such speech, as much as the act itself, is very much real. We hope that readers understand these chapters as also elaborating a discourse on race. Every time one speaks of race, one effects in reality what one says. The research on MSIs provides empirical knowledge about MSIs, but it also keeps "race" alive in discourse. We think it is important that race be kept alive in discourse, as the conservative backlash on racial gains is gaining ground in re-creating a world where it is logical, and even morally correct, to argue that race does not exist. Race very much exists, and this book, we seriously hope, will illustrate that we still have a very long to way to go before we can exalt its demise.

REFERENCES

Marx, K. (1959). Theses on Feurbach. In L. S. Feuer (Ed.), *Marx & Engels: Basic writings on politics & philosophy.* New York: Anchor Books.

Schmidt, P. (April 4, 2003). Behind the fight over race-conscious admissions. *Chronicle of Higher Education,* A22–A25.

CHAPTER 2

Minority-Serving Institutions

A Historical Backdrop

Marybeth Gasman

Minority-Serving Institutions (MSIs) are diverse in their type and makeup and divergent in their history. Their individual histories are tightly interwoven with the history of the United States and connected to the various racial and ethnic cultures within the country. In this chapter, I provide an historical backdrop upon which the rest of the book can be read. I will focus on historically Black colleges and universities (HBCUs), Hispanic-Serving Universities (HSIs), and tribal colleges. The historical backdrop that I will provide of these institutions is, in many ways, held captive by the lack of research on them. With regard to HBCUs, some of which date from the mid-19th century, there is ample historical research. However, with regard to HSIs and TCUs, there is a scarcity of research upon which to draw. As this book is trying to change these circumstances, we have included several chapters that are among the first comprehensive treatments of their institutional type. As such, I will touch briefly on HSIs and TCUs in an effort to provide a foundation for the other chapters and so as not to overlap with them. Since Asian American Pacific Islander Universities are a relatively new phenomenon, I will not discuss them in a historical context; chapter eight includes a comprehensive overview of these institutions.

HISTORICALLY BLACK COLLEGES AND UNIVERSITIES (HBCUS)

From their arrival on the shores of America, Black people have thirsted for knowledge and viewed education as the key to their freedom. These enslaved people pursued various forms of education despite rules, in all southern states, barring them from learning to read and write. A few Black colleges

(e. g., Cheney, Lincoln, and Wilberforce) appeared in the North immediately prior to the Civil War, but the majority were established in the postbellum period. After the Civil War the federal government, through the Freedmen's Bureau, took on the daunting task of providing education to over four million formerly enslaved people. As early as 1865, the Freedmen's Bureau began establishing Black colleges, drawing many of their staff and teachers from the ranks of the military. During the postbellum period, most Black colleges could barely be called institutions of higher education; they generally provided primary and secondary education, a feature that was true of most historically White colleges (starting with Harvard) during the first decades of their existence.

As noted, religious missionary organizations—some affiliated with northern White denominations such as the Baptists and Congregationalists and some with Black churches such as the African Methodist Episcopal and the African Methodist Episcopal Zion—were actively working with the Freedmen's Bureau. Two of the most prominent White organizations that helped Black colleges were the American Baptist Home Mission Society and the American Missionary Association, but there were many others as well. White northern missionary societies founded Black colleges such as Fisk University in Nashville, Tennessee and Spelman College in Atlanta, Georgia. Although these are among the most prestigious of the Black colleges, the benevolence of their missionary founders was tinged with self-interest and sometimes racism. The missionaries' goals in establishing these colleges were to Christianize the freedmen (i.e., convert former-enslaved people to their brand of Christianity) and to rid the country of the "menace" of uneducated African Americans (Anderson, 1988). Among the colleges founded by Black denominations were Morris Brown in Georgia, Paul Quinn in Texas, and Allen University in South Carolina. Unique among American colleges, these institutions were started by African Americans for African Americans (Anderson, 1988). Because they relied on less support from Whites, these colleges were able to design their own curricula; however, they also were more vulnerable to economic instability.

With the passage of the second Morrill Act in 1890, the federal government again took an interest in Black education, establishing public Black institutions. This act stipulated that those states practicing segregation in their public colleges and universities would forfeit federal funding unless they established agricultural and mechanical institutions for the Black population. Despite the wording of the Morrill Act, which called for the equitable division of federal funds, these newly founded institutions received less funding than their White counterparts and thus had inferior facilities.

At the end of the 19th century, private Black colleges had exhausted funding from missionary sources. Simultaneously, a new form of support emerged—White northern industrial philanthropy. Among the leaders of industry who initiated this type of support were John D. Rockefeller, Andrew Carnegie, Julius Rosenwald, and John Slater. These industry captains were motivated by both Christian benevolence and a desire to control all forms of production in the regions where their philanthropies operated (Anderson, 1988). The organization making the largest contribution to Black education was the General Education Board (GEB), a conglomeration of northern White philanthropists, established by John D. Rockefeller, Sr. but spearheaded by John D. Rockefeller, Jr. Between 1903 and 1964, the GEB gave over $63,000,000 to Black colleges—an impressive figure, but nonetheless only a fraction of what it gave to White institutions. The funding system that these industrial moguls created showed a strong tendency to control Black education for their benefit and to produce graduates who were skilled in the trades that served their own enterprises—(commonly known as industrial education); (Anderson, 1988). Above all, the educational institutions they supported were extremely careful not to upset the segregationist power structure that ruled the South by the 1890s. Black colleges that received support from these corporate leaders such as Tuskegee and Hampton were showcases of industrial education (Lewis, 1994). It was here that students learned how to shoe horses, make dresses, cook, and clean under the leadership of individuals like Samuel Chapman Armstrong (Hampton) and Booker T. Washington (Tuskegee). The philanthropists' support of industrial education was in direct conflict with many Black intellectuals who favored a liberal arts curriculum. Institutions such as Fisk, Dillard, Howard, Spelman, and Morehouse were more focused on the liberal arts curriculum favored by W. E. B. Du Bois than on Booker T. Washington's emphasis on advancement through labor and self-sufficiency (Lewis, 1994). Whatever the philosophical disagreements may have been between Washington and Du Bois, the two educational giants did share a goal of educating African Americans and uplifting their race. Their differing approaches might be summarized as follows: Washington favored educating Blacks in the industrial arts so they might become self-sufficient as individuals, whereas Du Bois wanted to create an intellectual elite in the top 10 percent of the Black population (the "talented tenth") to lead the race as a whole toward self-determination (Lewis, 1994).

Beginning around 1915, there was a shift in the attitude of the industrial philanthropists, who started to turn their attention to those Black colleges that emphasized the liberal arts. Realizing that industrial education could exist side by side with a more academic curriculum, the philanthropists opted to spread their money (and therefore their influence) throughout the educational system (Anderson, 1988). The pervasive involvement of industrial philanthropy in the early twentieth century created a conservative environment on many Black college campuses—one that would seemingly tolerate only those administrators (typically White men) who accommodated segregation. But attention from the industrial philanthropists was not necessarily welcomed by institutions like Fisk University, where rebellions ensued against autocratic presidents who were assumed by students to be puppets of the philanthropists (Anderson, 1988). In spite of these conflicts, industrial philanthropists provided major support for private Black colleges up until the late 1930s.

Until the *Brown v. Board of Education* decision in 1954, both public and private Black colleges in the South remained segregated by law and were the only educational option for African Americans there. Although most colleges and universities did not experience the same violent fall out from the *Brown* decision as southern public schools, they were greatly affected by the decision. The Supreme Court's landmark ruling meant that Black colleges would be placed in competition with White institutions in their efforts to recruit Black students. With the triumph of the idea of integration, many began to call Black colleges into question, labeling them vestiges of segregation. However, desegregation proved slow, with public Black colleges maintaining their racial makeup well into the current day. In the state of Mississippi, for example, the *Fordice* desegregation case was mired in the court system for almost 25 years, with a final decision rendered in 2004. The case, which reached the United States Supreme Court, asked whether Mississippi had met its affirmative duty under the Fourteenth Amendment's Equal Protection Clause to dismantle its prior dual university system. Despite ample evidence to the contrary, the high court decided that the answer was yes. Although the *Fordice* case only applied to those public institutions within the Fifth District, it had a rippling effect within most southern states, resulting in stagnant funding levels for public Black colleges and limited inroads by African Americans into predominantly White institutions (Brown, 1999).

After the *Brown* decision, private Black colleges, which have always been willing to accept students from all backgrounds if the law would allow, struggled to defend issues of quality in an atmosphere that labeled anything all-Black inferior. Many Black colleges also suffered from "brain drain" as predominately White institutions in the North and some in the South made efforts to attract the top 10 percent of their students to their institutions. This effect was especially pronounced once academic discourse proclaimed racial diversity a "value" within higher education.

The Black college of the 1960s was a much different place than that of the 1920s. The leadership had switched from White to Black and because Blacks had more control over funding there was greater tolerance for dissent and the stirrings of Black self-determination. On many public and private Black college campuses throughout the South, students were staging sit-ins and protesting against segregation and its manifestations throughout the region. Most prominent among the protesters were the four Black college students from North Carolina A&T who refused to leave a segregated Woolworth lunch counter in 1960.

During the 1960s, the federal government again took a greater interest in Black colleges (Gasman, 2007; Thompson, 1973). In an attempt to provide clarity, the Higher Education Act of 1965 defined a Black college as "any . . . college or university that was established prior to 1964, whose principal mission was, and is, the education of black Americans" (Higher Education Act, 1965). The recognition of the unique aspect and purpose of Black colleges implied in this definition has led to increased federal funding for these institutions.

Another federal intervention on behalf of Black colleges took place in 1980 when President Jimmy Carter signed Executive Order 12232, which established a national program to alleviate the effects of discriminatory treatment and to strengthen and expand Black colleges to provide quality education. Since this time, every United States president has provided funding to Black colleges through this program. President George H. W. Bush followed up on Carter's initiative in 1989, signing Executive Order 12677, which created the Presidential Advisory Board on Historically Black Colleges and Universities to advise the President and the Secretary of Education on the future of these institutions.

Currently, over 300,000 students attend the nation's 105 historically Black colleges (40 public four-year, 11 public two-year, 49 private four-year, and five private two-year institutions). This number amounts to 13 percent of all African American college students. Overall, the parents of African American students at Black colleges have much lower incomes than of parents of Black students at predominantly White institutions. However, many researchers who study Black colleges have found that African Americans who attend HBCUs have higher levels of self-esteem and find their educational experience more nurturing (Brown & Freeman, 2004; Fleming, 1984). Moreover, graduates of Black colleges are more likely to continue their education and pursue graduate degrees than their counterparts at predominantly White institutions. Despite the fact that only 13 percent of African American college students attend Black colleges, these institutions produce the majority of our nation's African American judges, lawyers, doctors, and teachers (AAUP, 1995).

Black colleges in the twenty-first century are remarkably diverse and serve varied populations. Although most of these institutions maintain their historically Black traditions, on average 13 percent of their students are White. Because of their common mission (that of racial uplift), they are often lumped together and treated as a monolithic entity, causing them to be unfairly judged by researchers, the media, and policy makers. Just as predominantly White institutions are varied in their mission and quality, so are the nation's Black colleges. Today, the leading Black colleges cater to those students who could excel at any top tier institution regardless of racial makeup. Other institutions operate with the needs of Black students in the surrounding region in mind. And some maintain an open enrollment policy, reaching out to those students who would have few options elsewhere in the higher education system.

HISPANIC-SERVING INSTITUTIONS (HSIS)

The term Hispanic-Serving Institution is really a misnomer; a better description would be Hispanic enrolling. When the Higher Education Act of 1965 was reauthorized in 1992, the federal government inserted a legal definition of HSIs under Title III—"Institutional Aid"—of the act (Hispanic Association of Colleges and Universities [HACU], 2005). As a result, HSIs were defined as accredited degree-granting colleges and universities with Hispanic students accounting for 25 percent or more of the undergraduate enrollment. However, in 1998 the Higher Education Act was reauthorized once again and HSIs were placed under Title V—"Developing Institutions"—largely as a concession to HBCU leaders who argued that HSIs were siphoning off their funding. Under Title V, the new definition was narrowed to include universities with 25 percent Hispanic full-time students in their undergraduate population. Moreover, in order to qualify for Title V federal grants, these HSIs had to provide evidence that a minimum of 50 percent of their Hispanic students fell below the U.S. Census's poverty level restrictions (Laden, 2004).

With the exception of a few institutions, most HSIs emerged in the last 30 years as a result of shifts and growth in the Hispanic population in the United States, including demographic shifts within large cities, the Civil Rights Movement of the 1960s, the opening of predominantly White campuses up to nontraditional populations, and the increased availability of need-based financial aid with the passing of the Higher Education Act of 1965 (Laden, 2004). The only institutions expressly established to educate Latino/a students are Hostos Community College (New York), National Hispanic University (California), and Boricua College (New York)—all established, as a result of the Civil Rights Movement in the 1960s and 1970s.

Originally, Hispanic populations were concentrated in urban areas of the United States. Over the past ten years, however, they have relocated to less populous regions of the country where employment and housing options are more readily available (Laden, 2004). In spite of these migratory patterns, HSIs are still clustered in relatively few states, particularly U.S. Border States like California, Florida, New Mexico, and Texas. Yet these HSIs are situated in some of the fastest growing regions of the country, and as a result, are rapidly expanding to meet the shifting demands of their geographic settings (Hirt, 2006).

Enrollments by Latinos are increasing quickly at HSIs, mainly due to the exceptional growth rate of this population, reportedly 55 percent between 1990 and 2000. As a result of this growth, the number of HSIs will likely increase. For example, since 1992, there has been close to a 100 percent increase in the number of institutions that report at least 25 percent Hispanic enrollment (HACU, 2005; Laden, 2004). With increased enrollment, HSIs have seen their funding increase. Whereas in 1995 appropriations were $12 million, by 2005 they had reached $95 million. Currently the average award amount is $500,000 per institution, these federal grants are flexible in nature with funds typically going toward program development, physical infrastructure, or faculty hiring (Laden, 2004).

Unlike HBCUs and TCUs, whose missions address the needs of their racial and ethnic constituencies, most HSIs were not established specifically to help Latinos. It cannot be assumed that HSIs provide either congenial or intimidating environments for students. Within institutions labeled HSI by the federal government, there is a mixed reaction to the designation. Some institutions use it in marketing and promotional materials, while others do not acknowledge it. This paradox makes it difficult to talk about HSIs as a group.

TRIBAL COLLEGES AND UNIVERSITIES (TCUS)

Very little is known about tribal colleges and universities (TCUs), most likely because these institutions are often remote, resource poor, two-year colleges, with little infrastructure for systemic research (Ambler, 2003a; Vernon, 2002). The Navajo Nation created the first tribal college in 1968, now Dine College in Arizona. Founded in response to the larger Civil Rights Movement of the 1960s, the college's purpose was to provide affordable and culturally specific education to American Indians, in hopes of providing new opportunities among Native American populations (Crum, 1991; Oppelt, 1990). During this period, many Native Americans realized the importance of building their own institutions and self-governance (Cunningham & Parker, 1998). In a conscious embrace of "self-determination"—Native

American leaders realized that their people were not reaching the level of education needed to be successful in the United States. The period following the Civil Rights Movement (the 1970s and 1980s) saw the creation of many new TCUs—mostly two-year institutions (Johnson, Conrad, and Perna, 2006).

In accordance with the Tribally Controlled College or University Assistance Act, a TCU is an accredited institution of higher education with a minimum of 50 percent of its enrollment consisting of Native American students. Today, there are 28 tribally controlled colleges and three federally chartered tribal colleges, all members of the American Indian Higher Education Consortium (AIHEC). Founded in 1972, AIHEC supports the work of tribal colleges and the movement for national tribal college self-determination (AIHEC, n.d.). These institutions are located in 12 states, with Montana, North Dakota, and South Dakota providing a home to sixteen of them. TCUs are also located in Minnesota, Michigan, Wisconsin, Nebraska, New Mexico, Arizona, California, Washington, and Kansas (Johnson, Conrad, and Perna, 2006). Traditionally, these tribal colleges are located on reservations or other tribally controlled lands, most of which are isolated communities. As a result of being part of close-knit neighborhoods, tribal colleges have a more interactive "town-gown" relationship than most American colleges and universities, and focus heavily on service to their communities (Cunningham & Parker, 1998; Pavel, Inglebret, & Banks, 2001).

Enrollment in TCUs has increased dramatically over the past 25 years. In 1982, enrollment at TCUs was 2,100; by the fall of 2001 enrollments grew to 13,961, an increase of 565 percent (Snyder, Tan, & Hoffman, 2003; Ambler, 2003a, 2003b; AIHEC, n.d.). These institutions offer open admissions. Using data from the National Center for Educational Statistics, Johnson, Conrad, and Perna (2006) estimate that two-thirds of TCUs are public two-year institutions. Currently all of the members of AIHEC are in the process of receiving regional accreditation. This is part of a move to encourage graduates to continue at four-year institutions and beyond (Ambler, 2003a, 2003b; Vernon, 2002).

Tribal colleges receive limited funding from Title III of the Higher Education Act, which includes the Strengthening Institutions Program and the American Indian Tribally Controlled Colleges and Universities Program. These programs help eligible Minority-Serving Institutions (MSIs) to become self-sufficient by providing funds to improve and make stronger their academic quality, institutional leadership, and fiscal stability. Funding in Title III for tribal colleges has increased considerably, from $6 million in 2000 to $24 million in 2005. This financial support, however, is well below what is necessary, and tribal colleges struggle with few resources, insufficient facilities, and little ability to recruit and retain faculty (Cunningham & Parker, 1998).

The challenges facing TCUs are similar to those of some Black colleges. Many of these institutions encounter financial problems that threaten their long-term stability. Because most TCUs are located on reservations—near the people they serve—local property taxes cannot be levied to support them; neither does the state have a financial responsibility toward them. As a result, TCUs must rely primarily upon tuition revenues and the federal funding mentioned previously. Despite these challenges, TCUs continue to expand their degree offerings. At present, many TCUs offer baccalaureate degrees, and two offer masters degrees (AIHEC, 2006).

Tribal Colleges and Universities assist their Nations in three important ways: (1) they educate American Indians living in geographically-isolated reservations; (2) they serve as centers for discovering, restoring, and strengthening tribal cultures and traditions; and (3) they encourage and enhance economic development within the tribal community (Pavel, Inglebret, & Banks, 2001). As with other U.S. community colleges, tribal colleges focus on teaching all levels of their populations, enhancing vocational training for local businesses, and participating in economic development activities. Because each tribal college is unique and approaches education from its own tribal and cultural understanding, comparing tribal colleges with other higher education institutions is problematic. Through their curricula, TCUs teach cultural values and preserve Native American traditions. In some tribal college courses, tribal elders instruct students on their language, history, art, folklore, and other cultural practices.

Currently, historically Black colleges and universities, Hispanic-serving institutions, and Tribal colleges and universities are the only Minority-Serving Institutions recognized by the federal government. However, as will be shown by Julie J. Park and Robert T. Teranishi in this book, other racial and ethnic populations are striving for this federal classification and the funding attached to it. As our nation changes and these Minority-Serving Institutions grow, their histories will develop and change. Hopefully, historians of higher education will capture these histories and share them with scholars interested in higher education and policy makers who make decisions pertaining to the support of these institutions.

REFERENCES

Ambler, M. (2003a). Cultural resistance. *Tribal College, 14*(4), 8–10.

Ambler, M. (2003b). Reclaiming native health. *Tribal College, 15*(2), 8–9.

American Association of University Professors. "Historically Black Colleges and Universities: A future in the balance." *Academe* (January–February 1995).

American Indian Higher Education Consortium (quest.aihec.org).

Anderson, J. D. (1988). *The education of Blacks in the south, 1860–1935*. Chapel Hill: The University of North Carolina Press.

Brown, M. C. (1999). *The quest to define collegiate desegregation: Black Colleges, Title VI compliance, and Post-Adams litigation*. Westport, CT: Greenwood.

Brown, M. C. and Freeman, K. (2004). *Black colleges. New perspectives on policy and practice*. Westport, CT: Praeger.

Crum, S. (1991). Colleges before Columbus. *Tribal College, 3*(2), 14–17.

Cunningham, A. F., and Parker, C. (1998). Tribal colleges as community institutions and resources. *New Directions for Higher Education, 102*, 45–56.

Fleming, J. (1984). *Blacks in College*. San Francisco: Jossey-Bass.

Gasman, M. (2004). "Rhetoric vs. reality: The fundraising messages of the United Negro College Fund in the immediate aftermath of the *Brown* decision." *History of Education Quarterly, 44*(1).

Gasman, M. (2007). *Envisioning black colleges: A history of the United Negro College Fund*. Baltimore, MD: Johns Hopkins University Press.

Higher Education Act, 1965. (www.higher-ed.org/resources/HEA.htm).

Hispanic Association of Colleges and Universities, 2005 (www.hacu.net).

Hirt, J. B. (2006). *Where you work matters: Student affairs administration at different types of institutions*. Lanham, MD: University Press of America.

Johnson, J., Conrad, C., and Perna, L. W. (2006). Minority-serving institutions of higher education: Building on and extending lines of inquiry for the advancement of the public good. In C. F. Conrad and R. C. Serlin (2006), *The SAGE handbook for research in education: Engaging ideas and enriching inquiry*. San Francisco, CA: Sage Publications.

Laden, B. V. (2004). Hispanic-serving institutions: What are they? Where are they? *Community College Journal of Research and Practice, 28*, 181–198.

Levering, Lewis D. (1994). *W. E. B. Du Bois. Biography of a race, 1868–1919*. New York: Henry Holt.

Oppelt, N. T. (1990). *The tribally controlled Indian college: The beginning of self-determination in American Indian education*. Tsaile, AZ: Dine Community College Press.

Pavel, D. M., Inglebret, E., and Banks, S. R. (2001). Tribal colleges and universities in an era of dynamic development. *Peabody Journal of Education, 76*(1), 50–72.

Snyder, T. D., Tan, A. G., and Hoffman, C. M. (2003). *Digest of education statistics 2003*. Washington, DC: National Center for Education Statistics, U.S. Department of Education.

Thompson, D. C. (1973). *Private Black colleges at the crossroads*. Westport, CT: Greenwood Press.

Vernon, I. S. (2002). Violence, HIV/AIDS, and Native American women in the twenty-first century. *The American Indian Culture and Research Journal, 26*(2), 115–133.

CHAPTER 3

Minority-Serving Institutions

Selected Institutional and Student Characteristics

Charmaine Jackson Mercer and James B. Stedman

Federal education policy recognizes different groups of Minority-Serving Institutions (MSIs) of higher education and targets financial resources to them. For example, in fiscal year 2005, MSIs collectively received approximately $895 million in direct institutional support from the federal government (Mercer, 2005). Among other things, the funding is intended to maintain and improve facilities, increase and establish endowments, and build academic programs. Thomas R. Wolanin (1998) characterizes the federal government's investment in MSIs as follows:

> Where minority-serving institutions—the HBCUs, the tribally controlled community colleges, and the HSIs—do a uniquely effective job in serving populations for which the federal government has a special responsibility or in which it has a special interest, and where these institutions lack adequate resources to carry out their mission, the federal government has adopted programs to directly support these institutions. (Wolanin, 1998, p. 30)

The "special responsibility" and "special interest" that Wolanin describes is evidenced by the legislation and funding that exists for these institutions. However, a better understanding of the diversity and range of attributes of these groups of institutions may assist in the consideration of programs and policies to assist these institutions and the students who attend them.

This chapter analyzes selected characteristics of the institutions and students making up five separate groups of MSIs: majority-minority institutions (MMIs), or institutions whose undergraduate and graduate enrollment of a single minority or a combination of minorities exceeds 50 percent of the total student enrollment; historically Black colleges and universities (HBCUs), Hispanic-Serving Institutions (HSIs), Alaska Native and Native Hawaiian-Serving Institutions (ANNHIs), and tribal colleges and universities (TCUs).

This chapter will address a number of basic background questions relevant to federal policy making for MSIs. How are MSIs defined and what are the implications of those definitions? What role do MSIs play in educating minority students, particularly with regard to number and proportion of minority students served? How different or similar are the several groups of MSIs? How do they differ within groups, across groups, and from predominantly White institutions in general? How many and what types of degrees do MSIs award? Do they award the full range of postsecondary degrees? How widely distributed are MSIs across the country? Are there states with no direct ties to MSIs? What are the racial, ethnic, and income characteristics of students served by these schools? The answers that emerge from this analysis help paint a more complete picture of MSIs—a picture that is necessary for policy development.

CURRENT STATUS AND DEFINITIONS OF INSTITUTIONS IN THE STUDY

This section defines the groups of Minority-Serving Institutions that are analyzed in this chapter. Although the groups of MSIs are distinct, membership is not exclusive. As a result, in some cases, a single institution can be classified in more than one group. To a large extent, all MSI groupings have been constructed using the definitions found in the Higher Education Act of 1965 as amended (HEA), specifically Titles III and V. All the institutions examined in this chapter (MSIs and a comparison group of institutions) are degree-granting, two-year and four-year institutions that are either public or private nonprofit. Proprietary institutions are not eligible to participate in HEA programs funded under Title III and Title V and therefore are excluded from the MSI designations. They are also excluded from the comparison group of schools in the study to allow for a more accurate comparison with MSIs. The MSIs and the institutions included in the comparison group are limited further to those that also meet the eligibility criteria for participation in the student aid programs under Title IV of the HEA.

Majority-Minority Institutions are identified by the percentage of the institution's student body that can be identified as a racial or ethnic minority. Specifically, MMIs are those institutions whose undergraduate and graduate enrollment of a single minority or a combination of minorities exceeds 50 percent of the total student enrollment. This follows the HEA's Minority Science and Engineering Improvement Program (MSEIP) definition of Minority-Serving Institution. For the purposes of our study, each institution's minority enrollment percentage was calculated by dividing the reported racial/ethnic minority student population by the total student enrollment, resulting in 474 institutions being defined as MMIs.

While MMIs are not a federally recognized group, these institutions have a critical number of characteristics in common. Collectively, these institutions educate a significant number of minority students and award a large number of the associate's degrees to minority students. Although MMIs also enroll a large number of low-income students (defined as having received a federal Pell Grant), by virtue of their largely public status, they avoid some of the financial trials of other MSIs that enroll large numbers of federal student-aid recipients.

Institutions are classified as HBCUs if they are eligible to receive a grant under Title III of the HEA. To qualify as an HBCU for the purpose of Title III, an institution must have been established prior to 1964 and have as its principal mission the education of African Americans. This is an historical designation, not one predicated on the current racial composition of the institution. There are 102 institutions classified as HBCUs for this study.

HSIs are unique among the MSI population because unlike the other groups of institutions, they enroll a substantial portion of the specific population used in identifying them (Hispanic students). More specifically, although HSIs represent approximately five percent of all institutions of higher education, they enroll nearly 50 percent of all Hispanic students. In addition, unlike their counterparts, most HSIs are public institutions, which means they are state-supported and thus, less likely to experience some of the financial challenges experienced by other MSIs.

Hispanic-Serving Institutions analyzed in this research are intended to approximate the definition of an eligible HSI appearing in Title V of the HEA. The ones included here were identified by the Department of Education (ED) in its Integrated Postsecondary Education Data System (IPEDS) for FY2001-FY2002. An institution received this designation if at least 25 percent of its full time, undergraduate student enrollment is Hispanic. There are 237 institutions identified as HSIs in our study.

The Tribal colleges and universities (TCUs) selected for inclusion in this study are the institutions that are eligible for grants under Title III, Section 316 of the HEA. Section 316 defines TCUs as institutions identified by Section 2 of the Tribally Controlled College or University Assistance Act of 1978 (25 U.S.C.1801) or those that are included in the Equity in Educational Land Grant Status Act of 1994 (7 U.S.C. 301). For this study, there are 30 institutions identified as TCUs.

ANNHIs are also very unique because there are a limited number of these institutions (approximately 8) and are all located in Alaska and Hawaii. Similar to HSIs, all ANNHIs are public institutions, thereby making the state responsible for their financial viability. Unlike HSIs, however, ANNHIs do not educate a majority of Asian American/Pacific Islander and Native American/Alaskan Native postsecondary students.

The Alaska Native and Native Hawaiian-Serving Institutions included in this group currently receive a grant under Title III, Part A, Section 317. An institution is eligible for a grant under this section if at least 20 percent of its undergraduate students are Alaska Natives or 10 percent are Native Hawaiians.

For the purposes of this analysis, MSIs include all Title IV eligible institutions that belong to at least one of the groups of institutions under analysis in this study: Majority-Minority Institutions, historically Black colleges and universities, Hispanic-Serving Institutions, tribal colleges and universities, or Alaska Native and Native Hawaiian-Serving Institutions. An institution can be in more than one MSI group. For example, an HBCU can also be an MMI because its undergraduate student population may be greater than 50 percent minority. There are 550 institutions classified as MSIs for this analysis.

For the purposes of comparing the characteristics of the different groups of MSIs, a "universe" of postsecondary education institutions (PSEIs) was created. The universe is defined as all Title IV eligible, two-year and four-year, public and private, nonprofit postsecondary education institutions. The type and control of the MSIs, as noted earlier, dictated the attributes of the comparison group. Our analysis was limited to institutions with these characteristics to allow for an accurate comparison between groups. There are 3,407 postsecondary education institutions included in our analysis. This "universe" of postsecondary institutions also includes any institution that is included in any of the MSI categories previously outlined.

The data presented are derived primarily from the IPEDS. IPEDS is a series of surveys of postsecondary education institutions that offers information on such variables as location, institutional control, types of degrees awarded, the number and minority status of enrolled students, and the number of degrees awarded by field. Institutions participating in the federal Title IV student aid programs are required to complete the IPEDS surveys annually.

The IPEDS data used for this analysis come from surveys of this universe of postsecondary education institutions and are not derived from survey samples. Nevertheless, some of the data reported in IPEDS have been inputted by the Department of Education to compensate for missing or erroneous data. Thus, all values presented in this report should be interpreted as estimates. The data on institutional characteristics, including student enrollment, are for fall 2001, while that for degrees completed apply to academic year 2001–2002.

The race/ethnicity categories used in this analysis are derived from IPEDS. Currently, IPEDS uses five basic racial/ethnicity categories: American Indian or Alaskan Native, Asian or Pacific Islander, Black (not of Hispanic origin), Hispanic, and White (not of Hispanic origin). These categories do not disaggregate data for American Indians, Alaskan Natives, Asians, or Pacific Islanders, separately. As a result, the student data presented in this report may differ somewhat from the institutional categories. For example, the exact number of Pacific Islanders cannot be ascertained from the IPEDS data because IPEDS groups Pacific Islanders and Asians together. The economic status of undergraduate students enrolled at these institutions was determined using Department of Education data on the number of Pell Grant recipients in postsecondary education institutions at any point during the award year 2001–2002.

CHARACTERISTICS OF MSIS

In the following sections, we provide analysis of selected institutional characteristics of MSIs—location, size, and highest degree offered—and selected data on students attending MSIs—racial and ethnic group membership of students, income status of students, and degrees awarded. Generally, for each variable, MSIs are compared among themselves and to the selected "universe" of PSEIs described earlier. As is explained below, some attributes characterize the majority of MSIs, with substantial differences among MSI groups.

A significant portion of MSIs are two-year public institutions (40.5 percent). Most notably, 53.3 percent of TCUs are two-year public institutions, as are nearly half of all HSIs (46.8 percent). In contrast, nearly half (47.1 percent) of all HBCUs are four-year private, nonprofit institutions and another 40.2 percent are four-year public schools. Information on institutional type and control is presented in table 3.1.

Analysis of MSIs by highest degree awarded reveals that, with the exception of HBCUs and ANNHIs, MSIs are more likely to award only undergraduate degrees. This is particularly true for TCUs; 80 percent of these institutions solely award associates degrees (table 3.2). In contrast, over a quarter (27 percent) of all HBCUs offer either a first professional degree and/or a doctorate as their highest degree, an even higher percentage than that of the comparison group of PSEIs (23.2 percent).

Most MSIs are small, enrolling fewer than 5,000 students. Further, a significant portion have fewer than 1,000 students (35.1 percent). For example,

Table 3.1 Groups of Institutions by Type and Control

Institutional group	Four-year public (%)	Four-year private, non-profit (%)	Two-year public (%)	Two-year private non-profit (%)
MMIs	18.9	32.1	38.4	10.5
HBCUs	40.2	47.1	10.7	1.9
HSIs	19.8	27.0	46.8	6.3
TCUs	16.7	3.3	53.3	26.7
ANNHIs	37.5	12.5	50.0	0.0
MSIs	20.3	30.0	40.5	9.0
Title IV PSEIs	18.7	45.8	31.7	3.8

Source: Estimates based on data from the U.S. Department of Education's Integrated Postsecondary Education Data System.

as illustrated by table 3.3, 90 percent of TCUs enroll fewer than 1,000 students. But there are some exceptions among the MSI groups. For example, 9.7 percent of HSIs enroll 20,000 or more students, a higher percentage than the comparable Title IV postsecondary institutions (4.4 percent).

MSIs are primarily located in southern and coastal parts of the country, though nearly all states have one or more MSIs. It is important to note that eight states have no MSIs—Idaho, Nevada, New Hampshire, Maine, Rhode Island, Utah, Vermont, and Wyoming (see figure 3.1).

Table 3.2 Highest Degree Awarded

Institutional group	AA (%)	BA (%)	MA (%)	Doctoral (%)	First prof. only (%)	BA and first prof. (%)	MA and first prof. (%)	Doctoral and first prof. (%)
MMIs	48.9	19.4	17.3	5.9	1.0	0.4	2.1	4.8
HBCUs	12.7	37.2	22.5	12.7	0.9	0.9	2.9	9.8
HSIs	53.1	12.2	19.8	7.6	0.0	0.4	1.6	5.1
TCUs	80.0	10.0	10.0	0.0	0.0	0.0	0.0	0.0
ANNHIs	50.0	12.5	12.5	12.5	0.0	0.0	0.0	12.5
MSIs	49.6	17.6	17.8	6.0	0.9	0.5	2.2	5.3
Title IV PSEIs	35.5	17.3	23.6	7.5	1.1	0.6	3.6	10.4

Source: Estimates based on data from the U.S. Department of Education's Integrated Postsecondary Education Data System.

Note: IPEDS makes a distinction between academic and first professional degrees. The academic degrees (e.g., AA and BA) are hierarchically ordered, with the doctorate being the highest. Institutions that award professional degrees are identified separately, and by academic degree they might also award. The degree categories are exclusive; a single institution can only be counted once.

Table 3.3 Distribution of MSIs by Enrollment Size, Fall 2001

	Students (%)				
Institutional group	0–999	1000–4999	5000–9999	10,000–19,999	20,000+
MMIs	38.4	31.8	14.5	9.9	5.2
HBCUs	32.3	48.0	17.6	1.9	0.0
HSIs	19.8	31.2	21.1	18.4	9.7
TCUs	90.0	10.0	0.0	0.0	0.0
ANNHIs	37.5	25.0	25.0	12.5	0.0
MSIs	35.1	32.5	15.6	11.1	5.6
Title IV PSEIs	30.7	42.5	13.5	8.7	4.4

Source: Estimates based on data from the U.S. Department of Education's Integrated Postsecondary Education Data System.

The different MSI groups are often located in the areas of the country where there are concentrations of citizens from the respective racial/ethnic group. This pattern can be observed, for example, among HSIs. Because there are a large concentration of Hispanics in the southern and western states, a majority of HSIs are located in the southern and western regions of the country (see figure 3.2). TCUs are located primarily in the west (figure 3.3). The ways in which MSIs are defined may also influence this distribution. For

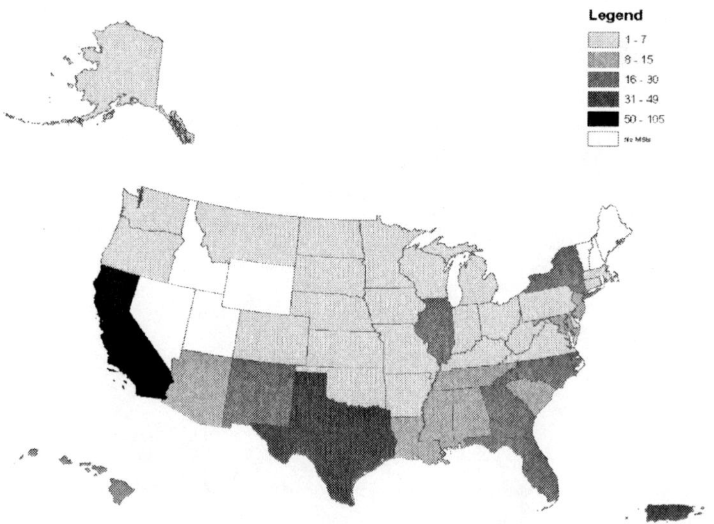

FIGURE 3.1 GEOGRAPHIC DISTRIBUTION OF MSIs
Source: Estimates based on data from the U.S. Department of Education's Integrated Postsecondary Education Data System.

example, in contrast to the HSIs, HBCUs are designated on an historical basis (founded prior to 1964 with a principal mission of educating African Americans), and are not necessarily located in places that necessarily have large concentrations of African Americans (see figure 3.4).

STUDENT CHARACTERISTICS

In 2001, the total number of students in all the MSIs in this study was over 2.8 million (2.6 million of whom were undergraduates). The number of students enrolled in each group of MSIs varied significantly. Some, such as the TCUs, enrolled few students, while others, such as the HSIs, had substantially higher numbers of students and accounted for significant percentages of total enrollment of Hispanics. Table 3.4 shows that undergraduate enrollment at MSIs ranged from almost 14,000 (TCUs) to over 2 million students (MMIs) (see figure 3.5).

Variation in MSIs' percentage share of undergraduate enrollment at comparable Title IV postsecondary institutions was from 0.1 percent (TCUs) to 16.0 percent (MMIs). MSIs in the aggregate accounted for 19.6 percent of total undergraduate enrollment.

Not surprisingly, the enrollment in each of the groups of MSIs is largely minority. In 2001, the percentage of undergraduate enrollment in each of the MSI groups that was minority ranged from 58.3 percent (ANNHIs) to 84.1

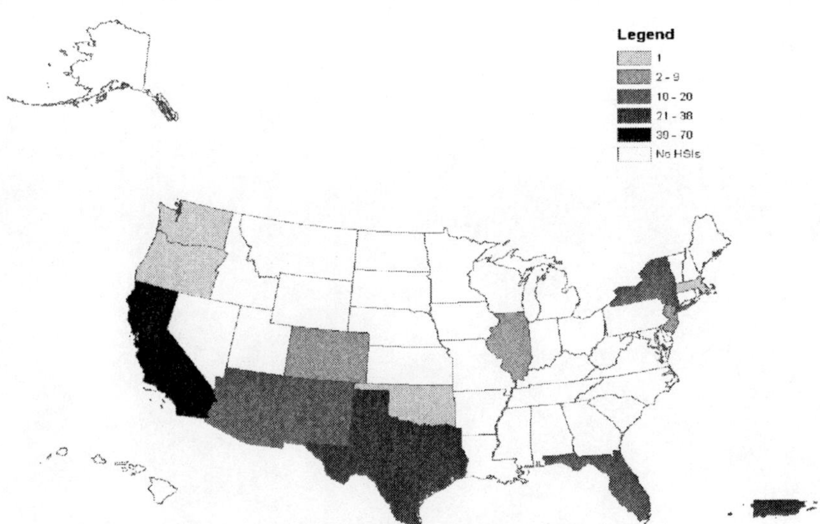

FIGURE 3.2 GEOGRAPHIC DISTRIBUTION OF HSIs
Source: Estimates based on data from the U.S. Department of Education's Integrated Postsecondary Education Data System.

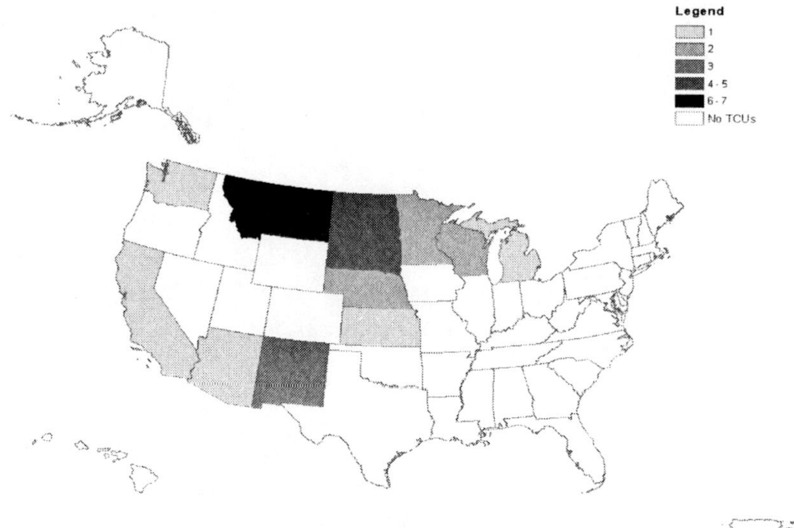

Figure 3.3 Geographic Distribution of TCUs
Source: Estimates based on data from the U.S. Department of Education's Integrated Postsecondary Education Data System.

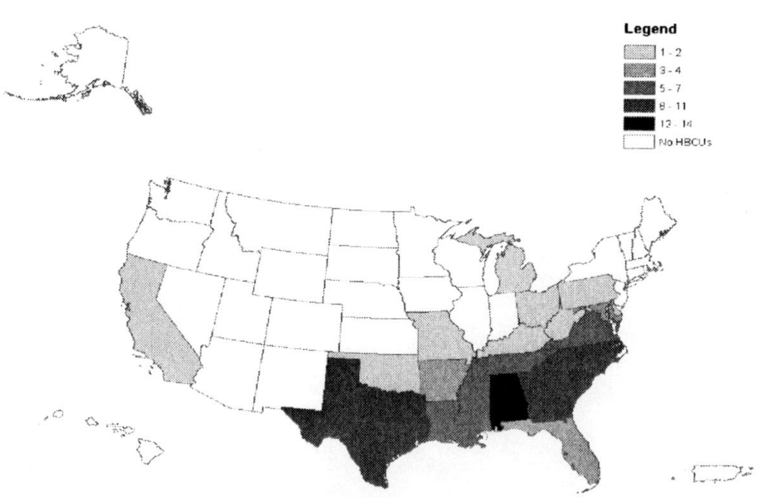

Figure 3.4 Geographic Distribution of HBCUs
Source: Estimates based on data from the U.S. Department of Education's Integrated Postsecondary Education Data System.

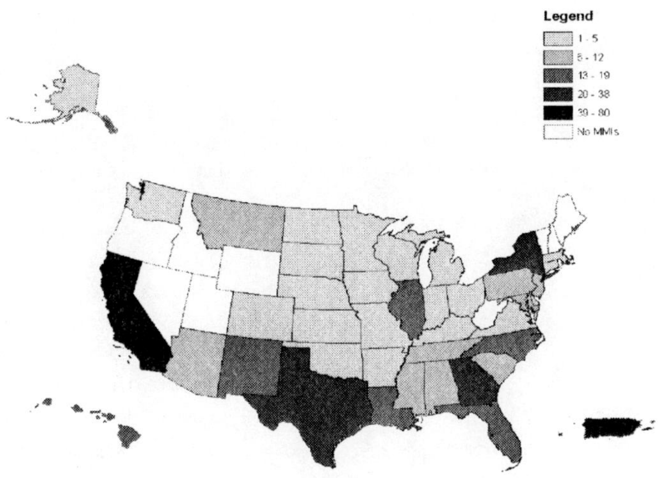

FIGURE 3.5 GEOGRAPHIC DISTRIBUTION OF MMIs
Source: Estimates based on data from the U.S. Department of Education's Integrated Postsecondary Education Data System.

percent (HBCUs and TCUs). At all MSIs, 67.1 percent of undergraduate enrollment was minority. In general, the predominant cohort of minority students within each MSI group reflected the specific minority focus of that institutional sector (e.g., HBCU's Black enrollment was 80.9 percent Black). In MMIs, there were two predominant racial/ethnic cohorts—Hispanic students (34.7 percent of MMI undergraduate enrollment) and Black students (25.0 percent of MMI undergraduate enrollment). These data are provided in table 3.5.

Table 3.4 MSI Undergraduate Enrollment, Fall 2001

Institutional group	Estimated undergraduate enrollment	Estimated share of all undergraduate enrollment in comparable Title IV institutions (%)
MMIs	2,150,799	16.0
HBCUs	260,466	1.9
HSIs	1,674,652	12.5
TCUs	13,800	0.1
ANNHIs	31,957	0.2
MSIs	2,623,641	19.6
Title IV PSEIs	13,414,552	100.0

Source: Estimates based on data from the U.S. Department of Education's Integrated Postsecondary Education Data System.

Table 3.5 Number and Percentage of Undergraduates by Institutional Group and Race/Ethnicity, Fall 2001

Institutional group	Black	Hispanic	Native American/ Alaska Native	Asian Pacific Islander	Total minority	Total undergraduate enrollment
Estimated number of undergraduate students						
MMIs	537,272	745,555	26,303	251,092	1,560,222	2,150,799
HBCUs	210,696	6,164	527	1,580	218,967	260,466
HSIs	160,750	788,679	14,955	130,875	1,095,259	1,674,652
TCUs	39	120	11,414	30	11,603	13,800
ANNHIs	430	661	2,023	15,531	18,645	31,957
MSIs	564,542	879,676	35,545	281,070	1,760,833	2,623,641
Title IV PSEIs	1,497,382	1,455,203	133,068	802,985	3,888,638	13,414,552
Estimated percentage share within each group of institutions						
MMIs	25.0	34.7	1.2	11.7	72.5	
HBCUs	80.9	2.4	0.2	0.6	84.1	
HSIs	9.6	47.1	0.9	7.8	65.4	
TCUs	0.3	1.0	82.7	0.2	84.1	
ANNHIs	1.3	2.1	6.3	48.6	58.3	
MSIs	21.5	33.5	1.4	10.7	67.1	
Title IV PSEIs	11.2	10.8	1.0	6.0	29.0	

Source: Estimates based on data from the U.S. Department of Education's Integrated Postsecondary Education Data System.
Note: The undergraduate enrollment totals include non-resident aliens and students whose race/ethnicity was reported as unknown. As a result, the difference between the total minority percentage for each group of institutions and 100% does not equal the non-minority enrollment percentage.

In comparison to their shares of undergraduate students, MSIs as a whole and thus many of the MSI subgroups of institutions, account for disproportionately large shares of undergraduate minority students. For example, in 2001, MSIs enrolled 19.6 percent of all undergraduate students (see table 3.4), but they enrolled the following shares of specific cohorts of undergraduate minorities—well over half (60.5 percent) of Hispanics, over a third (37.7 percent) of Blacks, more than a third (35.0 percent) of Asian/Pacific Islanders, and nearly half (45.3 percent) of all minority undergraduates (see table 3.6). Among Hispanic undergraduates, MMIs and HSIs enrolled 51.2 percent and 54.2 percent of Hispanic undergraduates, respectively, in fall 2001.

Significantly, table 3.6 illustrates that, with the exception of Hispanic undergraduates, undergraduate minority students are predominantly enrolled outside of the MSIs. In the fall of 2001, MSIs as a whole accounted for 45.3

Table 3.6 Share of All Minority Undergraduates in MSIs, Fall 2001

MSI group	Black (%)	Hispanic (%)	Native American/ Alaska Native (%)	Asian Pacific Islander (%)	Total minority (%)
MMIs	35.9	51.2	19.8	31.3	40.1
HBCUs	14.1	0.4	0.4	0.2	5.6
HSIs	10.7	54.2	11.2	16.3	28.2
TCUs	less than 0.1	less than 0.1	8.6	less than 0.1	0.3
ANNHIs	less than 0.1	less than 0.1	1.5	1.9	0.5
MSIs	37.7	60.5	26.7	35.0	45.3

Source: Estimates based on data from the U.S. Department of Education's Integrated Postsecondary Education Data System.
Note: The percentages for each minority group do not add to the total minority percentage. The total minority percentage represents the share of all undergraduate minority students at all Title IV comparable institutions.

percent of minority undergraduates, 35.0 percent of Asian/Pacific Islander undergraduates, 26.7 percent of Native American/Alaska Native undergraduates, and 37.7 percent of Black undergraduates. This disparity in where minorities are enrolled is even more pronounced for some MSI groups of institutions. For example, HBCUs enrolled only 14.1 percent of all Black undergraduates and TCUs accounted for just 8.6 percent of all Native American/Alaska Native undergraduates.

A substantial percentage of students at some groups of MSIs are low-income (using Pell Grant receipt as a proxy for low-income status). Undergraduates in certain MSIs groups are much more likely to receive Pell Grants—the largest federal need-based grant aid for undergraduates—than are their counterparts in other MSIs or in the comparison group of institutions analyzed in this chapter. As shown in table 3.7, in 2001–2002, this was particularly true for HBCUs and TCUs, where an estimated 46.8 percent and 40.9 percent of undergraduates, respectively, received Pell Grants. These percentages are more than twice that of Pell recipients across all PSEIs in the comparison group (18.9 percent of undergraduates).

In academic year 2001–2002, with the exception of the TCUs, each of the MSIs awarded more bachelors than associates degrees. Though more than half of the undergraduate degrees at MMIs and HSIs were bachelors degrees, both groups of institutions awarded significant numbers of associates degrees. Table 3.8 shows the number of associates and bachelors degrees awarded in 2001–2002 by the different types of MSIs.

As table 3.9 shows, MSIs account for significant portions of the undergraduate degrees earned by different racial and ethnic groups of students; this

Table 3.7 Share of Undergraduate Enrollment Receiving Pell Grants, 2001–2002

Institutional group	Pell Grant recipients as estimated percentage of undergraduate enrollment in the institutional group
MMIs	21.6
HBCUs	46.8
HSIs	18.8
TCUs	40.9
ANNHIs	12.3
MSIs	21.6
Title IV PSEIs	18.9

Source: Estimates based on data provided by the U.S. Department of Education's Office of Postsecondary Education, and the U.S. Department of Education's Integrated Postsecondary Education Data System.

Table 3.8 Undergraduate Degrees Awarded by MSIs, 2001–2002

Institutional group	Associates degrees	Bachelors degrees
MMIs	87,095	101,796
HBCUs	4,082	28,703
HSIs	65,217	77,911
TCUs	1,373	159
ANNHIs	1,201	2,867
MSIs	103,517	135,223
Title IV PSEIs	520,807	1,282,928

Source: Estimates based on data from the U.S. Department of Education's Integrated Postsecondary Education Data System.

is particularly true for MMIs and HSIs. For example, HSIs accounted for 55. 6 percent of all associates degrees and 42.0 percent of all bachelors degrees awarded to Hispanics. HBCUs and TCUs accounted for relatively large shares of the undergraduate degrees awarded to students from a single racial or ethnic group, at one level of degree—HBCUs accounted for 23.1 percent of the bachelors degrees awarded to Blacks; TCUs awarded 19.7 percent of the associate degrees to by Native American/Alaska Native students.

SUMMARY AND IMPLICATIONS

Minority-Serving Institutions play a special role in the education of minority and low-income students. This group of institutions annually receives a significant amount of federal funding to pursue their educational mission and educate minority students. The preceding analysis reveals

Table 3.9 Share of All Minority Undergraduate Degrees Awarded by Different Groups of MSIs, 2001–2002

MSI group	Black (%)	Hispanic (%)	Native American/ Alaska Native (%)	Asian/ Pacific Islander (%)
Estimated percentage share of all Associates degrees awarded at Title IV institutions to students from specified minority background				
MMIs	34.2	55.0	31.1	42.8
HBCUs	4.0	0.6	0.2	0.2
HSIs	13.0	55.6	9.9	21.0
TCUs	less than 0.1	less than 0.1	19.7	less than 0.1
ANNHIs	less than 0.1	0.1	1.0	2.5
MSIs	35.8	63.4	36.0	45.7
Estimated percentage share of all Bachelors degrees awarded at Title IV institutions to students from specified minority background				
MMIs	31.9	37.2	4.5	14.4
HBCUs	23.1	0.2	0.7	0.2
HSIs	5.8	42.0	5.1	6.5
TCUs	0	0	1.6	0
ANNHIs	less than 0.1	less than 0.1	0.7	2.1
MSIs	33.6	46.2	9.3	18.3

Source: Estimates based on data from the U.S. Department of Education's Integrated Postsecondary Education Data System.

that there are some institutional and student characteristics shared by MSIs. At the same time, there is a considerable diversity among these groups of institutions. Both findings are potentially important for policy making in this area.

In general, MSIs are disproportionately two-year public institutions. Yet, this attribute does not characterize all MSI groups—nearly all HBCUs are four-year public or private schools. Most MSIs are likely to be small institutions, often enrolling fewer than 1,000 students, though a few are large, enrolling 20,000 or more students. Most states have one or more MSIs within their borders, although several states have none.

Not unexpectedly, students in MSIs are predominantly from minority backgrounds. The proportion of undergraduates in these schools who come from minority backgrounds ranges from about 60 percent to in excess of 80 percent. MSIs play a significant role in educating minority students, often accounting for substantial shares of all postsecondary students from minority backgrounds. Nevertheless, with the exception of Hispanic students, the majority of undergraduate students from individual minority groups do not attend MSIs.

Substantial shares of undergraduate enrollment in MSIs are likely to be composed of low-income students. For some groups of MSIs, this low-income share of undergraduate enrollment is significantly higher than the comparable share of all undergraduates at PSEIs in the comparison group. More than 45 percent of undergraduates at HBCUs received a Pell Grant compared to 19 percent of undergraduates at all of the PSEIs analyzed.

This study was limited to examining selected characteristics of MSIs. Future research might consider exploring a wider range of issues that are potentially relevant to policy making for MSIs. For example, our analysis did not address the effectiveness of MSIs in educating minority students, an issue that could be part of a policy debate over continued federal support for these institutions. Further, future research might consider exploring the impact of current federal support for MSIs. As discussed, the federal government has been providing direct support to one or more of these institutions for more than 40 years; however, the impact of the funding remains unknown. What is known is that many of the MSIs rely heavily upon federal support in the form of both institutional and student aid. Many MSIs, especially the privately operated institutions, often struggle to maintain financial viability in spite of this funding.

REFERENCES

Mercer, C. N. (2005). *Federal Funding of Programs for Minority-Serving Institutions of Higher Education.* Washington, DC: Department of Education.

Wolanin, T. R. (1998). The Federal Investment in Minority-serving institutions. In Jamie P. Merisotis and Colleen T. O'Brien (eds.) (1998), *New Direction for Higher Education. Minority-serving institutions: Distinct Purposes, Common Goals.* San Francisco, CA: Jossey-Bass Inc., Publishers.

CHAPTER 4

Shall I Compare Thee?

Reflections on Naming and Power

Philo A. Hutcheson

Several years ago a doctoral student and I co-authored a chapter on minority-serving community colleges, and in a moment of audacity, I decided to frame part of the discussion in two terms: historically Black colleges and universities and essentially White institutions, the latter of which we abbreviated to EWI (Hutcheson & Christie, 1999) in an attempt to identify the presumed essentialism of White colleges and universities. This event rapidly became minor; no other scholars have cited my term, and I hardly know whether I originated it or silently borrowed it from an unremembered reading of someone else's work. While occasionally other publications will refer to historically White institutions of higher education (Kim, 2002, 2004), and others will refer to traditionally White institutions (Allen & Jewell, 2002; Fries-Britt & Turner, 2002), both of those terms are rarely used. It appears that scholars and practitioners face an important but seldom asked question about naming higher education institutions and the consequences of assumed comparisons.

Regardless of the impact, or lack thereof, of such terms as historically White colleges and universities, I am still often insistent on the subject, and indeed I rejoice at the occasional use of the term. In a scholarly world where many argue that the naming of the subject is a creation of subjugation, it seems obvious that the more likely usage of the White wording, the predominantly White institution (PWI), elicits knowledge that confirms not only racial and ethnic differences but also power relations. In simple terms, historically Black colleges and universities are historically minority, carrying a tradition that is simultaneously proud and named as lesser. As a poignant example, many scholars know the infamous exchanges that Jencks and Riesman (1967) had with many other scholars, culminating in a volume edited by Willie and Edmonds (1978), exchanges based on Jencks and Riesman's Olympian claim that Negro colleges were academic disaster areas and Willie and Edmond's counter that they served a substantially disenfranchised population and served it well.

This naming differential occurs in other ways. It is not uncommon for participants in at least one national association to argue that presidents of historically Black colleges and universities are far more autocratic than their colleagues at predominantly White institutions. Indeed, such claims also permeate discussions at some scholarly meetings, and certainly among some scholars. It is a troubling notion, one that is likely to result in a shrug, a casual acknowledgment that these institutions and their leaders are not especially on par with the White institutions. Such claims fail to acknowledge, however, the remarkable autocracy of such well-known White presidents as Robert Maynard Hutchins (Dzuback, 1991). Yet in Whiteness, the predominantly White of it all, other well-known academic leaders such as Clark Kerr proclaim that Hutchins may have been the last great university president. Charles W. Eliot is celebrated for his leadership in the supposed development of the elective system at Harvard (for competing and convincing arguments, see Hawkins, 1972); Eliot was in fact a product of a partial elective system when he graduated from Harvard College 16 years before he became its president. Far easier, apparently, to ignore is his autocratic behavior, as when he walked into a medical school faculty meeting and responded to a question about his attendance by simply noting that he was the president (Hawkins, 1972). Nor, in what can only be construed as a terrible irony, do such claims recognize the rule of historically Black colleges and universities by *White* presidents. For example Dittmer (1994), despite his overall respect for the *White* president of Tougaloo College, who refused to repress antisegregation activities among some Tougaloo students, faculty members, and administrators acknowledges that he ran a "tight ship" (p. 234). As James D. Anderson (1988) describes, in 1926 Black students at Fisk University demonstrated against the autocratic White president and his "Draconian code of student discipline" (p. 269), eventually resulting in his removal. Also disturbing is that such claims ignore the gendered autocracy of generations of men serving as presidents of women's colleges, or of the clear hierarchical expectations of many White religious institutions. If we are to place the argument on putatively equal footing, than we must pay greater attention, for example, to the ability of the Vatican to issue statements that it expects, even requires, Roman Catholic institutions of higher education in the United States to follow, and without question. In addition, there is many a small White liberal arts college where the president is in command. I recall all too well that in my first year of college, the faculty and the students worked for months to convince the board of trustees that the president had two ways of conducting business: his way or no way.

Despite the possible saliency of these examples, they rest dangerously close to the anecdotal, possibly mere moments of inductive reasoning or possibly mere moments of selective argument. In this chapter, I propose to provide evidence and argument, resting on claims of a theory of rhetoric, that the names "historically Black colleges and universities" and "predominantly White institutions" produce invidious, continuous distinctions that capture the former and free the latter.

RHETORIC, LOGIC, AND TROPES

In *Tropics of Discourse* (1978), Hayden White makes a number of arguments in several essays about language and history's use of language. His discussion of the underlying rhetorical theory is complex, and somewhat foreign certainly to the broad sweep of scholarship on higher education with which I am familiar. As a result, throughout this essay, I will rely heavily on his specific terms, so that some degree of certainty is perhaps attainable. As an indication of the complexity, his introduction offers the argument that the construction of historical language is both assumed and evasive. In terms of the former, he argues that "discourse itself must establish the adequacy of the language used in analyzing the field to the objects that appear to occupy it. And discourse effects this adequation by a prefigurative move that is more tropical than logical" (p. 1). So, in naming, for example, in a scholarly field such as the study of higher education, we engage in linguistic acts that establish acceptable analysis, but the naming is not an act of logic. It is an act of trope, a figurative use of speech. We assume that the language we use, such as historically Black colleges and universities and predominantly White institutions, is adequate as a trope for what we mean to state, but whatever logic exists in the naming is substantially limited in comparison to the prefigurative movement, the underlying assumptions about the institutions.

In terms of the evasive, White (1978) suggests that a trope "is the shadow from which all realistic discourse tries to flee" (p. 2). He points out that even the famed syllogism of logic falls under the shadow, since the minor premise is not a logical one; as he argues, in a well-known syllogism's major premise, all men are mortal, then the selection of Socrates as a man as the minor premise is a decision to move from the universal to a chosen particular. Understanding, then, our persistent use of tropes requires that we understand that the trope will not rationally capture the named person, place, or thing.

Beyond the dimensions of tropes, to which I will return, the issue of discourse is paramount. In this form of communication, White (1978) argues that

> discourse itself, as a product of consciousness's efforts to come to terms with problematical domains of experience, serves as a model of the metalogical operations by which consciousness, in general cultural praxis, effects such comings to terms with its milieux, social or natural as the case may be. (p. 5)

In essence, then, discourse seeks to solve problems of life by simultaneously reflecting and engaging the social or cultural context of the discourse. The naming is at once an attempt to reflect experience while being unable to divorce itself from that experience's context. Logical steps do not suffice. Discourse is, in many ways, narrative, for narrative uses discourses, however imprecise, to tell a story. Here I argue that White's (1978) arguments also account for narrative more generally, as in the narratives of the study and practice of higher education. White (1978) argues that historical narrative

> does not *reproduce* the events it describes; it tells us in what direction to think about the events and charges our thought about the events with different emotional valences. The historical narrative does not *image* the things it indicates; it *calls to mind* images of the things it indicates, in the same way that a metaphor does. (p. 91)

Thus, in extension of White's (1978) arguments about historians, scholars choose tropes to create and direct the argument with the discourse's cultural praxis and cultural milieu. He uses a remarkably droll example, a series of events, a, b, c, d, e, . . . n, and notes that the historian chooses which of the letters to capitalize to create the trope. There is nothing inherently tragic in any event until the historian makes it so, and communicates that tragedy to the reader. Scholars in other disciplines and fields also make those choices; even in supposed objective analysis, quantitative works create the same emphasis by, for example, ignoring outliers. As a relevant example of the consequences of choosing one event rather than another, in an essay curiously central to this essay's arguments, White argues in "The Noble Savage Theme as Fetish" (1978) that in the New World Western Europeans had to classify natives, a previously unexperienced group for Western Europeans. That classification was an act requiring metaphor in order to call to mind a direction to think, and metaphors in fact represent a simple form of trope. Specifically, White suggests, "Metaphors are crucially necessary when a culture or social group encounters phenomena that either elude or run afoul of normal expectations or quotidian experiences" (p. 184). We have often surrendered to the metaphor of the fetish, whether it is the Disney movie, *Pocahontas,* replete with scenes of British explorers unable to understand American Indian behaviors and values, or Buffalo Bill's Wild West Show portrayal of American Indians, brilliantly captured in the rendition of Chief Joseph's speech of resignation and surrender in Arthur Kopit's play, *Indians,* or photographs of stoic but proud American Indians in museum stores. White notes the cruelties inflicted on Native Americans and suggests that it is important to understand the development of the fetish and to analyze the ideologies which formed the fetish as underlying the justification for the cruelty. Those ideologies, grounded in centuries of Western thought, dichotomized those peoples in horizontal and vertical terms. Horizontally, as supposedly obvious choices for slaves, the natives were outsiders who were nomadic and lived in the wilderness, while Whites, slave owners, were stable and urban. Also according to the Europeans, the natives were closer to animal souls than human souls, thereby reflecting a vertical dimension of Western thought.

A similar fetish occurs in the ideology underlying the literary narratives about African slaves in the 1700s and 1800s. As Henry Louis Gates argues in *Loose Canons* (1992), White comprehension of Africans in those centuries produced a narrative of apparently necessary imitation, that African-American literature, for example, could only imitate the higher literature of Western Europe. Although Gates has provided far more serious considerations of the fetish of African slaves, *Loose Canons* is an especially powerful example for this essay because of his adroit use of irony, which, as I will argue, is an important trope. Thus, Gates shows that the first use of canon as a term to capture a literature uniquely belonging to the United States occurred in the mid-1800s, and it was a direct reference to slave narratives, particularly the lives of fugitive slaves. Those narratives had romance, trial, and tragedy. Yet an enduring problem resulted from the apparent necessity of imitation and the actual creation of Black literature: "Is 'Black' poetry racial in theme, or is 'Black' poetry any sort of poetry written by Black people" (p. 26)? Although Gates continuously argues for a shifting but selected Black literature canon that derives from Black experience, his arguments are always contextualized by conservative notions of the canon, by such scholars and intellectuals as Allan Bloom (1987) and Lynn Cheney (1989), who argue that Western European notions of great works are the most universal and articulate. Others have not had the higher souls, the higher level of reasoning that brings such universality and articulation. And Bloom, Cheney, and their supporters establish the context precisely because the power to create canon has been centered with Whites, and especially White males. So even though race as a biological fact is actually social and intellectual fiction, it is a very powerful fiction; Gates explicitly notes it as a "trope of ultimate, irreducible difference between cultures, linguistic groups, or practitioners of specific belief systems" (p. 49). Whites since the early 1600s questioned whether Africans could ever create a literature; if they could not, they were in the vertical dimension of Western thought, destined to be slaves. In fact, as Morrison (1993) argues, conceptions of White people in literature cannot exist in this country without conceptions of Black people, and in order to ensure a superior place, White authors think of Blackness as "a way of talking about and a way of policing matters of class, sexual license, and repression, formations and exercises of power, and meditations on ethics and accountability" (p. 7). In straightforward terms, Morrison states that Blacks are demonized, a clear indication of the conception of the noble savage, unable to achieve Christian grace.

Nevertheless, African Americans produced literature, poetry, and prose. As early as the 1770s Phillis Wheatley's volume of poetry was examined by Whites who determined that she was indeed the author, and slave narratives received attention from Whites—both in terms of praise and dismissal. Yet history as written here is cruel, and by the late 1800s developing literary theory was so racialized that Black literature did not even receive attention. Gates (1992) proposes, in something of an extension of the Harlem Renaissance of the 1930s, that no longer should Black writers imitate the Western canon; instead, they need to explore the variety of meanings in Black experience and reflect upon those meanings in creation of text.

These assumed imitative characteristics also reached into the narratives about education for Blacks. As James D. Anderson argues in *The Education of Blacks in the South* (1988), White-Black conceptions of education differed in both the horizontal and vertical dimensions suggested by White. Although Anderson's arguments focus on the economic and not the rhetorical conditions of life among southern Blacks, he identifies many characteristics of the arguments about Black education that reflect the ideological uses of rhetoric. At the outset of his work, Anderson notes that Thomas Jefferson's conception of a civilized, democratic society depended on a public education that excluded the slaves, for they were suited to sustaining the economy through life and work on the plantation. Even the more liberated, the northern missionaries, who journeyed south to teach the freed men and women, held "the preconceived idea that the slave regime was so brutal and dehumanizing that Blacks were little more than uncivilized victims who needed to be taught the values and rules of civil society" (p. 6), obviously reflecting a fetish of the noble savage. In a telling addition, Anderson notes that although the missionaries were stunned by the extent to which the freed slaves had already formed and staffed their own schools, the missionary perception of "uncivilized victims" persisted. Not only the missionaries, but also texts designed for the education of Blacks provided a direction of image that reinforced the ideology of the horizontal and vertical dimensions. Anderson reports: "These books portrayed Blacks in subservient roles and frequently assumed that Blacks were morally and mentally inferior" (p. 30). Nor did advocates of higher education for Blacks escape the fetish. General Samuel Chapman Armstrong, the founder of the Hampton Normal and Agricultural Institute, which was very influential in conceptions about Black higher education for several years after the Civil War, repeatedly argued that Blacks were both mentally and morally inferior to Whites, products of centuries of enslavement and their previous pagan beliefs. Well into the twentieth century such conceptions of the inferior Black persisted among historically Black College and University administrators; indeed, the revolt against the White autocratic president of Fisk University primarily resulted from President McKenzie's repeated efforts to prohibit organizations and activities promoting equality between Blacks and Whites. Yet Anderson concludes that eventually historically Black Colleges and Universities created an environment which supported the idea of equality, an environment which led in many ways, albeit sometimes indirectly, to the Civil Rights Movement.

TROPES AND NAMING INSTITUTIONAL TYPES

In view then of the underlying ideologies that construct White metaphors for Blacks, what are the tropes for historically Black Colleges and Universities and for predominantly White institutions? Hayden White (1978) draws upon Giambattista Vico to illustrate four tropes that dominate the construction of image, the direction for us to follow in developing an image. The first trope is metaphor; while the most simple of the tropes, it is also more complex than might be thought, because metaphors are not simple reflections but both attributions of senses to inanimate objects and the naming the unfamiliar by familiar discourse. In this sense, the common literary device of not naming an individual Black person but only calling him or her by race, or by racial slur, represents metaphor in the cruelest way (Morrison, 1993) in that the lack of a name identifies the individual in terms of a noble savage, someone not capable of human thought and identified as unfamiliar. Although metaphor in the act of naming is an act of classification, it is a classification that requires little in the way of comparison and contrast with other named images.

The second trope is metonymy, which is both binary and reductive. It is binary in that it classifies by such oppositions as cause and effect; in many traditional civilizations, thunder is caused by the anger of gods. Metonymy is reductive in that it therefore classifies the named object or event: "the thunder is endowed with all the characteristics necessary to permit the conceptualization of it as a powerful, willful, and purposeful being, a great spirit which, because it is similar to man in some of its attributes, can be treated with, served, and placated" (White, 1978, pp. 206–207).

At the risk of assigning too much power to the taxonomy of tropes, and therefore ignoring that classification schemes are only analytical tools (a danger that Hayden White recognizes), it seems that the naming of Black institutions of higher education as historically Black colleges and universities falls within the trope of metonymy. Such naming is somewhat distanced from the trope of metaphor; the noble savage, for example, does not provide adequate language for those institutions or the majority of the people who are part of those institutions. No longer are Blacks the unfamiliar and therefore requiring familiar discourse; they are familiar and classifiable. In fact, the name is insistently binary, for historically Black must more often than not call upon the legacy of slavery as a causal power in the past and present condition of Blacks. That is, obviously, a central condition of their history; those causal attributions are, however, not reflective of historical and contemporary resistance as documented by such scholars as Gates (1992), Anderson (1988), hooks (1989), Dittmer (1994), Shaw (1996), Lewis (1993), Baldwin (1963), Bell (1994), and Lefever (2005). Nevertheless, despite the powerful and growing scholarship on resistance, the public narrative is based on a discourse of the inheritance of slavery, as is the continuing scholarship that argues for the deficit created by slavery. (For a fascinating view of the deficit arguments, see Gasman, 2006, on the Jencks and Riesman claims about historically Black colleges and universities.) The binary condition continues to the present, with the persistently identified distinctions in levels of education, income, and status for Blacks in comparison with Whites. It is also simultaneously a binary statement and a classification for institutions, an image of institutions as a part of a narrative of differentiating within a whole, of institutions that are other and need special assistance. Finally, the use of the institutional names, colleges, and universities, is obviously familiar discourse that provides an acknowledgment of understandable conceptualization. Most readers recognize the attributes, however general, of the terms colleges and universities.

What, then, of predominantly White institutions? At first glance, they appear to direct the thought to the trope of metonymy as well, an obvious classification engaging the familiar. The binary condition persists as well, for without Black there is no White. (Ralph Ellison provides an exquisite, complex, necessarily ambiguous representation of this binary condition in a chapter on a paint factory that prides itself on the quality of its white paint, a color that can only occur with black tint. See chapter 10, *Invisible Man,* 1947/1990.) The issue of causal relationship is very much unclear in the name predominantly White institutions; while the resistance literature on Blacks is growing and in the scholarly world becoming powerful enough to at least at times counter scholarly assumptions of deficits arising from slavery, the notion that Blackness constitutes Whiteness as its opposite (or in another area, gender, femaleness constitutes maleness) is still somewhat under scholarly development, and an unknown argument for many academics. More important for this essay, there continues the public norms that White is defining in terms of behaviors and values. (Perhaps the most heartless of those defining norms is the extraordinary overrepresentation of Black children in special education, especially in emotionally and behaviorally disorder classifications; see, for example, Weikart, 1998. My first encounter with those data was very disheartening, but my heart fell when I heard a special education teacher report that hardly any students move out of special education.) So, for example, the strongest historically Black colleges and universities are often called the "Black Ivy League." They are not, for the most part, Ph.D.-granting institutions and are much less likely to have medical or law schools or other postbaccalaureate professional schools; nor do they share an athletic conference. Embedded in the naming is the defining Whiteness of behavior and values, of academic selectivity focused on standardized testing, of preparation for middle or even upper-class lives, of status. Neither the binary nor the classification appears to serve as meanings for the trope of predominantly White institutions.

Since the explanation of trope is dependent on power relations, as White (1978) argues as in the case of the fetish, it is therefore necessary to examine the third trope, synecdoche, in consideration of predominantly White institutions. Synecdoche extends metonymy by directing the image to unity; particulars, intrinsic to metonymy, rise into universals. So naming the universal in the social and cultural milieu reflects a power relation, as in naming a set of institutions as predominantly White. Imagine what we might name the Ivy League if we had a social and cultural milieu reflecting the universal of Black; I cannot, much as I have tried for the purposes of this essay. Most invidious, this power relation is not explicit. It is not clear from the naming of historically Black colleges and universities, the Ivy League, or the Black Ivy League. In his brilliant essay on forms of power, Stephen Lukes (1974) argues that power analyses based on who is voting, or even who is on the agenda, fail to recognize a robust but remarkably subtle form of power, its exercise when the participants do not recognize its existence. Most people use the term historically Black colleges and universities without reflection, without questioning what the term may represent in deep and enduring ways. The search for naming White institutions is more problematic, although the analysis of power often focuses on who is voting or who is on the agenda rather than the capacity of those institutions to empower themselves and disenfranchise other institutions. Thus, the Ivy League is a mirror of a fetish, employing the imitative for the Black Ivy League, and in social and intellectual terms establishing an obvious, almost reified, vertical dimension.

In view of the differences in tropic image for historically Black colleges and universities and predominantly White institutions, it really seems like a good idea to rename both groups of institutions. Furthermore, the renaming needs to reflect some level of consciousness about not only tropes, but also cultural praxis and cultural milieu, which leads to the fourth trope, irony. It is a process of self-knowledge at, perhaps, its worst and its best:

> Irony represents a stage in the evolution of consciousness in which language itself has become an object of reflection, and the sensed inadequacy of language to the full representation of its object has become perceived as a problem. Ironic speech presupposes an awareness of the possibility of feigning or of lying or dissimulating. (White, 1978, p. 207)

Institutional classification by social and cultural milieu is, of course, common: we know tribal colleges and women's colleges as we know historically Black colleges and universities and predominantly White institutions. Given the tendency to abbreviate, such as HBCU, to further classify into metonymy, there is at times an understandable sarcasm in the abbreviation of PWI; those institutions too can be reduced to letters. Yet the sarcasm does not direct the image of thought away from power relations. It does not establish irony.

Curiously, I think that in recent years we have achieved the ironic trope in the naming of one group of institutions, a naming that we should seriously consider elevating to the universal while understanding its irony. The first time that I heard the name Hispanic-Serving Institutions, I thought, "What?" It took some time for me to grasp the meaning, to recognize the inadequacy of language representing neither historically nor predominantly a racial or ethnic group, the institution could only serve. The explanations I heard made it clear that neither of the more common terms for Blacks or Whites provided an image that adequately directed thought or image. Rather than lodging the Black collegiate experience in its past, in essence responding to the White narrative, it is more powerful to explore—as Gates suggests for literature—the variety of meanings of Black experience in the present as well as the past. Serving a group is of course an inadequate expression because service cannot rise to all demands, for institutions are constantly reshaping themselves in the best of worlds to meet demands of constituents and they are constantly ignoring constituents in the worst of worlds. The serving designation becomes, then, a form of incivility (Mayo, 2002), a reminder that the power relations between institutions and constituents are continuously awkward, reaffirming and disrupting the norms of both dominant and disenfranchised groups. Mayo argues that traditional norms of civility are built upon centuries of deliberate differentiation, requiring the oppressed to be civil and allowing the oppressors to be polite without having to acknowledge that the social, economic, and political distances between groups are the products of unequal distributions of power. Overcoming those distances requires more than friendliness; it requires opposition, and incivility is a reminder that "there is a historical and political background that structures . . . perceptions and interactions" (p. 184). The practice of incivility is a reminder that power has multiple characteristics, and we need to question its exercise in many ways and realms. In literary terms according to Morrison (1993), what is necessary is not the replacement of one form of intellectual domination with another, but rather "how knowledge is transformed from invasion and conquest to revelation and choice" (p. 8). Understanding and challenging tropes, as assumptions of how we create language that sustains argument and assumption, is an important means to disrupting our norms of behaviors and expectations about race and ethnicity, although such disruption is a process and not simply an outcome.

Embedded in the inadequacy of service, of Hispanic-Serving Institutions, of Black-Serving Institutions, of White-Serving Institutions is, then, the irony of power relations, both between groups—such as Blacks and Whites—and even within the nature of institutions themselves and how they can only inadequately serve whichever group they presume to serve. The name, "-Serving," gives us, then, the power to question. Shakespeare asked: "Shall I compare thee?" in Sonnet 18, resting on metaphor to suggest that he would immortalize beauty by putting it into words. Perhaps we should consult one of his greatest works, *Othello,* which employs some of the Noble Savage fetish, thus, using irony in one narrative of the master's voice to create resistance.

REFERENCES

Allen, W. R. and Jewell, J. O. (2002). A backward glance forward: Past, present, and future perspectives on historically Black colleges and universities. *Review of Higher Education, 25,* 241–261.

Anderson, J. D. (1988). *The education of Blacks in the South, 1860–1935.* Chapel Hill, NC: University of North Carolina Press.

Baldwin, J. (1963). *The fire next time.* New York: Dial Press.

Bell, D. (1994). *Confronting authority: Reflections of an ardent protester.* Boston, MA: Beacon Press.

Bloom, A. (1987). *The closing of the American mind: How higher education has failed democracy and impoverished the souls of today's students.* New York: Simon and Schuster.

Cheney, L. V. (1989). *50 hours: A core curriculum for college students.* Washington, DC: National Endowment for the Humanities.

Dittmer, J. (1994). *Local people: The struggle for civil rights in Mississippi.* Urbana, IL: University of Illinois Press.

Dzuback, M. A. (1991). *Robert M. Hutchins: Portrait of an educator.* Chicago, IL: University of Chicago Press.

Ellison, R. (1947/1990). *Invisible man.* New York: Vintage Press.

Fries-Britt, S., and Turner, B. (2002). Uneven stories: Successful Black collegians at a Black and a White campus. *Review of Higher Education, 25,* 315B330.

Gasman, M. (2006). Salvaging "academic disaster areas": The Black college response to Christopher Jencks' and David Riesman's 1967 *Harvard Education Review* article. *Journal of Higher Education, 77,* 317–352.

Gates, H. L., Jr. (1992). *Loose canons: Notes on the culture wars.* New York: Oxford University Press.

Hawkins, H. (1972). *Between Harvard and America: The educational leadership of Charles W. Eliot.* New York: Oxford University Press.

hooks, b. (1989). *Talking back: Thinking feminist, thinking Black.* Boston, MA: South End Press.

Hutcheson, P., and Christie, R. (1999). The church-affiliated two-year college and issues of access. In Barbara Townsend (Ed.), *Community Colleges for Women and Minorities: Enabling Access to the Baccalaureate* (pp. 195–223). New York: Garland Press.

Jencks, C., and Riesman, D. (1967). The American Negro college. *Harvard Educational Review, 37,* 3–60.

Kim, M. M. (2002). Historically Black vs. White institutions: Academic development among Black students. *Review of Higher Education, 25,* 385–407.

Kim, M. M. (2004). The experience of African American students in historically Black institutions. *Thought and Action, 20,* 107–124.

Lefever, H. G. (2005). *Undaunted by the fight: Spelman College and the civil rights movement, 1957–1967.* Macon, GA: Mercer University Press.

Lewis, D. L. (1993). *W.E.B. Du Bois: Biography of a race 1868–1919.* New York: Henry Holt and Company.

Lukes, S. (1974). *Power: A radical view.* London: Macmillan Press.

Mayo, C. (2002). The binds that tie: Civility and social difference. *Educational Theory, 52,* 169–186.

Morrison, T. (1993). *Playing in the dark: Whiteness and the literary imagination.* New York: Vintage Books.

Shaw, S. J. (1996). *What a woman ought to be and to do: Black professional women workers during the Jim Crow era.* Chicago, IL: University of Chicago Press.

Weikart, L. A. (1998). Segregated placement patterns of students with disabilities in three states. *Educational Policy, 12,* 432–448.

White, H. (1978). *Tropics of discourse: Essays in cultural criticism.* Baltimore, MD: The Johns Hopkins University Press.

Willie, C. V., and Edmonds, R. R. (Eds.). (1978). *Black colleges in America: Challenge, development, survival.* New York: Teachers College Press.

Part II

Context-Specific Trends and Challenges

CHAPTER 5

Arguing For A Different View

Deaf-Serving Institutions as Minority-Serving

Noah D. Drezner

> We conclude that in the field of public education the doctrine of "separate but equal" has no place. Separate educational facilities are inherently unequal. Therefore, we hold that the plaintiffs and others similarly situated for whom the actions have been brought are, by reason of the segregation complained of, deprived of the equal protection of the laws guaranteed by the Fourteenth Amendment.
>
> —United States Supreme Court decision in *Brown v. Board of Education* (1954)

> No otherwise qualified handicapped individual in the United States—shall, solely by reason of his handicap, be excluded from the participation in, be denied the benefits of, or be subject to discrimination under any program of activity receiving federal financial assistance.
>
> —Section 504, Rehabilitation Act of 1973

Institutions such as Gallaudet University in Washington, D.C., the National Technical Institute for the Deaf (NTID) at the Rochester Institute for Technology (Rochester, NY), California State University at Northridge, and St. Paul Technical College in Minnesota, all of which serve the deaf and hard of hearing, are excluded from the definition of an MSI. While these postsecondary institutions do not primarily serve a racial or ethnic minority in the United States, they serve a portion of the population that historically has been marginalized within society, treated unequally, and has shared similar struggles for fair employment and admission to higher education.

Author Note: The author would like to thank the editors who commented on this chapter, particularly Marybeth Gasman and Benjamin Baez. In addition, the author is grateful to Shaun R. Harper, assistant professor at the University of Pennsylvania for his thoughtful words when this paper was presented at the Association for the Study of Higher Education annual conference in the fall 2005.

Opponents of HBCUs believe that access to traditionally White institutions (TWIs) makes the purpose of Minority-Serving Institutions less vital (Jencks & Riesman, 1968; Gasman, 2006). Similarly, some scholars argue that access to traditional colleges nullifies the importance of deaf-serving institutions. While the Rehabilitation Act of 1973 (Public Law 93–11) and subsequent federal acts require all institutions to provide interpreters or note takers and other needed facilities for deaf students, researchers debate the true access that deaf and hard of hearing students have to postsecondary education (Fleischer, 1975; Jacobs, 1977; Livingston, Singer, & Abramson, 1994; Schick, Williams, & Bolster, 1999; Marschark, Sapere, Convertino, & Seewagen, 2005a). Furthermore, one can ask, are deaf-serving institutions, which are primarily funded by the federal government, a good use of funds (Drezner, 2005)? The projected federal expenditure for fiscal year 2006 on deaf-serving institutions is $160 million; this is broken down as $105 million for Gallaudet and $55 million for NTID (Office of Management and Budget, 2005). When looked at per capita, this is a federal subvention of $64,000 per student. Throughout this chapter, I will argue that not only are these institutions necessary and a fair federal expense, but also that Gallaudet, NTID, and other deaf-serving institutions should be viewed as Minority-Serving Institutions, and therefore be moved from the Department of Education's Office of Special Education and Rehabilitative Services to a separate "initiative" office much like those offices that serve HBCUs, HSIs, and Tribal colleges and universities. At the end of this chapter, I propose a definition of the deaf-serving institution classification.

To understand the argument of deaf higher education as minority-serving rather than a form of special education or rehabilitation one must have an appreciation for Gallaudet, NTID, and the other deaf-serving institutions and the services they provide to their constituents. Higher education for the deaf in the United States is very similar to that of historically Black colleges and universities in its success graduating well-educated and productive citizens. After understanding the similarities to HBCUs, other Minority-Serving Institutions, and some learning differences within the Deaf community, the argument for the need of deaf-education will become apparent.

THE INSTITUTIONS

Gallaudet University, chartered by the U.S. Congress in 1864 as Columbia Institution for the Deaf and Dumb and reauthorized by the Education of the Deaf Act of 1986 (EDA), is a private university that provides primary (Kendall Demonstration Elementary School), secondary (Model Secondary

School for the Deaf), postsecondary, and continuing education programs for the deaf and hard of hearing. Gallaudet's undergraduate students, who are all deaf, receive a traditional liberal arts education. Additionally, the university has graduate programs for both deaf and hearing students in deaf-related disciplines (www.ed.gov).

Congress created NTID in 1965 to provide technical and professional education to deaf students. Rochester Institute of Technology (RIT) hosts NTID as one of its colleges. Through this relationship NTID students have access to more facilities, institutional, and career services then if NTID were its own institution. NTID confers various degrees (certificate, diploma, associate, and bachelor) in business, engineering, science, visual communications, and interpreting. Additionally, NTID began a master's degree in 1996 for secondary education of the deaf (www.ed.gov). Besides educating deaf students, Gallaudet and NTID faculty and researchers provide a majority of research related to deafness in the United States.

THE SIMILARITIES BETWEEN DEAF-SERVING AND MINORITY-SERVING INSTITUTIONS

In Gasman's (2007) history of the United Negro College Fund, she quotes F. D. Patterson, the founder of the United Negro College Fund, stating what Black colleges provide: "(*a*) congenial social atmosphere, (*b*) lower costs, (*c*) greater concern for [the] limitations of [the] academic background of Negro youth, and (*d*) participation in extra-curricular activities" (Patterson, 1952, p. 368). If I were to replace "Negro" with "deaf," Patterson's quote about historically Black colleges would perfectly describe the benefits of deaf-serving institutions to their underrepresented students.

When looking at the history of deaf education in the United States, it is hard not to see the parallels to Black education. While the segregation of deaf students was never legally binding—as it was with Black colleges in the Jim Crow South—it was not until 1973, nearly two decades after *Brown v. Board* (347 U.S. 483), that the federal government recognized the unique needs and issues that deaf and handicapped students had with regard to access to education. Congress passed the Rehabilitation Act of 1973 (Public Law 93–11), which included a short yet powerful paragraph, §504, quoted in the epigraph to this chapter. This, like *Brown* for African Americans, was the first time that those with differing abilities were accorded civil rights with respect to education.

Section 504 of the Rehabilitation Act mandated that any program receiving federal funds, including educational institutions, could not discriminate against handicapped persons. In other words, handicapped students could no longer be discriminated against in college admissions based on the lack of physical access to the campus. Furthermore, §504 required institutions to supply "auxiliary aids" for these students so that they could participate within the classroom and extracurricular activities. The rights afforded by §504 were delineated in more depth in the Individuals with Disabilities Education Improvement Act (IDEA) (Public Law 105–17) and increased by the passage, seventeen years ago, of the Americans with Disabilities Act of 1990 (ADA) (Public Law 101–336). The ADA required that all institutions become accessible, not only those receiving federal funding.

The similarities between historically Black colleges and universities and deaf-serving institutions go beyond their origin and mission to educate a marginalized portion of the U.S. population. Just as members of the White majority opened many of the Black colleges to "uplift" Blacks and school them in vocational skills, Gallaudet and NTID were started by an outside majority—the hearing majority. Black colleges were often lead by White presidents and administrators until the 1940s (Anderson, 1988; Cross Brazzell, 1992). Similarly, not until students, faculty, alumni, and other deaf individuals around the world protested in the 1988 "Deaf President Now" movement, did Gallaudet install its first non-hearing executive, Dr. I. King Jordan. Those involved believed that a deaf president could be the only effective leader of an academic institution whose mission is to serve the Deaf community. Interestingly Dr. Jordan was born hearing. An automobile accident, at age 21, left him profoundly deaf.

WHO IS ATTENDING?

Just as with African Americans in the two decades after *Brown* there was a "great migration" of deaf students after the opening of traditional education, both K-12 and postsecondary, through the Rehabilitation Act of 1973. According to Department of Education statistics, more than 80 percent of deaf children in the 1950s and 1960s attended residential or other special schools and programs, while today the same percentage attend local public schools (National Center for Education Statistics, 2002a; Lewis, Farris, & Greene, 1999). Higher education has seen a similarly dramatic influx of deaf students in "mainstream" institutions. Prior to 1973, very few deaf students attended colleges other than NTID, Gallaudet University, or California State University, Northridge. Bigman (1961) calculated that no more than 65 deaf students were in traditional schools in 1955. However, today nearly 89 percent of deaf and hard of hearing college students are attending traditional institutions (National Center for Education Statistics, 2002b).

The most current demographic information about deaf and hard of hearing students in postsecondary institutions is from a report by the National Center for Educational Statistics (Lewis, Farris, & Greene, 1999). This investigation was conducted over the 1996–98 academic years and reports numbers of students who identified themselves as deaf or hard of hearing. This report only looked at students at mainstream institutions and therefore did not include the enrollment at Gallaudet and NTID. Lewis, Farris, and Greene (1999) estimated 23,860 deaf and hard of hearing students. By adding in the enrollments at Gallaudet (1,400) and NTID (1,100) one finds approximately 26,360 deaf or hard-of-hearing students in college. Stuckless, Ashmore, Schroedel, and Simon (1997) found that nearly half of the students are deaf and the other half are classified as hard of hearing.

The estimates for the hard of hearing students are probably unreliable and low. This can be attributed to the fact that hard of hearing students are reluctant to self-identify to their institution. A 1989–90 National Postsecondary Student Aid study asked 70,000 college students if they had a hearing impairment. The respondents did not share their status with their institutions. Based on the self-reports, the U.S. Department of Education estimated more than 250,000 college students were hearing impaired (Lewis, Farris, & Greene, 1999).

Interpreting

The origins of sign language interpreting in college hail from the 1960s. Before the introduction of interpreting, few deaf students had access to traditional colleges. Gallaudet College, at the time, was the only institution in which deaf students could access lectures, unless they were able to lip-read at other colleges. This meant that few deaf students attended college at all. Interpreting, outside of academe, was not widespread until the 1960s as well. Hearing individuals, who were related to or worked with deaf people, such as family members, teachers, or clergy, offered nearly all of the interpreting. Additionally, interpreting was done on a voluntary basis. The establishment of the national Registry of Interpreters for the Deaf in 1964 helped interpreting emerge as a profession (Sanderson, Siple, & Lyons, 1997). The increased numbers of professional interpreters, combined with the federal laws requiring postsecondary institutions to provide "auxiliary aids," including interpreting, for their deaf students led to the dramatic increase in deaf students at traditional colleges.

Access to interpreting services was a great victory in the battle to increase access for deaf and hard of hearing students to higher education. However, we must be cautious when thinking that the battle is over. Countless researchers over the past nearly 30 years show that interpreting does not give deaf students "full access" to the classroom and the information that is being disseminated, no matter how experienced the interpreter or his or her knowledge of the student's needs (Caccamise, Blaisdell, & Meath-Lang, 1977; Cokely, 1990; Harrington, 2000; Jacobs, 1977; Karchmer & Mitchell, 2003; Marschark, Sapere, Convertino, & Seewagen, 2005a; Marschark, Sapere, Convertino, & Seewagen, 2005b; Redden, Davis, & Brown, 1978; Stewart & Kluwin, 1996; Stinson & Kluwin, 2003; Winston, 1994; Winston, 2005).

WHY WE NEED DEAF-SERVING INSTITUTIONS

Graduation and Retention Concerns

With estimates of 26,000 to a quarter million deaf and hard of hearing students in traditional colleges, and the two federally sponsored institutions for the deaf having a combined enrollment of only 2,500 students—or merely 1 to 10 percent of the total—why should deaf-serving institutions exist? One answer is simple: They are more successful than mainstream institutions at educating deaf postsecondary students.

Even with support services at traditional institutions providing access for deaf students to attend, persistence and eventual graduation is a concern. The average graduation rate for deaf and hard of hearing students at these institutions is 25 percent (Stinson & Walter, 1997; Walter, Foster, & Elliot, 1987). However, at deaf-serving institutions, the average graduation rate is higher: 41 percent at Gallaudet, and 61 percent at NTID and rising (U.S. Department of Education, 2004).

Some research identifies academic unpreparedness as the main reason for such low degree attainment for deaf students (Foster & Elliot, 1986; Franklin, 1988). Others found that students left college after having trouble deciding on a major (Scherer & Walter, 1988). However, using Vincent Tinto's (1987) work on student attrition as a conceptual frame, other researchers have attributed the college environment as having a major role in persistence, at least as important as academic integration (Stinson & Walter, 1997). Tinto (1987) cautioned:

> Rather than mirroring academic difficulties, they [students departing] reflect the character of the individual's social and intellectual experiences within the institution following entry. Specifically, they mirror the degree to which those experiences serve to integrate individuals into the social and intellectual life of the institution. Generally, the more integrative those experiences are, that is, the more they are seen as satisfying and leading to integration into the life of the college, the more likely are individuals to persist until degree completion. Conversely, the less integrative they are, the more likely are individuals to withdraw voluntarily prior to degree completion. (p. 53)

Foster, Long, and Snell (1999) find that deaf students often do not feel they are part of, or identify with, the university to the same extent as their hearing peers.

Social integration into college can be difficult for many students regardless of their ability to hear. However, for deaf and hard of hearing students it might be a greater challenge. Stinson and Walter (1997) note that deaf students from mainstream high schools often have limited social experiences in secondary school because of the communication gap between them and their hearing peers, making it even more difficult to integrate socially in college. This difficulty is confirmed by multiple studies. This is further complicated at traditional colleges with small deaf populations because there are few deaf peers to turn to for friendship (Murphy & Newton, 1987; Walter, Foster, & Elliot, 1987; English, 1993). Additionally, deaf students from residential schools might find it hard to adjust to "the social freedoms of college life, compared to a highly regulated dormitory life in high school" (Stinson & Walter, 1997, p. 19).

Traditional colleges and universities often do not think about deaf students' needs beyond the academic halls. Often, as required by legislation, these universities provide interpreting and note taking to their deaf students. But by stopping there, these institution do not provide for the whole needs of the student (Porter, et al., 1997). The institutions are under the impression that "deaf students can be made equal to hearing students if they are provided access to regular classroom communication" (Stinson & Walter, 1997, p. 22). Typically, after an interpreter or other service is provided, deaf students are expected to succeed at the same rates as hearing students. In cases where they do not, Stinson and Walter (1997) found that "failure is often attributed to a lack of innate ability or effort rather than to the educational environment or method of instruction" (p. 22).

Rarely is integration into the broader educational and social community in college considered by the administration. In fact, very few traditional colleges provide social programs or support for deaf students (Walter, et al, 1987). Stinson and Walter (1997) contend, rightfully so that:

> It is integration into the total educational community that . . . must be the goal of any program providing support services to deaf persons. We must constantly ask ourselves whether the academic and social needs of students are being met within the context of institutional environments where the typical hearing students to deaf students ratio is 500 to 1. (p. 22)

Deaf-serving institutions successfully attend to the entire student, providing not only classes and lectures that can be fully comprehended, but also affording the students with cocurricular activities, social interactions, and more access to student services than at traditional colleges and universities.

Earnings Effect of a College Degree

In a report looking at the effect of holding a college degree on a deaf person's earnings, Walter, Clarcq, and Thompson (2002) argue that degree completion is more important than attempting college. They found that if a deaf student does not persist, and never attains a college degree, their earnings would be lower than if that student never attended college in the first place. In contrast, earning a college degree has a greater effect on someone who is deaf than their hearing peer. Walter, Clarcq, and Thompson (2002) found that those who graduated are two to three times less likely to receive Supplemental Security Income (SSI) or Social Security Disability Insurance (SSDI) benefits—available to individuals with disabilities—than those who withdrew or were denied admission. Data presented shows that a large percentage of those who do not persist remain heavily dependent on federal income support throughout their lives. Walter, Clarcq, and Thompson (2002) make a clear case for the importance of a college degree for the deaf and hard of hearing.

ARGUING FOR A DIFFERENT VIEW OF DEAF-SERVING INSTITUTIONS

After understanding that Gallaudet and NTID do a better job at graduating deaf and hard of hearing students than traditional institutions, the question of the need for deaf-serving institutions is less important. However, why is it important to view these institutions as minority-serving rather than a form of "special education and rehabilitative services," as the U.S. Department of Education currently does? Does the classification really matter, as long as federal support continues? I argue yes!

The purpose of the classification of Minority-Serving Institutions is to make sure that underrepresented and underserved peoples have access to and funding to receive a college education. Such a classification should not and need not be given to all those populations that are non-majority, and it should not automatically be given to schools serving populations that were once excluded from higher education, such as women, Jews, or Catholics. While once excluded from U.S. higher education women, Jews, and Catholics were barred on an institutional level rather than through legislative segregation (Thelin, 2004). Deaf students were de facto excluded from higher education when universities lacked support services and classroom access. Our need to support Black, Hispanic, American Indian, and deaf education is different than those of other non-majority groups. By extending the classification to deaf-serving institutions, we will continue to support and further this marginalized group within society.

Minority-Serving Institutions are often credited as being empowering to the populations that they serve in terms of those who attend and the larger communities of their students (Freedman & Cohen, 2001; Nichols & Kayongo-Male, 2003; U.S. Department of Housing and Urban Development, 2003). Kassie Freedman and Rodney T. Cohen (2001) present a convincing argument that links education to cultural empowerment and therefore economic development of the African American community.

Historically Black colleges and universities have been empowering in many ways, among them by teaching cultural history, establishing an accepting environment, providing self-esteem, and creating personal and professional networks (Freeman & Cohen, 2001). Researchers (Allen, 1992; Anderson, 1988; Davis, 1998; Epps, 1972; Fleming, 1984; and Wilson, 1994) find that "HBCUs have historically and culturally filled a niche that no other higher education institutions were or are willing to serve and that students who attend these institutions are psychologically and professionally well served" (Freedman & Cohen, 2001, p. 588).

Deaf culture has its own history, shared values, social norms, customs, and technology which are transferred from generation to generation. Culturally deaf people do not look on deafness as a disability. Many deaf individuals see their deafness as a positive trait or asset that is strengthened by the strong sense of community. While not being able to hear excludes deaf people from some aspects of the hearing world, it further reinforces unity within the community. The concept of Deaf culture often extends to children. Many deaf parents wish to have deaf children and refuse to consider procedures like cochlear implants that would give the ability to hear to their children.

The sense of empowerment can be the most important result of identifying deaf-serving institutions as minority serving. The current federal classification of these colleges and universities as "special education and rehabilitative services" is not empowering to deaf individuals and the strong Deaf culture that exists (Erting, 1994; Holcomb, Holcomb, & Holcomb, 1994; Padden, 1988; Ladd, 2003; Padden, 2005). In fact, by viewing deaf students solely as disabled and in need of "special education and rehabilitation services," one is taking a view that was once believed of Blacks: that these students are not as capable of achievement as their peers. The federal government through its current classification is doing the opposite of empowering, and, as Freedman and Cohen (2001) suggest for Blacks this "can create feelings of inferiority, hopelessness and despair, entrapment, and disenchantment" (p. 587).

While classifying deaf-serving institutions as minority serving might be a change in name only, it is a significant way to show that the federal government sees deaf individuals no longer in need of special education, a term often reserved for students with developmental disabilities, or disabled in their own right, but rather as students with differing abilities, still able to succeed and be productive within society. This sense of empowerment will not only extend to those that attend these institutions, but also to all those in the Deaf community.

PROPOSED DEAF-SERVING INSTITUTION CLASSIFICATION

When defining deaf-serving institutions, I think that a combination of the number of deaf students attending the school and the additional special support services available for these students should be considered. Once central support system is the Postsecondary Education Programs Network (PEPNet), a national collaboration of the four regional centers that serve deaf and hard of hearing students and higher education institutions, with the mission to "assist postsecondary institutions across the nation to attract and effectively serve" deaf and hard of hearing students (www.pepnet.org). King, DeCaro, Karchmer, and Cole (2001), working with PEPNet published *College & Career Programs for Deaf Students* through both Gallaudet University and NTID. This book, in its 11th edition, lists over 100 postsecondary (two- and four-year, vocational, and technical) institutions in the United States and lists information about admissions, enrollment, costs, support services available, and degrees offered by the institutions.

I used this list of institutions, along with Gallaudet, NTID, and California State University—Northridge as the basis of my proposed new deaf-serving institutions classification. St. Paul Technical College was not included, even though it once received federal funding to support deaf education because of its low number of deaf students. Not all of the institutions identified by PEPNet are included; additionally other institutions were added. Those institutions with more than 25 full-time deaf students (combination of undergraduate and graduate), that provided special services for that population, and which conferred an associates degree or above to a deaf student are recognized as deaf-serving institutions. I decided on 25 full-time students because it is a critical mass of students that can create a social network that could support deaf students through their degree completion. It is important to note that depending on the definition of deaf used, only 0.18 percent to 0.49 percent of the U.S. population is deaf (Holt, Hotto, & Cole, 1994). Therefore, 25 deaf students within a college population is a significant amount.

I identified 23 schools that met this criteria based on the information available. While none of these institutions, besides Gallaudet and NTID, receive direct federal subvention for deaf students, it is important to include them in the new classification, as they provide extensive services for deaf and hard of hearing students.

Deaf education is often forgotten. The education of the deaf on a postsecondary level is taken up by only a small number of scholars and is rarely discussed within the literature or the media. By introducing deaf-serving institutions as minority-serving, an increased level of focus and attention will occur toward these institutions. With increased attention comes increased responsibility; however, this will only help the students that are served by deaf-serving institutions and the Deaf community in general.

REFERENCES

Allen, W. R., Epps, E. G., and Haniff, N. (Eds.). (1991). *College in Black and White: African American students in predominantly White and historically Black public universities.* Albany, NY: State University of New York Press.

Allen, W. (1992). The color of success: African American college student outcomes at predominately White and historically Black colleges. *Harvard Educational Review, 62,* 26–44.

Anderson, J. (1988). *Education of Blacks in the South 1860–1935.* Chapel Hill, NC: University of North Carolina Press.

Bigman, S. K. (1961). The deaf in American higher education. *Personnel and Guidance Journal, 107,* 417–420.

Caccamise, F., Blaisdell, R., and Meath-Lang, B. (1977). Hearing impaired persons' simultaneous reception of information under live and two visual motion media conditions. *American Annals of the Deaf, 122,* 339–343.

Cokely, D. (1990). The effectiveness of three means of communication in the college classroom. *Sign Language Studies, 69,* 415–439.

Cross Brazzell, J. (1992). Missionary-sponsored Black higher education in the postemancipation era. *Journal of Higher Education, 63*(1), 6–49.

Davis, J. E. (1998). Cultural capital and the role of historically Black colleges and universities in educational reproduction. In K. Freeman (Ed.), *African American culture and heritage in higher education research and practice* (pp. 143–154). Westport, CT: Praeger.

Drezner, Noah D. (2005). Advancing Gallaudet: Alumni support for the nation's university for the deaf and hard-of-hearing and its similarities to Black colleges and universities. *International Journal of Educational Advancement, 5*(4), 301–315.

English, K. M. (1993). *The role of support services in the integration and retention of college students who are hearing impaired.* Unpublished doctoral dissertation. San Diego State University: Claremont Graduate School.

Epps, E. G. (1972). Higher education and Black Americans: Implications for the future. In E. G. Epps (Ed.), *Black students in White schools* (pp. 102–111). Worthington, OH: Charles A. Jones.

Erting, C. J. (1994). (Ed). *The deaf way: Perspectives from the International Conference on Deaf Culture.* Washington, DC: Gallaudet University Press.

Fleischer, L. R. (1975). Language interpretation under four interpreting conditions. Unpublished doctoral dissertation. Brigham Young University.

Fleming, J. (1984). *Blacks in college.* San Francisco: Jossey-Bass, Inc., Publishers.

Foster, S., and Elliot, L. (1986). *The best of both worlds: Interviews with NTID transfer students.* Rochester, NY: Rochester Institute of Technology.

Foster, S., Long, G., Snell, K. (1999). Empirical paper. Inclusive instruction and learning for deaf students in postsecondary education. *Journal of Deaf Studies and Deaf Education, 4*, 223–235.

Franklin, E. L. (1988). Attrition and retention of hearing-impaired community college students. Unpublished doctoral dissertation. University of Kansas.

Freedman, K., & Cohen, R. T. (2001). Bridging the gap between economic development and cultural empowerment: HBCUs challenges for the future. *Urban Education, 36*(5), 585–596.

Gasman, M. (2006). Salvaging 'academic disaster areas': The Black college response to Christopher Jencks' and David Riesman's 1967 *Harvard Educational Review* Article. *Journal of Higher Education.*

Gasman, M. (2007). *Envisioning Black colleges: A history of the United Negro College Fund.* Baltimore, MD: The Johns Hopkins University Press.

Harrington, F. (2000). Sign language interpreters and access for deaf students to university curricula: The ideal and the reality. In R. P. Roberts, S. E. Carr, D. Abraham, and A. Dufour (Eds.), *The critical link 2: Interpreters in the community.* Amsterdam: John Benjamins.

Holcomb, R. K., Holcomb, S. K., and Holcomb, T. K. (1994). *Deaf culture, our way: Anecdotes from the Deaf community.* San Diego, CA: Dawn Sign Press.

Holt, J., Hotto, S., and Cole, K. (1994). Demographic aspects of hearing impairment: Questions and answers. Retrieved December 2, 2005 from: www.gri.gallaudet.edu/Demographics/factsheet.html#Q1/

Jacobs, L. R. (1977). The efficiency of interpreting input for processing lecture information by deaf college students. *Journal of Rehabilitation of the Deaf, 11*, 10–14.

Jencks, C., and Riesman, D. (1968). *The academic revolution.* New York: Transaction Press.

Karchmer, M. A., and Mitchell, R. E. (2003). Demographic and achievement characteristics of deaf and hard-of-hearing students. In M. Marschark and P. E. Spencer (Eds.), *Oxford handbook of deaf studies, language, and education* (pp. 21–37). New York: Oxford University Press.

King, S. J., DeCaro, J. J., Karchmer, M. A., and Cole, K. J. (2001). *College and career programs for deaf students, 11th Edition.* Washington, DC: Gallaudet University.

Ladd, P. (2003). *Understanding Deaf culture: In search of deafhood.* Buffalo, NY: Multilingual Matters.

Lewis, L., Farris, E., and Greene, B. (1999). *An institutional perspective on students with disabilities in postsecondary education.* Washington, DC: U.S. Department of Education.

Livingston, S., Singer, B., and Abramson, T. (1994). A study to determine the effectiveness of two different kinds of interpreting. Proceedings of the 10th *National Convention of the Conference of Interpreter Trainers—Mapping our course: A collaborative venture,* pp. 175–197. CIT.

Marschark, M., Sapere, P., Convertino, C., and Seewagen, R. (2005a). Access to postsecondary education through sign language interpreting. *Journal of Deaf Studies and Deaf Education, 10*(1), 38–50.

Marschark, M., Sapere, P., Convertino, C., and Seewagen, R. (2005b). Educational interpreting: Access and outcomes. In M. Marschark, R. Peterson, and E. A. Winston (Eds.), *Sign language interpreting and interpreter education: Directions for research and practice.* New York: Oxford University Press.

Murphy, J. S. and Newton, B. J. (1987). Loneliness and the mainstreamed hearing-impaired college student. *American Annals of the Deaf, 132*, 21–25.

National Center for Education Statistics (2002a). *Digest of education statistics, 2002.* Washington, DC: U.S. Department of Education.

National Center for Education Statistics (2002b). *Profile of undergraduates in US. postsecondary institutions: 1999–2000* (NCES-2002–168). Washington, DC: U.S. Department of Education.

Nichols, T. J. and Kayongo-Male, D. (2003). The dynamics of Tribal college-state university collaboration. *Journal of American Indian Education, 42*(3), 1–24.

Office of Management and Budget (2005). Projected FY 2006 budget. Retrieved August 1, 2005 from: www.whitehouse.gove/omb/budget/fy2006/sheets28_6.xls

Padden, C. (1988). *Deaf in America: voices from a culture.* Cambridge, MA: Harvard University Press.

Padden, C. (2005). *Inside Deaf Culture.* Cambridge, MA: Harvard University Press.

Patterson, F. D. (1952). The private Negro college in a racially-integrated system of higher education. *The Journal of Negro Education, 21*(3).

Porter, J., Camerlengo, R., DePuye, M., and Sommer, M. (1997). *Campus life and the development of postsecondary deaf and hard of hearing students: Principles and practices.* A report of the National Task Force on Quality of Services in the Postsecondary Education of Deaf and Hard of Hearing Students. Rochester, N.Y.: Northeast Technical Assistance Center, Rochester Institute of Technology.

Redden, M. R., Davis, C. A., and Brown, J. W. (1978). *Science for handicapped students in higher education: Barriers, solutions, and recommendations.* Washington, DC: American Association for the Advancement of Science.

Sanderson, G., Siple, L., and Lyons, B. (1997). *Interpreting for postsecondary deaf students.* A report of the National Task Force on Quality of Services in the Postsecondary Education of Deaf and Hard of Hearing Students. Rochester, N.Y.: Northeast Technical Assistance Center, Rochester Institute of Technology.

Scherer, M. J., and Walter, G. G. (1988). *College career programs for the deaf.* Washington, DC: Gallaudet University.

Schick, B., Williams, K., and Bolster, L. (1999). Skill levels of educational interpreters working in public schools. *Journal of Deaf Studies and Deaf Education, 4,* 144–155.

Stewart, D. A., and Kluwin, T. N. (1996). The gap between guidelines, practice, and knowledge in interpreting services for deaf students. *Journal of Deaf Studies and Deaf Education, 1,* 29–39.

Stinson, M. S., and Anita, S. D. (1999). Considerations in educating deaf and hard-of-hearing students in inclusive settings. *Journal of Deaf Studies and Deaf Education, 4*(3), 163–175.

Stinson, M. S., and Kluwin, T. N. (2003). Educational consequences of alternative school placements. In M. Marschark and P. E. Spencer (Eds.). *Oxford handbook of deaf studies, language, and education* (pp. 52–64). New York: Oxford University Press.

Stinson, M., and Walter, G. (1997). Improving retention for deaf and hard of hearing students: What the research tells us. *Journal of the American Deafness and Rehabilitation Association, 30*(4), 14–23.

Stuckless, R., Ashmore, D., Schroedel, J., and Simon, J. (1997). *Introduction:* A report of the National Task Force on Quality of Services in the Postsecondary Education of Deaf and Hard of Hearing Students. Rochester, N.Y.: Northeast Technical Assistance Center, Rochester Institute of Technology.

Thelin, J. R. (2004). *A history of American higher education.* Baltimore, MD: The Johns Hopkins University Press.

Tinto, V. (1987). *Leaving college: Rethinking the causes and cures of student attrition*. Chicago, IL: University of Chicago Press.

U.S. Department of Education (2004). Program performance plan. Retrieved August 1, 2005 from: www.ed.gov/about/reports/2004plan/

U.S. Department of Housing and Urban Development (2003). Minority-serving institutions of higher education: Developing partnerships to revitalize communities. Washington, DC: Government Printing Office.

Walter, G. G., Clarcq, J. R., and Thompson, W. S. (2002). Effect of degree attainment on improving the economic status of individuals who are deaf. *Journal of the American Deafness and Rehabilitation Association, 35*(3), 30–46.

Walter, G. G., Foster, S. B., and Elliot, L. (1987). Attrition and accommodations of hearing-impaired college students in the U.S. Paper presented at the 10th National Conference of the Association on Handicapped Student Services Programs in Post-secondary Education. Washington, DC.

Wilson, R. (1994). The participation of African Americans in American higher education. In M. J. Justiz, R. Wilson, and L. G. Bjérk (Eds.). *Minorities in higher education* (pp. 195–211). Phoenix, AZ: Oryx Press.

Winston, E. A. (1994). "An interpreted education: Inclusion or exclusion?" In R. C. Johnson and O. P. Cohen (Eds.), *Implications and complications for deaf students of the full inclusion movement* (pp. 55–62). Gallaudet Research Institute Occasional Paper 94–2. Washington, DC: Gallaudet University.

Winston, E. A. (2005). "Interpretability and accessibility of mainstream classroom." In E. A. Winston (Ed.), *Educational interpreting: How it can succeed*. Washington, DC: Gallaudet University Press.

CHAPTER 6

Hispanic-Serving Institutions

Closeted Identity and the Production of Equitable Outcomes for Latino/a Students

Frances E. Contreras, Lindsey E. Malcom, and Estela Mara Bensimon

As the demographic shifts for the Latino community continue to outpace other racial/ethnic groups, Hispanic-Serving Institutions (HSIs) represent a growing segment of higher education institutions in the United States. Given the newness of the Hispanic-Serving Institutions identity, this chapter addresses two interrelated questions. One question applies to institutional identity and the second question relates to educational outcomes for Latinos/as. In regards to identity, we were curious about the ways in which institutions reveal and acknowledge their status as Hispanic-Serving. How would an outsider or a newcomer to the institution know that it is Hispanic-Serving? More importantly, how would a newly appointed president or faculty member know what the expectations of leadership or teaching are in the context of an HSI? With respect to educational outcomes, we wanted to explore the additional value of attending Hispanic-Serving Institutions. Since the identity "Hispanic-Serving" implies a special mission, and given that the college outcomes of Latinos/as are unequal compared to Whites nationally, we asked, "Do Hispanic-Serving Institutions produce equitable educational outcomes for Latino/a students?" "Do Latino/a and White students attending HSIs achieve comparable outcomes?" In developing these questions, we were influenced by the knowledge that women's colleges and HBCUs produce a very large share of high-achieving individuals who rise to positions of leadership

---

Authors Note: Jennifer L. Hoffman, a doctoral candidate in the College of Education at the University of Washington, assisted with the IPEDS data collection.

and prominence and that their positive impact is attributed to these institutions' special mission, sense of purpose, and strong identity as colleges for women and for African American students (Drewry & Doermann, 2001; Kim & Alvarez, 1995; Outcalt & Skewes-Cox, 2002).

We conducted an exploratory study of ten two- and four-year HSIs in five states. All of the 10 institutions examined are among the 242 institutions eligible to apply for federal funding under the U.S. Department of Education Title V grant program. Specifically, we examined the incorporation of the HSI identity in their mission statement and their websites; we assessed the status of equity among Latinos/as using data on enrollment and degrees granted, and undergraduate major data. The study of these 10 institutions, it needs to be pointed out, is only intended to demonstrate alternative ways of examining the role and outcomes of HSIs for Latino/a students and to encourage more empirical research on this institutional sector. We start the chapter with an overview of HSIs in terms of types of institutions, various categories of HSI status, and their geographic distribution.

ASSUMING A HISPANIC IDENTITY

While the label "Hispanic-Serving" makes these institutions appear as the Hispanic equivalent of HBCUs or women's colleges, they are not a vestige of de jure segregation nor of that period when a women's place was thought to be at home rather than in college. To become an HSI and qualify for Title V funding an institution has to meet three criteria: (1) they must be accredited and nonprofit; (2) have at least 25 percent Latinos/as undergraduate full-time equivalent enrollment; and (3) at least 50 percent of the Latino/a students are low-income. Federal funding earmarked for HSIs has increased substantially since the first appropriation of $12 million in FY1995 (HACU, n.d.). In FY2005, over $95 million has been appropriated for distribution under Title V (U.S. Department of Education, 2005). Title V funds are distributed through an annual grant competition. The grant competition consists of two application processes: first, institutions must be designated as an HSI in accordance with Title V criteria. After an institution is determined to be eligible, it may submit a grant proposal to be considered for funding. Institutions apply for Title V funds for a variety of initiatives, including technology, improving retention, and so forth, all intended to better serve the needs of their students.

Although institutional-aid appropriations under Title V have increased over the past decade, HSIs remain underfunded compared to other degree-granting institutions (HACU, n.d.). This is due in part to the fact that so many of HSIs are two-year institutions, an already underfunded segment of postsecondary education.

Table 6.1 provides the number and geographic distribution of two- and four-year HSIs. The data on table 6.1 underscore well-known trends on the college participation of Latinos/as, namely, their high concentration in community colleges and their growing presence in California and the southwest.

First, the majority of HSIs, 53 percent, are community colleges, which is not surprising. In view of the overrepresentation of Latinos/as in the community college sector of higher education, it makes sense that these institutions would be the most likely to meet the criteria to acquire the HSI designation and become eligible for Title V funding. Second, the majority of the four-year colleges that have earned the designation, 40 percent, are located in Puerto Rico. These institutions are not comparable to Hispanic-Serving Institutions on the U.S. mainland. The identity of Puerto Rico's colleges is Puerto Rican, the language of instruction is Spanish, their leadership and faculty is Puerto Rican as are their students. Third, HSIs are spread over 13 states but more than half (54 percent) are in California, Texas, and New Mexico. Not shown in the table is that two-thirds of the HSIs are public institutions.

Curiously, in addition to these 242 formally designated HSIs, there is a much larger group of institutions that have assumed the designation according to a different definition used by the Office of Civil Rights (OCR), or that have assumed it voluntarily by becoming members of HACU. The OCR keeps its own list of HSIs, which includes the 242 that are certified by

Table 6.1 Number of 2-year and 4-year Title V Eligible Institutions by State

State or Commonwealth	Number of 2-year HSIs	Number of 4-year HSIs	Total number of HSIs
Arizona	10	2	12
California	54	19	73
Colorado	4	2	6
Florida	3	9	12
Illinois	7	3	10
Massachusetts	1	—	1
New Jersey	3	2	5
New Mexico	14	6	20
New York	4	8	12
Oklahoma	—	1	1
Oregon	—	1	1
Puerto Rico	6	43	49
Texas	22	16	38
Washington	1	1	2
Total	129	113	242

Title V and 118 more that have at least 25 percent enrollment of Latinos/as. OCR's list includes for-profit proprietary institutions. HACU, which is a dues-paying supported association, has a list that includes institutions with at least 25 percent Latino/a student enrollments that elect to become full members, and other institutions with 10–24 percent of Latino/a undergraduates, or at least 1,000 Latino/a undergraduates (head count) that elect to become associate members. For the purpose of this study, we utilize the "official" definition of Hispanic-Serving, which classifies any higher educational institution with at least 25 percent Latino/a enrollment as an HSI.

The multiple ways of becoming an HSI makes it possible for some institutions to appear as an HSI in one list but not in another; moreover, since most people are not aware of the differences among the many ways of becoming an HSI, it is commonly assumed that any institution with an enrollment of at least 25 percent Latino/a must be Hispanic-Serving. Another complication related to the criteria for becoming an HSI is that it is possible for an institution to cease being Hispanic-Serving if, for example, the percentage of Latinos/as drops below 25 percent or there is a change in the proportion of Hispanics who are low-income.

In sum, Hispanic-Serving is a manufactured identity that is highly variable. In the same way that an institution can gain the status of Hispanic-Serving from one year to the next if there is an increase in the percentage of Latino/a students, it can also lose its HSI designation if it experiences a decline of Latino/a enrollment. The unplanned and unstable nature of the HSI identity made us wonder about its importance and influence in the character of the institution. We wondered, "In what ways do the mission statements incorporate the HSI identity?" and "How do institutions demonstrate their HSI identity inside and outside of the campus?" We explore these two questions in the next section.

THE SIGNIFICANCE OF MISSION STATEMENTS

There is some disagreement about the significance of institutional mission statements. Some organizational theorists believe that ambiguity, a characteristic that is common to most institutional mission statements, makes it possible for colleges and universities to pursue competing goals without risking conflict among different factions (Cohen & March, 1986; Birnbaum, 1988). In contrast, scholars of organizational cultures view mission statements as the embodiment of an institution's values, commitment, and purpose (Caruthers & Lott, 1981; Chaffee & Tierney, 1988; Peeke, 1994). The perceived benefits of an ambiguous mission statement may have greater applicability to large and structurally complex research universities. In contrast, a special purpose institution would not be well served by an ambiguous mission statement that hides its distinctiveness and commitment to specific student populations or educational purposes. For example, Howard University refers to itself as a "historically Black, private university . . . with particular emphasis upon the provision of educational opportunities to promising Black students"; Wellesley College aims "to provide an excellent liberal arts education for women who will make a difference in the world"; and Tohono O'odham Community College is dedicated to enhancing the unique Tohono O'odham Himdag. Himdag is an all-encompassing word for the culture, way of life, and values of the Tohono O'odham people.

Mission statements serve many functions in postsecondary institutions. From a cultural perspective, the mission statement is the place where one can learn "what [the institution] is, and what it is not" (Caruthers & Lott, 1981, p. 26). In addition, if constructed meaningfully, the mission statement can be a guide for change, a consensus-builder and an assessment tool. Because the mission statement declares an institution's intent and direction (Dominick, 1990), mission statements are the starting place in strategic planning efforts (Gioia & Thomas, 1996), and an organization's participants typically spend a great deal of time deliberating on the content. The mission statement can guide long-term change efforts, reminding decision makers of institutional values and goals. If an institution's statement of mission prioritizes educating low-income students, for example, the mission statement serves as a tangible cue to university leadership to enact policies and practices, allocate resources, and take other necessary steps to meet this priority. When institutions experience major changes in their institutional identity (e.g., a single sex institution becomes coeducational; a religiously affiliated institution becomes secular) their mission statements are likely to change to signal new values and beliefs (Peeke, 1994) and provide stakeholders with a collective understanding of the institution (Chaffee & Tierney, 1988).

Given the cultural importance of mission statements we chose 10 two- and four-year HSIs in California, Texas, New Mexico, Colorado, and New York and examined how their HSI designation was incorporated into their mission. The 10 institutions were selected purposefully to reflect variability in institutional type, size, urban, and rural location. The sample included small institutions with enrollments of fewer than 5,000 students as well as institutions with more than 15,000 students. Among the four-year campuses, three granted only BAs and MAs and two were doctoral granting institutions. We also selected institutions based on high, low, or moderate Latino/a enrollment and created an institutional sample with varying levels of "latinization."

Institutional mission statements for the 10 colleges and universities were retrieved from institutional websites. For the purposes of consistency, only statements labeled "mission statement" were included in the analysis. We conducted the mission statement analysis on multiple levels. First, we searched for keywords related to HSI status (e.g., Hispanic-Serving Institution, Hispanic, diversity, equity, underrepresented minorities). Following this first-order analysis, we examined the mission statements in greater detail noting how these keywords were used and in what context. We then categorized each institution's mission statement by the salience of the HSI status and the manner in which the status was discussed.

THE SALIENCE OF HSI IDENTITY IN INSTITUTIONAL MISSION STATEMENTS

The most surprising and unexpected finding was that none of the 10 institutions explicitly mentioned their designation as a Hispanic-Serving Institution in their mission statement. Instead, three keywords emerged from our analysis: "diversity/diverse," "culture/multicultural," and "access." The mission statements of all 10 institutions examined include at least one of the aforementioned keywords. In some cases, however, it is not apparent that the keywords are used in a context related to racial or ethnic characteristics of their student body, and in some cases it was not clear if these words were used in relation to students. For example, CA–4 states that the university aims to prepare students for a "changing, multicultural world," but does not specifically make reference to the importance of a diverse student body to accomplish this goal. CO–4's mission states that the institution "offers programs, when feasible that preserve and promote the unique history and culture of the region," but there is no indication of what that culture is, nor any mention of the composition of the student body. And the mission statement of NM–4 refers to faculty, staff, and students' advancement of "understanding of the world, its peoples, and cultures," but does not make reference to, or identify the culture or diversity of faculty, staff, or students.

Six institutions use the keywords "diverse/diversity," and/or "culture" in relation to students or the entire campus population. The mission statements of CA–2, NY–4, NY–2, TX–4, TX–2 and NM–2 include statements about the importance of a "culturally diverse environment," "diverse population," or "diverse student body." In all but one case, these institutions referred to responding to the needs of a diverse student body or providing services and support to a diverse student body. Excerpts from each institutional mission statement are shown in table 6.2.

The final keyword identified in our analysis was "access." The missions of two institutions included this keyword; the mission statement of CO–2 refers to the institution's role to provide access to "underserved students,"

Table 6.2 Analysis of Institutional Literature and Website

Institution	Explicit mention of HSI Status in Mission Statement	Inclusion of related keywords (e.g. diversity, culture, access)	Excerpt from Institutional Mission Statement
CA-4	No	Yes	"[Our college's] mission is to . . . prepare students for lifelong learning, leadership, and careers in a changing, *multicultural* world."
CA-2	No	Yes	"We are responsive to the learning needs of our community and dedicated to a *diverse* educational and *cultural* campus environment . . ."
CO-4	No	Yes	". . . [Our college] offers programs, when feasible, that preserve and promote the unique history and *culture* of the region."
CO-2	No	Yes	"Programs and strategies that promote *access* and success for *underserved* students are the foundation of [our college] operations."
NM-4	No	Yes	"Faculty, staff, and students . . . advance our understanding of the world, its peoples, and *cultures*."
NM-2	No	Yes	"IHE offers a wide range of educational programs and services to meet the needs of . . . a *diverse* population."
NY-4	No	Yes	". . . the College provides a *diverse* student body with exceptional opportunities to participate in creative intellectual pursuits."
NY-2	No	Yes	"Located a transit hub that links . . . the most *ethnically diverse* borough with the world center of finance . . . the college provides *access* to higher education and serves New Yorkers of all backgrounds, ages, and means. [Our college] is committed to . . . providing extensive support services and opportunities for a highly *diverse* student population . . . enhanc[ing] the economic, social, cultural, and educational development of Western Queens and New York City."
TX-4	No	Yes	"The mission of the [college] is to provide a range of educational programs that foster an intellectually and *culturally diverse* environment . . ."
TX-2	No	Yes	"The mission of [the] Community College District is to provide educational opportunities and support services that prepare individuals . . . to contribute to their economically and *culturally diverse* community."

and NY–2's mission states that the institution "provides access to higher education and serves New Yorkers of all backgrounds, ages, and means."

Upon finding that none of the institutional mission statements made reference specifically to being a Hispanic-Serving Institution, we expanded our exploratory analysis beyond the mission statement. We used the search feature on each college's website and searched for "Hispanic-Serving Institutions" and "HSI" to identify substantive statements that might make reference to being a Hispanic-Serving Institution. This search resulted in links to the HSI acronym for all but one institution. However, in all but three of the institutions the HSI designation was used descriptively in information about Title V funded projects and in job announcements, which included the institution's HSI status as part of the college's description. The search typically led to a link that read as follows: "With an overall Hispanic enrollment in excess of 25 percent, [Name of Institution] has been an officially designated Hispanic-Serving Institution (HSI) since Congress established that designation in 1992." We found substantive statements about being an HSI in just one institution, a comparatively small four-year institution in Colorado. The link took us to a profile of the president, which said, "Dr . . . also puts a priority on the college's role as a Hispanic-Serving Institution" and quotes the president as saying, "We must respect the cultures that developed this region. Most importantly, if 30 percent of our students are Hispanic, 30 percent of our graduates will be Hispanic." In addition, we also used key identifiers like Latino/a, Hispanic, Mexican-American to assess direct efforts pertaining to this particular group of students, and found that references to Latino/a students were embedded in umbrella diversity literature for each of the respective campuses. Based on the website search we were not able to discern a Latino/a agenda across the Hispanic-serving institutions assessed.

HSIS AND LATINO/A EDUCATIONAL OUTCOMES

We concluded our exploration of these 10 institutions by examining their value-added to Latino/a students. Specifically, we asked: Do these institutions produce equitable educational outcomes for Hispanic students? We asked this question for two reasons. First, the approaches that have been used to assess the value-added of HSIs have focused on the percentage of total BA and MA degrees earned by Latinos/as that were conferred by HSIs (Stearns, Watanabe & Snyder, 2002); the percentage of Latino/a Ph.D. recipients who earned their BA at an HSI (Solórzano, 1995); and the number of HSIs that rank among the top 25 baccalaureate origins of science and engineering doctorate recipients (National Science Foundation, 2004). Based on these studies HSIs have been found to play a critical role in the education of Latinos/as in the following ways: (1) providing access to higher education: HSIs represent eight percent of postsecondary institutions but nearly half (48 percent) of all the Latino/a students enrolled in higher education attend an HSI (Stearns, Watanabe, & Snyder, 2002; Brown & Santiago, 2004); (2) community colleges in California that have the highest concentration of Latinos/as transferring to a four-year college are HSIs (Laden, 2000); (3) eight of the top 25 baccalaureate origins of 1997–2001 science and engineering doctorate recipients were HSIs (National Science Foundation, 2004); (4) seven of the top 10 baccalaureate origin institutions of all Chicana doctorate recipients between 1980 and 1990 were HSIs (Solórzano, 1995); (5) HSIs conferred 25 percent of the master's degrees earned by Latinos/as in 1999–2000 (Stearns, Watanabe, & Snyder, 2002).

The two empirical studies that we came across examined whether HSIs produce more engaged and satisfied students (Laird, et al., 2004) and faculty attitudes, opinions about students and levels of job satisfaction at HSIs (Stage & Hubbard, 2005). Laird et al. (2004) found that Latino/a students attending predominantly White institutions and Hispanic-Serving Institutions had similar scores in the National Survey of Student Engagement (NSSE) in terms of engagement, satisfaction with college, and gains in overall development. In contrast, the authors reported that a comparable analyses of African Americans at HBCUs revealed they are more engaged and feel that they gain more from college than their counterparts at predominantly White institutions. Similarly, Stage and Hubbard (2005) found only a few differences between HSIs and predominantly White institutions in terms of faculty attitudes, practices, and satisfaction. Conversely, there were differences in these measures between HBCUs and predominantly White and Hispanic-Serving Institutions.

The second reason that prompted us to examine the outcomes of Latinos/as compared to other racial and ethnic groups who also attend HSIs is that unlike other special mission institutions, HSIs, particularly BA granting institutions also have high concentrations of White and Asian American students. Thus, these institutions are largely multicultural in their student composition. Studies have shown that compared to these groups, Latinos/as generally experience unequal educational outcomes (Bensimon, Hao, & Bustillos, 2006). Thus, we wondered how the outcomes for Latinos/as at HSIs would compare to those of groups that typically experience greater equity. To explore this question we used fall 2004 IPEDS data to construct indicators of access, degree completion, and degrees earned in high demand fields. Below we describe the Equity Index method that was used to determine the value-added context for Latinos/as that attend HSIs.

ASSESSING EQUITY IN EDUCATIONAL OUTCOMES FOR LATINOS/AS IN HSIS

The analysis for assessing equity at the four-year institutions that we conducted is largely exploratory. For this analysis we applied an Equity Index method (Hao, 2005), a measure of proportionality to establish how far or how close a particular group (e.g., Latinos, Latinas, African American males, White women, etc.) is from reaching representation on a particular indicator of attainment that is equal to their representation in a specified population pool. The index does not assess cohorts, but rather proportionality at a single point in time. Hao's equity index method has been used to assess the state of equity in college readiness and participation for Latinos in California and Texas (Hao, 2005); Perna and colleagues (2005) have used a similar index to measure the equity for African American students in admission and BA degree attainment in the southern states; Contreras (2003, 2005) utilized a parity index to assess the level of representation of minority students post 209 in select California UC institutions (as applicants and admits), compared to their composition in California high schools, graduation rates, and percent of those UC eligible for admission; and Bensimon, Hao, and Bustillos (2006) have used it to construct an academic equity scorecard for California's postsecondary education system. The Equity Index formula is depicted in figure 6.1.

$$\text{Target Group's \textbf{Equity Index} for the educational outcome of interest} = \frac{\text{Target group with the educational outcome} \div \text{Total students with the educational outcome}}{\text{Target group in the reference population} \div \text{Total students in the reference population}}$$

The percentage in the numerator consists of the share of Latino/a students who have achieved a particular educational outcome, such as earning the BA degree. The denominator consists of the share of Latino/a students who make up the reference population for the particular educational outcome, such as the Latinos' share in the freshman cohort four years prior to the year BA degree attainment was examined. Equity is achieved when the value of the numerator equals the value of the denominator, which means the value of the index equals "1.0." A number below 1.0 indicates inequity.

DO HSIS PRODUCE EQUAL ACCESS TO HIGHER EDUCATION FOR LATINOS/AS?

The enrollment tables provided earlier in the chapter revealed that the 10 HSIs enroll very large percentages of Latinos/as. For our analysis we examined whether the enrollment of Latinos/as was proportional to Latino/a high school graduates in the state where each institution is located, using the formula in figure 6.2:

$$\frac{\text{Number of Latino (or White, Black, etc.) degree recipients/all degree recipients}}{\text{Target group undergraduate enrollment/Total undergraduate enrollment}}$$

Our analysis revealed that three of the four-year colleges are performing extremely well in terms providing access to Latinos/as in proportion to their representation among high school graduates in their respective states. Notably, Latinos/as do not have equitable levels of access to the two most selective four-year institutions in the sample. The important role these institutions play in serving minorities is evident in the equity scores for Asian Americans and Blacks; both groups are above equity in all institutions except one. On the other hand, Whites are below equity in all but one institution. Detailed results of the equity index for enrollment versus the composition of high school graduates in each of the five states are provided in table 6.3a–g.

Similar to the accessibility that four-year Hispanic-Serving Institutions provided for Latino/a students, the two-year institutions played a greater role in access. Given that the majority of Latinos/as are enrolled in community

Table 6.3 Equity Index—Various Institutions

Table 6.3A Equity Index for Access to 4-year Institutions, 2004

	White	Black	Latino	Asian/Pacific Islander	American Indian
ACCESS: Undergraduate Enrollment vs. High School Graduates					
CA-4	.557	.521	.775	2.37	NA
NM-4	1.10	1.30	.789	2.53	.591
TX-4	.463	2.0	1.10	2.91	3.0
NY-4	.237	1.93	2.62	2.03	.100
CO-4	.728	1.30	1.89	.344	1.50

Table 6.3B Equity Index for Access to 2-year Institutions, 2004

	White	Black	Latino	Asian/Pacific Islander	American Indian
ACCESS: Enrollment vs. High School Graduates					
CA—2	.567	.394	1.53	.523	.01
CO—2	.543	3.58	1.96	1.63	.588
NM—2	1.15	.004	.934	1.15	.300
NY—2	.259	1.30	3.09	1.87	.100
TX—2	.173	.176	2.64	.003	.300

Table 6.3C Equity Index for BA Degrees Conferred, 2004

	White	Black	Latino	Asian/Pacific Islander	American Indian
RETENTION: BA Degrees Conferred vs. Total Enrollment					
CA-4	1.05	.784	.796	.938	.333
NM-4	1.19	.733	.910	.970	.277
TX-4	1.48	.996	.722	.980	.667
NY-4	.905	1.38	.831	1.26	NA
CO-4	1.26	.589	.832	.006	.004

Table 6.3D Equity Index for AA Degrees Conferred, 2004

	White	Black	Latino	Asian/Pacific Islander	American Indian
RETENTION: AA Degrees Conferred vs. Total Enrollment					
CA-2	1.01	1.82	.994	1.23	140
CO-2	1.24	.824	.718	1.13	.882
NM-2	.913	NA	1.11	.004	1.30
NY-2	.930	.857	.896	1.02	1.0
TX-2	1.41	1.22	.967	.8	.667

Table 6.3E Equity Index for Degrees Conferred in Math at 4-Year Institutions, 2004

	White	Black	Latino	Asian/Pacific Islander	American Indian
RETENTION: Degrees Conferred in Math vs. Total Enrollment in Math Major					
CA -4	1.09	0	.677	2.22	2.57
NM -4	1.15	0	1.198	0	.593
TX -4	2.57	.737	.606	1.03	NA
NY -4	1.21	1.21	1.94	.725	NA
CO -4	1.31	0	0	0	NA

Note: The data for Math was comprised of very small ns, essentially illustrating a large drop off of students in the Math major across all racial/ethnic categories.

Table 6.3F Equity Index for Degrees Conferred in Engineering at 4-Year Institutions, 2004

	White	Black	Latino	Asian/Pacific Islander	American Indian
RETENTION: Degrees Conferred in Engineering vs. Total Enrollment in Engineering Major					
CA-4	1.02	1.07	.616	1.06	1.33
NM-4	1.11	.002	.889	1.48	.632
NY-4	.787	1.53	.885	.844	NA

Note: The Texas and Colorado institutions did not have engineering degrees.

Table 6.3G Equity Index for Degrees Conferred in Biology/Life Sciences at 4-Year Institutions, 2004

	White	Black	Latino	Asian/Pacific Islander	American Indian
RETENTION: Degrees Conferred in Biology/Life Sciences vs. Total Enrollment in Biology/Life Sciences Major					
CA -4	1.19	1.89	.841	.686	NA
NM -4	1.30	.500	.795	2.0	.467
TX -4	1.07	1.53	.397	.580	NA
NY -4	.813	.737	.698	1.42	NA
CO -4	1.23	NA	.312	NA	1.45

colleges nationally (close to half), and the fact that two-year institutions are essentially open enrollment campuses, the equity index for access to two-year colleges can be interpreted as positive or negative news. The good news is that community colleges in four states are providing more than equitable access to Latinos/as. However, this is central to the mission of community colleges in general and not unique to HSIs. The bad news is that the significant concentration of Latinos/as in two-year HSIs can also be interpreted as a sign of segregation and diminished opportunity for educational advancement, depending on these institutions' track record in preparing and facilitating transfer to four-year colleges. Given that they are the primary point of entry into higher education for Latinos/as and students of color, the key issues for two-year institutions include persistence, transfer, and preparation for academic success (degree completion).

DO HSIS PRODUCE EQUITABLE ATTAINMENT OF DEGREES FOR LATINOS/AS?

The previous section conveyed that HSIs add value to Latinos/as by providing them with access to higher education. In this analysis we consider the value of access by examining whether HSIs produce equitable results in baccalaureate and associates degrees earned by Latinos/as. To compute the equity index for degrees earned we applied the following formula to the ten institutions (Detailed results of our calculations appear in table 6.3a–g):

$$\frac{\textit{Number of Latino (or white, black, etc.) degree recipients/all degree recipients}}{\text{Target group undergraduate enrollment/Total undergraduate enrollment}}$$

Surprisingly, the BA equity index for Latinos/as revealed them to be below equity at all five four-year HSIs included in our analysis. In contrast, Whites exceed equity in all but one institution. In addition, while White students were found to be below equity in terms of access at four of the five institutions, they are earning a disproportionately higher share of BA degrees earned. These results suggest that Latinos/as may be experiencing unequal outcomes compared to Whites even at Hispanic-Serving Institutions. Admittedly, this analysis has limitations in that we are comparing two different populations, and it is possible that the same analysis applied to a cohort of students to assess BA attainment four and six years after first enrolling may have produced different results. Although IPEDS does not permit a cohort analysis of equity in BA attainment, HSIs have access to their own institutional data and could easily assess themselves on this indicator.

Even more surprising, the equity index results for AA attainment for Latinos/as in two-year HSIs were not much different from the findings for BA attainment. We found that Latinos/as achieved equity in AA degree attainment at only one community college. In contrast, Whites achieved equity at three of the two-year HSIs. The outcomes for the AA equity index suggest that starting postsecondary education in two-year colleges may not yield optimal returns for Latino/a community college students and concurs with the research on Latinos/as in the community colleges, which suggests high attrition rates (Contreras & Gandara, 2005; Saenz, 2002).

DO HSIS PRODUCE EQUITABLE ATTAINMENT OF DEGREES IN FIELDS IN WHICH THERE IS AN UNDERREPRESENTATION OF LATINOS/AS?

The Hispanic-Serving Institutions reviewed also had higher levels of access to science, technology, engineering, and math majors in which students of color are severely underrepresented. What appeared unclear is whether access to science, technology, engineering, and mathematics (STEM) majors translates into equitable results in degrees earned by Latinos/as. We therefore examined equity in BA degrees granted in mathematics, engineering and biology/life sciences by comparing them to the number of students who declared themselves as mathematics, engineering, or biology/life science majors. The equity index results for mathematics degree attainment revealed Whites as achieving equity in all five HSIs, whereas Latinos/as achieved equity in only two of the HSI institutions examined. Even though Latinos/as comprised over 20 percent of the math majors at three of the Hispanic-Serving Institutions, they were still below equity in earned degrees, and White students constituted the majority of mathematics degree recipients. In addition, Latinos/as were found to be below equity among engineering degree recipients in three institutions for which data were available.

Finally, of the Latinos/as enrolled in STEM majors, our analysis of IPEDS data revealed that the majority are likely to be enrolled in the biological/life sciences. In our review of the percentage of students enrolled in the biology/life science major at the five HSI institutions, we found that four of the five institutions had at least 25 percent of Latinos/as. However, our analysis revealed that at all five HSIs, Latino/a students fell below this proportion in terms of degree attainment in biological and life sciences. Conversely, White students experienced inequity in this major in only one of the HSI institutions.

In sum, the exploratory study showed that the websites of HSIs contain almost no symbolic representations that call attention to their Hispanic-Serving identity and make it immediately recognizable to the outside world. The search of the 10 institutions' websites revealed that the HSI identity was typically acknowledged in descriptions of programs and special initiatives supported by Title V. The assessment of access and success through the analytical lenses of the Equity Index revealed that four- and two-year HSIs produce equitable access for Latinos/as but unequal attainment of degrees generally, particularly in high-income fields from which Latinos/as are locked out (Davis, 2001). These findings underscore the fact that access is hardly sufficient to close the educational opportunity gaps in higher education.

Even though these findings are exploratory and applicable to 10 representative institutions, they bring to light questions about the purpose, role, and outcomes of Hispanic-Serving Institutions that merit further in-depth study and analysis. In the next section, we consider some of these questions and the implications of the findings in relation to the educational condition of Latino/a students.

CONCLUSION

Why is the Hispanic identity of HSIs invisible? There are several plausible answers to this question. First, institutions are transformed into Hispanic-Serving purely on the basis of changing demographics. Their conversion seems to be accidental and evolutionary rather than strategically planned, which may explain the silence about being Hispanic-Serving. It is possible that the Hispanic identity is so new that for most institutions there has not been enough time to reconsider their mission in light of their newly acquired identity. We have no way of knowing whether the institutions have had strategic planning processes since becoming HSIs and what role, if any, the HSI status played in deliberations about future direction and mission implementation. Another possibility is that the absence of symbols signifying the Latinization of institutional identity is symptomatic of internalized racism. The mention of Hispanic may conjure stereotypical images in which Latinos/as appear, even if subconsciously, as the "negative other"—the "illegal immigrant," impoverished, uneducated, day laborer who speaks little or no English. Or, possibly, institutional leaders may be apprehensive about embracing the Hispanic-Serving identity too enthusiastically for fear of alienating students from other racial or ethnic groups and discouraging them from applying to the institution. In a post-*Grutter* context, institutions that target, or are perceived to be targeting, specific underrepresented racial groups increasingly face a backlash from those who oppose affirmative action and the diversity movement in general.

Institutions may be hesitant to publicize their HSI designation, despite its legitimacy as a federally recognized institutional type, because of possible negative reactions from anti-diversity forces. Alternatively, HSIs may be fearful that in being openly Hispanic-Serving there will be repercussions such as the loss of prestige, or that they will be stigmatized as different from "normal" or mainstream institutions. Unfortunately, this fear is likely warranted given the larger social context of this country, which deems "Hispanic-Serving" as a negative characteristic. In the current climate of American higher education, prestige is everything. Colleges and universities are attempting to become more selective, engaging in marketing campaigns, and working to maximize their prestige. Thus, it is not surprising that leaders of HSIs feel that the costs of publicizing the Hispanic-Serving status outweigh the benefits, particularly when these benefits (i.e., Title V funds) do not require public proclamations of the designation. It is possible that the lack of acknowledgement of the HSI designation may be simply an oversight. The Hispanic identity might be taken for granted and the fact that it is essentially missing from institutional documents may not be noticeable to institutional members.

What might be the implications of not acknowledging the Hispanic-Serving identity? We recognize that mission statements are not the most widely read documents of an institution nor are they likely to be scrutinized regularly for relevance. We also recognize that the apparent non-acknowledgement of the Hispanic-Serving identity in the website may not be as important if, for example, the institutional leaders repeatedly and consistently articulate its importance and interpret its meaning to the campus community and external constituencies. It is also possible that an institution's website is not an accurate reflection of an institution's values and commitments or actual practices. However, we contend that this venue presents an opportunity for HSIs to market themselves and disclose the niche they fulfill.

Notwithstanding the limitations of the web search method used to determine the salience of Hispanic-Serving identity, our findings introduce the divergence between meeting a demographic requirement to qualify for Title V funds and producing equitable results for the very students who are the basis for the HSI designation. The examination of the status of Latinos/as on measures of access and success showed that these 10 HSIs do extremely well in attracting and enrolling Latino/a students. However, on success measures, the patterns of unequal outcomes that are typical of Latinos/as in predominantly White institutions are reproduced in the HSIs. On just about every measure of success, including overall attainment of AA and BA degrees, and degree completion in high demand fields, Latinos/as were below equity and Whites were above equity. It is possible that the non-transparency of the Hispanic-Serving identity in the mission statements of the 10 institutions is an indication that not enough attention is being given to student outcomes. Another plausible interpretation for our findings with respect to the institutions' closeted identity is that being an HSI has yet to create a sense of collective responsibility and accountability among institutional leaders and faculty members for producing equitable educational outcomes for Latino/a students.

To conclude, we offer four sets of recommendations for HSIs, the U.S. Department of Education, accrediting associations, and researchers. The purpose of these recommendations is to start framing an agenda for institutional self-assessment, policy development, and knowledge creation designed for HSIs.

For institutional self-assessment we recommend that the meaning of Hispanic-Serving be considered in relation to: (1) mission and values that guide academic decision making and resource allocation; (2) roles and responsibilities of faculty members, administrators, staff, and trustees; (3) knowledge and competencies that are expected of academic leaders, faculty members, staff, and trustees; (4) criteria for appointing and evaluating the performance of institutional leaders, faculty members, and staff; (5) assessment of institutional performance and effectiveness and student outcomes; and (6) the needs of the regional economy with respect to contributing to the development of sustainable communities.

Currently institutions that apply to be designated a Developing Hispanic-Serving Institution and to be eligible to receive a grant under the Strengthening Institutions Program (Title V) are required only to provide data on Hispanic student enrollment and on the proportion that are classified as needy. The U.S. Department of Education could do two things to influence HSIs. First, it could require them to report student outcomes disaggregated by gender within racial-ethnic categories on specific measures of success such as year-to-year persistence, six-year BA degree attainment and three-year AA attainment, transfer rates from community colleges to four-year colleges, majors and degree recipients in STEM fields, GPA for graduating students, postbaccalaureate enrollment in professional and graduate programs. Second, HSIs could be required to provide benchmarks to monitor institutional effectiveness in producing equitable educational outcomes for Latinos/as such as the methods and processes of the Equity Scorecard pioneered by the Center for Urban Education at the University of Southern California (Bensimon, 2004; Bensimon et. al., 2004; Dowd, 2005). Related to the above recommendations regarding institutions that accept Title V funding, accrediting associations can ensure that these HSIs fulfill their obligation to serve Latino/a students by requiring Title V recipients to include the HSI designation in the institutional mission statement and evaluating these institutions along the metric of equity in educational outcomes for Latinos/as during the accreditation process.* The evaluation approach should also include an examination of the academic support that exists within the infrastructure of the institution.

Lastly, it has been observed that while there is a considerable body of research on the collegiate experience of Latino/a students, actual empirical work that is specific to HSIs is practically nonexistent (Laird, et al., 2004, p. 4). Indeed, as we mentioned earlier, the only two studies we located were a paper by Laird and several of his colleagues which compared student engagement at predominantly White and HSIs and HBCUs (Laird, et al., 2004) and a paper by Stage and Hubbard that explored attitudes and practices of faculty at HSIs (Stage & Hubbard, 2005). In light of the very large concentration of Latino/a students at HSIs (48 percent of all undergraduates, including Puerto Rico), particularly in the two-year college sector, there is an urgent need to develop an agenda for qualitative and quantitative studies to address topics such as: the academic culture of HSIs; the attitudes, values, and commitments of HSI faculty members; faculty members' awareness of the HSI status and the meanings they ascribe to it; the academic outcomes HSIs produce for Latino/a students (cohort analyses); and the role of HSIs in increasing college enrollment and degree attainment for Latinos/as.

We are cognizant that leaders of Hispanic-Serving Institutions may view our analysis as a critique coming from outsiders who have limited experience with these institutions. In anticipation of this criticism, we conclude that it is precisely because we value the critical role that HSIs play in increasing the numbers of college educated Latinos/as that we chose to test the meaning of Hispanic-Serving in relation to identity and equity in student outcomes. We have attempted to make unexamined aspects of these institutions visible, and hope to contribute to the discussion of the increasingly

* The authors thank Frances K. Stage for this insightful suggestion.

important purpose Hispanic-Serving institutions might play within the Latino community, specifically the potential for maximizing their impact on raising the levels of Latino/a postsecondary attainment.

REFERENCES

Ben-David, J. (1977). *Trends in American higher education*. Chicago, IL: The University of Chicago Press.

Bensimon, E. M. (2004). The diversity scorecard: A learning approach to institutional change. *Change, 36*(1), 45–52.

Bensimon, E. M., Hao, L., and Bustillos, L. T. (2006). Measuring the state of equity in higher education. In Gandara, P. Orfield, G., & Horn, C. (Eds.). *Leveraging promise and expanding opportunity in higher education*. Albany: State University of New York Press.

Bensimon, E. M., Polkinghorne, D. P., Bauman, G. L., and Vallejo, E. (2004). Doing research that makes a difference. *Journal of Higher Education, 75*(1), 104–126.

Birnbaum, R. (1983). *Maintaining diversity in American higher education*. San Francisco, CA: Jossey-Bass Inc., Publishers.

Birnbaum, R. (1988). *How colleges work: The cybernetics of academic organization and leadership*. San Francisco, CA: Jossey-Bass Inc., Publishers.

Brown, S. E., and Santiago, D. (2004, December 27). Latino students gravitate toward HSIs. *Hispanic Outlook in Higher Education, 15*(7), 21.

Caruthers, J. K., and Lott, G. B. (1981). *Mission review: Foundation for strategic planning*. Boulder, CO: National Center for Higher Education Management Systems.

Chaffee, E. E., and Tierney, W. G. (1988). *Collegiate culture and leadership strategies*. New York: American Council on Education and Macmillan Publishing.

Cohen, M. D., and March, J. G. (1986). *Leadership and ambiguity* (2nd ed.). Boston, MA: Harvard Business School Press.

Contreras, F. (2003). College admissions in the affirmative action era and post Proposition 209: Assessing the impact of public policy on college access in California (Doctoral dissertation, Stanford University, 2003). *Dissertation Abstract International*, 71–73.

Contreras, F. (2005). The Reconstruction of Merit Post Proposition 209. *Educational Policy*, Sage Publications, 19, 371–395.

Contreras, F., and Gandara, P. (2005). Latinas/os in the Ph.D. pipeline: A case of historical and contemporary exclusion. In J. Castellanos and A. Gloria (Eds.), *Journey to a Ph.D.:The Latina/o experience in higher education*. Sterling, VA: Stylus Publishing.

Davis, M. (2001). *Magical urbanism: Latinos reinvent the U.S. city*. London: Verso.

Dominick, C. A. (1990). Revising the institutional mission. *New Directions for Higher Education, 71*, 29–36.

Dowd, A. C. (2005). *Data don't drive: Building a practitioner-driven culture of inquiry to assess community college performance*. Indianapolis, IN: Lumina Foundation for Education.

Drewry, H., and Doermann, H. (2001). *Stand and Prosper: Private Black colleges and their students*. Princeton, NJ: Princeton University Press.

Gioia, D. A., and Thomas, J. B. (1996). Identity, image and issue interpretation: Sensemaking during strategic change in academia. *Administrative Science Quarterly, 41*(3), 370–403.

Hao, L. (2005). Assessing equitable postsecondary educational outcomes for Hispanics in California and Texas. Unpublished Dissertation. University of Southern California.

Higher Education Amendments of 1998, Pub. L. No. 105–244, §§ 501–518, 112 Stat. 1581 (1999).

Hispanic Association of Colleges and Universities. (n.d.). *HACU—HEA background.* Retrieved July 30, 2005, from http://www.hacu.net/hacu/HEA_Background_EN.asp?SnID=311953099

Institutional Development and Undergraduate Education Service. (n.d.). Hispanic-Serving Institution List. Retrieved June 12, 2005, from http://www.ed.gov/programs/idueshsi/hsilist0102.xls

Kim, M., and Alvarez, R. (1995). Women-only colleges: Some unanticipated consequences. *Journal of Higher Education, 66*(6), 641–668.

Laden, B. V. (2000). *Hispanic-Serving two-year institutions: What accounts for their high transfer rates?* Paper presented at the annual meeting of the Association for the Study of Higher Education, Sacramento, CA.

Laden, B. V. (2004). Hispanic-serving institutions: What are they? Where are they? *Community College Journal of Research and Practice, 28,* 181–198.

Laird, T. F., Bridges, B. K., Holmes, M. S., Morelon, C. K., and Williams, J. M. (2004, November). *African American and Hispanic student engagement at minority serving and predominantly White institutions.* Paper presented at the Annual meeting of the Association for the Study of Higher Education, Kansas City, MO.

National Science Foundation. (2004). *Women, minorities, and persons with disabilities in science and engineering: 2004* (NSF 04–317) Arlington, VA: Author.

Outcalt, C., and Skewes-Cox, T. (2002). Involvement, interaction and satisfaction: The human environment at HBCUs. *Review of Higher Education, 25*(3), 331–347.

Peeke, G. (1994). *Mission and change: Institutional mission and its application to the management of further and higher education.* Buckingham, England: Open University Press.

Perna, L. W., Milem, J., Gerald, D., Baum, E., Rowan, H., and Hutchens, N. (2005, May). *The status of equity for Black undergraduates in public higher education in the south: Still separate and unequal.* Paper presented at the annual meeting of the Association for Institutional Research, San Diego, CA.

Saenz, V. B. (2002). Hispanic students and community colleges: A critical point for intervention. ERIC Digest. Los Angeles, CA: Eric Clearinghouse for Community Colleges. (ERIC Document Reproduction Service No. ED 477908)

Solórzano, D. G. (1995). The baccalaureate origins of Chicana and Chicano doctorates in the social sciences. *Hispanic Journal of Behavioral Sciences, 17*(1), 3–32.

Stage, F. K., and Hubbard, S. M. (2005, November). *Conditions, practices and attitudes of faculty at Hispanic-serving institutions.* Paper presented at the Annual meeting of the Association for the Study of Higher Education, Philadelphia, PA.

Stearns, C., Watanabe, S., and Snyder, T. (2002). *Hispanic-serving institutions: Statistical trends from 1990–1999.* National Center for Education Statistics (NCES 2002–051). Washington, DC: U.S. Department of Education.

Title V of the Higher Education Act, 20 U.S.C. §§ 1100 *et seq.* (2005). U.S. Department of Education. (2005). *Funding status—Title V developing Hispanic-serving institutions program.* Retrieved August 2, 2005, from http://www.ed.gov/programs/idueshsi/funding.html

CHAPTER 7

Tribal Colleges and Universities

Identity, Invisibility, and Current Issues

Justin P. Guillory and Kelly Ward

If you ask a student or even a faculty member at a mainstream institution if they can name one tribal college, chances are, the answer would be no. Ironically, the obscurity of tribal colleges and universities (TCUs) and their impact on reservations across America make their story that much more important. Over the past 30 years, TCUs have experienced a dramatic growth in a relatively brief amount of time, yet despite their ability to provide unprecedented educational access to Native American students their success has been overlooked beyond the borders of Indian Country.

TCUs comprise an intriguing and little-studied phenomenon within higher education. For years, mainstream institutions have failed to meet the unique needs of Native American students due to governmental neglect and miseducation. Today, Minority-Serving Institutions (MSIs) such as TCUs provide unprecedented access to historically marginalized groups such as Native Americans, African Americans, and Hispanic Americans. The emergence and growth of MSIs has much to teach mainstream institutions given their ability to attract and retain students who consistently have the lowest graduation rates and who are often the most difficult to retain. TCUs, in particular, have been able to successfully tap into their own respective Indian populations where mainstream school systems are often viewed with antipathy and skepticism because of their historical association with the U.S. government's relentless efforts to assimilate Indians into mainstream society. The grim reality of the government's unyielding assault on Indian people have left permanent scars. However, the tenets of cultural pride and hope that did survive are remarkably being resurrected and revitalized at TCUs.

The purpose of this chapter is to delineate how TCUs have found a unique niche within the Minority-Serving Institution umbrella. This chapter begins with a brief overview of the history of Indian education and how its legacy of failure spurred the genesis and growth of the tribal college movement. Second, we discuss several issues that TCUs are currently facing. And third, the chapter offers an analysis of how TCUs negotiate the needs of tribal communities and broader needs of higher education.

HISTORICAL OVERVIEW OF INDIAN EDUCATION

To better understand the purpose and significance of TCUs, it is helpful to think of the history of Indian education in the context of three overarching eras: colonial, federal and self-determination (Carney, 1999; McClellen, Fox, & Lowe, 2005). For over 350 years, Native Americans have been encouraged to participate in the ritual of higher education (Carnegie Foundation for the Advancement of Teaching, 1989). Indian education was misguided from the beginning because the American higher education system that Indians would later be coerced into was modeled after the European system, which meant that the system was initially designed by and for White males. But the initial motives of the colonists for educating Native Americans were not about the empowerment of Indian people, but rather about cloning Indian versions of themselves (Stein, 1999).

The founding of Harvard symbolizes the early efforts of the colonists to educate Native Americans. Listed among the original goals of Harvard was the "Education of the English and Indian youth of this country in knowledge and Goodness" (Carnegie Foundation for the Advancement of Teaching, 1989, p. 8). In fact, a "college within a college" was erected on the Harvard campus in 1654 for the primary purpose of educating Indian youth (Stein, 1988). This ambitious endeavor, however, was a colossal failure, as only two of the original twenty Indian youth survived and received their bachelor's degree. Sadly, the lives of the other eighteen Indian students ended in tragedy. They "died from sickness, change in lifestyle (food, clothing), and loneliness" (Stein, 1988, p. 31). Other colonial colleges such as Dartmouth and William and Mary also listed the education of the American Indian as part of their original mission statements; however, in a combined 80 years of operation between their founding and the American Revolution, these three colonial colleges enrolled only 47 Native American students, with only four graduating (Carney, 1999).

The federal era spawned a new mentality toward the American Indian—governmental paternalism and forced assimilation. In 1824, the Bureau of Indian Affairs (BIA) had been created and placed within the Department of the Interior and gradually replaced missionaries as the primary educator of Native Americans (Prucha, 1979). According to Stein (1988) education for Indian people became a federal responsibility when treaties were signed between tribes and the federal government in exchange for Indian land and trade concessions. These treaties established what is known as a "trust relationship" between tribes and the federal government. With Indian education under the paternalistic watch of the BIA, this would later prove to be a responsibility the government underestimated, misunderstood and ultimately mismanaged.

In response to the perceived "Indian problem," the federal government formalized the practice of relocating Indian people onto reservations as a solution to assuage the conflicts between Indian tribes and White settlers. The "out of sight, out of mind" mentality was thought to be the panacea as Indians were viewed as the thorn in the side of the White man. This resulted in the "checker boarding" of sacred lands that many tribes used to fish, hunt, and gather as a way of life. Indian people watched with agony as their beloved "mother earth" was chopped up into small parcels of land and turned into reservations as a result of the General Allotment Act—also known as the Dawes Act—(Reyhner & Eder, 1989).

By the late 1800s, the federal government's strategy regarding Indian education turned to the boarding school concept. The majority of boarding schools could be characterized as a system of forced acculturation, as many Indian children were taken from their families and thrust into a repressive, militaristic work environment and received an education that "emphasized agricultural and manual skills for boys and domestic skills for girls over academic training" (Lomawaima, 2004, p. 3). Some boarding schools were located on the reservation but most were located great distances away. Indian children were given short hair cuts and were forbidden to speak their indigenous language. The main objective of boarding schools, such as the Carlisle Indian boarding school founded by General Richard Henry Pratt in 1879, was to "de-Indianize" Indian children and assimilate them into White society, a goal shared by most of his contemporaries (Oppelt, 1990).

Although boarding schools such as Carlisle equipped many Indians with valuable skills to become productive members of mainstream society, the long-term results were futile as many Indians returned to the reservation only to find few opportunities to utilize their skills back on the reservation (Oppelt, 1990). The Indians who attended boarding schools found themselves caught between two completely different worlds—they were too "Indian" to fit into the White man's world and too "White" to fit back into their tribal culture. Within a few decades of the founding of Carlisle, the failure of assimilation was clear as Indians of the boarding school experience were left despondent and disillusioned.

In 1928, the Meriam Report sent shockwaves throughout the BIA and federal government as it exposed the deplorable condition of Indian education. The report sharply criticized the boarding school system and other educational programs designed by the BIA because of their "absence of Indian involvement in the planning and management of all federal Indian schools" (Oppelt, 1990, p. 24). Lomawaima and McCarty (2002) describe the report as "an excoriating critique of the work of the Office of Indian Affairs, and because of its impact the Meriam Report is still viewed as a watershed in Indian education" (p. 284). The report was responsible for casting Indian education back into the political spotlight and swung the pendulum of public opinion in favor of ameliorating the condition of Indian education. This spurred a period of change as the Indian Reorganization Act in 1934 (also known as the New Indian Deal) subsequently terminated the Dawes Act and authorized federal financial aid to secondary schools established on Indian reservations.

This promising trend, however, was truncated some twenty years later when the federal government decided to return to the assimilationist programs of the past and tried to get out of the Indian business by ending its relationship with Indian tribes (Lomawaima, 2004). The period between the 1940s and 1950s, known as the termination period, resulted in the termination of the government-to-government or "trust" relationship between many tribes and the federal government. The severing of this relationship affected Indian education significantly as many schools on reservations that depended upon federal funding soon found their funding cut and had to shut down. Indian students that were enrolled in off-reservation schools were either dropping out or being "pushed out" at alarming rates due to the unfriendly learning environment and cultural incongruity with the school system. By the early 1960s, Indian education was at its nadir, as nine out of every ten Native Americans dropped out of college (Szasz, 1974). Moreover, in 1961, only 66 Native Americans graduated from four-year mainstream institutions *combined* (Szasz, 1974).

The tides began to change as the spirit of the Civil Rights Movement and the passing of the Higher Education Act in 1965 galvanized American Indian leaders, educators, and elders to take action and initiated the era of self-determination. With a renewed sense of purpose, they wanted to erase the atrocities of the past and create their own version of Indian education—a version defined by Indians, for Indians. In 1968, Indian education was reborn with the establishment of Navajo Community College (now Diné Community College) on the Navajo Indian reservation in Tsaile, Arizona—the college that marked the beginning of the Tribal College movement.

As America's first and now the largest tribally controlled institution of higher learning, Diné "was the flagship school full of possibility and hope for Indian people" (Brewer, 2003, p. 90). Other tribes immediately took notice and started their own colleges. Members of reservation communities gathered in living rooms and backyards to form ad hoc committees and to lay out their plans (Brewer, 2003). With limited staff and scarce equipment and facilities, but plenty of cynics, five other colleges soon followed: Oglala Lakota College in Pine Ridge, South Dakota; Sinte Gleska University in Rosebud, South Dakota; Sitting Bull College in Fort Yates, North Dakota; Turtle Mountain Community College in Belcourt, North Dakota; and Deganawidah-Quetzalcoatl University (known as DQ University) in Davis, California. These six colleges laid the foundation and blueprint for the future of TCUs.

The early years of the tribal college movement were very difficult as the first tribal colleges were set up in abandoned houses, trailers, old storefronts, condemned buildings, barracks, and warehouses, or any structure where students and teachers could gather for classes. Mann (2003) describes TCUs as having to "build their institutional foundations dollar-by-dollar, grant-by-grant, program-by-program, and literally brick by brick" (p. xix). It was not unusual to find students studying in their cars because there was no place on campus with heating (Brewer, 2003). In order to survive these difficult beginnings, the presidents of the first six tribal colleges formed the American Indian Higher Education Consortium (AIHEC) in 1973 to provide political support for TCUs. In turn, AIHEC created the American Indian College Fund in 1989. Over the next decade, AIHEC was instrumental in establishing the AIHEC Student Congress in 1990, and the Alliance for Equity in Higher Education in 1999, all of which have contributed to the development and success of tribal colleges and the students they serve (Gipp, 2003). The American Indian College Fund has been particularly successful in raising millions of dollars earmarked for scholarships for students attending tribal colleges.

The self-determination era was fueled by the passing of the Indian Self-Determination and Education Assistance Act of 1975 and Tribally Controlled Community College Act of 1978. The passing of the Tribally Controlled Community College Act had the most significant impact on the growth of tribal colleges. This Act (renamed the Tribally Controlled Community College and University Assistance Act in 1998) authorized Congress to provide funding for higher education institutions controlled by tribal governments (Oppelt, 1990). Before the 1978 Act, there were only a handful of Indian colleges. After its passage, the number grew to 24 in a little more than a decade (Carnegie Foundation for the Advancement of Teaching, 1989). In 1994, TCUs achieved another significant milestone when they were granted Land Grant status. This designation helped secure additional funding, broaden offerings in the food and agricultural sciences, and expand institutional missions of teaching to include research and extension activities (Nichols & Kayongo-Male, 2003).

In 1996, President Clinton continued the trend of federal support as he proposed an executive order that directed all government agencies to establish specific linkages with TCUs, an Executive Order that was renewed by President Bush in 2002. Funding opportunities for tribal colleges have also expanded, with support from organizations such as the United States Department of Agriculture (Tribal Colleges Endowment Fund, Tribal College Education Equity Grants, Tribal College Research Grants Program) and the W. K. Kellogg Foundation.

Today, there are 36 TCUs which serve over 30,000 Native American students, representing more than 250 tribal indigenous groups across the United States and Canada. The majority of TCUs are chartered by one or more tribes and locally managed. There are three federally charted institutions which are governed by national boards (AIHEC, 1998). Many tribes across the United States are currently discussing plans of starting their own tribal colleges and this number will likely increase in the near future. Three of the newest TCUs include Comanche Nation College in Oklahoma (established in 2002), Little Priest Tribal and Community College of the Winnebago Tribe in Nebraska (established in 1997), and the Wind River Tribal College of the Arapaho Nation in Wyoming (established in 1997).

At the heart of the tribal college movement is a commitment by Native Americans to reclaim their cultural heritage (Carnegie Foundation for the Advancement of Teaching, 1989). The cultural focus on the rebuilding and preservation of Native American culture has had a dramatic impact on the enrollment of TCUs. Nichols and Kayongo-Male (2003) state that "Enrollment at tribal colleges has grown from approximately 2,100 undergraduates in 1982 to 24,363 undergraduates and 250 graduate students in 1996" (p. 2). In addition, in the states with tribal colleges, the proportion of American Indian students being educated rose 62 percent between 1990 and 1996. Enrollment growth has been accompanied by expanded academic offerings, so that several tribal colleges now offer baccalaureate and graduate degrees, in addition to associate degrees and certificate programs (American Indian Higher Education Consortium, 1999; Stein, 1992; Nichols and Kayongo-Male, 2003). Indeed, one can argue that more has been accomplished since the founding of the first tribal college to meet the higher education needs of the tribes and their members than in the two hundred years since the first Indian graduated from Harvard University (Oppelt, 1990).

Despite the remarkable ability of these "underfunded miracles" to provide and expand access to those who might otherwise not pursue a higher education, TCUs continue to be marginalized and dwell on the fringe of higher education. Beyond the prestige and bright lights of mainstream colleges and universities, TCUs are quietly changing the educational and social topography of reservations. Indian students are flocking to TCUs in unprecedented numbers to begin and/or continue to pursue a postsecondary education. Using innovative and resourceful means and with a commitment to restore and preserve the indigenous pride that was lost during years of assimilation-driven policies, TCUs have found a way to meet the unmet needs of Indian people by providing an education that makes one proud, and not ashamed, to *be* Indian.

MISSION AND IDENTITY

So what does it mean to be a TCU and how do they differ from mainstream community colleges and other institutions of higher learning? According to Stein (1999), TCUs can be described as small, persistent institutions of higher education that serve the smallest and poorest minority group in the United States. Though initially modeled after and similar in many ways to mainstream community colleges, TCUs are different in their cultural identities, which are reflected in virtually every aspect of college life (AIHEC, 1998; Oppelt, 1990; Stein, 1992). The mission of TCUs is not to "mimic mainstream institutions but to reflect and sustain a unique tribal identity" (Boyer, 2002, p. 18).

Tribal colleges support and teach curricula, cultures, and languages related to their Indian nations (Stein, 1999). As part of their missions, tribal colleges (1) respond to community needs, (2) empower communities, (3) preserve and revitalize Native culture and language, and (4) facilitate community healing (Pavel, Inglebret & Banks, 2001; Stein, 1999). Szasz (1999) describes TCUs as "cultural intermediaries" for Native American college students, reaffirming Native identity and training for survival in a contemporary world. Another trait that distinguishes them from other community colleges is their dual mission: (1) to rebuild, reinforce, and explore traditional tribal cultures, using uniquely designed curricula and institutional settings; and (2) to address Western models of learning by providing traditional disciplinary courses that are transferable to four-year institutions (AIHEC, 1999).

Another unique aspect of TCUs is that approximately 30 percent of the faculty are American Indian, whereas at mainstream institutions, Indians make up less than 1 percent of the faculty (AIHEC, 1999). TCUs provide educational, cultural, emotional, and monetary support for Indian students while at the same time bolstering community efforts for cultural revitalization, health and social needs, and economic development (Fann, 2002). The idea behind the tribal college movement was not only to educate students so that they reap the economic advantages of a college degree, but also to provide an education that reinforced tribal culture and identity (Tierney, 1992). For example, Bay Mills Community College offers a traditional tribal literature class—only in the winter term because the stories are supposed to be told when the snow is on the ground—and Fort Belknap College offers a course on the economic history of the reservation (AIHEC, 1998). Each college is designed in the image of each particular tribe.

All TCUs offer associates degrees, seven colleges offer bachelor's degrees, and two offer master's degrees (AIHEC, 2006). TCUs support Indian learning styles and foster a family-like atmosphere of respect and cultural sensitivity. Whereas the early European educators and the federal government viewed Indian culture as an obstacle for the education of Indian youth, tribal colleges view culture as the key to unlocking the genius of the Native intellect. For example, it is common for tribal elders and other nontraditional faculty members to teach classes ranging from tribal language emersion classes, arts and crafts, and indigenous medicine. Furthermore, TCUs take a holistic view of students, as people situated within a history, culture, and nuclear and extended family. Students' family and personal concerns are not irrelevant to the college but central to it, a complete reversal of many educational institutions (Pavel, 1992).

Like most mainstream community colleges, TCUs provide open admission, low tuition, general education, vocational preparation, and on-the-job training and are dedicated to their mission of meeting the needs of the reservation community. Many TCUs also offer adult basic education, as well as remedial and high school equivalency programs.

Although tribal colleges vary considerably, they share some basic characteristics (Boyer, 1997; American Indian Higher Education Consortium, 1999). Most TCUs are less than twenty-five-years-old, have relatively small student bodies (often fewer than five hundred students) that are predominantly American Indian, were chartered by one or more tribes, have open admissions policies, began as two-year institutions, and are located on reservations.

Given the overall focus of this book on Minority-Serving Institutions, it is important to situate the mission and identity of TCUs in the larger MSI context and to discuss how they are distinct. Like other MSIs, the mission and identity of TCUs is firmly rooted in serving the unique needs of a particular racial and ethnic group (in this instance Native Americans). All MSIs play an important role in access to higher education for the particular populations they serve (O'Brien & Zudack, 1998). TCUs are unique as MSIs given their history and origin. The majority of TCUs are located on reservations and chartered by a particular tribe (i.e., Sitting Bull College is located on the Standing Rock Sioux Reservation and was chartered by the Standing Rock Sioux Tribal Government). TCUs are inextricably tied to tribal sovereignty. Tribal sovereignty refers to the inherent sovereignty of Indian nations and their right to self-governance, self-determination, and self-education (Lomawaima, 1999; Lomawaima & McCarty, 2002). This legal and political status was solidified by the signing of legal binding agreements between the U.S. government and American Indian tribes called "treaties." TCUs are an example of how tribal sovereignty is exercised. These colleges play a role in maintaining the health, vitality, and cultural traditions of particular tribes (and of Indian people as a whole). This stands in contrast to HBCUs that were founded under the premise of "separate but equal" to provide access to higher education for African Americans given the context of racial segregation and the denial of access at mainstream institutions. The Morrill Act of 1890 established governmental support for HBCUs in order to keep African Americans separate from their White counterparts. In contrast, TCUs were founded by Indian people for Indian people as a way to maintain Indian identity and sovereignty in light of government and educational systems that sought for centuries to assimilate American Indians into mainstream society.

In light of similarities to meet the ongoing educational needs of a particular racial and ethnic group, from a historical perspective TCUs are also distinct from HSIs. HSIs as a type of MSI were not established with the particular purpose of educating people of Hispanic descent, instead the missions of these campuses evolved in response to demographic trends and shifts that included greater Hispanic participation on a particular campus (O'Brien & Zudack, 1998). We point out these similarities and differences as a way to think about the origins of particular types of MSIs because these origins in turn shape the current and future of these institutions. While it is helpful to have the umbrella term "MSI" to convey the purpose of these institutions to serve minorities, "the lumping together of Native American peoples with other marginalized groups denies the central and critical difference of American Indians as tribal peoples of distinct nations with sovereign status and treaty rights" (Grande, 2000, p. 344). As we continue our discussion of TCUs and the current issues they face, it is important to keep in mind the Native American mission and identity of these institutions.

CURRENT ISSUES

What are some of the issues facing TCUs? Like all sectors of higher education TCUs have many challenges they grapple with on a daily basis and as they move into the future. These issues include, but are not limited to funding, student preparation, politics, service, accountability, and assessment.

Funding. Like many mainstream higher education institutions today, funding is the major hurdle that TCUs are scrambling to overcome. Most TCUs are geographically located among some of the worst socioeconomic conditions in America and have access to very limited funds from local sources. Most TCUs are located on reservation lands held in "trust" by the BIA, which prevents the levying of local property taxes to support higher education—an important source of revenue for most mainstream colleges (AIHEC, 1999). The limited federal support they receive, which is their primary source of funding, fails to keep pace with their enrollment. For example, in fiscal year 2002, TCUs received only $3,900 per Indian student, compared with the $6,000 authorized by Congress, far below the amount used by state colleges (Ambler, 2002). Further exacerbating this issue, there has been a recent increase in non-Native students, for which TCUs do not receive federal support. If TCUs fall below 51 percent of federally recognized Indian students, they lose a percentage of their BIA funding. TCUs are victims of their own success. Although TCUs receive help from private sources, grants, and endowments such as the American Indian College Fund for scholarships and building renovation, continued funding efforts are critical to ensure ongoing operation and success.

Students. Since many TCUs are located in remote areas, the tribal college is not just an option for many Native Americans, but the *only* option for higher education. The typical student has characteristics that are far different than traditional campuses. The average student is a single mother in her early thirties, part-time, and Pell Grant eligible (AIHEC, 1998). Students bring with them the emotional baggage of many years of failure—failed marriages and relationships, periods of unemployment and welfare dependency, and, for some, histories of drug and alcohol addiction (HeavyRunner & Ortiz, 2003). Many of the social ills that plaque reservations are reflected in the TCU student body leaving educators and administrators faced with the task of rebuilding self-esteem, remediating deficits in past education, and preparing students for the future.

Politics. Tribal politics, internal and external, also present unique challenges for tribal colleges. Politics within tribal communities can be puzzling to outsiders because although the culture and unity does resonate powerfully on reservations, it can divide just as easily. The intimate connection that tribal college leaders such as presidents and boards of trustees (which are comprised of nearly 100 percent local American Indian community members) have with their communities can be a double-edged sword (Stein, 1999). It is not uncommon, for example, for a member of a tribe to get elected to the board and to use the appointment to further personal concerns rather than those of the college. These types of personal and ulterior motives can lead to tribal college presidents being suddenly fired without cause based on personal issues and personality. During a two-year period, either boards or tribal councils or both removed tribal college presidents at nine institutions, or 27 percent of the total members of AIHEC (Archambault & Allen, 2002). Such "cut-throat" politics put the tribal college on precarious ground in the eyes of accrediting agencies that closely examine the relationships that tribal colleges have with outside political entities such as tribal councils. While all institutions encounter politics to some degree, TCUs exist in insular communities where politics can become personal, damaging, and lose perspective of the educational interest of the college.

Service. Similar to other Minority-Serving Institutions including HBCUs and HSIs, the relationship that exists between TCUs and their communities supporting them is unique (Ward, 2003). "Tribal colleges, like larger Native American communities in which they dwell, are deeply rooted in an ethic of service. The concept of neighbor helping neighbor is part of life on both the reservation and in tribal colleges" (Ward & Wolf-Wendel, 2000, p. 772). TCUs are actively involved in a broad range of community efforts—including adult basic education, alcohol prevention programs, counseling services, and economic development initiatives—that are specifically focused on communities that would otherwise be completely isolated from such resources (AIHEC, 1998). Another aspect of service at TCUs is the role they play in maintaining repositories for cultural and sacred archival items (Edinger & Ambler, 2002). The unique exercise of the TCU service mission provides an example as all colleges and universities seek greater social responsibility.

Accountability and Accreditation. Full accreditation has been a goal for TCUs since their founding. With the support of AIHEC, all of the 36 tribal colleges are accredited or seeking accreditation. TCUs have to meet the same rigorous standards as mainstream institutions. Yet, because TCUs are different than the average mainstream college due to their dual missions, meeting the standards set by non-Indian accrediting agencies can be a challenge.

In the past two decades, all American higher education institutions have come under increased scrutiny as consumers and policy makers want to know that their investments of time and money are worthwhile (Boyer,

2003). This new era of accountability is of great concern for tribal colleges because the criteria they are being measured by are directed by Western definitions of quality (Boyer, 2003). Given the dual mission of TCUs, it is often difficult to use traditional indicators of quality such as those present in most accreditation and accountability measures. While these measures can assess student development in a particular subject, they can fail to overlook indigenous ways of knowing. The question then becomes: How does one accurately measure or assess the non-Western culture that is omnipresent at tribal colleges using Western methods? Dilemmas such as this have tribal college presidents now considering an alternative accreditation process led by the colleges (Boyer, 2003). While no models for alternative accreditation currently exist in the American higher education context, tribal college leaders have looked at models emanating from the international education arena to find ways to be true to their indigenous mission while meeting the needs of students who move into mainstream systems (Johnson, Benham & VanAlstine, 2003).

Analysis of these issues as well as the history and mission of TCUs leads us to the root challenge these institutions face: invisibility. Invisibility in funding formulas, invisibility in the media, and a general invisibility in the overall higher education landscape. We argue that while TCUs are not unique in having to address issues associated with funding, student preparation, politics, and accreditation, they are unique, however, in their invisibility and relative unknown status in the world of higher education.

INVISIBILITY

As a form of summary and analysis we offer seven considerations that contribute to the invisibility of TCUs. These considerations emerge based on a review and analysis of existing literature and research related to TCUs. First, special focus institutions associated with a particular "race" continue to be invisible to some degree in the American higher education arena, and TCUs are no exception. Because American higher education has a legacy of exclusionary practices, many groups that were historically excluded, such as women, African Americans, and American Indians created their own colleges to gain access to higher education. These special focus colleges are "dedicated to meeting the unique needs of particular ethnic minority groups" (Ward, 2003, p. 91). In addition, Townsend (1999) surmises that special focus colleges—like tribal colleges—are unique because they "strive to create a climate conducive to the academic success of their particular racial or ethnic student body or their all-female student body" (p. 3). However, this uniqueness relegated them into the "other" category which in this case meant anything other than the traditional American mainstream colleges or universities. Consequently for TCUs, the designation of being a special focus college and their association with being "tribal" has contributed to them being perceived as inferior or second-rate when compared to mainstream colleges and universities (Tierney, 1992).

Second, TCUs are still "young" when compared with the more mature American college and universities. Most Ivy League colleges, for example, have had over 200 years to grow and develop their elite reputations prior to the creation of the first tribal college in 1968. Since most TCUs were created in the last twenty-five years, a mere blink in time for American higher education (Carnegie Foundation for the Advancement of Teaching, 1989), this contributes to their invisibility because they are so new to the higher education world, and they do not have legacies that other institutions have established.

Third, the geographical isolation of TCUs contributes to their invisibility. TCUs are simply difficult to find. One has to literally drive 50 or more miles off a major highway to locate them. Most TCUs are located on rural Indian reservations where few state highways run nearby. This lack of visibility is a disadvantage because the average person—if not a member of that particular tribe, a member of the community, or not from the area—will not know that TCUs even exist. Do you know where Lame Deer is? How about Belcourt?

Fourth, stereotypical images of American Indians in textbooks and mass media in contemporary society compromise educational legitimacy. Based on television shows, movies, and sports entertainment today, one would think that Native Americans still live in teepees, walk around dressed in traditional regalia with their face covered with paint while singing and chanting to the cacophonous rumble of a rhythmic drum beat. Although many Indian people today still actively practice their traditional cultures and speak their indigenous languages, Indian people no longer live in teepees and no longer rely on horses as their primary means of transportation. Rarely (if ever) does one see Indian role models in the media who are successful educators, business people, or politicians. A recent campaign ad by the American Indian College Fund appears to mock the modern image of Indians promulgated by the media. Their campaign slogan is "Have you ever seen a *real* Indian?" This iconoclastic slogan comes off as a news flash to mainstream America that Indian people are not stuck in a time warp and there are "real" contemporary Indians who are lawyers, teachers, professors, and doctors—and yes, they actually do drive a *car* to work. As long as images of Indians in the mass media and textbooks are misrepresented or connected to vestiges of the past—such as cowboys and Indians—the tribal college struggle for educational legitimacy will continue.

Fifth, given that all TCUs began as community colleges, TCUs have not been able to shake the "image" that comes with being a community college. Since their inception in the early 1900s, mainstream community colleges have since struggled to maintain their legitimacy as viable institutions of higher education. Community colleges, whether substantiated or not, have been chastised for maintaining the social stratification of American higher education by sidetracking students of lesser academic ability and lower socioeconomic status from four-year schools (Cohen & Brawer, 2003). Even though campuses like Sinte Gleska University and Oglala Lakota College offer master's level degrees, they are still primarily associated with community colleges which, by default, relegate them to the lower end of the higher education hierarchy. Although TCUs are similar to mainstream community colleges on many levels, there are significant differences when closely examined. But the perception of an institution, however, often outweighs reality.

Six, the names of TCUs do not register with mainstream America due to unfamiliarity or lack of public recognition. Most TCUs are named after great leaders of their respective tribes and/or use names of their traditional tribal language, both of which were never taught or given scant recognition in American history. For example, tribal college names like Chief Dull Knife College are probably only known by members or descendants of their respective tribes or by scholars or people who are curious about the history of American Indians. It is highly unlikely that the majority of Americans would know that Chief Dull Knife is a highly revered chief among the Northern Cheyenne tribe in Lame Deer, Montana. Mainstream society would likely be more familiar with colleges named after "American" heroes such as George Washington (George Washington University) or Meriwether Lewis and William Clark (Lewis-Clark State College, ID or Lewis & Clark College, OR). Even the "state" schools that were established with the passing of the Morrill Acts in 1862 and 1890 such as Iowa State University or A&M schools such as Texas A&M gives one a general sense of where they are located because of their association with a particular state. But TCUs such as Stone Child College or Si Tanka University, which are names that have great significance to their respective tribes, are often foreign to the majority of mainstream America.

Finally, TCUs lack sufficient funding needed for promotion and advertising, which keeps them under the radar screen of higher education in America. Mainstream institutions are willing to spend millions of dollars in advertising and promotional costs to attract students ranging from local to international students. Many TCUs simply lack the array of funding resources to place ads in the major national magazines and newspapers or the television market on a consistent basis. Big time college athletics such as football or basketball is another major promotion tool that generates national attention and mass appeal. Much to the chagrin of some academics, research studies show a direct correlation between an increase in student enrollment at an institution the year after their football or basketball team had a successful season—such as winning a conference championship or national championship—(Sperber, 2000). Although there are TCUs such as Haskell Indian Nations University and United Tribes Technical College that have successful athletic programs and compete against other community colleges within their region, they suffer because of their lack of size and resources. Unlike some mainstream institutions which have teams that compete in high-profile conferences with multimillion dollar television contracts, TCUs do not have national, regional, or local fan bases (and/or alumni) that enable them to generate massive revenue dollars to market and promote their success.

In summary, the factors discussed here contribute to the ongoing invisibility of TCUs and their place and role in the larger higher education landscape. However, when we delve deeper into this invisibility and look at it from the perspective of TCUs and Indian people, we may see something different. As indicated at the outset, TCUs were founded by Indian people for Indian people as a way to preserve culture and language and improve the educational offerings in their communities. The dual mission of the tribal college movement was (and still is) to provide access to higher education for American Indians and revitalize Indian culture. Some of the issues associated with invisibility discussed here can be attributed to the values that tribal colleges are built upon. These values at times stand in opposition to the values upon which mainstream colleges are founded. For example, Tierney (1992) states that TCUs value cooperation whereas mainstream colleges value competition. In this light, when one considers the urgency and desperation that breathed life into the tribal college movement and the painful history of Indian education in general, one could assume that tribal college leaders do not mind being overlooked because Indian education was never about personal achievement. Instead, education was used to develop a greater understanding of who Indian people are and in this regard they have been extremely successful.

Formal methods of European education, therefore, were (and are) fundamentally incongruous with Indian ways of life because they tried to take the "Indian" out of Indian education whereas Indians taught that education lies within themselves. In other words, the more Indians were exposed to Eurocentric methods of education, the further they got from themselves (Dansie, 2004). This does not mean that TCUs are unaware of the ways and means of traditional higher education. As participants in the larger milieu of higher education, TCUs must stay abreast of the ways of traditional and predominantly White colleges and universities since many students transition between sectors of higher education. Yet, it is important to recognize simultaneously the unique nature of TCUs given their unique dual mission. This dual mission leaves TCUs standing in a unique position. On the one hand, they need to meet the typical needs of any college student (e.g., requirements for particular majors) while at the same time supporting students as Indian people (e.g., language, history).

TCUs are often overlooked (read: invisible) in the larger higher education community given their dual mission. While this invisibility can be problematic, one could argue that the success of tribal colleges was *because* they were ignored and left alone, which allowed tribes to define their own colleges based on the values of Indian people—not on the values of Europeans. One should not be surprised if the leaders of the tribal college movement choose to remain in the shadows of mainstream higher education. As the late prominent Indian scholar Vine Deloria, Jr. said in his famous Indian Manifesto, "Custer Died for Your Sins": "Any movement which begins to exert a significant influence in America is subjected to publicity. Too much attention from the press can radically change conceptions and goals simply by making the process appear commonplace" (p. 267).

As we have pointed out, the unique mission and identity of TCUs is far from commonplace and tribal college leaders have fought to maintain this identity. This raises some critical questions. How do tribal college leaders negotiate issues that contribute and lead to invisibility? What can tribal college leaders do to attract quality students to tribal colleges and support these students in their transition to other aspects of higher education? Such questions can present a dilemma for tribal college leaders. These leaders need to simultaneously balance calls from the local tribal community to serve the cultural needs of Indian people while preparing students to navigate the world of higher education (often away from reservations) and life in general. These leaders, just like all higher education leaders, also need to pay attention to the contemporary higher education landscape and the need to worry about funding, quality of students, and student success.

Given their history, mission, and origin tribal colleges find themselves standing in a unique and invisible place in higher education. On the one hand they have the benefit of their history and of their success. These campuses have existed alongside traditional American higher education, but have maintained a clear identity. In this way invisibility has had its benefits. Yet for tribal colleges to survive and grow into the future they need to pay attention to the issues outlined throughout this chapter. These issues, however, are not easily resolved due to the double consciousness that tribal colleges must maintain. These campuses have the dual purpose of providing access to higher education for Indian people and maintaining cultural identity.

The dual mission of TCUs can lead them to a state of liminality. Turner (1967) uses the term *liminality* to explain the contradictions, ambiguity, and creative tensions that emerge from inhabiting a space between two distinct categories (in this case tribal identity and mainstream higher education). According to Turner, liminal beings exist in an undefined cultural space. They are "necessarily ambiguous" and "can slip through the network of classifications that normally locate states and positions in cultural space" (Lape, 1998, p. 260). Turner's use of the term liminal helps us understand the "betwixt and between" location of tribal colleges. To survive and thrive tribal colleges need to embrace the liminality afforded by a grounding in traditional Native American culture *and* a location in mainstream higher education. The future success of tribal colleges calls for embracing the inevitable tension of liminal existence. These campuses cannot turn their backs on their cultural identity nor can they ignore the realities of higher education as a whole.

TRIBAL COLLEGES: PROSPECTS FOR THE FUTURE

This chapter is our attempt to provide insight into the urgency, struggle and subsequent success of the tribal college movement. For Indian people, the tribal college movement was, and continues to be, a tangible sign of progress on Indian reservations across America. Their existence alone has resurrected the educational dreams and aspirations of people who, at one time, thought going to college was an impossible dream (Boyer, 1997). Prior to the creation of tribal colleges, Indian education was not only moribund, it was described as a "national tragedy" and needed a prayer to stay alive—a prayer that was answered during the self-determination era which gave tribes control of their own destiny. Tribal colleges are now rewriting the odyssey of Indian education, and this time they are playing a lead role.

Tribal college pioneers have made many intelligent steps in the last three decades, and their substantial progress is a testament to their wisdom. The dual mission of TCUs is fundamental to their identity, and as we have pointed out in this chapter, this has also contributed to their invisibility. TCUs are a model for mainstream institutions and other MSIs in how they have successfully integrated cultural diversity into their curriculum and into the fabric of their institutions. TCUs have masterfully navigated their dual mission and their ongoing success calls for them to be innovative in how they communicate their mission and in how they prepare students for further higher education and leadership in their cultural communities.

REFERENCES

Ambler, M. (2002). Thirty years strong. *Tribal College Journal, 14,* 6–9.

American Indian Higher Education Consortium and the Institute for Higher Education Policy. (1998). What makes tribal colleges unique? Washington DC: Authors.

American Indian Higher Education Consortium and the Institute for Higher Education Policy (1999). Tribal Colleges: An Introduction. Washington DC: Authors.

American Indian Higher Education Consortium. (2006). *Top five majors.* Retrieved January 13, 2006 from http://www.aihec.org/AIHEC/Documents/Research/DCNA report.pdf.

Archambault, D., and Allen, T. (2002). Politics and the presidency: Tribal college presidents share their thoughts. *Tribal College Journal, 13,* 14–19.

Boyer, P. (1997). *Native American colleges: Progress and prospects.* Princeton, NJ: Princeton University Press.

Boyer, P. (2002). Defying the odds: Tribal colleges conquer skepticism but still face persistent challenges. *Tribal College Journal, 14,* 12–18.

Boyer, P. (2003). Building tribal communities: defining the mission and measuring the outcomes of tribal colleges. In M. K. P. Benham and W. J. Stein (Eds.), *The renaissance of American Indian higher education: Capturing the dream* (pp. 137–148). Mahwah, NJ: Lawrence Erlbaum Associates.

Brewer, S. (2003). *In Real Indians: Portraits of contemporary Native Americans and America's tribal colleges.* New York: Melcher Media, Inc.

Carney, C. M. (1999). *Native American higher education in the United States.* New Brunswick, NJ: Transaction Publishers.

Carnegie Foundation for the Advancement of Technology. (1989).

Cohen, A. M., and Brawer, F. B. (2003). *The American community college (4th ed.).* San Francisco, CA: Jossey-Bass Inc., Publishers.

Dansie, R. (2004, July 22). *Education in Indian country. Indian Country Today,* pp. 1–2.

Deloria, V., Jr. (1988). *Custer died for your sins: An Indian manifesto.* Norman, OK: University of Oklahoma Press.

Edinger, A., and Ambler, M. (2002). If I had a hammer (and several million dollars). *Tribal College Journal, 14,* 28–31.

Fann, A. (2002). Tribal colleges: An overview. Los Angeles, CA: ERIC Clearinghouse for Community Colleges.

Gipp, G. E. (2003). Foreword. In M. K. P. Benham and W. J. Stein (Eds.), *The renaissance of American Indian higher education: Capturing the dream* (pp. xiii–xvi). Mahwah, NJ: Lawrence Erlbaum Associates.

Grande, S. (2000). American Indian identity and intellectualism: The new quest for a new red pedagogy. *Qualitative Studies in Education, 13,* 343–359.

HeavyRunner, I., and Ortiz, A. M. (2003). Student access, retention, and success: Models and inclusion and support. In M. K. P. Benham and W. J. Stein (Eds.), *The renaissance of American Indian higher education: Capturing the dream* (pp. 215–240). Mahwah, NJ: Lawrence Erlbaum Associates.

Johnson, V., Benham, M. K. P., and VanAlstine, M. J. (2003). Native leadership: Advocacy for transformation, culture, community, and sovereignty. In M. K. P. Benham and W. J. Stein (Eds.), *The renaissance of American Indian higher education: Capturing the dream* (pp. 149–165). Mahwah, NJ: Lawrence Erlbaum Associates.

Lape, N. G. (1998). "I would rather be with my people, but not live with them as they live": Cultural liminality and double consciousness in Sarah Winnemuca Hopkins's life among Piutes. *American Indian Quarterly, 22,* 259–280.

Lomawaima, K. T. (1999). The unnatural history of American Indian education. In K. G. Swisher and J. W. Tippeconnic (Eds.), *Next steps: Research and practice to advance Indian education (*pp. 1–31). Charleston, WV: AEL, Inc.

Lomawaima, K. T. (2004). Educating Native Americans. In J. A. Banks and A. M. B. Cherry (Eds.), *Handbook on research in multicultural education* (pp. 331–347). San Francisco, CA: Jossey-Bass Inc., Publishers.

Lomawaima, K. T. and McCarty, T. L. (2002). When tribal sovereignty challenges democracy: American Indian education and the democratic ideal. *American Educational Research Journal, 39,* 279–306.

Mann, H. (2003). Prologue: Elder reflections. In M. K. P. Benham and W. J. Stein (Eds.), *The renaissance of American Indian higher education: Capturing the dream* (pp. xvii–xxix). Mahwah, NJ: Lawrence Erlbaum Associates.

McClellen, G. S., Fox, M. J. T., and Lowe, S. C. (2005). Where we have been: A history of Native American higher education. In M. J. T. Fox, S. C. Lowe, and G. S. McClellen (Eds.), *Serving Native American Students* (pp. 7–15). San Francisco, CA: Jossey Bass Inc., Publishers.

Nichols, T. J. and Kayongo-Male, D. M. (2003). The dynamics of tribal college-state university collaboration. *Journal of American Indian Education, 42,* 1–24.

O'Brien, E.M. and Zudak, C. (1998). Minority serving institutions: An overview. In J. P. Merisotis and C.T. O'Brien (Eds.), *Minority serving institutions: Distinct purposes, common goals* (pp. 5–16). San Francisco, CA: Jossey-Bass Inc., Publishers.

Oppelt, N. T. (1990). *The tribally controlled Indian colleges: The beginnings of self determination in American Indian education.* Tsaile, AZ: Navajo Community College Press.

Pavel, D. M., Inglebret, E., and Banks, S. R. (2001). Tribal colleges and universities in an era of dynamic development. *Peabody Journal of Education, 76,* 50–72.

Pavel, D. M. (1992). The emerging role of tribal college libraries in Indian education. Charleston, WV: Clearinghouse of Rural Education and Small School.

President Bush Signs Executive Order for TCUs (2002). *Tribal College Journal, 14,* 65.

Prucha, F. P. (1979). *The churches and the Indian schools.* Lincoln, NE: University of Nebraska Press.

Reyhner, J., and Eder, J. (1989). A history of Indian education. Billings, MT: Council for Indian Education.

Sperber, M. (2000). *Beer and circus: How big-time college sports is crippling undergraduate education.* New York: Henry Holt.

Stein, W. J. (1988). *A history of the tribally controlled community colleges: 1968–1978.* Unpublished doctoral dissertation. Pullman, WA: Washington State University.

Stein, W. J. (1992). *Tribally controlled colleges: Making good medicine.* New York, NY: Peter Lang.

Stein, W. J. (1999). Tribal colleges: 1968–1998. In K. G. Swisher and J. W. Tippeconnic, III (Eds.), *Next steps: Research and practice to advance Indian education* (pp. 259–270). Charleston, WV: ERIC Clearinghouse on Rural Education and Small Schools. (E 9755N48).

Szasz, M. (1974). *Education and the American Indian.* Albuquerque, NM: University of New Mexico Press.

Szasz, M. (1999). *Education and the American Indian: The road to self-determination since 1928* (3rd ed.). Albuquerque, NM: University of New Mexico Press.

The Carnegie Foundation for the Advancement of Teaching. (1989). *Tribal Colleges: Shaping the future of Native American.* Lawrenceville: Princeton University Press.

Tierney, W. G. (1992). *Official encouragement, institutional discouragement: Minorities in academe—the Native American experience.* Norwood, NJ: Ablex.

Townsend, B. (1999). *Two-year colleges for women and minorities: Enabling access to the baccalaureate.* New York: Falmer Press.

Turner, V. (1967). *The forest of symbols.* Ithaca, NY: Cornell.

Ward, K. (2003). *Faculty service roles and the scholarship of engagement.* Hoboken, NJ: Jossey-Bass Inc., Publishers.

Ward, K., and Wolf-Wendel, L. (2000). Community-centered service learning: Moving from doing for to doing with. *American Behavioral Scientist, 43,* 767–780.

CHAPTER 8

Asian American and Pacific Islander Serving Institutions

Historical Perspectives and Future Prospects

Julie J. Park and Robert T. Teranishi

There has been a stubborn and persistent divide that separates the educational issues of Asian American and Pacific Islanders (AAPIs) from other communities of color. It is often assumed that AAPIs are high academic achievers who do not need special assistance (Nakanishi, 1995) and that their educational experiences are more often aligned with those of White students, rather than with other minorities (Teranishi, 2005). As a result, the introduction of federal legislation to create an Asian American and Pacific Islander Serving Institution designation in the Higher Education Act has faced many challenges. Among the challenges is persuading Congress to reject the "model minority" narrative that has defined Asian Americans in education for so long.

The purpose of this chapter is to outline some of the historical factors that contributed to the introduction of the AAPI serving institutions legislation, as well as explore theoretical implications of the resolution. In this chapter, we examine the creation of an AAPI Serving Institution designation as a *racial project*. Omi and Winant (1994) state: "A racial project is simultaneously an interpretation, representation, or explanation of racial dynamics, and an effort to reorganize and redistribute resources along particular racial lines" (p. 56). Racial projects are situated within the trajectory of *racial formation,* which Omi and Winant define as "the sociohistorical process by which racial categories are created, inhabited, transformed, and destroyed" (p. 55). The creation of an AAPI Serving Institution designation presents a unique representation of the ongoing evolution of Asian American racial positioning within American society. We contend that this policy is itself a racial project within an evolution of Asian American racial politics that seeks to reinterpret Asian American racial positioning.

This chapter begins with a brief discussion of the racialization of Asian Americans. We then provide an historical overview of the AAPI Serving Institutions legislation. Finally, we examine how the legislation seeks to reinterpret racial dynamics by challenging the model minority image and carving out a unique space for Asian Americans in the racial spectrum.

THE RACIALIZATION OF ASIAN AMERICANS AND PACIFIC ISLANDERS

Although Asian American students were originally viewed as a yellow peril threat in California schools (Wollenberg, 1978) and later a danger to national security during World War II, Asian Americans have been more recently lauded for their perceived exceptional studiousness, diligence, and intelligence. In the meantime, the Asian American population in higher education has spiked (Hsia & Hirano-Nakanishi, 1989). The number of AAPIs in U.S. colleges and universities more than doubled in a decade, from 271,006 in 1980 to 570,873 in 1990 (Teranishi, 2005).

The "model minority" image preceded the growth of AAPIs in U.S. higher education, and was coined in 1966 (Petersen, 1966). The term model minority suggests that Asian Americans serve as an exemplar for other minorities, who evidently exhibit less than desirable behavior. The timing of the label was no accident; its emergence in the mid-1960s highlighted the supposed self-reliant achievements of Asian Americans while implicitly denigrating the agitation for racial justice led by other minority groups (Chun, 1980). As deficit thinking models blame Latino, Black, Native American "culture" for not valuing education and hard work (Valencia, 1997), Asian Americans stand as a beacon of the American Dream, an example that other minority groups *could* get it right if they only tried harder and complained less.

Since the origination of the model minority stereotype, Asian American and Pacific Islander communities have become even more demographically complex due to variations in immigration patterns, socioeconomic status, educational attainment, and ethnicity, among other factors. Despite major qualitative differences, Pacific Islanders are often lumped together with Asian Americans for the purposes of political representation. Beginning in 2000, the U.S. Census Bureau separated the formerly "Asian or Pacific Islander" category into two categories, "Asian" and "Native Hawaiian or Other Pacific Islander" (Harris & Jones, 2005). Despite this variation, the monolithically successful image prevails (Chew, 1994).

As the model minority image became the dominant narrative of Asian American identity in education, Asian American racial positioning was simultaneously developing in a way that aligned Asian Americans more closely in relation to White interests (Robles, 2004; Takagi, 1992). Although Asian Americans still faced discrimination like other minority groups, their perceived ability to overcome barriers and succeed was seen as further proof that they were an ideal model for other minorities (Chun, 1980). As our overview of the development of AAPI Serving Institutions legislation will point out, AAPI policy makers and educators were frustrated at how the model minority myth overshadowed the concerns of and resources available for AAPI communities. They saw the legislation as a way to reposition AAPIs as racial minorities with distinct needs.

THE DEVELOPMENT OF THE AAPI SERVING INSTITUTIONS LEGISLATION

The development of an Asian American and Pacific Islander Serving Institution designation has gone through several stages. U.S. Congress, H.R. 4825, "a bill to amend the Higher Education Act of 1965 to authorize grants for institutions of higher education serving Asian Americans and Pacific Islanders," was introduced by Congressman Robert Underwood (D-Guam) in 2002 as a proposed amendment to Title III of the Higher Education Act, which provides federal funding to Minority-Serving Institutions (MSIs). Title III designations already exist for historically Black colleges and universities (HBCUs), Tribally Colleges and Universities (TCUs), Alaska Native Serving Institutions, and Native Hawaiian Serving Institutions. Hispanic-Serving Institutions (HSIs) were originally introduced into Title III but are now funded through Title V. Although MSI funding was largely compensatory, given the history of federal and state-sponsored discrimination against Blacks and Native Americans in education, a shift occurred with the 1992 inclusion of HSI federal designation and funding. Unlike HBCUs and TCUs, HSI eligibility was determined by the proportion of Latino students (25 percent or higher), low-income students, and general low educational expenditures.

As noted earlier, AAPIs were largely absent from discussions on MSI, although Espiritu (1992) notes that in 1986, Congressmen Robert Matsui and Norman Mineta protested the exclusion of AAPI students from minority student counts in determining MSI status. AAPIs did not begin to push for a serving institution designation until the late 1990s. The release of a College Board report, "Reaching the Top, the College Board's National Task Force on Minority High Achievement" (1999) that grouped Asian

Americans with Whites in terms of educational attainment served as somewhat of a catalyst for AAPI policy makers to address the lack of recognition towards the AAPI presence in higher education and in particular, underserved subgroups such as Southeast Asian Americans and Pacific Islanders (Adhikary & Eav, 2004; Yang & Niedzwiecki, 2003). On January 21, 2000, the Congressional Asian Pacific American Caucus (CAPAC) held a forum on misperceptions regarding AAPIs in higher education (SEARAC, 2001). As a follow-up, CAPAC and the Southeast Asia Resource Action Center (SEARAC) organized the "Summit on the Status of Pacific Islander and Southeast Asian Americans in Higher Education" on May 18, 2001.

In their interim report released on January 19, 2001, among other policy recommendations, the White House Initiative on Asian Americans and Pacific Islanders recommended a federal designation for "Asian American and Pacific Islander Serving Institutions and organizations" that would create productive partnerships between the federal government, community networks, and schools (President's Advisory Commission, 2001, p. 16). Similar ideas are linked in a 2001 concept paper:

> As part of an overall strategy to enhance the objectives of Executive Order (EO) 13125 [White House Initiative on AAPIs], the Coordinating Committee on Asian Americans and Pacific Islanders is in the process of developing a set of criteria to enable federal agencies to identify those educational institutions and organizations that are potential partners in increasing participation of Asian Americans and Pacific Islanders (AAPIs) in federal programs where they may be underserved. (concept paper, April 16, 2001)

AAPI serving institutions were seen as a means to "enhance the objectives" of the White House Initiative on AAPIs. The paper also mentions the key role that community-based organizations would have in partnering with AAPI serving institutions. Federal agencies are encouraged to collaborate with MSIs, as are community-based organizations (O'Brien & Zudak, 1998; U.S. Department of Health and Human Services, 2003). Thus, the stakeholders in the AAPI Serving Institutions legislation are not limited to the institutions eligible for the designation. In particular, AAPI health and community development organizations played a key role in shaping the legislative strategy.

Finally, H.R. 4825 was introduced by Congressman Robert Underwood (D-Guam) in May 2002. It was reintroduced as H.R. 333 by Congressman David Wu (D-OR) on January 8, 2003 and again as H.R. 2616 in May 2005. Senators Barbara Boxer (D-CA) and Daniel Akaka (D-HI) introduced a senate companion bill, S. 2160, the Asian American and Pacific Islander Serving Institutions Act, on December 21, 2005. The legislation states that eligible institutions must have an AAPI enrollment of at least 10 percent. Additionally, the legislation requires that either 50 percent of students receive federal financial aid *or* the proportion of students receiving Pell Grants meets or exceeds the national median. Funds can be used for general institutional expenditures (Section 318) such as renovation of libraries and laboratories, as well as specific needs of the community, such as conducting research on AAPI students and establishing partnerships with community based organizations.

Thus, in the policy realm, the fight for AAPI Serving Institutions largely came out of a desire to increase the capacity of AAPI organizations and institutions, as well as a frustration that AAPI needs in education were ignored or unknown. We will now turn to two ways in which the AAPI Serving Institutions legislation seeks to reinterpret racial dynamics. It does so through challenging the model minority image and carving out a unique space for AAPIs in the racial landscape. Whether or not these efforts will be successful or not is unclear, but in this context, we speak of what the legislation is *trying* to do, rather than its success or failure as a legislative movement or racial project.

CHALLENGING ASSUMPTIONS ABOUT SUCCESS

One way in which the AAPI Serving Institution legislation challenges the racial status quo is through a refutation of the model minority myth. The dominant representation of Asian Americans in education is that they are successful to the point of "out-whiting the Whites" (Chun, 1980). The aggregate success of the community continues to overshadow the unique needs of AAPI subgroups (Hune & Chan, 1997; Hune, 2002; U.S. Dept. of Health and Human Services, 2001), and AAPI students continue to be perceived as "not educationally disadvantaged" (Nakanishi, 1995).

Furthermore, neoconservatives are quick to point out that if anything, affirmative action at highly selective institutions punishes the success of AAPI students (Takagi, 1992). In an article published in *Forbes Magazine,* University of California Regent John Moores argues that the University of California Comprehensive Review admissions policy is guilty of "blatantly discriminating against Asians" (APAHE, 2004). *Brian Ho v. San Francisco Unified School District,* an affirmative action case brought by Chinese American plaintiffs who felt that the SFUSD school assignment process discriminated against Chinese Americans, also reflects a neoconservative embrace of Asian Americans as victims of continued race conscious policies (Robles, 2004). This depiction of Asian Americans is disrupted by two phenomena: how the broad AAPI community is hurt by the model minority myth and the continuing salience of class and ethnicity. Both of these issues are explicitly documented in the language of H.R. 2616.

The backlash of the model minority myth on AAPI students is noted in research on the underutilization of counseling services (Fong, 1998; U.S. Dept. of Health and Human Services, 2001), mental health issues (Okazaki, 2002), negative campus climate (Bennett & Okinaka, 1990; Cress & Ikeda, 2003), suicide (Arenson, 2004), and hate crimes (Kotori & Malaney, 2003). Further countering reports of monolithic Asian American success are reports of students feeling underserved because of resistance towards Asian American studies programs, the underrepresentation of AAPI faculty and administrators, and a lack of student services that specifically address the AAPI population (Campus Advisory Commission, 2001).

These issues find their way into the legislation in Section 1 of H.R. 2616, sub-points 4 and 5:

> (4) The "model minority myth" assumption adversely effects AAPI youth, who are perceived as being academically successful and not in need of outreach, academic support systems, or other support services.
>
> (5) The "model minority myth" and lack of disaggregated data may prevent student services offices from conducting intentional outreach efforts, such as through TRIO programs including Upward Bound and Educational Talent Search, to AAPI students, because they are perceived to not be in need of support. (H.R. 2616, Section 1, 4–5)

As part of the rationale for AAPI Serving Institutions, the legislation specifically makes note of the harmful effects of the model minority stereotype on the educational experiences of Asian American students. By explaining how the way in which AAPI students are stereotyped in higher education adversely affects AAPI students, the AAPI Serving Institution legislation works as a racial project to make the case for increased resources to remedy this issue. On a literal level, H.R. 2616 seeks to authorize 30 million dollars in funding. The legislation can be interpreted as a call for other resources such as increased attention toward and understanding of AAPI experiences in education.

A second critical disruption of the model minority myth represented by H.R. 2616 occurs along class and ethnicity lines, as educational attainment rates and levels of poverty vary drastically among AAPI subgroups (Reeves & Bennett, 2004). Unlike the previous discussion of how the model minority myth hurts AAPI students because of the stereotyping of Asian Americans, much of the concern with disparities within the AAPI community has to do with the fact that many subgroups do not even have adequate access to higher education. Section 1, subpoints 6 and 7 note:

(6) Additionally, disaggregated data indicates that 25.0 percent of Vietnamese Americans, 63.6 percent for Hmong Americans, 42.6 percent of Cambodian Americans, 34.7 percent Laotian Americans, 17.7 percent of Pacific Islander live in poverty. Such socioeconomic disparities within the community are often overlooked, as only 12.6 percent of the total AAPI population lives in poverty.

(7) While Asian Americans and Pacific Islanders overall have the highest college graduation rates of any group (44 percent in 2000), certain subgroups have much lower rates of degree attainment. Only 13.8 percent of Vietnamese Americans, 5.8 percent of Laotian Americans, 6.1 percent of Cambodian Americans, and less than 5.1 percent of Hmong Americans had college degrees. Only 13.8 percent of Pacific Islanders had degrees.

By and large, H.R. 2616 challenges the model minority image by rejecting neoconservative claims that align Asian Americans with Whites as victims of affirmative action and reverse discrimination in higher education. The legislation uses disaggregated data to depict how contrary to popular belief, certain AAPI subgroups are desperately in need of special services. By seeking entry into Title III alongside other MSIs, H.R. 2616 is a legislative rejection of the model minority myth and an alignment with other communities of color from which AAPIs have traditionally been distanced from in the educational realm. H.R. 2616 draws on the experiences of AAPIs who feel the negative effects of the model minority myth on campus and the intersection of class and ethnicity for AAPI subgroups underrepresented in higher education. The emphasis on underserved AAPI subgroups attempts to draws attention to the overall complexity and diversity of the AAPI community, as Section 1, subpoint 4 of the legislation states:

(4) The distinct cultural, linguistic, socioeconomic, and historical experiences that affect educational attainment of different AAPI subpopulations are often overlooked because programs and policies are based on aggregated data and the assumption that AAPIs are a monolithic group . . .

By refuting the model minority myth, advocates are embracing a more nuanced understanding of what it means to be AAPI and a community with special needs. In turn, the departure from assumptions of monolithic AAPI success serves as an alternative interpretation and representation of AAPI educational experiences.

THE RACIAL REPOSITIONING OF ASIAN AMERICANS AND PACIFIC ISLANDERS

In addition to challenging the model minority stereotype, the AAPI Serving Institutions legislation also works as a racial project to reposition how AAPIs are viewed by carving out a unique space for AAPIs in the American racial landscape. Takagi (1992) argues that the polarization of race in higher education and American society affects how Asian Americans are perceived in education: "[R]acial politics in higher education are determined and shaped by Black experiences, on one hand, and White experiences, on the other. Asians are perceived to be either like Whites or not like Whites; or alternatively, like Blacks or not like Blacks" (p. 11). She describes Asian Americans as the "wild card" of American education, with an inconsistent racial status (p. 11). On one hand, the aggregate AAPI population mirrors and even exceeds the academic success of Whites. However, AAPIs are still subject to discrimination, aligning them with other traditionally disenfranchised minorities. AAPIs and the country's rapidly changing demographics confound simplistic explanations for supposed racial difference. Unfortunately, the mainstream American discourse has responded all too often by omitting in-depth discourse on AAPIs altogether, grouping them with Whites, and ignoring cultural-specific issues.

Two scholars provide additional insight helpful in framing AAPI Serving Institutions. Chang (1999) makes the case for a Critical Asian American Legal Studies that abandons the traditional American racial Black/White binary. He argues that because of the qualitative differences between Asian Americans, other communities of color, and Whites, Asian Americans cannot simply be defined in relation to other racial groups. Furthermore, he contends that the Black/White binary omits or marginalizes the experiences of Asian Americans, Latinos/as, Native Americans, and multiracial Americans from discussions in the law. While noting the contributions of Critical Race Theory in foregrounding race in the law, he states that the experiences of Asian Americans still lack adequate coverage within Critical Race Theory.

Kim (1999) responds to Chang in her provocatively titled essay, "Are Asians Black?: The Asian American Civil Rights Agenda and the Contemporary Significance of the Black/White Paradigm," in which she refutes his rejection of the Black/White paradigm. Kim argues that the fact that the historical Black/White paradigm is rooted in the fundamental American legacy of Black/White race relations does not limit its ability to include other racial groups in the American racial dialogue. She contends that Chang's call for a Critical Asian American Legal Studies is primarily an issue of coverage, which can be remedied without rejecting the Black/White paradigm. Kim suggests that because of their aggregate high educational attainment, Asian Americans actually have a unique opportunity to subvert the racial hierarchy of the Black/White paradigm, which has shifted over time to deem them as "almost-'White'" (p. 2403). For instance, by rejecting model minority status, Asian Americans can destabilize the hierarchy that pits their interests against other communities of color. However, she notes that such a subversion of the set pecking order requires a deep understanding, not rejection, of the continuing salience of the Black/White paradigm in American racial dynamics.

The trajectory leading up to the AAPI serving institutions legislation reflects Takagi's (1992) assessment of Asian American concerns in education as being a "wild card," with Asian Americans maintaining a somewhat inconsistent identity as minorities or people of color. The legislation calls for a greater recognition of the lack of coverage of Asian American needs in discussions concerning communities of color, as Chang (1999) highlights in his call for a Critical Asian American Legal Studies. Finally, following Kim (1999), as it attempts to subvert the model minority myth and destabilize imposed identities, the AAPI Serving Institutions legislation reflects the need for a deep understanding of the Black/White paradigm, its effect on higher education, and continuing legacy of racism in America.

These analyses of Asian American racial positioning in education all contribute to the current question of how the AAPI Serving Institutions legislation creates a unique space for Asian Americans within educational discourse and identity politics as a racial project. (For another helpful analysis of Asian American racial positioning, see Claire Jean Kim's [1999] discussion on Asian Americans and racial triangulation.) As Takagi (1992) articulates, little or no unique space currently exists for Asian Americans in education, as their experiences are always defined in relation to Whites or Blacks. Kim's (1999) discussion of the continuing significance of the Black/White paradigm is essential in understanding H.R. 2616's attempt to expand Title III of the Higher Education Act to include Asian Americans. The legislation rejects neoconservative overtures that align Asian Americans with Whites in education. On the other hand, Asian Americans have certain needs that differ from Blacks, Latinos/as, Native Americans, Alaska Natives, and Native Hawaiians, who are currently served by Title III and Title V institutions.

The racial repositioning of one group cannot happen without altering the configuration of other racial groups. The depiction of Asian Americans as the success story of America is powerful evidence in support of the case for American meritocracy and opportunity. As the model minority myth distances Asian Americans from the presumed failure of other minority groups, a rejection of the myth, as presented in H.R. 2616, is implicitly a rejection of America as a completely fair and colorblind society. Seeking a closer alignment with other minority groups by seeking a MSI classification is one step further away from Asian Americans as the "middleman" minority (Kim, 1999) and a step towards a more complex American racial hierarchy.

In order to understand how racial positioning plays into the push for federal recognition of AAPI Serving Institutions, we must understand how the intent of H.R. 2616 stands vis-à-vis other MSIs. The legacy of slavery,

Jim Crow, and federally sponsored discrimination against Blacks is paramount to the origins of Title III funding. HBCUs existed before Titles III, V, or even before the Higher Education Act itself came to being. The original rationale for funding was the federal government's obligation to create educational opportunity for freed slaves (Wolanin, 1998). In later years, the rationale shifted toward strengthening the institutions themselves, but federal support for Black higher education was unstable (Wolanin, 1998). While the original Title III provided direct support for "Developing Institutions," there were no explicit references to HBCUs, although they were eligible for funding.

In 1986, Part B, "Strengthening historically Black colleges and universities" was added to Title III. Although HBCUs benefited from Title III prior to 1986, the funds that HBCUs received were inconsistent because other institutions competed for funds (Wolanin, 1998). According to Willie (1991), HBCUs had been "pushed out of competition" for Title III funds by the early 1980s, receiving "only about one-third" of Title III funds. In response, Part B was part of a strategy by HBCUs to create specific allocations for HBCUs. HBCUs continue to play a critical role, educating a disproportionately high number of Black students and other underserved populations.

Although H.R. 2616 would create a MSI designation for AAPI students, it is clear that such a designation would differ remarkably from the original MSI designation for HBCUs. Because of the historical compensatory rationale behind HBCUs and later, Tribally Controlled Colleges and Universities, the inclusion of HSIs into the Higher Education Act was met with some resistance from minority educators and policy makers. Of particular concern was that funding HSIs based on the percentage of Hispanic/Latino/a students departed from the historical rationales for separate funding of HBCUs, that funding HSIs could take away from aid given to HBCUs, and that funding HSIs would be subject to anti-affirmative action forces and thus put HBCUs at risk (Laden, 2001). In a letter to the editor (1991), William Blakey, legal representative from the United Negro College Fund (UNCF), objected to one article's presentation of the debate: "I strongly object to the article's characterization of my position as opposing any attempts to provide Title III or other federal aid to predominantly Hispanic institutions. Further, the article's attempt to pit the two major minority populations against each other in this context is neither accurate nor helpful." However, in a time of perceived limited funding, conflicts in the competition for resources seem inevitable. MSIs have since created several joint collaborations, including the founding of the Alliance for Equity in Higher Education in 1999 and the recent Kellogg MSI Leadership Fellows Program (Institute for Higher Education Policy, 2004). Native Hawaiian/

Alaska Native Serving Institutions appear to be absent from these networks, and one wonders how AAPI Serving Institutions would be received.

The concept behind AAPI Serving Institutions is much closer to the rationale for HSIs because of their mutual dedication to serving a population that has been shaped by immigration, as well as the proposed percentage-based eligibility for designation. However, the educational needs of the AAPI community remain distinctly different from the needs of Latinos/as in higher education. In the public imagination, the needs of Latino/a students are more closely aligned to Black and Native American educational trends than Asian American students due to the aggregate group's lower socio-economic status and rates of educational attainment, as well as cultural stereotypes and expectations of different groups. Within the overall Latino/a population, 10.4 percent of those ages 25 and older held at least a bachelor's degree, in contrast to 44.1 percent of the aggregate Asian American population (Ramierez, 2004; Reeves & Bennett, 2004). Research on HSIs supports the need for federal funding under Title V because of the average low-educational expenditures of institutions that serve a disproportionately high number of Latino/a students (Benitez, 1998). However, little is known about the characteristics of institutions that would be eligible for the AAPI Serving Institution designation. Many, like HSI, may have generally low-educational expenditures. The nature of H.R. 2616 raises the need for recognition of the types of institutions that AAPI students attend.

Teranishi (2001) suggests that by default, many large public institutions on the West Coast already exist as AAPI Serving Institutions because of their sheer number of AAPI students. Popular conception affirms the AAPI presence at highly selective institutions throughout the country ("MIT: Made in Taiwan") but fails to associate AAPI students with the type of schools that they attend the most: large, public institutions (Chang & Kiang, 2002). AAPIs actually have their largest concentration of total higher education enrollment in community colleges. In 2002, 47 percent of AAPI undergraduates attended community colleges (*The Chronicle of Higher Education,* 2005). Moreover, enrollment in two-year institutions is increasing faster than enrollment in four-year colleges—public or private—(Teranishi, 2005). Still, little is known about the AAPI presence and growth in two-year institutions, although many potential AAPI Serving Institutions would be community colleges (Laanan & Starobin, 2004). Regardless of educational expenditures, these institutions would differ in some ways from HSIs simply because of the different needs of their respective student populations.

Thus, AAPI Serving Institutions would carve out a unique position for the Asian American community in the racial landscape that diverges from the current model minority image that aligns them with Whites. Neither White nor Black, Asian Americans have needs of their own, although the effort for inclusion into Title III appears to mark an attempt towards solidifying the position of Asian Americans as people of color or minorities. H.R. 2616's attempt to redefine Asian American racial positioning within education requires a contextual understanding of how AAPIs can subvert the racial hierarchy by refuting the model minority stereotype and asserting the needs of the AAPI community. Kim's (1999) discussion of the Black/White paradigm of American race relations, and how AAPIs can subvert it, is useful here. At the same time, the educational needs of Asian Americans differ markedly from the community needs of Blacks, Latinos, and Native Americans. In this respect, Chang's (1999) call for a unique racial positioning for Asian Americans is appropriate, as AAPIs have unique political and social identities.

FUTURE CHALLENGES AND PROSPECTS

The push for a federal designation of AAPI Serving Institutions is situated within a process of racial formation for AAPIs in which Asian American racial positioning and identity is continuously contested and evolving. This effort marks an attempt to break away from the pervasiveness of the model minority stereotype and align more closely with other minority groups, due to the stereotype's tendency to overshadow the unique needs of the broader AAPI community and underserved subgroups. Furthermore, the push reflects ongoing attempts by the AAPI policy and education communities to subvert a racial positioning that lumps AAPIs with Whites and to establish a more distinct space for AAPIs in the American racial spectrum. Because one racial group cannot be repositioned without affecting how other racial groups are situated in relation to each other, the proposed AAPI Serving Institutions legislation also has ramifications for how the educational experiences of other minority groups are understood.

Much of the compelling interest in protecting affirmative action revolves around the need for a critical mass of Black, Latino/a, and Native American students, particularly at the highly selective institutions where affirmative action policies in admissions are most contested (Solórzano, Allen & Carroll, 2002). However, the AAPI student population is unique because while a critical mass of AAPI students exists at many of these institutions, students are still marginalized (Campus Advisory Committee, 2001). Cho (1996) also highlights the deceptiveness of the parity based on structural diversity, specifically in the case of faculty. The seemingly healthy numeric representation of Asian American faculty on many college campuses draws attention away from issues such as continuing racial and sexual harassment, denial of tenure, and the lack of high-level Asian American administrators.

Proponents of the AAPI education success story may herald the high persistence rates of AAPI students, but AAPI students are known to persist even when they have negative perceptions of campus climate (Bennett & Okinaka, 1990). Even though campuses may be structurally diverse and students of color are academically achieving, they still may face a hostile campus climate if other aspects of diversity are not addressed (Hurtado et al., 1998).

The fact that AAPI students at even highly resourced institutions still feel underserved is a highly troubling issue, and one that if passed, H.R. 2616 may help remedy. However, the implementation of H.R. 2616 must guarantee that the needs of students who already have access to higher education are balanced with the needs of AAPI students, particularly underserved subgroups, who face strong barriers to accessing higher education. Kiang (2004) and Ong and Espiritu (1994) refer to the challenges of adequately addressing the needs of subgroups who are marginalized within the AAPI community because of class and ethnicity. Kiang (2004) does not refer to H.R. 2616, but his basic argument that Southeast Asian American communities have been neglected within the pan-AAPI agenda is a useful call for accountability to underserved populations if the AAPI Serving Institutions legislation does pass. Under the proposed legislation, institutions that apply for funding must have a five-year plan for improving assistance for AAPI students. This stipulation may be helpful in making sure that Southeast Asian American and Pacific Islanders are not shortchanged during the implementation process.

H.R. 2616 certainly faces an uphill battle as a legislative attempt to refute the model minority myth, as it seeks to carve out a unique space for Asian Americans in the educational and political realms. Racial formation is often imposed from the outside, with racial identity being largely dictated by the dominant group. Thus, the AAPI Serving Institutions legislation is a critical opportunity for the AAPI community to take ownership of its racial formation, redefining racial positioning on its own terms.

Addendum: In September 2007, Congress passed the College Cost Reduction Act which included a designation for AAPI serving institutions.

REFERENCES

Adhikary, P., and Eav, M. (2004). *(Draft) Designating Asian American Pacific Islander serving institutions: A vehicle for Southeast Asian American advancement?* Washington, DC: National Asian Pacific American Legal Consortium.

APAHE. (2004). *Resolution of the APAHE board on UC admissions.* Resolution presented at the Asian Pacific Americans in Higher Education, San Francisco, CA.

Arenson, K. (2004, December 3). Worried colleges step up efforts over suicide. *New York Times.*

Benitez, M. (1998). Hispanic-serving institutions: Challenges and opportunities. In *Minority-serving institutions: Distinct purposes, common goals* (Vol. 102, pp. 57–68). San Francisco, CA: Jossey-Bass Inc., Publishers.

Bennett, C., and Okinaka, A. (1990). Factors related to persistence among Asian, Black, Hispanic, and White undergraduates at a predominantly White university: Comparison between first and fourth year cohorts. *The Urban Review,* 22, 33–60.

Blakey, W. A. (1991, June 19). Letter to the editor: New model needed to aid Hispanic colleges. *The Chronicle of Higher Education.*

Campus Advisory Committee for Asian American Affairs. (2001). *Asian Pacific Americans at Berkeley: Visibility and marginality.* Berkeley, CA: University of California.

Chang, M. J., and Kiang, P. N. (2002). New challenges of representing Asian American students in U.S. Higher education. In W. A. Smith, P. G. Altbach and K. Lomotey (Eds.), *The racial crisis in American higher education* (pp. 137–158). Albany: State University of New York Press.

Chang, R. S. (1999). *Disoriented: Asian Americans, law, and the nation-state.* New York: New York University Press.

Chew, P. (1994). Asian Americans: The "reticent" minority and their paradoxes. *William and Mary Law Review,* 38(1).

Cho, S. (1996, March). *Confronting the myths: Asian Pacific American faculty in higher education.* Paper presented at the Asian Pacific Americans in Higher Education, San Francisco, CA.

The Chronicle of Higher Education (2005). College enrollment by racial and ethnic group, selected years. *The 2005–6 Almanac.* Retrieved 11/15/05, 2005, from *http://chronicle.com/weekly/almanac/2005/nation/0101503.htm*

Chun, K. (1980). The myth of Asian American success and its educational ramifications. *IRCD Bulletin,* 15(1 & 2). New York: Teachers College, Columbia University.

The College Board. (1999). *Reaching the top: A report of the national taskforce on minority Achievement.* New York: The College Entrance Examination Board.

Cress, C. M., and Ikeda, E. K. (2003). Distress under duress: The relationship between campus climate and depression in Asian American college students. *NASPA Journal,* 40(2), 74–97.

Espiritu, Y. L. (1992). *Asian American Panethnicity: Bridging institutions and Identities.* Philadelphia, PA: Temple University Press.

Fong, T. P. (1998). *The contemporary Asian American experience: Beyond the model minority.* New Jersey: Prentice Hall.

Harris, P. M., and Jones, N. A. (2005). *We the people: Pacific Islanders in the United States.* Washington, DC: U.S. Census Bureau.

H.R. 333, 108th Cong., 1st Sess. (2003).

H.R. 2616, 109th Cong., 1st Sess. (2005)

H.R. 4825, 107th Cong., 2nd Sess. (2002).

Hsia, J., and Hirano-Nakanishi, M. (1989). The demographics of diversity. *Change,* 20–27.

Hune, S. (2002). Demographics and Diversity of Asian American College Students. In M. McEwen, C. Kodama, A. Alvarez, and C. Liang (Eds.), *Working with Asian American College Students* (pp. 11–20). San Francisco, CA: Jossey-Bass Inc., Publishers.

Hune, S. and Chan, K.S. (1997). *Special focus: Asian Pacific American demographics and educational trends.* In D. Carter and R. Wilson (Eds.) Minorities in Higher Education (Vol. 15). Washington, DC: American Council on Education.

Hurtado, S., Milem, J. F., Clayton-Pedersen, A. R., and Allen, W. R. (1998). Enhancing campus climates for racial/ethnic diversity: Educational policy and practice. *The Review of Higher Education, 21*(3), 279–302.

The Institute for Higher Education Policy. (2004). *Leading the way to America's future: A monograph about the launch and implementation of the Kellogg MSI leadership fellows program, 2002–2004.* Washington, DC: The Alliance for Equity in Higher Education.

Kiang, P. N. (2004). Checking Southeast Asian American realities in pan-Asian American agendas. *AAPI Nexus, 2*(1), 48–76.

Kibria, N. (1998). The contested meanings of 'Asian American': Racial dilemmas in the contemporary US. *Ethnic and Racial Studies, 21*(5).

Kim, C. J. (1999). The Racial Triangulation of Asian Americans. *Politics and Society, 27,* 105–38.

Kim, J. Y. (1999). Are Asians Black? The Asian-American civil rights agenda and the contemporary significance of the Black/White paradigm. *The Yale Law Journal, 108*(8), 2385–2412.

Kotori, C., and Malaney, G. D. (2003). Asian American students' perceptions of racism, reporting behaviors, and awareness of legal rights and procedures. *NASPA Journal, 40*(3), 56–76.

Laanan, F. S., and Starobin, S. S. (2004). Defining Asian American and Pacific Islander-serving institutions. In B. V. Laden (Ed.), *Serving minority populations: New directions for community colleges* (Vol. 127, pp. 49–59). San Francisco, CA: Jossey-Bass Inc., Publishers.

Laden, B. V. (2001). Hispanic-serving institutions: Myths and realities. *Peabody Journal of Education, 76*(1), 73–92.

Lee, S. (1996). *Unraveling the "model minority" Stereotype: Listening to Asian American Youth.* New York: Teachers College Press, Columbia University.

Nakanishi, D. T. (1995). Growth and diversity: The education of Asian/Pacific Americans. In D. T. Nakanishi and T. Y. Nishida (Eds.), *The Asian American educational experience* (pp. xi–xx). New York: Routledge.

O'Brien, E. M., and Zudak, C. (1998). Minority-serving institutions: An overview. In J. P. Merisotis and C. T. O'Brien (Eds.), *Minority-serving institutions: Distinct purposes, common goals* (Vol. 102, pp. 5–16). San Francisco, CA: Jossey-Bass Inc., Publishers.

Okazaki, Sumie. (2002). Self-Other Agreement on Affective Distress Scales in Asian Americans and White Americans. *Journal of Counseling Psychology, 49*(4), 428–437.

Omi, M., and Winant, H. (1994). *Racial formation in the United States* (2nd ed.). New York: Routledge.

Ong, P., and Espiritu, Y. L. (1994). Class constraints on Racial solidarity among Asian Americans. In P. Ong, E. Bonacich, and L. Cheng (Eds.), *The new Asian immigration in Los Angeles and Global Restructuring.* Philadelphia, PA: Temple University Press.

Petersen, W. (1966, January 6). Success story, Japanese-American style. *New York Times Magazine,* p. 20ff.

Ramirez, R.R. (2004). *We the people: Hispanics in the United States.* Washington, DC: U.S. Census Bureau.

Reeves, T. J., and Bennett, C. E. (2004). *We the people: Asians in the United States.* Washington, DC: U.S. Census Bureau.

Robles, R. (2004). Articulating race—Asian American neoconservative renditions of equality. *AAPI Nexus, 2*(1), 77–104.

SEARAC. (2001). Summit on the status of Pacific Islanders and Southeast Asian Americans in higher education. Retrieved November 25, 2004, from http://www.searac.org/highedsummit.html

Solórzano, D. G., Allen, W. R., and Carroll, G. (2002). Keeping race in place: Racial microaggressions and campus racial climate at the University of California, Berkeley. *Chicano-Latino Law Review, 23,* 15–112.

Takagi, D. (1992). *The retreat from race: Asian-American admissions and racial politics.* New Brunswick, NJ: Rutgers University Press.

Teranishi, R.T. (2001). 'Raced' perspectives on College Opportunity: *The intersectionality of ethnicity and social class among Asian Pacific Americans.* Unpublished doctoral dissertation, University of California, Los Angeles.

Teranishi, R. T. (2005). *Asian American and Pacific Islander participation in U.S. higher education: Status and trends.* New York: The College Board.

U.S. Census Bureau. (1994). *1990 Census of Population: Education in the United States.* Washington, DC: U.S. Department of Commerce, Economics and Statistics Administration. http://www.census.gov/prod/cen1990/cp3/cp-3-4.pdf.

U.S. Census Bureau. (2003). *Educational Attainment: 2000.* Washington, DC: U.S. Department of Commerce, Economics and Statistics Administration.

U.S. Department of Education, National Center for Education Statistics. (2003). Higher Education General Information Survey (HEGIS), "Fall Enrollment in Colleges and Universities" surveys, 1976 and 1980; and Integrated Postsecondary Education Data System (IPEDS), "Fall Enrollment" surveys, 1990 through 1999, and Spring 2001 and Spring 2002 surveys.

U.S. Department of Health and Human Services. (2003). Minority-serving institutions of higher education: Developing partnerships to revitalize communities. Washington, DC: U.S. Department of Health and Human Services, Office of Policy Development and Research. Office of Urban Partnerships.

U.S. Department of Health and Human Services. (2001). Mental Health: Culture, Race, and Ethnicity—A Supplement to Mental Health: A Report of the Surgeon General. Rockville, MD: U.S. Department of Health and Human Services, Substance Abuse and Mental Health Administration. Center for Mental Health Services.

Valencia, R. (Ed.). (1997). *The evolution of deficit thinking.* Washington, DC: Falmer Press.

Walker-Moffat, W. (1995). The other side of the Asian American success story. San Francisco, CA: Jossey-Bass Inc., Publishers.

Willie, C. V. (1991, December 4). Universal programs in education are unfair to minority groups, we must again focus aid on the students who need it most. *The Chronicle of Higher Education.*

Wolanin, T. (1998). The federal investment in minority-serving institutions. In J. P. Merisotis and C. T. O'Brien (Eds.), *Minority-serving institutions: Distinct purposes, common goals* (Vol. 102, pp. 17–32). San Francisco, CA: Jossey-Bass Inc., Publishers.

Wolanin, T. (2003). *Reauthorizing the Higher Education Act: Issues and options.* Washington, DC: The Institute for Higher Education Policy.

Wollenberg, C. M. (1978). *All deliberate speed: Segregation and exclusion in California schools, 1855–1975.* Berkeley, CA: University of California Press.

Yang, K., and Niedzwiecki, W. R. (2003). *Southeast Asian Americans and Higher Education: Prepared for the Congressional Forum Entitled Evaluation of Asian Pacific Americans in Education,* 108th Cong. (2003).

CHAPTER 9

¿Dónde Están Los Hombres?

Examining Success of Latino Male Students at Hispanic-Serving Community Colleges

Berta Vigil Laden, Linda Serra Hagedorn, and Athena Perrakis

Rapid population growth among Hispanics in the United States over the past three decades has led them to become the largest minority group in the twenty-first century. Additional projections assert that this rapid growth will continue well into the first half of the current century causing concern among educational and policy leaders for the social and economic well-being of Hispanic students. Despite their burgeoning size as the emergent majority group, Hispanics remain significantly underrepresented in higher educational attainment and lag behind every other population group in attaining college degrees, in spite of numerous intervention efforts by various educational, government, and policy leaders (Fry, 2002; National Center for Education Statistics [NCES], 2005). Given that college enrollment and attainment of a bachelor's degree are now the norms for young adults aged 18–20, educators cannot afford to be idle while a large segment of the population opts out of the higher educational pipeline or falls into an economic downward spiral (Goncharoff, et al., 2000; Hagedorn, Maxwell & Hampton, 2001).

There is a marked need to study specifically *male* enrollment and performance in light of the recent sharp drop of Latino male students receiving high school and college diplomas. Since large numbers of Latinos attend community colleges, many of them Hispanic-Serving Institutions (HSIs), this chapter explores factors related to retention and success of Latino males in community college HSIs. The chapter begins with a detailed review of the literature. We then move beyond the extant knowledge to explore the academic success of Latino males within a very large urban community college district—the Los Angeles Community College District (LACCD). In the latter part of the chapter, we provide analyses performed as part of the Transfer and Retention of Urban Community College Students Project (TRUCCS). All analyses were based on transcripts and questionnaire data from over 18,000 students across the six LACCD HSIs. We choose the LACCD because of its large size and the number of Latinos served; six of the district's nine campuses have been identified as HSIs. The district resides in a county with a very high Latino proportion (46 percent) of residents (State of California, 2005). This chapter is one of several emerging research efforts that recognize the importance of HSIs, particularly community college HSIs, for Latinos and emphasizes the role that HSIs may play in advancing the educational achievement of a significant segment of the population.

REVIEW OF THE LITERATURE

As Mortenson (1995) and others have pointed out, the sharpest declines in the share of degrees have been among Hispanic males. Thus we ask the question: Is the increasing Latino gender imbalance resulting from Latinas (females) outpacing Latinos (males) in high school completion, college enrollment, and graduation rate? This imbalance has created an alarming and widening 60/40 percentage achievement gap between Latinas and Latinos in higher education. Even in HSIs, where Latino students represent at least 25 percent or more of the student population, Latinas are outperforming their male counterparts in enrollment numbers and academic achievement with a similar 60/40 gender gap (U.S. Census Bureau, 2003). Higher education is increasingly serving a brown populace wherein Latina students are more likely to outperform their male counterparts (Hernandez & Lopez, 2004–2005; Perrakis, 2005).

Latino Demographics

Hispanics, a heterogeneous population that can be of any race, have become the largest and fastest growing racial/ethnic group in the United States. In fact Hispanics have already achieved majority status in some areas of the nation. In March 2002, Hispanics represented 37.4 million or approximately 14 percent of the total American population (U.S. Census Bureau, 2003). Two in five Latinos are foreign born, and over half entered the United States in the recent period between 1990 and 2002. Although Latinos can be found moving into all geographic areas of the United States in search of a better life, they are largely concentrated in two major areas: 44.2 percent in the west and 34.8 percent in the south. In California alone, the most racially and ethnically diverse state in the nation, Hispanics represent 32.4 percent of the population

(U.S. Census Bureau, 2003). Although the majority of Latinos prefer living in metropolitan areas, they are also moving into other rural areas.

Larger families are more common for Latinos as over a quarter (26.5%) of Latino households consist of five or more persons, compared to only 10.8 percent of non-Hispanic White family households (U.S. Census Bureau, 2003). They are the youngest population group in the nation, with 34.4 percent under the age of 18 years as compared with 22.8 percent of non-Hispanic Whites. At the other end of the age spectrum, Latinos represent only 5.1 percent of the population aged 65 and over.

Latino Educational Attainment

Given their large numbers, while the educational attainment of the Hispanic population is of great national importance, the current data reveal a grim picture. More than a fourth (27%) of all Hispanics have less than a ninth grade education, and 57 percent of the population aged 25 and older are unlikely to have graduated from high school. The statistics become more dismal when one considers that only 11.1 percent of the Latino population has completed and earned a bachelor's degree. It is no surprise, therefore, that Latinos are more likely than Caucasians to be employed in low-paying, low-skilled service occupations and as laborers. Furthermore, more than one-fifth of all Latinos are living below the poverty level (U.S. Census Bureau, 2003).

Amidst the grim statistics, there is some good news. According to other recent data, Hispanic students made the biggest gains among all minority groups in achieving higher overall college enrollment in a ten-year period ending in October 2003. Specifically, Hispanic college enrollment rose from 4 percent in 1993 to 10 percent in 2003 (American Council on Education [ACE], 2005). In comparison, African American enrollment increased from 10 percent in 1993 to 13 percent in 2003, while Asian American/Pacific Islander student enrollment rose from 4 percent to 7 percent in the same period (ACE). Approximately one-fourth of these minority students were enrolled in four-year institutions while more than one-third were enrolled in community colleges. Approximately 12 percent of African American college students enrolled in historically Black colleges and universities (HBCUs). Nearly half (47%) of all Latino college students were enrolled in HSIs where they constituted at least a minimum of 25 percent of the students in the institutions (NCES, 2005).

California. Although Latinos represented 42.5 percent of the California population between the ages of 18–24, only one-third (32.9%) of these young adults were high school graduates (U.S. Census Bureau, 2003). Of the 2.6 million students enrolled in California's vast higher education system, Latinos represented only one in four (24.1 percent) of all students overall and slightly more, 26.8 percent, of all students in the state's 109 community colleges (CPEC, 2005).

The Integral Role of Hispanic-Serving Institutions

Were it not for the presence of HSIs, especially community college HSIs that create a vital pipeline to four-year HSIs and the baccalaureate degree, the overall college participation rates of Latinos would be even lower. California leads nationally with the highest number of HSIs overall and of these nearly 70 percent are community colleges (Hagedorn & Cepeda, 2004; Laden, 2004). Often labeled as nontraditional students by researchers and educators alike due to some of their personal and academic characteristics, many Latino students are first-generation college students in need of academic and financial support, guidance in course planning, and assistance with orientation and socialization to college. It is not uncommon for Latinos to be enrolled part-time and work at least part-time, to be academically underprepared for college, and to come from low- or lower middle-income families where knowledge of how to survive and succeed in the college culture is vague or absent. In order to succeed academically, Latino students require culturally inclusive orientation and socialization to college; comprehensive and appropriate curricula; supportive student and instructional services; accurate and consistent counseling and mentoring; understanding of and assistance with financial aid; quality transfer programs with strong articulation agreements; and caring, sensitive faculty and innovative administrative leaders (Laden, 1999b).

Yet, despite the potential academic at-risk characteristics of Latino students, community college HSIs successfully produce approximately 40 percent of all Latino associate degree graduates compared to less than 10 percent in non-HSIs, while four-year HSIs produce another 40 percent of all Latino baccalaureate degree graduates compared to 6 percent in non-HSIs (NCES, 2002). Together, these community college and four-year HSIs also form an important and direct pipeline for Latinos into doctoral granting institutions (Santiago, Andrade, & Brown, 2004; Solórzano, 1995). Santiago and colleagues contend that HSIs with their large Latino student bodies are now "at the forefront of higher education because of the shift in demographics and thus have an opportunity to be trendsetters" (p. 3). These researchers argue that the current Latino student enrollment patterns and diverse pathways to degree completion challenge HSIs—and other higher education institutions with large enrollments of Latino and other racial and ethnic students—to reconsider their traditional measures of success and how they deliver academic programs, student support services, and outreach into their communities. Certainly, these words of caution bear consideration, particularly when addressing the decline of Latino males in higher education.

Latino Male Academic Performance

A shadow side exists to Latino student success in terms of course completion rates in the HSI context. As evidenced by IPED graduation rates, it must be acknowledged that as a group, HSIs do not traditionally have high success rates. Thus, while the participation of Latinos in HSIs may be lauded in the literature, there may also be a substantial drawback when Latinos are directed to HSIs if their success could be hampered. Furthermore, HSIs are not exempt from the gender gap of female students exceeding male students in college enrollment and completion rates (Perrakis, 2005). Recent articles in well-regarded academic publications cite the alarming enrollment decline of male students with provocative, eye-catching headlines such as, "What's Wrong with the Guys?" (Mortenson, *Postsecondary Education Opportunity,* 1995), "Where the Boys Aren't" (Jones, *National Crosstalk,* 2005), and "College Enrollments Grow More Diverse, More Numerous, and More Female, 2 Government Reports Say" (Evelyn, *Chronicle of Higher Education,* 2005). While some researchers (Brownstein, 2000; King, 2000) argue that little has changed regarding the personal profiles of entering college first-year students and that the typical college student is still a White male from a relatively advantaged background, others are concerned about the population projections of increasing minority student enrollment (Brown, 1996) and decreasing male enrollment in the American college-age population (Jones, 2005).

In 2002, men constituted a declining portion of students enrolled in higher education, with 48.6 percent male enrollment and 43 percent as degree recipients, respectively (NCES, 2002). Enrollment projections suggest that a further downward enrollment trend for male students will reach 42 percent by 2010 (NCES)—although California community colleges already have reached 42.6 percent for Latino males (CPEC, 2005). King's (2000) analysis of national data, however, reveals that the gender gap varies rather considerably by age, race/ethnicity, and SES, which highlights a "class gap" (p. 12). Specifically, King reports that the gender/class gap is concentrated among low-income and minority male students: White males comprise 46 percent of all low-income students enrolled in higher education, 32 percent are African American males, 23 percent are Native American males, while 43 percent are Latino males. Furthermore, although the percentage of low-income Latino males enrolled in higher education is higher than that of low-income African Americans, Latino males are far less likely than either White or African American low-income students to finish high school

(King), enroll in college immediately after high school graduation, or persist to degree completion when they do enroll in college (NCES, 2005).

Some four-year institutions with selective admissions processes, in response to declining male enrollment, have responded to the rising 60/40 female/male imbalance by offering admissions preference to male applicants (Gose, 1999); but with its open-door admissions policy, the community college cannot follow suit. While the scholarly literature makes little mention of this mammoth issue, Latino male students are falling between the educational cracks.

Researchers such as Gándara (1995) argue that the gender difference between Latinos and Latinas favors males due to a cultural bias toward male achievement. However, the U.S. Department of Education (NCES, 2005) notes that Latinos are substantially more likely than Latinas to have dropped out of high school. The literature on male college retention is sparse, and the literature on Latino male persistence is virtually nonexistent. Few researchers have taken as their subject of investigation this population for reasons one can only hypothesize. Perhaps, until recently, it was politically incorrect to question the performance in college of male students in general, and Latino males in particular, because it was assumed that female students overall and Latinas in particular, struggled to persist and achieve in academic settings. Moreover, it may also have been assumed that men of color, including Latinos, faced only the obstacle of their race, when in fact issues of gender, class, and SES compounded the importance of race in terms of college achievement.

The decline of male enrollment leading to a 60/40 gender imbalance (Evelyn, 2002) and the subject of male achievement have caught the attention of some who cite two trends they perceive as responsible for decreased male interest in college: One, the rising divorce rates and corollary rates of single-mother households; and, two, the disproportionate number of female teachers in elementary schools, where young men find fewer role models to emulate (Brownstein, 2000). Recent NCES data (as cited in Evelyn, 2002) reveal that in 2002, 131 women received a bachelor's degree for every 100 men enrolled in four-year institutions; and 151 women received associate degrees for every 100 men enrolled in community colleges in the United States. While these figures are attracting widespread attention of officials at four-year colleges and universities, the gap between genders at the community college level has yet to generate as much scholarly concern.

Nevertheless, a few community colleges are concerned about the male student achievement crisis and seek to better understand the causes for their low enrollment and poor persistence. Yet, even these concerned faculty and administrators admit that "We know that male enrollment is a problem for education at large, but we've only scratched the surface in terms of looking at our specific problems here" (Chand, cited in Evelyn, 2002, p. 4). For example, Lakeland Community College in Ohio created a men's resource center originally to provide continuing education programs. Abysmal male graduation rates led to an in-depth examination of gender discrepancies in enrollment patterns and academic performance. The director of the men's resource center found that male students are 58 percent more likely to be placed on academic notice, and 40 percent more likely to be dismissed outright; male students' grade point average is approximately 2.64 compared to 2.85 for women, and men are less likely to use college tutorial services or visit faculty during their office hours (Evelyn, 2002).

Latino male students in particular lack the social, cultural, and capital resources to navigate successfully in predominantly White institutions; these men must therefore develop skills and attitudes in order to succeed despite the odds against them (Perrakis 2003; 2005). Family support as a means of developing these skills and attitudes is crucial for Latino students because their peers may be less supportive of academic achievement than the friends of their Caucasian counterparts (Maton et al., 1996). As a subset of social support, family support has only recently been the subject of research in studies on racial and ethnic student achievement. Maton and colleagues adopt a cultural specificity perspective, which takes as given the notion that ethnic groups have different cultural norms, experiences, and world views that differ from—and often collide with—those of other ethnic or racial groups in society. The effects of family support can mediate the challenges of conflicting social norms for students of color, whose friends often adopt a culturally based view that succeeding academically is akin to "acting White" (Fordham & Ogbu, 1986, as cited in Maton, et al.). Rendón (1995) observes that peer pressure *not* to succeed can make the act of educational achievement appear as a breach of loyalty to friends of the student who are neither enrolled in nor planning to attend college. Thus, without the support of peers or friends, students of color depend on parental guidance in the absence of institutional support mechanisms as the main source of encouragement to persist and graduate from college.

Hispanic Enrollment in the Los Angeles District

In California Latinas outnumber their male counterparts in all sectors of higher education. Across the 109 California community colleges, in the fall, 2003 Latinas represented 53.6 percent of Hispanic student enrollment compared to 46.4 percent Latino males (CPEC, 2005). Within the nine-campus LACCD, overall Hispanic enrollment has increased fairly rapidly. In 1972, Latinos represented only 16.1 percent of the student population; in 2004, nearly three decades later, their proportion of the student population reached a record high of 46.5 percent (LACCD, 2005). At one of the district's six HSIs, Hispanic enrollment skyrocketed to 75.9 percent in the same year. Nevertheless, despite a pattern of overall growth for Hispanics of both genders, the proportion of Latino male enrollment has steadily decreased in the LACCD. In 1972, Latino males represented 56 percent of the overall LACCD enrollment, but by 1980, only 45.9 percent of the enrollment was of Latino males (LACCD). Their enrollment percentage decreased slightly to 44.5 percent a decade later, but plummeted to 39.2 percent in 2004.

Transfer rates are an indicator of movement from the community college to the university in pursuit of the baccalaureate degree. Transfer rates for racial and ethnic students are very carefully scrutinized by policy leaders and researchers as an indicator of both student and institutional success. Like all of the 74 community college districts in California, the LACCD maintains data on the ethnic distribution of transfers from its nine campuses to the state's nine University of California campuses and 25 California State University campuses. While there has been some recent improvement in Latino transfer rates, data from the 2002–2003 academic year indicate that only 25.1 percent of transferring students were Latino, thus emphasizing their under representation with respect to transfer and revealing severe leakage in the transfer pipeline for this group.

ANALYSES

As indicated earlier, our data is from the TRUCCS Project and based on the transcripts and questionnaire data from over 18,000 students. In the fall of 2000, the LACCD administered a 103-question instrument during classroom time to a randomly selected group of classes. The sampling was accomplished through a random number generator and applied to the fall 2000 semester inventory of classes. This procedure maximized participation and representation. Sampling frames were varied by college so as to ensure large enough samples for the smaller colleges while limiting sizes (and costs) at the large institutions. Although the purpose of our analyses is to understand better the success specific to Latino males, for reasons of comparison we include African American and White male students. Table 9.1 provides demographic characteristics of this sample. Data analyses revealed that within each ethnic group, males were more likely than females to be in a comparatively higher income bracket. Also of interest is that among the three male groups, Latinos were more likely to be in the lower income bracket.

Table 9.1 illustrates additional and important aspects of the sample. We note that the White students in the sample do not fit many of the stereotypes of nonminorities; for example, less than 60 percent of the students are U.S. citizens and/or speak English as a first language. Other interesting differences are the low proportion of African Americans in the traditional age bracket (less than 25 years). However, regarding Latino males, the true focus of these analyses, we note that while the majority express a desire to transfer to a four-year institution, less than half reported a successful high school GPA and the majority came from homes where parents did not even finish high school. Typical of community college students, as noted earlier, few students attended college on a full-time basis. While African American male students were less likely than Latino males to attend full-time, it is important to note that White male students were much more likely to be enrolled on a full-time basis. Also included in table 9.1 are cumulative college GPA and course success ratios. The course success ratio represents the proportion of

Table 9.1 Demographics of Latinos in the Los Angeles Community College District

	Hispanic		African Americans		White	
	Males (n=3,146)	Females (n=5,214)	Males (n=912)	Females (n=2,037)	Males (n=272)	Females (n=379)
U.S. Citizens (%)	68.4	71.8	88.7	94.3	58.9	56.5
English as first language (%)	49.8	47.8	93.1	96.8	56.7	54.4
Under 25 years of age (%)	57.6	58.0	42.8	34.5	58.5	58.0
Desire to transfer (%)	78.6	80.0	82.1	80.4	75.4	80.0
High School GPA 'B' or better (%)	47.7	53.7	41.9	56.9	56.1	75.8
Father: less than high school graduate (%)	65.1	66.8	26.1	26.6	7.9	10.0
Mother: less than high school graduate (%)	66.5	69.1	20.9	23.7	8.4	13.4
College GPA (Std. dev.)	2.42 (.796)	2.45 (.750)	2.30 (.793)	2.39 (.758)	2.52 (.813)	2.63 (.828)
Attend full time (%)	34.4	35.3	37.2	30.9	42.9	41.4
College course success ratio (std. dev.)	.681 (.218)	.691 (.214)	.639 (.230)	.660 (.223)	.710 (.241)	.744 (.228)
Transfer-prepared (%)	24.9	26.8	16.4	20.0	20.6	25.6

courses enrolled that were passed with a grade of "C" or better. Latino males had slightly lower GPAs and course completion ratios than either Latinas or Whites, regardless of gender for the latter.

Based on the fact that a very significant aspect of the community college mission is to ready underprepared students for transfer to a four-year college or university, we included a measure of "transfer-prepared." We defined "transfer-prepared" as the earning of 64 or more college level credits, including at least one transfer level English and Mathematics course. It is important to note that 24.9 percent of the Latino males in the sample fit the definition of "transfer-prepared." While at first blush this proportion seems low, it must also be stated that 77.7 percent of the Latino males began in a "less than college level" math course; 68.8 percent began in a "less than college" English course; and 64.4 percent began in *both* an English and Math course below college level.

To assess the success of Latino males in an urban community college system, we performed a two-way analysis of variance by gender and ethnicity across the measures of college GPA and course completion ratio. We also performed a chi-square analysis on the proportions of students, as grouped by ethnicity and gender, readied for transfer.

RESULTS

The test of the multivariate general linear model for GPA and successful course completion ratio indicated a significant interaction by ethnicity and gender (Wilks' Lambda=.999; F=4.126; p<.01). We therefore split the sample by gender and performed the statistical tests for comparison. We used the Tukey post hoc test to distinguish statistical differences for pairwise comparisons among ethnic groupings. All tests were highly significant indicating that both females and males differed by ethnic groups. The results of all comparisons via the Tukey post hoc were also statistically significant. Therefore, the results indicated that regardless of gender, African American students had the lowest GPA and course completion success ratio followed by Hispanics. White students had the statistically higher GPA and course completion ratio.

Interestingly, the chi-square analysis by gender for proportion of transfer-prepared was also statistically significant (female chi-square=105.877; df=2; p<.001; male chi-square=35.8556; df=2; p<.001). Regardless of gender, the pattern remained the same—the lowest proportion of transfer-ready students was African American, followed by White students. The highest proportion was for Hispanic students.

CONCLUSION

Community colleges have been the frequent target of discontent regarding low proportions of students, particularly students of color and those from lower socioeconomic brackets, who ultimately transfer to four-year universities. Our analyses of a large urban district with six HSIs indicated that many students of color enter the college with histories of lower academic performance (i.e., low high school GPA), and may not speak English as a first language; moreover, they often come from families without a history of higher education. Indeed, when viewing the academic success of the students in our sample, the average community college GPA was between a C+ and B–. While these grades denote "passing," they may indicate that students are not sufficiently readied for transfer to a four-year campus.

Our findings regarding the measure of "transfer-prepared" by ethnic group offer some very interesting interpretations. Latino students in our sample were statistically *more likely* to be prepared than their African American or White counterparts. This finding is in stark contradiction to the fact that Hispanic students from the district were *less likely* to actually transfer. The difference lies in the two measures of importance. Transfer-prepared only represents the earning of credits to be transfer-eligible, whereas actual transfer requires specific actions coupled with financial obligations and changes in lifestyle. While there are several public and private four-year colleges and universities in driving distance from the community college campuses, they may not offer courses at times convenient for these students.

While our conclusions highlight interesting dilemmas, they do little to facilitate the development of appropriate policies to assist Latino students in crisis. One way community colleges can help abate the crisis is to focus attention and resources on poor male academic performance. As the example of Lakeland Community College in Ohio makes clear, tutoring centers and other academic help arenas do not typically attract Latino males. Moreover, research shows that few Latino males are likely to study in groups in a cooperative fashion. Therefore it may be helpful to provide faculty with focused development and mentoring activities that teach and encourage Latino males—as with all students—to work and study collaboratively rather than individually. Since we know that the Latino culture favors a communalistic rather than individualistic ethic (Delpit, 1988, as cited in Perrakis, 2003) the encouragement of collaborative work might help Latino students overcome the battle between utilitarian individualism and their culturally affirmed sense of communal responsibility (Stanton-Salazar & Spina, 2000).

Our analyses in one community college district have uncovered both encouraging and discouraging data regarding Latino males. While their performance in community college is less strong than that of their White counterparts, they are more likely to be transfer-prepared. The serious caveat to this finding is that Latinos, especially Latino males, do not actually transfer in expected proportions despite measures of transfer readiness. Thus, there remain many important issues with respect to community college HSIs that should be explored and considered, including the extent to which the community college be held accountable for student success, and how. Do the HSIs in particular have a greater responsibility than non-HSIs to actively promote the success of both Latino and Latina students? Further, one may question if enrollment and attendance in community college HSIs is the best way to serve Latino/a students.

It may be that for some Hispanic students attendance at an HSI is ill-advised or even detrimental; some students may simply fare better in institutions with higher transfer and graduation rates and more opportunities. It may also be argued that the comfort of having an overrepresentation of Hispanics at community college HSIs does not prepare students for the reality of being a "minority" at a typical four-year college. The majority of the Hispanic students at HSI community colleges has lived in predominantly Hispanic neighborhoods and has attended majority Hispanic K–12 schools. While attendance at a HSI community college may have been well within these students' initial comfort zone, the next move, most likely a transfer to a four-year, predominantly White college or university, may cause distress. Ultimately, we must acknowledge that HSIs, like all minority-serving and specific focus institutions, were created to compensate for national inequalities in opportunities. Until our nation can provide true equality for all, such compensations may alleviate some of the symptoms of the nation's illness but will not cure it.

REFERENCES

American Council on Education. (2005). *Minorities in higher education: Twenty-first annual report.* Washington, DC: American Council on Education.

Brown, S. V. (1996). Responding to the new demographics in higher education. In L. I. Rendon and R. O. Hope (Eds.). *Educating a new majority: Transforming America's educational system for diversity* (pp. 71–96). San Francisco, CA: Jossey Bass Inc., Publishers.

Brownstein, A. (2000, November 3). Are male students in short supply, or is this crisis' exaggerated? *The Chronicle of Higher Education,* p. A47.

California Postsecondary Education Commission. (2005). *University eligibility as a percentage of all high school students.* Sacramento, CA: California Postsecondary Commission, March, FS 05–04.

Evelyn, J. (2002). Community colleges start to ask, where are the men? *The Chronicle of Higher Education.* Accessed June 28, 2002, *http://chronicle.com/prm/weekly/v48/i42/42a03201.htm.*

Evelyn, J. (2005). College enrollments grow more diverse, more numerous, and more female, 2 government reports say. *The Chronicle of Higher Education.* Accessed June 2, 2005, *http://chronicle.com/prm/daily/2005/06/2005060203n.htm.*

Fry, R. (2002). *Latinos in higher education: Many enroll, too few graduate.* Pew Hispanic Center. Los Angeles: University of Southern California Annenberg School of Communication.

Gándara, P. (1995). Over the ivy walls: The educational mobility of low-income Chicanos. New York: State University of New York Press.

Goncharoff, T., Nook, M. A., Kane, M., Wu, J., and Quaranto, D. (2000, January 14). Should we be alarmed when women outnumber men on campuses? [Letters to the Editor]. *The Chronicle of Higher Education,* p. B3.

Gose, B. (1999, November 26). Colleges look for ways to reverse a decline in enrollment of men. *The Chronicle of Higher Education.*

Hagedorn, L. S., and Cepeda, R. (2004). Serving Los Angeles: Urban community colleges and educational success among Latino students. In B. V. Laden (Ed.), Special Issue on Hispanic-serving community colleges. *Community College Journal of Research and Practice,* 28(3), 199–212.

Hagedorn, L. S., Maxwell, W., and Hampton, P. (2001). Correlates of retention for African American males in community colleges. *Journal of College Student Retention Research, Theory, and Practice, 3*(3).

Hernandez, J. C., and Lopez, M. A. (2004–2005). Leaking pipeline: Issues impacting Latino/a college student retention. *Journal of College Student Retention: Research, Theory and Practice, 6(1).* 37–60.

Jones, R. A. (2005). Where the boys aren't. *National Crosstalk.* San Jose, CA: National Center for Public Policy and Higher Education, Spring.

King, J. E. (2000). *Gender equity in higher education: Are male students at a disadvantage?* Washington, DC: American Council on Education.

LACCD. (2005). LACCD Research and Statistics website at http://research.laccd.edu/all-reports.htm Retrieved July 5, 2005

Laden, B. V. (1999a). Two-year Hispanic-serving community colleges. In B. K. Townsend (Ed.), *Two-year colleges for women and minorities* (225–243). New York: Garland Publishing, Inc.

Laden, B. V. (1999b). Celebratory socialization of culturally diverse students in academic programs and support services. In K. M. Shaw, J. R. Valadez, and R. A. Rhoads (Eds.), *Community colleges as cultural texts: Ethnographic explorations of organizational culture* (pp. 173–194). New York: State University of New York Press.

Laden, B. V. (2004). Hispanic-serving institutions: What are they? Where are they? In B. V. Laden (Ed.), Special Issue on Hispanic-serving community colleges. *Community College Journal of Research and Practice,* 28(3), 181–198.

Maton, K. I., Douglas, M. T., Corns, K. M., Viera-Baker, C. C., Lavine, J. R., Gouze, K. R., and Keating, D. P. (1996). Cultural specificity of support sources, correlates and contexts: Three studies of African American and Caucasian youth. *American Journal of Community Psychology, 24*(4), 551–587.

Merisotis, J. P., and O'Brien, C. T. (Eds.) (1998). *Minority-serving institutions: Distinct purposes, common goals.* New Directions for Higher Education, 102. San Francisco, CA: Jossey-Bass Inc., Publishers.

Merisotis, J. P., and Goulian, K. A. (2004). The alliance for equity in higher education. In B.V. Laden (Ed.), *Serving minority populations* (pp. 127, 89–96). New Directions for Community Colleges, 127, 89–96. San Francisco, CA: Jossey-Bass Inc., Publishers.

Mortenson, T. (1995). What's wrong with the guys? *Postsecondary Education Opportunity.*

Mortenson, T. (2005). Cited in interview with Jones, R. A., Where the boys aren't: *National Crosstalk.* San Jose, CA: National Center for Public Policy and Higher Education (Spring).

National Center for Education Statistics. (2002). *Digest of Education Statistics.* Washington, DC: U.S. Department of Education.

National Center for Education Statistics. (2005). *Contexts of postsecondary education: Characteristics of postsecondary students. Indicator 31.* Washington, DC: U.S. Department of Education.

Perrakis, A. I. (2003). *When the majority becomes the minority.* Unpublished manuscript.

Perrakis, A. I. (2005). *A few good men: Factors that encourage retention and persistence of male community college students.* Paper presented at the annual meeting of the Council for the Study of Community Colleges, Boston, MA.

Rendón, L. I. (1995). Facilitating retention and transfer for first generation students in community colleges. *National Center on Postsecondary Teaching, Learning and Assessment.* PA: University Park, PA.

Santiago, D. A., Andrade, S. J., and Brown, S. E. (2004). *Latino success at Hispanic-serving institutions: Findings from a demonstration project.* Fund for the Improvement of Postsecondary Education. Washington, DC: U.S. Department of Education.

Solórzano, D. G. (1995). The baccalaureate origins of Chicano and Chicana doctorates in the social sciences. *Hispanic Journal of Behavioral Sciences, 17*(1),3–32.

Stanton-Salazar, R. D., and Spina, S. U. (2000). The network orientations of highly resilient urban minority youth: A network-analytic account of minority socialization and its educational implications. *The Urban Review, 32*(3), 227–261.

State of California (2005). California's demographics. Retrieved January 5, 2006, from http://www.lao.ca.gov/1998/1998_calfacts/1998_calfacts_demographics.pdf.

U.S. Census Bureau. (2003). The Hispanic population in the United States: March 2002. *Current Population Reports,* P20–545. Washington, DC: U.S. Census Bureau.

CHAPTER 10

Another Side of the Percent Plan Story

Latino Enrollment in the Hispanic-Serving Institutions Sector in California and Texas

Stella M. Flores and Otoniel Jiménez Morfín

The end of affirmative action in higher education admissions in California and Texas led a number of researchers to investigate the effects of this event on the college enrollment patterns at selective universities in these states (Anderson, 2002; Horn & Flores, 2003; Orfield & Miller, 1998; Tienda, Leicht, Sullivan, Maltese, & Lloyd, 2003). Of major concern were the effects that the end of affirmative action would have on the college-eligible Latino and African American population. For example, citing the desire to admit a student body as socially and geographically representative as the residents of Texas, both flagship universities in the state instituted a number of programs informally associated with the recruitment, admission, and enrollment of minority students during a race-neutral policy era (Horn & Flores, 2003). Soon after, the University of California (UC) instituted similar long-term outreach programs with the intent of increasing diversity in the UC System via a California legislative initiative. However, minimal attention has been given to the enrollment effects experienced by what are termed "non-selective" or "second to third-tier" public four-year institutions as a result of anti-affirmative action legislation, admissions plans such as the percent plans, and changes in race-conscious outreach and recruitment policies.

This chapter examines the statewide enrollment patterns of Latino students in California's and Texas' "non-selective" public four-year universities, with a focus on the Hispanic-Serving Institution (HSI) sector in the race-neutral admissions policy period of 1998 to 2002. California and Texas are specifically examined since they are the states that have (1) the largest Latino and Mexican-origin population in the United States (U.S. Census, 2000); (2) the highest number of high school graduates in the nation (Mortenson, 2002); (3) the largest number of Hispanic-Serving Institutions (HSIs) in the country (Hispanic Association of Colleges and Universities, 2005); and (4) implemented a version of a percent plan admissions policy during the time period examined.

Although the issue of why so few Latinos are attending selective public universities remains a critical topic, our concern in this chapter lies in determining *where* the majority of Latino students are attending *four-year* institutions. For this reason, we examine enrollment trends of Latino and other race and ethnic groups in the four-year systems that are most likely to enroll underrepresented minority students in each state's higher education landscape: the California State University System and the non-flagship university system in Texas. Since our focus is on Latino students, we also evaluate enrollment by institutional sector within each state's system: the Hispanic-Serving Institution sector and the non-Hispanic-Serving Institution sector. It is estimated that nearly half of all Latino students in U.S. higher education enroll in an institution designated as an Hispanic-Serving Institution (Santiago, Andrade & Brown, 2004).

We provide a descriptive enrollment trend analysis and evaluate whether "cascading," a process by which minority students (Latino and Black) in the eligible admissions pools in these states' higher education systems end up in the lower-tier institutions as a result of restrictive admissions policies, may be occurring (Selingo, 1999). We also consider an additional angle to this sparsely documented phenomenon of cascading: whether White and Asian students, who are also affected by race-neutral percent plan policies, may also be increasingly attending these second-tier/non-selective institutions thereby increasing the capacity and selectivity levels of traditionally accessible four-year institutions. Since this analysis is descriptive in nature, we do not make causal inferences and do not account for other factors potentially affecting higher education enrollment, such as capacity, financial aid, and state economy issues.

This chapter begins with a review of the educational demographic context for Latino students. Next, we provide a brief portrait of the role of the Hispanic-Serving Institution in the United States as these are the institutions Latino students often attend (Santiago et al., 2004). We then present our main data: average enrollment trends from 1998 to 2002 in the California State University System and the Texas public non-flagship university system by race and ethnicity and by HSI sector. We follow with a discussion of these results and end with policy implications and concluding thoughts.

EDUCATIONAL DEMOGRAPHIC CONTEXT

Even though the Latino population in the United States continues to increase, and has surpassed that of African Americans, their educational status does not reflect their growing demographic power. Nationally, Latino students have high school completion rates of just over 50 percent (53.2%) compared to a rate of 74.9 and 76.8 percent for their White and Asian student counterparts, respectively (Swanson, 2004). Of those students who do graduate and participate in higher education, college enrollment patterns indicate that Latino students are more likely to enroll in a community college (Adelman, 2005; Chapa & De La Rosa, 2004; Hagy & Staniec, 2002) and, in some states, are more likely to attend an institution in close proximity to their home residence (Jones & Kauffman, 1994). In addition, just over 10 percent of Latinos have a bachelor's degree, compared to 27 percent of the White population (U.S. Census Bureau, 2003). The percent of Latinos with advanced degrees is also far below that of their White counterparts, at a rate of 3.8 percent compared to the 9.8 percent of Whites in the United States (U.S. Census Bureau, 2003). In assessing the higher education institutions where Latino students are more likely to enroll, if they enroll at all, the Hispanic-Serving Institution (HSI) becomes a critical policy point to explore in the higher educational pipeline. The HSI is defined as a college or university that enrolls at least 25 percent Hispanic full-time equivalent students (Benitez & DeAro, 2004).

A PORTRAIT OF THE HISPANIC-SERVING INSTITUTION IN CALIFORNIA AND TEXAS

The Hispanic Association of Colleges and Universities (HACU) documents the existence of 63 Hispanic-Serving Institutions in California and 38 in Texas (HACU, 2005). An HSI can be either a two or four-year institution and can also be both public and private. Of the 63 institutions in California, 10 are part of the California State University System with only one institution in the UC System, UC Merced, currently pursuing an HSI designation. In Texas, 10 of the 38 institutions examined are public four-year Hispanic-Serving Institutions, although there are six additional private four-year schools that are HSIs. A majority of the HSIs in both states are community colleges, a figure that is not surprising given where Latinos are most likely to enroll. Finally, the federal government reports that 46 percent of all HSIs in the United States are located in California and Texas alone (U.S. Department of Education, 2005a). Other U.S. states and territories with a large number of HSIs include Puerto Rico (33), New Mexico (17), New York (13), Florida (10), and Arizona (8) (HACU, 2005).

A variety of geographic, social, and demographic factors characterize Hispanic-Serving Institutions. Nationally, the geographic distribution of these institutions follows that of Hispanic residence in the United States (Benitéz, 1998, p. 59). Furthermore, not all of these institutions were originally created as HSIs, as were their counterpart historically Black colleges and universities (HBCUs), but instead gained this designation as a result of migratory and demographic patterns (Gillet-Karam, 1995). As a result, a majority of these institutions are located in California, Texas, New Mexico, Florida, New York, and Arizona (and Puerto Rico). Given this trend, it is not surprising that a similar pattern is mirrored within a state. In Texas, for example, eight of the 10 four-year HSIs are located in the area identified as the Texas-Mexico border region.

METHOD

The California data are from the California Postsecondary Education Commission (CPEC) and represent the universe of 22 four-year public higher education institutions in the California State University System (CSU), 10 of which are designated as Hispanic-Serving Institutions. The figures for the California data represent "Enrollment of First-Time Full-Time Freshmen Age 19 and Under in Public Institutions by Ethnicity" for the years 1998 to 2002. The data for Texas is from the state's governing higher education entity, the Texas Higher Education Coordinating Board (THECB). This sample represents the universe of 29 four-year public institutions of higher education with the exception of The University of Texas at Austin and Texas A&M University. Ten of the Texas institutions examined are classified as Hispanic Serving Institutions. The main outcome examined for the Texas data is "Summer/Fall First-Time Undergraduate Enrollment by Race and Ethnicity" from 1998 to 2002. The race and ethnic groups examined are White, Latino/Hispanic, African American/Black, Asian/Pacific Islander (but does not include Filipino students for CSU), and Native Americans.

We examine the average enrollment of students per institution by race and ethnicity over the selected five-year period for each state. The enrollment trends represent average student enrollment per institution per year and do not take into account variation in size.

RESULTS

The California State University System (CSU)[1]

Overall, the CSU System has seen an increase of 29 percent in total average enrollment from 1998 to 2002. Regarding changes in race and ethnicity in total enrollment, the data show that White students experienced the largest average enrollment growth over this five-year period at 33 percent, followed by Latino students at 26 percent. African American students grew by an average of 24 percent, followed by Asian and Native American students at 22 and 21 percent, respectively. However, it is important to note that on average there are more than twice as many Asian students than Black students enrolled in the CSU system.

ENROLLMENT OF FIRST-TIME FULL-TIME FRESHMEN BY HSI SECTOR IN THE CSU SYSTEM

Table 10.1 shows that on average CSU schools designated as HSIs experienced an increase in average enrollment per institution of 40 percent, while non-HSIs in the CSU System experienced approximately half the growth of their HSI counterparts at 22 percent from 1998 to 2002. A description of enrollment by HSI sector by race and ethnicity follows.

California Four-Year HSI Enrollment by Race and Ethnicity. Table 10.1 shows that White students also experienced the largest average enrollment growth in HSIs at a rate of 50 percent. Latino students experienced an average enrollment rate increase of 34 percent from 1998 to 2002. African American students made the most surprising average enrollment gains at HSIs, with a rate of 47 percent. This is especially noteworthy because, as will be discussed later, Black students experienced a 2 percent increase in average enrollment in non-Hispanic Serving Institutions, indicating an increasing presence of underrepresented minority students at already predominantly Minority-Serving Institutions. Asian-Pacific Islander students (not including Filipino students) experienced an average total enrollment growth of 25 percent at CSU Hispanic-Serving Institutions.

California Four-Year Non-HSI Enrollment by Race and Ethnicity. CSU non-Hispanic-Serving Institutions show a less dramatic change in the distributive enrollment of all race and ethnic groups. For example, table 10.1 shows that none of the groups in this sector show an average total enrollment increase over 27 percent compared to their counterpart students in the HSI institutions, which showed higher averages. Instead, the non-HSIs experienced the greatest average enrollment growth from Whites at 27 percent, Asians at 18 percent, and Latinos at 17 percent. African American student enrollment grew the least at 2 percent from 1998 to 2002 and is also the group to have experienced the most severe fluctuations in average enrollment in non-HSIs throughout this time period. For example, from 2000 to 2001, average Black

Table 10.1 Total Mean Enrollment of First-Time Full-Time Freshmen at HSIs (n=10) and Non-HSIs (n=12) in California State University System (CSU), 1998–2002

	1998		1999		2000		2001		2002		% Change 1998–2002	
	HSI	Non-HSI	HSI	Non-HSI	HSI	Non-HSI	HSI	Non-HSI	HSI	Non-HSI	HSI	Non-HSI
Hispanic/Latino	381	232	406	245	439	253	474	295	509	271	34	17
White	310	636	353	667	378	747	401	819	464	807	50	27
Black	94	86	104	82	116	82	123	98	138	87	47	2
Asian	178	200	203	217	215	237	204	262	223	236	25	18
Native American	8	12	9	13	9	12	7	12	9	15	19	22
Total Enr.	1,167	1,450	1,290	1,583	1,390	1,644	1,468	1,813	1,634	1,765	40	22

Source: Authors' calculations from California Postsecondary Education Commission, 2004.
Note: Unit of measurement is students. Figures have been rounded to whole numbers.

student enrollment rose by 20 percent but dropped by 10 percent in 2002. In comparison, during the time period when Black enrollment decreased at non-HSIs, their average enrollment increased by 12 percent at Hispanic-Serving Institutions. Asian students were the group to experience the second largest average enrollment growth in the non-HSI sector of the CSU system while Native American average enrollment grew similarly in each of the three sectors (CSU Total, CSU HSI and CSU non-HSI) examined. Although tribal colleges and universities enroll a large number of Native American students, there is only one private, two-year college of this type in California.

THE TEXAS NON-FLAGSHIP PUBLIC HIGHER EDUCATION SYSTEM[2]

Overall, the non-flagship Texas public four-year system experienced an average enrollment increase of 26 percent from 1998 to 2002, a growth that was consistently large since 1999. In examining enrollment data by race and ethnicity in the Texas public non-flagship sector, it is worth noting that, on average, White students outnumber Latino students by more than 2 to 1. However, Latino students experienced an average increase of more than twice that of White students (36 to 15 percent respectively) during the time period examined. Surprisingly, Asian students (defined broadly to include all Asian-origin students in Texas), who make up a small percentage of overall students in the state, experienced the largest average enrollment growth of all racial and ethnic groups at 44 percent from 1998 to 2002. The average enrollment rate for African American students grew at a similar rate as Latino students at 36 percent during this period. Native American students experienced an average enrollment increase of 31 percent during this period. There are currently no tribal colleges or universities in Texas (U.S. Department of Education, 2005).

FIRST TIME UNDERGRADUATE ENROLLMENT BY HSI SECTOR IN TEXAS NON-FLAGSHIP INSTITUTIONS

The HSI sector of Texas public higher education experienced an average enrollment increase of 41 percent while the non-HSI sector saw an increase of half this rate at 20 percent, although average enrollment is slightly higher in the non-HSI sector.

Texas Four-Year HSI Enrollment by Race and Ethnicity. Table 10.2 shows that the HSI sector in Texas experienced significant increases in average enrollment by all groups except African Americans during this period. Most notably, the average enrollment rate for Asian students grew by 94 percent from 1998 to

Table 10.2 Total Mean Enrollment of First-Time College Freshmen at HSIs (n=10) and Non-HSIs (n=19) in Texas Public Colleges and Universities, 1998–2002

	1998		1999		2000		2001		2002		% Change 1998–2002	
	HSI	Non-HSI	HSI	Non-HSI	HSI	Non-HSI	HSI	Non-HSI	HSI	Non-HSI	HSI	Non-HSI
Hispanic/Latino	566	153	572	150	628	169	690	183	805	192	42	25
White	222	890	218	913	238	933	248	985	309	998	39	12
Black	63	240	64	241	58	275	57	307	70	335	11	40
Asian	21	73	22	75	22	86	31	90	40	99	94	37
Native American	3	7	3	7	2	8	2	9	4	9	40	30
Total Enrollment	902	1,381	914	1,411	986	1,497	1,074	1,607	1,272	1,660	41	20

Source: Authors' calculations from the Texas Higher Education Coordinating Board, 2004.
Note: Unit of measurement is students. Figures have been rounded to whole numbers.

2002, followed by Latino and White students at 42 and 39 percent, respectively. The average enrollment rate for African American students grew by only 11 percent, although as discussed later, this group of students experienced a much larger rate of growth of 40 percent in the non-HSI sector. It is important to note that Texas has a number of four-year HBCUs, two public and six private, so a more comprehensive analysis that includes these institutions is needed to make further conclusions and reliable comparisons regarding the specific enrollment trends of this racial group.

While Latino enrollment grew consistently, this group experienced its largest average enrollment growth from 2001 to 2002. The average White student enrollment dropped from 1998 to 1999 and grew more significantly from 2001 to 2002. Black student enrollment experienced important declines from 1999 to 2001 before finally rising in 2002. Average Asian enrollment grew by small proportions from 1998 to 2000, and then rose dramatically from 2000 to 2002 in the HSI sector. Native American enrollment stayed relatively constant, although the overall increase looks large (40%) due to their small numerical representation in the state.

Texas Four-Year Non-HSI Sector by Race and Ethnicity. Table 10.2 also shows that although overall average enrollment in the non-HSI sector increased by 20 percent, Black and Asian students experienced the highest average enrollment increases during this five-year period at 39 and 37 percent respectively. Latino students in Texas experienced an average increase of 25 percent while White students experienced an average enrollment increase of 12 percent. Although this sector saw the most differences in enrollment from African American and Asian students, further research is required to examine exactly *where* Black and Asian students are enrolling. The presence of HBCUs in Texas, such as Prairie View A&M University, as well as the general location of the African American population in certain areas of the state (East and North Texas) may be factors in this analysis. Overall, average enrollment by all race and ethnic groups increased steadily, with no reversals in enrollment growth during this five-year period in the non-HSI sector of Texas public four-year higher education.

ANALYSIS

While California and Texas differ in many respects with regard to the higher education landscape, economic industries, and geography, their diverse and growing racial minority populations remain a consistent trend throughout the last decade (Chapa & De la Rosa, 2004). As states that experienced similar race-neutral policy environments in this specific period of analysis

(1998 to 2002), the effects of enrollment on colleges and universities with less selective admissions policies should also be a general concern for the higher education community and the families that invest in these systems.

The data show that different racial groups in California and Texas are enrolling in the CSU and non-flagship higher education system in distinctive patterns in each state. Moreover, the overall enrollment growth of these non-flagship systems has been generally consistent and strong from 1998 to 2002. A discussion by state follows.

CALIFORNIA

A major enrollment pattern worth noting in California is the growing average enrollment rate of African American students in the state's various Hispanic-Serving Institutions. This trend is particularly specific and important to California given the lack of any HBCUs in the state as well as the state's geographic residential patterns. Further evaluation as to where exactly these HSIs are located in relation to the college-eligible population of Latinos, African American, and other underrepresented minorities should be conducted for a more comprehensive analysis.

By race and ethnicity, the data show that the average White student enrollment has increased in large percentages in all of the three sectors evaluated (CSU total, CSU-HSI, and CSU-non-HSI), but especially in the HSI sector of the CSU system. Asian enrollment seemed to be distributed almost evenly between the HSI and non-HSI sector. Although the current method of analysis does not allow us to detect the exact direction or even clear existence of a cascading effect without further quantitative analyses, the enrollment trends suggest a shift in attendance by ethnic groups to particular types of four-year institutions. The issue of "cascading" should therefore also be considered more comprehensively beyond the University of California System into the less selective sectors of California disaggregated by sector and level (e.g. HSI v. non-HSI and four-year v. two-year).

TEXAS

The most surprising trend in the non-flagship Texas system is the growth of the average enrollment rate of Asian students in the HSI sector. Since a majority of these HSIs are located on the Texas-Mexico border, West Texas, and the Houston area, these trends indicate the growing migration of Asian students to institutions with high Latino student enrollment in the state. Moreover, the state trends also indicate an increasing average enrollment in HSIs by Latino students, with a small but unimpressive growth in the non-HSI sector. There data also show an increase of White students in the HSI sector of Texas, although there is an even greater increase in the average enrollment of African American students in the non-HSI sector. This latter finding is not surprising given that the regional residential patterns of African Americans in the state have traditionally not been near areas where the state's largest share of Latinos reside or where HSIs exist, with the exception of a few urban centers such as Houston.

The cascading story in Texas, however, is not as visibly evident as it may be in California, or it may be taking on a different pattern, as a result of the state's particular higher education structure and policies. For example, it is important to note that although Texas was also operating under a race-neutral policy environment during this period, it also applied a much more liberal version of a percent-plan admissions policy that allowed admission into any Texas public university in the state, in contrast to California, which functioned (and continues to function) under a more restrictive percent plan admissions policy (Horn & Flores, 2003). The California percent plan does not guarantee enrollment into a specific UC campus, hence, it is probable that the student may be admitted to a less selective UC campus rather than the institution of first choice. Moreover, the percent plan in California was only functional if the student met the rigorous UC criteria for admission. Texas had no such additional curricular requirements during this period of analysis (Tienda et al., 2003). Finally, Texas has a different structural landscape of higher education institutions than California. While both states have a public four- and two-year college system, the number of selective institutions in the state varies, as do issues of size and history of higher education planning models (Horn & Flores, 2003). Since enrollment in a Hispanic-Serving Institution is also closely related to geographic patterns of Latino communities in the state, the historical settlement patterns of Latinos in each state may also be playing a role in the incorporation of this group into higher education.

Nonetheless, it appears that Latinos are continuing to attend Hispanic-Serving Institutions at greater and more consistent rates. While this seems like a positive trend for institutions that may be better equipped to serve Latino college students, at least from a cultural perspective (Benitez & DeAro, 2004; Santiago et al., 2004), this also leads us to question whether there are unnecessary higher education segregation trends in both the California and the Texas Higher Education systems due to restrictive admissions policies.

DISCUSSION

Although descriptive in nature, the data for both states suggest interesting enrollment patterns and institutional developments for Hispanic-Serving

Institutions in high Latino population states. We suggest that particular attention be paid to two main implications from our findings: (1) the cascading of students *within* and *between* higher education systems so that additional stratification of students by race and ethnicity does not occur; (2) the role of institutional identity of the HSI as they respond to multiple and combined changes in demographics, admissions requirements, and capacity of a state's higher education system. As some of these forces are external and therefore cannot be directly controlled by university officers and administrators, the responsibility of promoting a committed agenda of academic success and equity of postsecondary institutions designated to serve Latino students must also be shared with state and federal actors (Flores, Horn, and Crisp, 2006).

First, the issue of cascading seems to be largely determined by a state's higher education structure and governing board, making generalizations of these patterns across different states inaccurate without a clear understanding of the capacity, demographics, and selectivity for each context under review. For example, California's Master Plan for Higher Education requires differential access restrictions for its three sectors of higher education (the UC, the CSU, and the community colleges,) guaranteeing a stratification of, and competition for, places in its most competitive University of California System (Pusser, 2004). To what extent a "zero-sum" admissions game is occurring in the next competitive sector in higher education, the California State University System, is currently unknown. Our data documents the increased enrollment of White students into previously high Latino enrolling CSU institutions, suggesting additional cascading trends within the CSU system as well as the potential for increased stratification outcomes by race and ethnicity between and within California higher education. While increased selectivity levels of an institution may be good news for some college and university administrators, the commitment these institutions hold to Latino students via their HSI designation becomes even more critical during a race-neutral admissions policy era.

The combination of Texas' four-year higher education structure and historical residential patterns, however, suggest a slightly different pattern of potential cascading in the state. The data indicate that the Latino student population in non-selective four-year universities is growing at a rate twice that of White students but continues to enroll in predominantly Hispanic-Serving Institutions despite a relatively permissive percent-plan admissions policy compared to that of California. Whether or not this trend is considered negative, the pattern may have overall negative consequences for college retention and completion if these institutions are quantitatively and qualitatively different in resources and capacity than their non-Hispanic-Serving counterparts. Although some research has noted that the segregated nature of Texas' housing and educational systems have allowed at least one flagship institution, the University of Texas at Austin, to continue enrolling a somewhat consistent number of racial and ethnic minorities via its version of the percent plan (Tienda & Niu, 2004), additional research is needed to examine whether there may be racially segregated patterns extending into the non-selective public four-year system. Therefore, although the manner and direction in which student enrollment cascades in Texas may vary from that of California, the negative outcomes of stratification and increased segregation within and between systems of higher education for students already underrepresented in these systems are equally problematic issues with which to contend.

Second, as institutions respond to changes in demographics, selectivity, and capacity, the role of an HSI's identity and responsibility continues to surface with additional educational implications. The data suggest that HSIs in the CSU system may not always have a static enrollment identity, with the influx of additional White and Black students into their student bodies. Institutions such as the CSU HSIs that appear to be constantly responding to demographic change, admissions restrictions, and capacity are therefore in great need of attention on how to appropriately serve Latino students and the additional student groups they enroll. If these trends were to remain consistent, one could imagine a situation in which the number of HSIs in the CSU system could fluctuate in either direction—gain or lose HSI status—based on the combined changes in demographics, admissions policies, and capacity. In Texas, where more Latino students appear to keep choosing to attend an HSI despite a more permissive percent-plan policy, the question of identity is also one for the state's higher education system and not for institutions alone. For example, does a state want a system of four-year institutions easily identified by race alone? These larger questions of identity are a responsibility for all practitioners and beneficiaries of higher education to consider as the state's Latino population continues to grow at unprecedented rates.

CONCLUSION AND FURTHER RESEARCH

Although we have seen some progress in the college enrollment rate of Latinos over the last few decades, four-year completion rates by the turn of the century remained dismal (Kurlaender & Flores, 2005), with most Latinos still concentrated in the community colleges (Adelman, 2005) and in institutions designated as Hispanic-Serving Institutions in both states (Santiago et al., 2004). These trends, as well as others analyzed in this chapter, lead us to a series of questions: what is the role of the HSI regarding the enrollment of Latino students in graduate and professional schools? How are Latino students faring in these areas and are these institutions the places most likely to grant advanced graduate degrees to this population? Does selectivity play a different role at this level of higher education? Regarding the crucial issue of finances, what is the financial aid role of the HSI at the state and federal level? Since HSI is a federal designation, what is the state's role in promoting Latino student success in these institutions?

This chapter sought to explore the potential of a cascading trend story in both California and Texas. Although descriptive in nature, the data and resulting policy implications suggest that cascading may affect various levels of analysis of U.S. higher education, and that questions of selectivity and identity are also prevalent in the four-year sectors considered to be technically "nonselective" in admissions requirements.

NOTES

1. Original calculations available from author upon request.
2. Original calculations available from author upon request.

REFERENCES

Adelman, C. (2005). Moving into town—and moving on: The community college in the lives of traditional-age students. Retrieved 11/16/2005, 2005, from http://www.ed.gov/print/rschstat/research/pubs/comcollege/index.html

Anderson, J. D. (2002). Race in American higher education: Historical perspectives on current conditions. In W. A. Smith, Phillip Altbach (Eds.), *The racial crisis in American higher education: Continuing challenges for the twenty-first century.* Albany, NY: State University of New York Press.

Benitéz, M. (1998). Hispanic-serving institutions: challenges and opportunities. In J. P. Merisotis and C. T. O'Brien (Eds.), *Minority-serving institutions: Distinct purposes, common goals* (pp. 57–68). San Francisco, CA: Jossey-Bass Inc., Publishers.

Benitéz , M., and DeAro, J. (2004). Realizing student success at Hispanic-serving institutions. In B. V. Laden (Ed.), *Serving minority populations* (pp. 35–49). San Francisco, CA: Jossey-Bass Inc., Publishers.

Chapa, J., and De La Rosa, B. (2004). Latino population growth, socioeconomic and demographic characteristics, and implications for educational attainment. *Education and Urban Society, 36*(2), 130–149.

Flores, S. M., Horn, C. L., and Crisp, G. (2006). Community colleges, public policy, and Latino student opportunity. *New Directions for Community Colleges, 133*(2), 71–80.

Gillet-Karam, R. (1995). Women and Minorities in Rural Community Colleges: Programs for Change. *New Directions in Community Colleges, 23* (2), 43–53.

Grutter v. Bollinger (02–241) 2.88 f. 3d 732 affirmed (U.S. 2003).

Hagy, A., and Staniec, J. F. O. (2002). Immigrant status, race, and institutional choice in higher education. *Economics of Education Review, 21,* 381–392.

Hispanic Association of Colleges and Universities. (2005). HACU member Hispanic-Serving Institutions (HSIs). Retrieved November 26, 2005, from http://www.hacu.net/assnfe/CompanyDirectory.asp?STYLE=2andCOMPANY_TYPE=1,5.

Hispanic Association of Colleges and Universities. (2005). HACU member Hispanic-Serving Institutions (HSIs). Retrieved October 8, 2006 from http://www.hacu.net/assnfe/cv.asp?ID=1411andSNID=878486621

Hopwood v. Texas, 78 F. 3d 932 (5th Cir. 1996); cert denied, 518 U.S. 1033 (1996).

Horn, C., and Flores, S. (2003). *Percent plans in college admissions: A comparative analysis of three states' experiences.* Cambridge, MA: Civil Rights Project at Harvard University.

Jones, R. C., and Kauffman, A. (1994). Accessibility to comprehensive higher education in Texas. *The Social Science Journal, 31*(2), 263–283.

Kurlaender, M., and Flores, S. M. (2005). The racial transformation of higher education. In G. Orfield, P. Marin, and C. L. Horn (Eds.), *Higher education and the color line: College access, racial equity, and social change* (pp. 11–32). Cambridge, MA: Harvard Education Press.

Mortenson, T. (2002). Chance for college by age 19 by state in 2000. *Postsecondary Education OPPORTUNITY, 123,* 1–10.

Niu, S., Tienda, M., and Cortes, K. (2004). College selectivity and the Texas top 10 percent law. *Annual meetings of the Population Association of America,* Boston, MA.

Orfield, G., and Miller, E. (Eds.). (1998). *Chilling admissions; the affirmative action crisis and the search for alternatives.* Cambridge, MA: Harvard Education Publishing Group.

Pusser, B. (2004). *Burning down the house: Politics, governance, and affirmative action at the University of California.* New York: State University of New York Press.

Santiago, D. A., Andrade, S. J., and Brown, S. E. *Latino Student Success at Hispanic-Serving Institutions.* Washington, DC: Excelencia in Education, 2004. Retrieved Nov. 4, 2005 from http://www.cierp.utep.edu/projects/lss/pbrief.pdf.

Selingo, J. (1999). A quiet end to the use of race in college admissions in Florida. *The Chronicle of Higher Education,* p. A31.

Swanson, C. B. (2004). Sketching a portrait of public high school graduation: Who graduates? Who doesn't? In G. Orfield (Ed.), *Dropouts in America* (pp. 13–40). Cambridge, MA: Harvard Education Press.

Tienda, M., Leicht, K., Sullivan, T., Maltese, M., and Lloyd, K. (2003). Closing the gap? Admissions and enrollments at the Texas public flagships before and after affirmative action (pp. 69): Princeton, NJ: Texas Top 10% Project.

Tienda, M., and Niu, S. (2004). Capitalizing on segregation, pretending neutrality: College admissions and the Texas top 10 percent law. Retrieved August 22, 2005, from http://www.texastop10.princeton.edu/reports/forthcoming/capitalizing_on_segregation

U.S. Census Bureau. (2001). The Hispanic population: Census 2000 brief. In E. A. S. Administration (Ed.):U.S. Department of Commerce.

U.S. Census Bureau. (2003). Educational attainment: 2000. In U. S. D. of Commerce (Ed.).

U.S. Department of Education. (2005). White house initiative on tribal colleges and universities. Retrieved August 13, 2005, from http://www.ed.gov/about/inits/list/whtc/edlite-tclist.html.

U.S. Department of Education. (2006). White house initiative on tribal colleges and universities. Retrieved December 1, 2006 from http://www.ed.gov/about/inits/list/whhbcu/edlite-list.

CHAPTER 11

Faculty Development at Historically Black Colleges and Universities

Current Priorities and Future Directions

Andrea L. Beach, Phyllis Worthy Dawkins, Stephen L. Rozman, and Jessie L. Grant

Faculty development has increasingly played an important role in change at HBCUs, and has been credited with helping to increase Black student enrollment at HBCUs in recent years (Drewry & Doermann, 2001). However, no research has yet focused on the unique development needs of faculty at HBCUs, and the ways that faculty development programs can meet those needs.

In this chapter, we explore the perceptions of faculty developers at HBCUs regarding the issues their faculty and institutions face, and their ability to address the issues they identify. We outline the history of faculty development in HBCUs and the progress made by the HBCU Faculty Development Network and other organizations and initiatives. We then present key results of a survey of HBCU faculty developers regarding current and future practices and challenges and compare them to a national survey of faculty developers at a wide range of colleges and universities. Research on faculty at HBCUs has been sparse (Johnson & Harvey, 2002), and research on faculty development at HBCUs almost nonexistent (Worthy Dawkins, Beach & Rozman, 2005). We hope through this chapter to spark greater interest in the unique faculty development needs at HBCUs and the efforts that have been underway to address them.

CHALLENGES OF FACULTY AT HBCUS

HBCUs succeed in educating African American students because they provide a climate in which the students feel welcome, supported, and encouraged to take part in both the academic and social life of the campus (Outcault & Skewes-Cox, 2002). Faculty at HBCUs bear a large role in creating this welcoming climate (Beach, 2002) by getting to know students well, interacting with them inside and outside the classroom, participating in campus and community events, and seeing it as their primary responsibility that students persist and succeed (Drewry & Doermann, 2001; Thompson, 1978). This is the historic mission and strength of Black colleges (Allen & Jewell, 2002; Brown & Freeman, 2002; Thompson, 1978).

Because of HBCUs' commitment to educating students "regardless of academic preparation, test scores, socioeconomic status, or environmental circumstances" (Brown & Freeman, 2002, p. 238), the teaching challenges facing faculty at HBCUs include the necessity for student enrollment in remedial courses, and addressing a mix of student learning styles and readiness. Research on Black faculty at HBCUs has found that they enjoy a strong socialization into the values and expectations of their institutions and that they feel supported in their work, but that their heavy workloads (they average 12 credit hours of instruction per semester) are a barrier to their success (Johnson & Harvey, 2002). Contributing to these heavy workloads are a change in institutional emphasis toward a greater research focus while maintaining the traditional focus on student achievement. HBCUs have historically been teaching focused, and scholarship did not play a large part in faculty work. Faculty in Johnson and Harvey's study (2002) reported increased pressure from accreditors and their institutions to publish, while maintaining their already high teaching loads and community engagement.

FACULTY DEVELOPMENT AT HBCUS

Although as long as 70 years ago, Florence (1932) described the development of faculty at HBCUs (as in-service training consisting of extension courses, correspondence courses, study clubs, professionalized faculty meetings, syllabus preparation, research and investigation, and leaves of absence), the faculty development movement in private Black colleges really began to gain momentum in the 1980s (Drewry & Doermann, 2001). Many of these programs were funded by Title III, private grants, and foundation grants such as the Andrew Mellon Foundation and Bush-Hewlett grant programs. Senior Program Officer of the Andrew Mellon Foundation, Henry Drewry, and former President of the Bush Foundation, Humphrey Doermann, were pioneers in promoting and supporting faculty development efforts within their foundations. Bush-Hewlett grants, in particular, touched the professional lives of many of the faculty in the participating colleges. Project activities concentrated on meeting the needs of students rather than focusing on research or faculty sabbaticals, and helped to improve the quality of teaching (Drewry & Doermann, 2001).

Two other organizations have significantly contributed to curriculum and faculty development at private Black colleges: The United Negro College Fund (UNCF) and the Southern Education Foundation (SEF). UNCF, founded in 1944 by Frederick D. Patterson, is the nation's largest, oldest, most successful and comprehensive minority higher education assistance organization (UNCF, n.d.). Aside from the primary goal of providing operation funds for 38 member HBCUs, the program activities of the organization include a focus on providing student scholarships, technology instruction for faculty members, service learning, HIV/AIDS and minority health disparities education, and other curriculum development and faculty development programs. The Southern Education Foundation was founded in 1867 to improve educational excellence and equity in the South. In recent history, the higher education programs sponsored by SEF (n.d.) have included a focus on improving the use of technology by faculty to support student learning at selected HBCUs.

Finally, the Bush Foundation itself funds faculty development at tribal institutions in the Midwest and historically Black colleges and universities (mainly in the southeast) that are members of the United Negro College Fund (UNCF). It also funded The Collaboration for the Advancement of College Teaching and Learning (The Collaboration). The Collaboration has been giving travel grants to faculty from UNCF-affiliated HBCUs to attend their semiannual faculty development conferences since the 1980s. The experience of attending The Collaboration conferences helped germinate the seeds of the HBCU Faculty Development Network.

THE HBCU FACULTY DEVELOPMENT NETWORK

The HBCU Faculty Development Network was created in 1994 with a grant from the Bush Foundation to Tougaloo College. The Network was founded by Stephen Rozman, a faculty member and the director of the Tougaloo College faculty development. Rozman has continued to serve as the Network's co-director since its inception. Phyllis Worthy Dawkins, the other co-director, from Johnson C. Smith University, and members from Fisk University, LeMoyne-Owen College, Xavier University, and Florida Memorial College served on the Steering Committee that founded the Network.

The mission of the HBCU Faculty Development Network is derived from the rich legacy of HBCUs in providing educational opportunities for underrepresented students. Building on this heritage, the Network is committed to promoting effective teaching and student learning through a variety of collaborative activities that focus on faculty enhancement. These collaborative activities are designed to make a connection between teaching, research, and service (HBCU FD Network, n.d.).

Over 100 people—nearly all serving as presenters—attended the first HBCU Faculty Development Symposium in 1994, which featured presentations in a variety of areas related to faculty development. The response to the initial Call for Proposals was very positive, with proposals submitted by faculty from a wide variety of HBCUs—and a few non-HBCUs. It became clear to all that this effort was filling an important gap in professional development by focusing specifically on the faculty development needs at HBCUs. Back then, when there was far less focus on faculty development at Minority-Serving Institutions, it was hard to imagine that a start-up organization on a shoestring budget could become successfully established. With the success of the initial conference, the steering committee was committed to making the symposium an annual event and moving it around to other cities in the southeast, given the location of most HBCUs. The HBCU Faculty Development Symposium has been attracting between 150 and 200 participants every year. A large majority of HBCUs have been represented at the symposium over the past 12 years by faculty as well as faculty developers and chief academic officers.

In 2002, with additional funding from the Bush Foundation, the Network added a summer institute to focus on areas of faculty development of particular interest to HBCUs. These focus areas have included learning communities, instructional technology, information literacy, service-learning, and civic engagement. Academic institutions are invited to send teams of faculty, administrators, and staff to address these topics and develop action plans. The summer institute has likewise become an annual event and has been moved from city to city where HBCUs are located. Supplemental funding from the Bush Foundation also enabled the Network to hold annual retreats for the purpose of developing and strengthening its vision and mission statements, and five-year strategic plan.

The vision of the HBCU Faculty Development Network is to empower faculty to promote effective teaching and learning practices that will enable students to become engaged lifelong learners in an ever-changing society. An aim of the Network is to be recognized as the main organization among the 105 historically Black colleges and universities for advancing the following strands of effective teaching and learning: Collaborative Models, Teaching and Learning Styles/Instructional Strategies and Techniques, Curriculum

Design and Revision, Diversity and Globalization, Learning Across the Curriculum, Educational Technology, Evaluation of Assessment and Learning: Outcome Based Assessment, and Community Service/Service Learning. The goals of the Network are to enhance the teaching and learning process based on the collective experience of HBCUs and to provide leadership and coordination efforts among HBCUs.

During its fourteen years of existence, the HBCU Faculty Development Network has established linkages with a wide variety of organizations, including other faculty development networks, government agencies, and nongovernmental organizations. Many of these organizations have participated in the annual HBCU Faculty Development Symposium, either as presenters or exhibitors. The United Negro College Fund and United Negro College Fund Special Programs (UNCFSP) have been actively involved in both the Symposium and Summer Institute, through their service-learning and health-related programs. This relationship initially led to their co-sponsorship of Network conferences, and in the summer of 2005, to a formal partnership between the Network and UNCFSP. The Network will provide the infrastructure and a pedagogical framework for UNCFSP outreach activities related to the grants they manage. The two organizations will also collaborate on a consultant training program in which Network members will be recruited to serve as consultants for UNCFSP grants. In addition to this endeavor, the Network has established a partnership with the Professional and Organizational Network (POD) and the Association for General and Liberal Studies (AGLS). In 2003, the Network and AGLS held a joint conference, hosted by Johnson C. Smith University in Charlotte, North Carolina.

As the Network matures, the steering committee wants to better understand the unique needs, influences, practices, and challenges of HBCU faculty developers. This understanding can help the Network focus its efforts to serve the unique needs of HBCUs in the future. The next section presents details of a survey of faculty developers within the Network undertaken in 2004 to assess the current influences on and issues addressed by faculty development, as well as future needs.

CURRENT PRACTICES AND FUTURE DIRECTIONS OF HBCU FACULTY DEVELOPERS

The survey reported here was conducted during the spring semester of 2004 using the mailing list of the HBCU Faculty Development Network. Of the 105 surveys sent to faculty or administrators representing each institution that was involved in the network, 49 responses were received after two mailings, resulting in a response rate of 47 percent.

The survey was composed of 18 questions with some sub-questions or follow-up questions, using Likert-type scales, rankings, and open-ended questions. It was developed by Sorcinelli, Austin, Eddy, and Beach (2006) and administered to the members of POD in 2001. The instrument was not modified for this administration, so that direct comparisons between HBCU responses and responses of POD members could be made. Following demographic statistics on the responders, we present results of the major questions in the survey and comparisons among HBCUs, where appropriate, and to the national response set.

Demographics

In terms of demographics, the titles given by respondents included senior-level administrator, director or program coordinator, or faculty member. Most (69%) reported two or more titles, often an administrative title first, and faculty or some other role second or third.

The mean of their years in faculty development was 7.5, and at their institution was 10 years. Forty-six percent of respondents worked in liberal arts colleges, 32 percent in comprehensive universities, and the rest in community colleges, research/doctoral institutions, and others. In terms of institutional status, 49 percent of the respondents were from public and 51 percent were from private institutions, exactly mirroring the number of public and private HBCUs in the country.

The structure of faculty development programs at the institutions included: a centralized unit with dedicated staff offering a range of programming and services (31%); a "clearinghouse" for programs and offerings that are sponsored across the institution, but offering few programs itself (11%); a committee charged with supporting faculty development (17%); an individual faculty member or administrator charged with supporting faculty development (31%); and some other kind of structure (10%). These structures differed somewhat from the structures found in the national sample of POD respondents, in that there were fewer centralized units (national—59%), and more individuals charged with responsibility for faculty development (national—15%). However, they match more closely the national liberal arts college structures (central unit—24%; individual—30%). Overall, there are a variety of structures for faculty development at HBCUs, and for a movement that started only in the 1980s, these structures are evidence of the swift growth of faculty development on these campuses.

CURRENT PRACTICES

The survey sought to determine the extent to which faculty development programs are currently offering services pertaining to 21 different issues that potentially affect faculty. Respondents were asked to indicate the extent to which they believe it is important for their programs to offer services pertaining to those issues (1=not at all, 2=to a slight extent, 3=to a moderate extent, 4=to a great extent). They also reported on the same scale the extent to which their faculty development programs offer services to address those issues. Table 11.1 compares the ratings of HBCU faculty developers with the responses of the national group. ANOVAs were run comparing the HBCU responses to the responses from the national sample, as well as from different types of institutions. Significant differences are reported for the comparisons.

The three most important issues to HBCU faculty developers—assessment of student learning, integrating technology into traditional teaching and learning settings, and teaching for student-centered learning—are the same as those for the POD faculty developers. HBCU faculty developers reported offering services to address assessment more than the POD group, and the POD group reported addressing teaching for student-centered learning to a greater extent. New faculty development, active or inquiry-based teaching and learning, and the scholarship of teaching were also equally important to the two groups. Interestingly, both judged addressing multiculturalism and diversity as important to offer, but were equal in their assessment that services to address the issue were far below the perceived need for them.

The next most important issues for HBCUs diverge strongly from the POD respondents' priorities, and are also addressed by HBCU faculty development programming to a greater extent. These include: writing across the curriculum, teaching underprepared students, addressing the changing characteristics and demographics of students, community service learning, course and curriculum reform, general education reform, and teaching adult learners. These issues closely match the strands developed by the Network to improve teaching and learning at HBCUs.

Interestingly, there are differences among HBCUs, both in terms of the current practices perceived as most important to address and in terms of the issues that are addressed. Public HBCU developers rated teaching in distance and on-line formats (3.63 vs. 2.47, $p<.01$), teaching adult learners (3. 47 vs. 2.53, $p<.01$), mentoring faculty of color (3.47 vs. 2,47, $p<.01$), and graduate student teaching development (2.44 vs. 1.50, $p<.05$) as statistically significantly more important than did developers at private HBCUs. They also indicated that they offered services to address teaching in on-line and distance formats (3.05 vs. 1.94, $p<.01$), the shifting characteristics of students (2.68 vs. 1.75, $p<.01$), and teaching adult students (2.79 vs. 1.88, $p<.01$) to a significantly greater extent, as well as course and teaching portfolios (2.74 vs. 1.82, $p<.05$), peer review of teaching (2.47 vs. 1.71, $p<.01$),

Table 11.1 Current Issues for Faculty Development

Issue	HBCUs Important	HBCUs Offer	POD Important	POD Offer
Assessment of student learning outcomes	3.66	3.00*	3.43	2.57
Teaching underprepared students	3.32**	2.63**	2.75	1.98
The shifting characteristics/demographics of students	3.21*	2.32	2.85	2.24
Integrating technology into "traditional" teaching and learning settings	3.61	3.55	3.51	3.28
Teaching in on-line and distance environments	3.05	2.53	2.96	2.63
Multiculturalism and diversity related to teaching	3.43	2.74	3.36	2.75
Teaching for student-centered learning	3.58	2.89	3.69	3.25*
Teaching adult learners	3.05*	2.39	2.63	2.08
Active, inquiry-based or problem-based learning	3.37	2.84	3.51	3.00
Writing across the curriculum/writing to learn	3.53**	2.89*	3.06	2.46
Team teaching	3.00**	2.13	2.49	1.91
Scholarship of teaching	3.26	2.58	3.28	2.57
New faculty development (e.g., mentoring)	3.45	2.82	3.60	3.03
Mentoring faculty from underrepresented populations	3.00	1.92	2.86	1.90
Course/teaching portfolios	3.16	2.37	2.97	2.46
Peer review	2.95	2.13	2.93	2.26
Post-tenure review	2.89**	1.92	2.33	1.62
Graduate student teaching development	2.11	1.47	2.46	2.07**
Course and curriculum reform	3.37*	2.45	2.98	2.40
General education reform	3.16**	2.51**	2.60	1.98
Community service learning	3.26**	2.47*	2.67	2.08

*p = .05; **p = .01

and post-tenure review (2.28 vs. 1.47, $p<.05$). Private college developers rated writing across the curriculum as more important than their public institution colleagues (3.65 vs. 3.37, $p<.05$), but did not report offering services addressing the issue to a statistically greater extent.

PERCEPTIONS OF IMPORTANT FUTURE DIRECTIONS

HBCU Network developers were asked to respond to a number of new challenges and pressures on institutions which affect faculty work, both in how important they think it is to address those issues through faculty development, and the extent to which their institutions are already responding (1=not at all, 2=to a slight extent, 3=to a moderate extent, 4=to a great extent). Table 11.2 contains a comparison of HBCU developer responses with

Table 11.2 New Challenges and Pressures for Faculty Development

Issue	HBCUs Important	HBCUs Offer	POD Important	POD Offer
Departmental leadership and management	3.47*	2.17	3.10	1.94
Changing faculty roles and rewards	3.30	2.17	3.18	2.12
Training and support for part-time/adjunct faculty	3.38	1.88	3.26	2.11
Ethical conduct of faculty work	3.38**	2.17*	2.81	1.84
Preparing the future professoriate	3.26*	2.11	2.87	2.20
Support of institutional change priorities	3.26*	2.46	2.89	2.34
Balancing multiple faculty roles	3.33	2.28	3.08	2.12
Community-based research	2.89**	1.91	2.18	1.64
Outreach/service activities	3.22**	2.45**	2.37	1.99
Faculty and departmental entrepreneurship (e.g., consulting on behalf of the institution)	2.59**	1.64	1.75	1.44
Unit/program evaluation	3.54**	2.58*	2.70	2.20
Program assessment (e.g., accreditation)	3.50**	3.09**	2.76	2.47
Collaborative departmental work teams	3.11**	2.30**	2.60	1.76
Interdisciplinary collaborations	3.20	2.37	3.05	2.24
Commitment to civic life/the public good	3.06*	2.42**	2.60	1.97
Post-tenure review	3.02*	1.98	2.37	1.69
Faculty roles in learning communities	3.15	2.21	2.83	1.95

* $p <= .05$; ** $p <= .01$

those of the POD respondents. Again, ANOVAs were run to assess the differences between HBCU and POD responses, and statistically significant differences are noted with asterisks.

For both groups, the training and support of adjunct and part-time faculty, the changing roles and rewards for faculty, and balancing multiple faculty roles were important. For HBCUs, however, other issues were of equal or greater importance. Unit and program evaluation and assessment, departmental leadership and management, the ethical conduct of faculty work, and supporting institutional change priorities were all rated significantly higher by HBCU respondents than the POD respondents. Further, HBCUs appear to be addressing those pressing new challenges to a much greater degree than their national counterparts. HBCU respondents rated preparing the future professoriate as a greater concern than did POD respondents, but the national sample indicated that their campuses are addressing this issue to a greater extent than the HBCU developers.

Again, differences among HBCUs emerged, although not as many as with the current offerings. Program assessment and accreditation was rated far more highly by public institutions than private (3.76 vs. 3.22, $p<.05$) and was also addressed to a greater extent (3.45 vs. 2.74, $p=.01$). Faculty and departmental entrepreneurship was also considered to be more important by public institutions (2.95 vs. 2.26, $p<.05$), and they reported addressing post-tenure review to a greater extent (2.33 vs. 1.61, $p=.05$).

GREATEST CHALLENGES

Finally, we asked the faculty developers to indicate, from the lists of current issues and new directions, those they considered to be the greatest challenges faced by the faculty at their institutions and by their institutions themselves, as well as the challenges they believed could be addressed through faculty development. Their responses spread across the issues offered in the survey, and as such there were no overwhelming responses. There did emerge, however, a clear set of challenges that are rather unique to HBCUs. They also point to the difficulties HBCUs face in helping faculty with their greatest challenges. No differences were found among types of institutions for these responses.

Faculty developers felt they could address only some of the top challenges they saw their faculty and institutions facing. Other challenges, such as helping faculty address the needs of underprepared students and balancing multiple roles, or helping institutions with program assessment and change, were not among the top issues these faculty developers believed they could address.

CONCLUSION

HBCUs have had unique cultures, missions, and challenges throughout their 100-plus years of existence, and in recent decades have had to become very creative in supporting themselves and their missions as changes in society have threatened their survival. Many students at HBCUs are first-generation college students with considerable challenges in adapting to a rigorous academic environment. Moreover, most HBCUs have very limited endowments and serious financial challenges. Consequently, HBCUs are under considerable pressure to be innovative in their teaching approaches, both to retain existing students and to attract new ones. The pressure for innovation and accommodation of student needs may help explain the differences in responses between the HBCU and POD respondents regarding the importance of "assessment of student learning outcomes," "teaching underprepared students," "the shifting characteristics/demographics of students," "writing across the curriculum," "team teaching," "course and curriculum reform," and "general education reform."

Of particular interest is the very significant difference between the HBCU sample and the POD sample regarding the importance of "Community service learning." Given the unique historical circumstances of African Americans in their encounters with racism and racial injustice, they may have developed a greater sense of community than Whites. Consequently, HBCUs have tended to have stronger identifications with their (African American) communities.

The program structures reported by HBCUs depict movement toward institutionalization of faculty development. Over two-thirds of respondents are part of a centralized unit with dedicated staff who are responsible for faculty development programming, and the number of senior-level administrators and directors involved indicates the centrality of faculty development on these campuses.

The program influences, current issues, and new challenges reported here highlight the unique missions and strengths of HBCUs, and reinforce the idea that different types of institutions have different needs in terms of faculty development (Austin et al., 2003; Sorcinelli et al., 2006). HBCU faculty developers indicated areas of concern and of services that were not high priorities for the national sample; in particular, issues of program and institutional assessment and support, community service learning, outreach, commitment to civic life, and writing across the curriculum. Interestingly, these are currently being addressed by the Network through the strands of the annual HBCU Faculty Development Symposium and summer institute. As noted earlier, these strands consist of: collaborative models, teaching and learning styles/instructional strategies and techniques; curriculum design and revision; diversity and globalization; learning across the curriculum; educational technology; evaluation of assessment and learning; outcome based assessment; and community service/service learning

HBCUs are not a monolithic group of institutions, however. There are differences in focus among them, particularly between public and private institutions, that will be important for the Network and other faculty development initiatives to further explore and address. Further, the top challenges identified in the survey include issues that go beyond the traditional teaching and learning focus of faculty development at HBCUs. Helping faculty balance their multiple roles and responsibilities, building program assessment capacity for accreditation, and acting as an important voice and resource in institutional change are all areas faculty developers at HBCUs may find themselves needing to address in the near future. Additionally, in order to create and sustain change, the Network and HBCUs will need to revise their mission statements to address some of the top challenges, especially in the areas of technology integration and the scholarship of teaching and learning. Faculty developers will also need to work with Black college presidents to produce strong leaders at HBCUs that will address important areas of concern and change the future direction of the institutions, the faculty, and the students they serve.

The HBCU Faculty Development Network has always been responsive to the needs of faculty in these institutions. HBCUs are known, according to many of their mission statements, to address the needs of the underprepared students. In order to continue to do this effectively, Drewry and Doermann (2001) argued that Black colleges must continue to assist motivated but less well-prepared students to overcome earlier educational deficits. For example, it is incumbent upon the Network to continue to address the issue of the underprepared student by providing faculty development strategies to effectively assess student learning outcomes. The outcomes should be used by faculty developers to assist them with strengthening the teaching and learning process.

Overall, the results of the survey can be used to assist member institutions in planning future activities, including the annual symposium and the summer institute. Furthermore, the results can be shared with administrators and faculty to assist them with their own institutional planning. It is important that administrators recognize that to support institutional change and student learning, it is critical to invest in the continued professional development of faculty through a systematic campus-based faculty development program.

REFERENCES

Allen, W. R., and Jewell, J. O. (2002). A backward glance forward: Past present and future perspectives on historically Black colleges and universities. *The Review of Higher Education, 25*(3), 241–261.

Austin, A., Sorcinelli, M. D., Eddy, P. L., and Beach, A. L. (2003, April). *Envisioning responsive faculty development: Perceptions of faculty developers about the present and future of faculty development.* Paper presented at the American Educational Research Association annual meeting, Chicago, IL.

Beach, A. L. (2002). *Strategies to improve college teaching: The role of different levels of organizational influence on faculty instructional practices.* Unpublished doctoral dissertation, Michigan State University, East Lansing.

Brown, M. C., III, and Freemen, K. (2002). Guest editors' introduction. *The Review of Higher Education, 25*(3), 241–261.

Browning, J. E., and Williams, J. B. (1978). History and goals of Black institutions of higher learning. In C. V. Willie and R. R. Edmonds (Eds.), *Black colleges in America* (pp. 68–93). New York: Teachers College Press.

Drewry, H. N., and Doermann, H. (2001). *Stand and prosper: Private Black colleges and their students.* Princeton, NJ: Princeton University Press.

Florence, C. W. (1932). Critical evaluation of present policies and practices of Negro institutions of higher education. In T. E. McKinney, *Higher education among Negroes* (pp. 39–58). Charlotte, NC: Johnson C. Smith University Publisher.

HBCU Faculty Development Network (n.d.). *Mission.* Downloaded December 2004 from http://hbcufdn.org/.

Johnson, B. J., and Harvey, W. (2002). The socialization of Black faculty: Implications for policy and practice. *The Review of Higher Education, 25*(3), 297–314.

Outcault, C. L., and Skewes-Cox, T. E. (2002). Involvement, interaction, and satisfaction: The human environment at HBCUs. *The Review of Higher Education, 25*(3), 241–261.

Sorcinelli, M. D., Austin, A., Eddy, P. L., and Beach, A. L. (2006). *Creating the future of faculty development: Learning from the past, understanding the present.* Bolton, MA: Anker Publishing.

Southern Education Foundation (n.d.). *Programs.* Downloaded, December 2004 from http://www.sefatl.org/.

Thompson, D. C. (1978). Black college faculty and students: The nature of their interaction. In C. V. Willie and R.R. Edmonds (Eds.), *Black colleges in America* (pp. 180–194). New York, NY: Teachers College Press.

United Negro College Fund (n.d.). *About us.* Downloaded December 2004, http://www.uncf.org/aboutus/index.asp.

Worthy Dawkins, P., Beach, A. L., and Rozman, S. L. (2005). Perceptions of Faculty Developers about the Present and Future of Faculty Development at Historically Black Colleges and Universities (HBCUs). *To Improve the Academy, 24,* 104–120.

CHAPTER 12

Groundwork for Studying Governance at Historically Black Colleges and Universities

James T. Minor

For more than three decades governance and decision making at colleges and universities has been a contentious issue (Allan, 1971; Baldridge, 1982). Controversy associated with academic governance is based on the premise that the extent to which an institution can effectively make decisions has significant consequences for institutional quality and vitality (Gerber, 2001; Longin, 2002). Therefore, issues related to how decisions are made, who has decision-making authority, and over what, represent a constant quandary. Conversations about governance encompass the involvement of governing boards, accreditation bodies, and campus constituents (i.e, the president, faculty, and alumni). Yet, university faculty in all sectors of higher education are considered a cornerstone of campus governance (AAUP, 1966; Burgan, 1998). Although higher education scholars arrive at various conclusions about the state of academic governance and the need for reform, the notion that effective governance is an essential component for institutional quality is well established.

Governance at historically Black colleges and universities (HBCUs) represents an enigma of sorts for the higher education community. This is due, in part, to a lack of general understanding about the operation of HBCUs and a subsequent shortage of governance research within this institutional sector. The importance of institutional quality and vitality at HBCUs (vis-à-vis governance) is understood in light of a few facts. Although HBCUs represent just 3 percent of all higher education institutions, they grant approximately 25 percent of baccalaureate degrees awarded to African Americans (National Center for Educational Statistics, 2003). A significant body of research exists supporting the notion that African American students who attend HBCUs report greater satisfaction with their college experience compared to their counterparts who attend predominantly White institutions (Allen, 1992; Fleming, 1984; Fries-Britt and Turner, 2002). From another vantage point, African Americans (along with Native Americans) have the lowest graduation rates (41%) of all participants at predominantly White institutions (Harvey, 2003). The vitality of HBCUs is critical; approximately half of all Black Ph.Ds earn bachelor degrees at HBCUs (Brown and Davis, 2001).

Despite these facts, one common perception is that HBCUs are still less stable, less productive, or less educative compared to predominantly White campuses. One reason for such negative perceptions results from questions surrounding governance policies and practices employed at HBCUs (Phillips, 2002). Financial fragility, accreditation challenges, and even closures are associated with poor governance practices (Hamilton, 2002). Yet, virtually no research exists regarding the state of governance at HBCUs, the involvement of faculty, or the relationship between governance and institutional quality. Using a national data set, I present findings that help establish a foundational understanding about the state of academic governance at HBCUs, with particular emphasis on the involvement of faculty. To begin, I contextualize the study and describe a culturally sensitive approach I use to frame it.

FACULTY GOVERNANCE AND HBCUS

Literature on faculty governance is embedded in a much larger discussion about the virtues of shared governance on college and university campuses. Universities able to effectively share authority are said to be better situated to advance institutional quality while, at the same time, exemplifying the doctrine of democracy valued by most institutions (Mortimer and McConnell, 1978; Hirsch and Weber, 2001). The American Association for University Professors (AAUP), since the early 1900s, has upheld faculty involvement in decision making as critical to preserving the academic and moral integrity of universities. Disagreements associated with shared governance in higher education do not concern whether the idea is important but rather how to employ such a concept. More specifically, in what areas should faculty have decision-making authority? How should faculty influence be expressed?

Collectively, the literature on faculty governance provides three central themes. First, faculty involvement in decision making is essential for academic quality and faculty satisfaction (Floyd, 1994). However, the most effective ways to involve faculty vary according to institutional context which include a host of cultural, political, and structural variables (Jordan, 2001; Pusser and Ordorika, 2001). Second, although the faculty senate is the most common venue for faculty participation, it is not the only means by which faculty are involved in decision making (Birnbaum, 1989; Tierney and Minor, 2003). Third, although many campuses promote the value of shared governance and faculty involvement in decision making, the practice of such creates contention due to multiple interpretations of what shared governance means and the structural complexity of many campuses (Baldwin and Leslie, 2001; Keller, 2001; Tierney, 2004). The literature, however, does not provide clues about differences that may exist across institutional sectors, models of effective faculty governance, or much research on plausible approaches to the challenges that exist.

Research on faculty governance at HBCUs is virtually nonexistent. The majority of research related to HBCUs is on students. There are, however, a handful of studies that lend governance-related understanding about these institutions and their faculty. One frequently discussed theme is the distinctiveness of HBCUs. Scholars have established the fact that HBCUs, from their beginning, were distinctly different institutions based on their founding mission of access and student development (Brazzell, 1992; Merisotis and O'Brien, 1998; Peeps, 1981). During the antebellum period "every Southern state except Tennessee prohibited the formal instruction of slaves or freed Blacks" (Roebuck and Murty, 1993, p. 21). The majority of HBCUs were started by churches or missionary societies that sought to provide educational opportunities to Blacks marginalized by society (Drewery and Doermann, 2001). The founding of these institutions, and the purpose they now serve, distinguishes HBCUs from all other sectors of higher education. Still, HBCUs are expected to operate according to conventional tenets of academic governance.

Other relevant studies reveal that faculty at HBCUs are among the most diverse in the country (Foster, 2001). Faculty at HBCUs also report differences in socialization patterns (Johnson and Harvey, 2002). From the institutional perspective, obstacles to developing "strong faculty" at HBCUs have been identified. Among them are: (*a*) the pool of available qualified faculty willing to work at HBCUs; (*b*) the ability to offer competitive salaries; (*c*) working conditions; and (*d*) working relationships among faculty, administrators, and other constituencies (Billingsley, 1982). Although there is a scarcity of research on academic governance at HBCUs, the institutions and the role faculty play within them is described as characteristically different. These differences call into question the appropriateness of conventional governance practices. At the very least one would expect the effects of employing the same practices used at predominantly White institutions to produce varying results at HBCUs.

Differences in the nature of faculty work at HBCUs does not suggest that their involvement in decision making or effective governance is less important. HBCUs are often accused of employing more autocratic styles of leadership, which is often linked to accreditation challenges and financial difficulties (Phillips, 2002). One dilemma, however, is that much of the discussion about governance at HBCUs is speculative. Because these conversations can influence perceptions, policy, and practice, the need for scholarship based on empirical data is necessary as are theoretically sound approaches. For these reasons it is important to establish the state of faculty governance at HBCUs. To what extent is shared governance valued at HBCUs? In what areas do HBCU faculty have decision-making authority? How satisfied are HBCU constituents with the operation of faculty governing bodies? In the following section, I describe the theoretical perspectives and research methods used to examine faculty governance at HBCUs.

A NATIONAL STUDY OF GOVERNANCE AT HBCUS

One common criticism about much of the research on HBCUs is that it is usually done out of context or uses inappropriate concepts (Freeman, 1998). To theoretically frame this study, I employ a "culturally sensitive" research approach. Researchers of ethnic populations in school settings use culturally sensitive approaches to recognize and, when possible, account for cultural difference that exist among groups (Tillman, 2002). In an educational context and others more generally, African American culture has always been described as differing significantly from European American culture. Such differences include (but are not limited to) value orientations based on historical experiences, the use of language(s), and even epistemological foundations (King, 1995). These differences are believed to establish cultural distinctiveness that must be recognized when conducting research on ethnic populations, in this case African Americans at historically Black institutions.

The use of a culturally sensitive approach provides a framework to interpret differences more accurately. Using this approach one might expect differences influenced by cultural aspects at institutions comprised predominately by African Americans. Conventional approaches tend to interpret differences at HBCUs as inherent organizational flaws without much attention to what might simply be cultural differences. The advantage of this approach is that it at least considers cultural differences or nuances often noted at HBCUs as potentially influencing outcomes.

THE DATA

Data for this study were gathered as a part of a larger project to examine challenges associated with academic governance at four-year colleges and universities. In 2002, a national survey on faculty governance was administered to 763 institutions, of which 27 were HBCUs (U.S. Department of Education, 2002). In 2003, the survey was readministered to the remaining 61 four-year HBCUs. The data represented here combines cases from the 2002 and 2003 surveys. Among the 88 HBCUs sampled, 7 were doctoral universities, 32 were masters institutions, and 49 were baccalaureate colleges. The institutions in this survey are only categorized by the U.S. Department of Education classifications. Consequently, some institutions that fall within the masters category may offer doctoral degrees in limited areas. Likewise, some baccalaureate colleges (as classified) may grant masters degrees.

From each campus five participants were sampled: (*a*) the chief academic officer (or provost), (*b*) the chair of the faculty senate, and (*c*) three department chairs/faculty from various academic disciplines. At face value, one might question whether department chairs accurately reflect the views of faculty members. One could argue, for example, that department chairs (depending on the institution) represent the administration. Yet, one could just as easily argue that department chairs are faculty. The results from both surveys show significant variation in responses between department chairs/faculty and chief academic officers, which indicates distinctiveness within the sample. For the purpose of this study, I proxy department chairs for faculty.

The web-based survey was designed to gain understanding about perceptions of shared governance that exist on campuses and areas in which faculty participate in decision making. The survey included more than 40 items, with a response rate of 68 percent. The term "faculty senate" is used generically to mean the primary faculty governing body. Faculty council, faculty assembly, or other terms may be alternatively used by campuses. As a prelude to more sophisticated analyses, the data presented here are descriptive in nature used to establish fundamental understanding about faculty governance at HBCUs.

FINDINGS

A portion of the survey was designed to gain understanding about perceptions related to campus governance. For example, the extent campus constituents expressed confidence in the employment of shared governance, the level of trust and communication between constituents, and administrative commitments to sharing authority. Findings show that perceptions about the quality of shared governance on campus vary by institutional type and constituency. Overall, 69 percent of all HBCU respondents agreed or strongly agreed that shared governance is an important part of their institutions' value and identity. Sixty-nine percent of all respondents agreed that the president and administrators are genuinely committed to shared governance. Sixty-four percent agreed that the faculty senate is an important governing body. By comparison, doctoral universities reported lower levels of trust and quality communication between campus constituents. Those at baccalaureate colleges reported higher levels of trust and confidence, and more frequently reported that presidents and administrators were genuinely committed to shared governance.

The most striking comparison of perceptions was by constituent groups. Across all institutions, 77 percent of chief academic officers agreed that shared governance was an important part of their institutions' value and identity compared to just 24 percent of faculty. Over 90 percent of chief academic officers agreed that trust and communication were sufficient for making progress on campus compared to approximately 62 percent of senate chairs and faculty. Even compared to senate chairs, a higher percentage of chief academic officers agreed that the faculty senate was an important governing body.

The survey was also designed to gain understanding about which areas of the institution faculty exercise substantial decision-making authority. Over 70 percent of respondents reported that faculty maintain substantial influence over the undergraduate curriculum. This is especially the case at baccalaureate colleges, which reported having the most (78%) influence over undergraduate curriculum; doctoral universities reported having the least (63%). Respondents reported faculty have considerably less influence over issues related to tenure and promotion (60%), strategic or budgetary priorities (22%), distance education (28%), evaluation of the chief academic officer (11%), and selection of the president (16%). Although provosts were still more optimistic, the responses between constituent groups were considerably less divergent for these items.

Consonant with the issue of where faculty exercised influence over decision making is the issue of how. That is, the venues or forums faculty use to participate in governance. Although the faculty senate represents the primary venue for faculty participation at most colleges and universities, the survey findings show that at HBCUs just 48 percent of faculty meaningfully participate in decision making via the senate. At doctoral universities 39 percent reported substantial faculty participation via the senate, compared to 51 percent at baccalaureate colleges and masters institutions. More than 70 percent of respondents at all institutions reported that faculty participate in decision making through their academic departments. Those at doctoral universities reported more participation through venues at the school/college level compared to baccalaureate colleges or masters institutions.

Participation by way of standing faculty committees assigned to specific tasks, standing committees that combine administrators and faculty, and ad hoc committees represent other alternatives. Seventy-nine percent of respondents reported that faculty substantially participate in decision making via standing faculty committees assigned to specific tasks such as tenure and promotion. Over 50 percent of all institutions reported participation through ad hoc committees. Yet, only 34 percent reported faculty participation in standing committees that involved faculty and administrators. Additionally, the findings showed no notable differences between campuses with collective bargaining units and those where unions are absent.

As a measure of the cultural and institutional distinctions that exist at HBCUs, the survey included two items that allowed participants to fill in short answers. One item asked: "How are HBCUs governed differently than predominantly White institutions?" Another asked: "What is the most critical challenge to successful faculty participation in governance?" The responses to the first question indicate that governance at HBCUs is less formal and more communicative. "HBCUs appear to be governed much more in a cultural fashion . . . compared to predominantly White institutions. There is less attention paid to the written processes and procedures at HBCUs than at other institutions," asserted one senate chair. Another claimed that

> Faculty at HBCUs tend to prefer the cultural form of governance and faculty at White institutions prefer greater formality. Many HBCUs have had paternalistic administrations in their history and HBCU faculty seem to have difficulty embracing their own power. In contrast, faculty at predominantly White institutions are more accustomed to using their power in open opposition to the administration.

Twenty-six percent of the written responses suggested that cultural or informal processes influence governance at HBCUs. This was the largest category of responses for this item.

Concerning the most critical challenges to successful faculty participation, the largest group of responses point toward faculty. Thirty-two percent of respondents suggested that the lack of faculty involvement was problematic. "Getting the faculty to voice their opinions about certain concerns and following through with their concerns" was the most critical challenge, according to one faculty member. Another claimed that "more faculty need to be involved." A provost reported that "there is a high level of apathy and disengagement among faculty concerning governance. Few are willing to take full responsibility for being involved in governance." The lack of participation was in some cases attributed to structural qualities. According to one faculty member, "because the president of the university or his designee is also the chair of the faculty senate, many faculty don't believe it's really their representative body." Another noted structural challenges by pointing out that time and teaching commitments represent a critical challenge. "The majority of my time is spent teaching and with students. I can't imagine sitting in a committee meeting that *might* influence a decision. Many faculty simply don't have time to substantially participate."

Another 21 percent suggested cultural challenges such as "faculty overcoming the perception of fear of the president." "Getting the administration to listen to the faculty" was the most critical challenge according to one faculty member. The issue of "trust" was simply stated by a provost. "The absence of institutional culture that constrains the administration to share its power and privileges with faculty" was the problem according to a senate chair. Another senate chair illustrated a challenge calling attention to both structural and cultural aspects of the institution. "The administration trusting faculty members outside of the 'designated group' to share in governance processes is a problem. The 'designated group' is made up of those individuals who the President trusts to be loyal to his initiatives."

DISCUSSION

A secondary objective of this study was to consider a conceptual or theoretical framework for studying governance issues at HBCUs. From a comparative perspective, one could interpret these findings as negative given that HBCUs, in general, report less confidence in governance compared to predominantly White institutions in the larger study. Utilizing a culturally sensitive approach, however, one might interpret these findings differently. Before moving forward, two qualifying statements must be made in order to neutralize common criticisms that arise when discussing governance at HBCUs. First, in spite of differences in decision-making context at HBCUs, there are challenges associated with governance and even evidence of poor practice exhibited at some institutions. The assessment of such, however, should be conducted with appropriate measures. Second, I recognize that all campuses have unique decision-making contexts. My discussion addresses differences that might be commonly shared among HBCUs. In the following discussion, I use the issues of faculty participation in governance and the challenge of collectively defining shared governance to advance understanding about faculty decision-making.

RETHINKING FACULTY PARTICIPATION AT HBCUS

Faculty participation serves as one example of how institutional differences can influence outcomes. The challenges of faculty participation in governance affect most campuses. Apathy, illegitimate governing bodies, administrative dispositions, or any number of factors could contribute to low participation (Floyd, 1994). At HBCUs, a few factors should be taken into account. First, the survey reveals that faculty participate in decision making via multiple venues. Consequently, a weak or dysfunctional senate, although problematic, does not mean faculty are not involved in decision making. More than 70 percent participate in academic departments and almost 80 percent report that faculty participate by way of standing committees. One prevailing assumption has been that if the faculty senate is inoperative or dysfunctional then faculty involvement in decision making is dead. Governance and decision making takes place on multiple levels within an institution. Therefore, the senate should not serve as the only measure of faculty participation. From a culturally sensitive approach, one could question whether the senate is the most effective mechanism for faculty participation in governance at HBCUs. Many respondents spoke of a more tribunal or communicative approach to faculty involvement. "Dealing with our senate has been the most inhibitive challenge . . . our best work seems to happen when we get together outside of the formal pretense and deal with each other as individuals who care about the college rather than being a dean, chair, and so forth."

The data reveal that HBCU faculty are involved in decision making yet report high levels of dissatisfaction with shared governance. In considering faculty participation at HBCUs more attention must be given to the potential influence of structural challenges, such as time, and cultural challenges such as tradition. HBCU faculty are known to commit significant amounts of time and energy to students (Allen, Epps, and Haniff, 1991). The very aspect of faculty involvement on campus that has led to positive student outcomes also may have created challenges for faculty participation in governance. No one would consciously ask faculty to be less committed to students, yet the expectation that faculty be more involved in governance represents a potential contradiction. In order to preserve the benefits of positive faculty/student interaction, it is important to consider potential trade-offs for increased faculty involvement in governance. Conventional wisdom suggests that increased faculty participation in governance enhances institutional quality. A culturally sensitive view considers whether this is the case for HBCUs if increased participation meant less emphasis on students.

It is equally important to recognize priority inconsistencies that institutions experience. Many HBCUs (especially masters and doctoral institutions), due to external pressures, have begun to focus on the recruitment and development of research faculty versus those more dedicated to teaching. Concerning faculty participation in governance, one assumption is that research faculty, being socialized differently, are more apt to participate in governance. However, new faculty members still operate within an institutional context that is student—not faculty-centered. Ironically, those at doctoral universities, which have the highest percentage of "research faculty" reported the lowest participation in the senate. When considering the role faculty play in governance at HBCUs, the possible contradictions between institutional traditions and contemporary expectations should also be taken into account.

COMMUNICATION AND RECONCILING PERCEPTIONS

One striking comparison is between chief academic officers (77%) and faculty (24%) responses to the question concerning whether shared governance was an important part of their institutions' value and identity. Chief academic officers were also significantly more positive about the quality of communication among constituents. One does not need to be an organizational expert to surmise the challenges such gaps represent. Differences in perception can be linked to communication. Such a gap in perception concerning the value of shared governance is usually due to divergent definitions of what shared governance actually means. One challenge many institutions of higher education face is that shared governance has not been collectively defined (Keller, 2001). Where constituents are situated within an institution influences their perceptions about the quality of governance. Consequently, it is important for campus leaders to articulate the meaning of shared governance in way that promotes a collective understanding. Much of determining how well shared governance operates is dependent on how one defines it.

In another open-ended question that asked participants to define briefly shared governance, respondents across constituent groups defined shared governance in three ways. Approximately one-third defined shared governance as collaborative process whereby administrators, faculty, and staff collectively are involved in the decision-making process across various areas of the institution. Another 29 percent defined shared governance as a stratified process. That is, different constituency groups have authority over specific areas of the institution. For example, faculty make decisions on curriculum or other academic matters and administrators make decisions on nonacademic issues such as the budget. A smaller portion of the sample (19%) defined shared governance as a consultative process in which the president is expected to make decisions but not before consulting faculty and other campus constituents on a particular issue.

Given that a significant portion of HBCU respondents reported their decision-making processes were more communicative, research on the relationship between perceptual gaps and communication represents a useful direction. A culturally sensitive perspective assumes that the communicative styles that mediate decision making at HBCUs are important variables for understanding the quality of shared governance. However, given the current gaps in perception among HBCU constituents, it is difficult to determine whether the most pressing challenges are related to structural elements of organization, more cultural elements such as communication, or a combination of both.

CAREFUL COMPARISONS

Overall, governance at HBCUs does not appear inoperable. Respondents in the original sample, which included 763 institutions, reported similar patterns of faculty influence and involvement in decision making. However, HBCU respondents report significantly lower levels of confidence in governance and decision-making processes. From a comparative perspective one might deem governance at HBCUs less effective. From a culturally sensitive perspective one might reconsider the appropriateness of using governance precepts at predominantly White institutions at HBCUs. Governance activity at HBCUs is usually understood in relation to predominantly White institutions and is assessed accordingly. Yet, if we accept that HBCUs are distinct institutions, we must also consider how such distinctions influence the practice of decision making.

There is a need to reconsider what governance principles or expectations are appropriate for HBCUs. At religious institutions where clergy serve as trustees one would expect that such a dynamic would influence how decisions are made. The intent is not to excuse poor practice but to develop more accurate frames to conduct research and evaluate academic governance at HBCUs.

Responding to the question of how are HBCUs governed differently, one participant claimed that "governance on some White campuses could be just as bad or good, but somehow our actions are always perceived as inferior." Reflecting a more internal perspective, another added that "sometimes I think we [campus constituents] hear so many negative things about this campus that we start to believe them and get duped into thinking that we're worse off than we really are." Many responses implicated race, or racial perceptions of others, as influential in assessing the quality of governance on campus. Although this warrants more careful analysis, critical race theory or other alternative theoretical frame that account for race may be useful for understanding governance activity at HBCUs. Such frameworks might also be used for examining various policies and the actions of external agencies such as system boards and accreditation bodies.

As previously noted, assuming that all HBCUs are the same can also thwart understanding. HBCUs are considered collectively here in the interest of developing fundamental knowledge under the presumption that there are similarities. However, just as unqualified comparisons between HBCUs and predominantly White institutions are problematic, making across-the-board generalizations about HBCUs is similarly limiting. Being able to better identify and articulate governance related differences that exist across institutional sectors also represents a viable area for research that would enhance understanding.

CONCLUSION

The well-being of HBCUs depends significantly on state and federal policy to support them. This support is, in part, based on the ability of proponents to define the virtues of HBCUs and better influence perceptions about governance activity. The perception that HBCUs are mismanaged due to poor leadership and tradition sets the stage for continued discussions that question their existence. However, the ability to demonstrate the need for diverse governance practices more consistent with institutional and cultural characteristics can help neutralize cynicism. This does not suggest that governance practices at HBCUs need not be responsible and effective. Rather, research that can determine relationships between institutional quality and governance, while accurately identifying challenges, can guide discourse and policy making.

Given the importance of HBCUs as an institutional sector that produces a disproportionate number of Black graduates, their vitality is essential. The practice of effective governance represents one way to promote stability and growth. However, before reform or other actions are proposed, there is a need to determine accurately where the most pressing challenges lie. Challenges that confront a small private liberal arts college with only 2,500 students will likely be different than those at a doctoral granting research university with 12,000 students. This study represents a starting point from which more in-depth, issue-specific research can be undertaken. For now, two important challenges have been identified. The discrepancy between campus constituents concerning the value of shared governance, trust, and communication is glaring. As are the potential challenges for faculty participation which contrasts with faculty commitments to teaching and to students. Establishing baseline data on faculty governance and considering appropriate frameworks provides necessary footing for future research that advances understanding about how HBCUs can be more effectively governed.

REFERENCES

Allan, G. (1971). Twixt terror and thermidor: Reflections on campus governance. *Journal of Higher Education, 42*(4), 292–309.

Allen, W. R., Epps, E., and Haniff, N. Z. (Eds). (1991). *College in Black and White: African American students in predominantly White and historically Black public universities.* Albany, NY: State University of New York Press.

Allen, W. (1992). The color of success: African American college student outcomes at predominantly White and historically Black colleges. *Harvard Educational Review, 62,* 26–44.

American Association of University Professors. (1966). *Statement on government of colleges and universities.* (AAUP). Retrieved March 15, 2005 from http://www.aaup.org/statements/Redbook/Govern.htm

Baldridge, J. V. (1982). Shared governance: A fable about the lost magic kingdom. *Academe, 68*(1), 12–15.

Baldwin, R., and Leslie, D. (2001). Rethinking the structure of shared governance. *Peer Review, 3*(3), 18–19.

Billingsley, A. (1982). Building strong faculties in Black colleges. *The Journal of Negro Studies,* 5(1), 4–15.

Birnbaum, R. (1989). The latent organizational functions of the academic senate: Why senates do not work but will not go away. *Journal of Higher Education, 60*(4), 423–443.

Brazzell, J. C. (1992). Bricks without straw: Missionary-sponsored Black higher education in the post-Emancipation era. *Journal of Higher Education, 63* (1), 26–49.

Brown, M. C., and Davis, J. E. (2001). The historically Black college as a social contract, social capital, and social equalizer. *Peabody Journal of Education, 76 (1),* 31–49.

Burgan, M. (1998). Academic citizenship. *Liberal Education, 84*(4), 16–21.

Drewry, H. N., and Doermann, H. (2001). *Stand and prosper: Private Black colleges and their students.* Princeton, NJ: Princeton University Press.

Fleming, J. (1984). *Blacks in college.* San Francisco, CA: Jossey-Bass Inc., Publishers.

Floyd, C. E. (1994). Faculty participation and shared governance. *The Review of Higher Education, 17*(2), 197–209.

Foster, L. (2001). The not-so-invisible professors: White faculty at the Black college. *Urban Education, 36*(5), 611–629.

Freeman, K. (Ed.). (1998). *African American culture and heritage in higher education research and practice.* Westport, CT: Praeger.

Fries-Britt, S., and Turner, B. (2002). Uneven stories: Successful Black collegians at a Black and a White campus. *The Review of Higher Education, 25*(3), 315–330.

Gerber, L. G. (2001). 'Inextricably linked': Shared governance and academic freedom. *Academe, 87*(3), 22–24.

Hamilton, K. (2002). When the campus becomes a battle ground: Shared governance can seem a distant dream when needs for faculty freedoms, speedy decisions clash. *Black Issues in Higher Education, 19*(14).

Harvey, W. (2003). Minorities in higher education. Annual status report 2002–2003. Washington DC: American Council on Education.

Hirsch, W. Z., and Weber, L. E. (Eds.). (2001). *Governance in higher education: The university in a state of flux.* London: Economica, Ltd.

Johnson, B., and Harvey, W. (2002). The socialization of Black college faculty: Implications for policy and practice. *Review of Higher Education, 25*(3), 297–314.

Jordan, R. (2001). The faculty senate minuet. *Trusteeship (September/October),* 18–23.

Keller, G. (2001). Governance: The remarkable ambiguity. In P. G. Altbach, P. Gumport, and B. Johnstone (Eds.), *In defense of higher education* (pp. 504–522). Baltimore, MD: Johns Hopkins University Press.

King, J. (1995). Culture-centered knowledge: Black studies, curriculum transformation, and social action. In J. A. Banks and C. M. Banks (Eds.), Handbook of research on multicultural education (pp. 265–290). New York: Macmillan.

Longin, T. C. (2002). Institutional governance: A call for collaborative decision-making in American higher education. In W. G. Berberet and L. A. McMillin (Eds.), *A new academic compact* (pp. 211–221). Boston, MA: Anker Publishing Co.

Merisotis, J. P., and O'Brien, C. T. (Eds.) (1998). *Minority-serving institution, distinct purposes, common goals.* San Francisco, CA: Jossey-Bass Inc., Publishers.

Mortimer, K., and McConnell, T. (1978). *Sharing authority effectively.* San Francisco, CA: Jossey-Bass Inc., Publishers.

National Center for Education Statistics. (2003). Status and trends in the education of Blacks. Washington, DC.: U.S. Department of Education.

Peeps, J. M. S. (1981). Northern philanthropy and the emergence of Black higher education: Do gooder's, compromisers, or co-conspirators? *Journal of Negro Education, 50*(3), 251–269.

Phillips, I. P. (2002). Shared governance on Black college campuses. *Academe, 88*(4), 50–56.

Pusser, B., and Ordorika, I. (2001) Bringing political theory to university governance. *Higher Education: Handbook of Theory and Research, 16,* 147–194.

Roebuck, J. B., and Murty, K. S. (1993). *Historically Black colleges and universities: Their place in American higher education.* Westport, CT: Praeger.

Tierney, W. (2004). *Competing conceptions of academic governance: Negotiating the perfect storm.* Baltimore, MD: Johns Hopkins University Press.

Tierney, W. G., and Minor, J. T. (2003). *Challenges for governance.* (Monograph available from The Center for Higher Education Policy Analysis, Rossier School of Education, The University of Southern California, WPH 701, Los Angeles, CA 90089).

Tillman, L. (2002). Culturally sensitive research approaches: An African American perspective. *Educational Researcher, 31(9),* 3–12.

U.S. Department of Education (2002). *White House initiative on historically Black colleges and universities.* Retrieved January 21, 2004 from the World Wide Web: http://www.ed.gov/about/inits/list/whhbcu/edlite-index.html.

CHAPTER 13

HBCU's Institutional Advantage

Returns to Teacher Education

Brooks B. Robinson and Angela R. Albert

From the outset, Historically Black Colleges and Universities (HBCUs) assumed roles as "normal schools" or "teacher colleges." Given the value placed on education and the fact that serving as an educator was a highly prized position in the Black community, many of the students who attended HBCUs did so for the express purpose of becoming educators. For the over 150 years of their existence, one would expect HBCUs to develop institutional advantages in producing high-quality elementary and secondary school teachers. Theoretically, these teachers, in turn, would experience superior outcomes in the classroom (i.e., they would produce relatively higher performing students), which would result in relatively higher level earnings for these teacher than for teachers who study at non-HBCUs. For certain, one would not expect earnings to be lower for HBCU-trained teachers than for teachers trained at other institutions of higher learning. This conjecture constitutes the authors' hypothesis about returns to HBCU teacher education. This hypothesis emerges from the literature on increased productivity and increased quality that can result from "learning by doing" (LBD) (see Bahk & Gort, 1993, for a survey of the literature and an enhancement to it), and from the literature on the positive effects of education quality on earnings (see Heckman et al., 1996, for an analysis of the literature and their own contribution). Generally, these two literatures infer that HBCUs could experience significant increases in productivity and quality in the production of teachers based strictly on LBD by HBCU professors; typically, HBCUs have not enjoyed abundant opportunities to achieve these outcomes through generous investments in physical capital or formal training. It is assumed that the resulting increases in the quality of education at HBCUs were transmitted to

HBCU-educated teachers, who have gone on to experience higher levels of earnings than they would have otherwise incurred. We test this hypothesis using a data set from the National Center for Education Statistics (NCES) Baccalaureate and Beyond Longitudinal Study (B&B).

This chapter provides background information on HBCUs, including information about recent financial crises that these MSIs have experienced. It reviews key literature on the determinants of earnings. It explores the development of institutional advantages for HBCUs vis-à-vis the production of elementary and secondary school teachers. Finally, it presents our data sources, research methodology, and the results of our analysis.

HBCUS AND TEACHER EDUCATION INCLUDING RECENT FINANCIAL CRISES

African Americans in United States have consistently sought success through their intense efforts to obtain education. Since 1837, HBCUs have provided a haven for fostering educational, economic, and cultural leadership for Blacks and the society at large. In the twenty-first century, this remains true and is a primary focus for thousands of Black students who continue to pursue the "American Dream." HBCUs were established to address the educational needs of Blacks who had gained their freedom during the pre- and post-Emancipation Proclamation period. Although these havens for freed slaves were referred to as "universities" or "institutes," the education that they provided was at the elementary and secondary levels. It was not until the twentieth century that HBCUs began implementing postsecondary level courses (U.S. Department of Education, 1991).

Despite their differing curricula, HBCUs have been consistent on three major fronts: (1) educating Black youth; (2) preparing teachers; and (3) perpetuating the Anglo-Saxon missionary tradition. They have been a refuge for Black students and have a long history of confronting major challenges. Philips (2002) and Anderson (1988) indicate that these challenges include, but are not limited to: (1) tight fiscal budgets and scarce physical resources; (2) faculty salary inequities; (3) lagging technological advances; (4) ill-prepared incoming freshmen; and (5) governance sharing.

Amid the struggle to contribute to the success of Black students specifically and students generally, HBCUs have disproportionate credit for the production of Black graduates of four-year and graduate-level institutions. The over 100 HBCUs account for about 3 percent of all institutions of higher learning in the nation; however, they account for a staggering 28 percent of all Black students in America's higher education system that complete their undergraduate degrees (Roscoe, 2001). Fifteen percent of Blacks who earn master's and professional degrees and 10 percent of those who earn doctoral degrees matriculate at HBCUs (U.S. Department of Education, 1991).

Despite these striking statistics, HBCUs are experiencing retention and completion problems that are not easily discerned by the casual observer. Freedman (2005) reported that, nationally, HBCUs have a six-year graduation rate of 38 percent. This rate is moderately lower than the statistic for Black students at all other institutions and is approximately 40 percent lower than for Blacks at prestigious and elite schools.

An important factor that impinges on the critical reality of low retention and completion rates is the increasing responsiveness of high achieving Black students to the now perceived less-threatening environment at traditionally White institutions. At an increasing rate, high-quality Black students (based on competitive grade point averages and test scores) are opting to attend institutions of higher learning other than HBCUs. As the pool of college-prepared Black students shrink, HBCUs have reacted by instituting lower thresholds for both incoming freshmen's GPAs and standardized test scores in order to maintain enrollment. They are paying for these lowered admission standards with remedial courses and college-readiness programs (Allen and Jewell, 2002). Financial woes and an inferior technological infrastructure exacerbate already troublesome conditions. Freedman (2005) noted the following:

> With the desegregation of colleges and universities in the South and the increased recruiting of Black students by top universities, what W. E. B. Du Bois famously called the "talented tenth"' no longer heads to places like Texas Southern by default. In fact, the top 10 percent of graduates from any Texas high school are guaranteed admission to the state university system. (p. B7)

After considering all challenges that confront HBCUs today, it is noteworthy that some of the brightest citizens of America graduated from HBCUs. Eighty percent of Black federal judges, 60 percent of Black attorneys, 70 percent of Black dentists, and 50 percent of Black teachers in public schools graduate from HBCUs. Additionally, 50 percent of Black faculty members at White research universities earn their undergraduate degrees from HBCUs. Spelman College and Bennett College produce more than half of the African American female doctoral students in the field of science (United Negro College Fund, 2005).

DETERMINANTS OF EARNINGS

Theoretically, in a monopsonistic (one buyer) economic environment, teacher wages are set equal to the value of their marginal revenue product. That is, teachers earn an amount equal to their factor input share of the revenue received by a school system for the marginal (final) student that is enrolled. More realistically, from an employer's perspective, teacher earnings are determined by a variety of factors, including, but not limited to, student outcomes, tenure, the subject matter taught, and so forth. These factors broadly indicate teacher quality. Indeed, Rivkin et al. (2002) state that teacher quality is the key ingredient that determines variation in student academic achievement. NCES (2000) reports that teacher quality may be characterized by the following four factors: (1) academic skill, (2) assignment, (3) experience, and (4) professional development.

Because there is variation in teacher quality, one expects that there should be variation in teacher earnings. Therefore, if a certain subset of teachers has higher levels of teacher quality, then one expects these teachers to accrue higher earnings—ceteris paribus. Given the foregoing evidence, we advance the falsifiable hypothesis that teachers trained at HBCUs should possess superior amounts of the first of these four factors—academic skills. That is, HBCU-trained teachers should have superior teaching skills relative to teachers trained at non-HBCU institutions and should, therefore, be able to obtain superior returns to their education.

Constantine (1995) finds that, for students with similar characteristics or option sets, there are higher returns for those graduating from HBCUs than for those graduating from non-HBCU institutions. These findings conflict with those presented by Ehrenberg and Rothstein (1994), who contended that HBCU-graduates do not incur higher returns compared with similar graduates of non-HBCUs. Constantine's (1995) analysis is statistical and is not restricted to persons employed in the field of education; no qualitative interpretation is provided in defense of these findings. Nevertheless, the literature is replete with analyses of existing White-Black differences in returns to education or training—irrespective of the academic institution attended. Important contributors who seek to explain this difference include Mason (1997); Neal and Johnson (1996); Constantine (1995); Maxwell (1994); Hirsch and Schumacher (1992); Griliches (1977) and Oaxaca (1973). Given that HBCUs often enroll poorer quality students than do certain non-HBCU institutions, it is with caution that we hypothesize that HBCU-trained teachers obtain higher returns to education than do non-HBCU-trained teachers. Our hypothesis is based on the principles of "institutional advantage."

INSTITUTIONAL ADVANTAGE EFFECTS, GENERALLY, AND THE HBCU CASE SPECIFICALLY

The concept of "institutional advantage" is akin to the economic concepts of "absolute" or "comparative" advantage. Based on the work of Adam

Smith (1776) and David Ricardo (1817), the latter two concepts embody the idea that one economic agent (*x*) requires fewer inputs (e.g., labor and physical capital) to produce two goods, say trained elementary and secondary school teachers, than another economic agent (*y*). If agent *x* can produce trained elementary school teachers using fewer inputs than agent *y*, then we say that agent *x* has comparative advantage in producing that good. If, on the other hand, agent *x* can produce both elementary and secondary school teachers using fewer inputs than agent *y*, then we say that agent *x* has an absolute advantage over agent *y* in producing these two goods. In this case, because economic agent *x* is an institution, we say that the institution has comparative or absolute advantage in producing teachers.

What we know about nations, firms, or institutions that have comparative or absolute advantage in production and that operate in a competitive market environment is that, because their goods are produced relatively cheaply, these national, firm, or institutional producers normally have an opportunity to expand their production to meet increased demand in response to the willingness of consumers to purchase the cheaply produced goods. The opportunity to expand production or simply to remain operational for an extended period of time facilitates prospects for reaping the benefits of LBD and for being able to refine and improve production techniques; thereby becoming more and more efficient and proficient in production. This process of "specialization" can lead to an improvement in the quality of the goods produced. In the case of a monopsonistic (one buyer) market environment, the opportunity to expand production may not occur, but producers with comparative or absolute advantage may have the opportunity to remain in production and to experience the type of continued quality improvements that occur under similar circumstances in a competitive market environment.

HBCUs reflect the characteristics of institutions with absolute or comparative advantage in the production of elementary and secondary school teachers. Initially, due to racial segregation, HBCUs were the primary source of teachers for a growing Black population in the United States. Strong demand for Black teachers provided HBCUs with an opportunity to expand production of trained teachers and to develop, on a LBD basis, the formula for producing high-quality teachers. There was no obvious economic incentive for Black teachers to exhibit professional excellence, but professional pride drove this outcome nonetheless. HBCUs and their teacher graduates were part of a culture of "being better than Whites, just to be considered equal" (Mason, 1997, p. 7). In addition, over the years, subpar physical plants and budgets forced HBCUs to learn to do more with less. Consequently, a culture of efficiency and excellence evolved at HBCUs—especially in the production of teachers.

After the onset of racial integration when HBCUs no longer held a virtual monopoly on the training of teachers for Black students, it is logical to conclude that these institutions called on their efficiency and history of superior performance to refine further their formula for producing high-quality teachers. They used expertise gained from decades of LBD to develop quality-centered teaching programs. They were driven to achieve this result because, if they were unsuccessful, one of two outcomes would ensue: (1) HBCU-trained teachers would not be able to compete in the market place, and HBCUs would no longer attract students headed for the field of education; and/or (2) Black students who desired to teach would opt to attend non-HBCU institutions to obtain training and HBCUs would no longer be needed to train teachers.

Consequently, we must surmise that HBCUs have evolved from monopoly providers of Black teachers, to efficient producer of high-quality teachers in the face of severe fiscal constraints, to quality-centered teacher training institutions that compete vigorously for prospective students in response to desegregation. A by-product of this evolution must be the development of the types of institutional advantages to which we have referred. These institutional advantages, in turn, should help produce high-quality elementary and secondary school teachers. HBCUs' continued existence today is, in fact, prima facie evidence of excellence and efficiency in producing high-quality teachers.

It is with this background in mind that we form the falsifiable hypothesis that, given the underlying monopsonistic structure of the market for public school teachers in the United States, teachers trained at HBCUs exhibit comparatively superior performance and, therefore, accrue superior returns to their education. At a minimum, such HBCU-taught teachers accrue earnings that are generally greater than or equal to, but no less than, earnings of non-HBCU-taught teachers.

We form this hypothesis despite evidence concerning the resource constraints that HBCUs have confronted and continue to confront, and the fact that HBCUs quite often produce teachers from students that begin their higher-learning experience with an inferior skill set when compared with students that enter certain non-HBCUs. Those who would adopt the antithesis of our hypothesis may use the generally lower pre-college skill set of HBCU enrollees as an indicator of HBCU's inability to produce high-quality teachers because certain HBCU enrollees are taught by HBCU-taught elementary and secondary school teachers.

DATA SOURCES AND ANALYTICAL FRAMEWORK

Using participants in the National Postsecondary Student Aid Study (NPSAS), NCES' B&B data set provides information on education and work experience after completion of bachelor's degrees (see http://nces.ed.gov/B&B/). The B&B data set captures information on baccalaureate degree holders who completed their degree in the 1992–93 academic year and who were followed up in 1994 and 1997 (B&B 93/97). B&B data are linked to data collected from NPSAS participants at the end of their secondary school experience. It is a rich source of data typically required for the study of returns to education. Our analysis focuses primarily on B&B data for 1997, because four years may be sufficient time for graduates to settle into the workforce. On the other hand, Griliches (1977, p. 3) recommends that a decade be allowed to elapse after college graduation before attempting to analyze returns to education; Constantine's (1995, p. 542) wage observations are for the tenth year after graduation. Nevertheless, it is possible that the data used in our analysis may not reflect undue influence from the types of economic uncertainties and volatility that characterize new graduates' lives.

Table 13.1 provides test variables that we use to identify factors that influence earnings outcomes, including attendance and/or graduation from an HBCU. The variables include a variety of demographic (race and gender), background (mother's and father's education, family income, attendance at an HBCU, college GPA, formal training beyond college, work experience, and education major), and direct-determinant (region of residence, employment status, multiple jobs, and placement) variables that could influence earning outcomes.

Variable selection for our analysis is consistent with the previously cited literature. Clearly, demographic variables are standard fare. Use of background and direct-determinant variables is mixed. Mason (1997) controls for educational achievement, work tenure, age, health, marital status, union participation, parents' income, education, and regional origin, position in the family hierarchy vis-à-vis siblings, citizenship status, regional indicators, and religion as variables in his models. Neal and Johnson (1996) only use test scores in combination with demographic variables in their models. Constantine (1995) uses all of the background variables included in our model; except that test scores replace GPA. Maxwell (1994) controls for parents' education, number of siblings, and years of schooling in his models. Hirsch and Schumacher (1992) use years of schooling, experience, current job tenure, union membership, marital status, employment status (full-time), location, and a racial density variable in their effort to explain White-Black wage differences. Griliches (1977) models earnings as a function of age,

Table 13.1 Model Variables

Line No.	Variable type*	Variable description	Model variable name	Variable B&B code	Expected signs on parameter estimates: Models 1	2
1	Dep	Annual salary for April 1997	Earnings	B2APRS1		
2	D	Race/ethnicity: Black, 1, 0 otherwise	Race	RETHNI1	+	+
3	D	Gender: Male, 1; 0 otherwise	Gender	Gender1	+	+
4	B	Highest level of mother's education: Bachelors degree or higher, 1; 0 otherwise	Mother's education	MOTHED1	+	+
5	B	Highest level of father's education: Bachelors degree or higher, 1; 0 otherwise	Father's education	DADEDU1	+	+
6	B	Total income of parents and independent student (while in undergraduate program)	Family income	CINCOM1	+	+
7	B	Historically black institution: Attended or graduated from and HBCU, 1; 0 otherwise	Graduated from or attended an HBCU	HBCU1	+	+
8	B	Cumulative grade point average as an undergraduate	College GPA	GPACUM1	+	+
9–12	B	Highest degree received after Bachelor's: Some formal training; Bachelor's degree; Master's degree; professional or doctoral degree	Formal training beyond first degree	B2HDGP 1, 2, 3, and 4	?	?
13	DD	Region of residence in 1997: Southeast, 1; 0 otherwise	Region	B2REGI1	–	–
14	DD	Employment status in April 1997: Less than full time, 1; 0 otherwise	Employment status	B2EM971	–	–
15	DD	Employed in multiple jobs: Multiple jobs, 1; 0 otherwise	Multiple jobs	B2MJOB1	–	–
16	DD	Relationship between April 1997 job and degree field: Closely, 1; 0 otherwise	Placement/job in degree field	B2AJRE1	+	+
17	B	Total teaching experience in years	Experience	B2SPEX1	+	+
18	B	Undergraduate major: Education, 1; 0 otherwise	Education major	UGMJCO1	+	+
19	DD	April industry code: Education, 1; 0 otherwise	Teacher Industry	B2AJOB1	+	+

* Dep=Dependent; D=Demographic; B=Background; and DD=Direct Determinant

schooling, desired wages, wages earned at last job, test and I.Q. scores, father's occupation, culture, experience, location, and region. Finally, Oaxaca (1973) explains White-Black wage differences using experience, schooling, class of worker, industry, occupation, worker health, employment status, mobility, marital status, location, and region. This eclectic mix of variables for the various models indicates that there is no "golden" variable set, and that certain included variables may be an artifact of which variables are available in a particular data set.

A relatively uncommon variable in our models is "placement/job in degree field," which captures the relationship between current employment and formal training. One would be expected to exhibit higher performance and achieve higher earnings in jobs that are closely related to one's formal training than in jobs that are unrelated to one's formal training. We augment this variable in certain models with an "education major" variable, which should also signal superior performance as an educator.

Our models are not as intricate as those presented by Mason (1997), Constantine (1995), and Griliches (1977), who employ more "conditional" approaches to estimating White-Black wage differences; conditional-type models employ systems of equations to account for pre-market factors that can influence earnings. However, our task is primarily constrained to determining whether attending an HBCU adversely affects teachers' earnings. Concerned only with those who have arrived at the teaching profession using many routes, we ask, "Does HBCU attendance/graduation result in higher or lower earnings relative to the earnings of non-HBCU educated teachers?"

To answer this question, we developed two models (see tables 13.2 and 13.3). Model 1 features observations from the B&B data set that reflect primary employment in the education industry; that is, elementary or secondary school teachers. This model permits us to focus only on educators and to assess the effects of attendance and graduation from an HBCU on earnings. Model 2 represents two sub-models from Model 1: One for White educators and one for Black educators. Model 2 results provide the ingredients for a Oaxaca decomposition (see Oaxaca, 1973). The analytical results from the two Model 2 sub-models along with the mean values of the variables in the sub-models are used to decompose White-Black earnings differences into those that are explained by the average characteristics of White versus Black teachers (including attendance at an HBCU), and those earnings differences that are attributable to other, "unexplained," factors.

The last two columns of table 13.1 reflect our expectations concerning the nature of the relationships between earnings and the remaining variables in Models 1 and 2. Generally, earnings are expected to be higher for males than for females, for HBCU attendees and/or graduates who are teachers than for non-HBCU attendees and/or graduates who are teachers, and for those employed in their degree field than for those not so employed. It is also expected that earnings will be positively influenced by higher levels of parental education, greater family income, and by a higher college GPA. Earnings are expected to be lower for teachers who are residents of southern versus northern states, for the unemployed than for the employed, and for those who have multiple jobs than for those with one job. In addition, earnings are expected to be higher for educators who are trained in the field of education and who possess higher levels of teaching experience. There is uncertainty, however, concerning the effect of formal training beyond college on earnings. On one hand, additional formal training could produce more effective teachers, which could contribute positively to higher earnings. On the other hand, additional formal training is likely to reduce experience in the classroom, which could adversely affect earnings.

RESULTS

We adopt the following general approach when conducting our analysis of earnings: First we consider a basic framework (A) that includes all of the aforementioned variables except for race and HBCU attendance and/or graduation; next we consider a framework (B) that accounts for race; finally we add the variable for HBCU attendance and/or graduation framework (C). The goal is to clearly assess the impact of graduating from or attending an HBCU on earnings. This stepwise process is shortened somewhat for Model 2 because it is based on race specific data; that is, framework B is excluded from the analysis in Model 2.

Model 1

Model 1 results represent respondents whose primary employment was as educators in 1997 (see table 13.2). The relationship between earnings and all of the variables in Model 1 meet expectations, except for the "race," "father's education," "graduated from or attended an HBCU," and "education major" variables. To reject our falsifiable hypothesis, we expected to identify an overall, inverse relationship between earnings and race; that is, Blacks would generally accrue less earnings than non-Blacks, which is a stylized fact of studies on White-Black wage differences. The positive relationship between earnings and race that was identified is statistically reliable. Our expectation was that earnings would be higher when fathers achieved a bachelor's degree or higher. It turns out that higher education by fathers is correlated with lower earnings in the model; however, this result is not statistically reliable. If it were reliable, then it would imply that

Table 13.2 Model 1 Results [All Teachers in B&B Data Set]

Line no.	Variables	Model 1.A		Model 1.B		Model 1.C	
		Parameter estimates	t-statistics	Parameter estimates	t-statistics	Parameter estimates	t-statistics
1	Intercept	21182.00*	8.70	19453.00*	7.86	19375.00*	7.81
2	Race			4691.82*	3.56	5000.33*	3.42
3	Gender	2452.04*	3.50	2611.72*	3.73	2621.75*	3.74
4	Mother's education	1322.78	1.72	1156.56	1.50	1179.93	1.53
5	Father's education	−1136.47	−1.61	−995.78	−1.41	−1010.30	−1.43
6	Family income	0.00	0.07	0.00	0.36	0.00	0.34
7	HBCU					−902.05	−0.49
8	GPA	10.99	1.55	14.70+	2.06	14.94+	2.09
9	Some formal training beyond first degree	1288.86	0.80	1604.74	1.00	1591.98	0.99
10	Second Bachelor's degree	197.55	0.15	242.18	0.18	248.12	0.19
11	Master's degree	2243.00*	2.61	2293.44*	2.68	2283.81*	2.67
12	Professional or doctoral degree	−2092.59	−0.66	−1823.96	−0.58	−1838.69	−0.58
13	Region	−1330.95	−1.85	−1680.39+	−2.32	−1659.72+	−2.28
14	Employment status	−11014.00+	−13.76	−10970.00*	−13.75	−10973.00*	−13.75
15	Multiple jobs	−2366.30*	−2.74	−2321.67*	−2.70	−2309.07*	−2.68
16	Placement/job in degree field	2301.81*	3.09	2346.28*	3.16	2366.69*	3.18
17	Experience	0.40	0.19	0.20	0.10	0.17	0.08
18	Education major	−696.77	−0.96	−390.51	−0.53	−389.22	−0.53
19	Adjusted R-square	0.1300		0.1359		0.1355	
20	N	1719		1719		1719	
21	F-statistic	18.13		17.90		16.85	
22	Root mean square error	12599		12556		12559	

* Statistically significant at the one-percent level.
+ Statistically significant at the five-percent level.

there was a preponderance of respondents who had relatively high earnings, and whose father did not possess bachelor's degrees. The model also signals a negative correlation between earnings and HBCU attendance or graduation; however, this result is also statistically unreliable. The apparent negative relationship between earnings and the "education major" variable is somewhat surprising, but it is consistent with a stylized fact that teachers holding undergraduate degrees in education are often paid less than teachers who receive undergraduate training in certain specialized fields, particularly mathematics or the sciences. Notably, the latter negative relationship is not statistically reliable, and does not warrant acceptance.

Model 2

Model 2 comprises two sub-models: A sub-model for White educators (2.1); and a sub-model for Black educators (2.2) (See tables 13.3A and 13.3B). The race specific nature of these sub-models permit analyses only for frameworks A and C, and there are no results for the "race" variable in the sub-models.

The relationships between earnings and the remaining variables in sub-model 2.1 (table 13.3A) are consistent with those identified for Model 1, except for the "graduated from or attended an HBCU" variable. Sub-model 2. 1 reflects a positive relationship between earnings and the "graduated from or attended an HBCU" variable, which is consistent with our hypothesis, but the relationship is not statistically reliable. If it were reliable, it might be interpreted to mean: (1) White students who attend HBCUs develop unique academic and/or social skills that facilitate the acquisition of high earnings as teachers; (2) these students may be products of underprivileged backgrounds and are motivated to work smarter and harder to garner higher earnings; or (3) these results may simply imply that training institutions have little effect on earnings.

Sub-model 2.2 (See table 13.3B), which restricts the analysis to Black educators, is slightly different from the previously discussed models. The number (N) of respondents for the sub-model is 83, and no respondents reported "some formal education beyond the first degree" or "professional or doctoral degrees." Although this sub-model passes a goodness-of-fit test, such a relatively small sample size should prompt cautious consideration of results that are derived.

The estimated relationships between earnings and the variables in sub-model 2.2 are as anticipated for 50 percent of the variables. For example, there are apparent negative relationships between earnings and the "mother's education" and "graduated from or attended an HBCU" variables, but both relationships are statistically unreliable. We find that while "multiple jobs" was indicative of lower earnings in the previously discussed models, it appears to

Table 13.3A Model 2 Results [All White Teachers in B&B Data Set]

		Model 2.1.A		Model 2.1.C	
Line no.	Variables	Parameter estimates	t-statistics	Parameter estimates	t-statistics
1	Intercept	17693.00*	7.59	17817.00*	7.62
2	Race				
3	Gender	1713.94*	2.62	1672.09+	2.55
4	Mother's education	1382.53+	1.98	1353.81+	1.94
5	Father's education	−983.28	−1.53	−931.86	−1.44
6	Family income	0.00	0.43	0.00	0.43
7	Graduated from or attended an HBCU			1680.76	0.76
8	GPA	18.01*	2.71	17.55*	2.63
9	Some formal training beyond first degree	1991.44	1.36	2017.08	1.37
10	Second Bachelor's degree	264.76	0.22	277.49	0.23
11	Master's degree	2293.34*	2.93	2319.91*	2.96
12	Professional or doctoral degree	−1244.99	−0.44	−1238.03	−0.44
13	Region	−906.65	−1.36	−915.10	−1.37
14	Employment status	−10651.00*	−14.29	−10642.00*	−14.27
15	Multiple jobs	−2172.27*	−2.83	−2185.14*	−2.84
16	Placement/job in degree field	2472.39*	3.51	2460.58*	3.49
17	Experience	3.23	1.63	3.19	1.61
18	Education major	−1377.25+	−2.05	−1361.90+	−2.03
19	Adjusted R-square	0.1742		0.1740	
20	N	1405		1405	
21	F-statistic	20.76		19.49	
22	Root mean square error	10522		10524	

* Statistically significant at the one-percent level.
+ Statistically significant at the five-percent level.

be indicative of higher earnings in this sub-model although this apparent positive relationship is not statistically reliable. In addition, two related variables—"placement/job in degree field" and "education major"—flip-flop on the direction of their relationship with earnings in this sub-model when compared with previously discussed models. Earnings appear to be negatively correlated with "placement/job in degree field," but appear to be positively correlated with "education major;" yet both relationships are statistically unreliable and do not warrant acceptance. Nevertheless, if they were statistically reliable, these relationships could be interpreted, on a combined basis, to mean that Black teachers who are not trained as educators are not as successful in securing higher earnings as those who hold degrees in education. One of the most striking results from sub-model 2.2 is a negative, but

Table 13.3B Model 2 Results (cont'd) [All Black Teachers in B&B Data Set]

Line no.	Variables	Model 2.2.A Parameter estimates	Model 2.2.A t-statistics	Model 2.2.C Parameter estimates	Model 2.2.C t-statistics
1	Intercept	34949.00*	5.36	34936.00*	5.33
2	Race				
3	Gender	6416.96*	3.06	6227.78*	2.89
4	Mother's education	−212.31	−0.06	−71.09	−0.02
5	Father's education	308.64	0.10	418.89	0.13
6	Family income	−0.01	−0.34	−0.01	−0.40
7	HBCU			−896.88	−0.45
8	GPA	−18.43	−0.88	−17.53	−0.83
9	Some formal training beyond first degree				
10	Second Bachelor's degree	−4510.29	−1.18	−4514.41	−1.17
11	Master's degree	4264.73	1.61	4175.40	1.57
12	Professional or doctoral degree				
13	Region	−3425.34	−1.72	−3364.57	−1.67
14	Employment status	−12861.00*	−5.03	−12604.00*	−4.79
15	Multiple jobs	1775.54	0.62	1888.66	0.65
16	Placement/job in degree field	−1224.42	−0.58	−1123.57	−0.53
17	Experience	3.71	0.62	3.48	0.57
18	Education major	588.79	0.24	664.47	0.27
19	Adjusted R-square	0.2752		0.2669	
20	N	83		83	
21	F-statistic	3.42		3.16	
22	Root mean square error	8009		8055	

* Statistically significant at the one-percent level.

statistically unreliable, relationship between earnings and the GPA variable. If the relationship were statistically reliable, it would lend credence to the theory that grades and test scores are not perfect predictors of job performance and the ability to accrue high earnings.

A Oaxaca Decomposition

As a final step in this analytical process, we use the results from framework C of sub-models 2.1 and 2.2 to prepare a Oaxaca (1973) decomposition of the difference between White and Black teacher earnings. The decomposition permits us to separately identify and value how differences in Black-White earnings are determined by the average characteristics of Black versus White teachers and by other, unexplained, factors. Quite often, the unexplained portion of the decomposition is linked to discrimination.

Our decomposition is somewhat uncharacteristic because it is performed with Whites serving as the "discriminated group." This is a result of the surprising fact that the B&B data set reports the mean annual earnings for Black educators at $27,383 in 1997, while it is $23,773 for Whites; this Black-White difference in earnings is $3,610 or about 15 percent. Mean earnings for all educators in the B&B data set is $24,270. These results are inconsistent with statistics provided by the NCES (2004, p. 94), which reports that White teachers' total earned income (derived from teaching and other pursuits) exceeded that of Black teachers by $2,249 for the 1999–2000 school year. However, the B&B data set results are consistent with Bureau of Labor Statistics Current Population Survey (CPS, 2005) data for 2004, which reflect usual weekly earning of salary workers in the educational services industry. The mean weekly earnings for Blacks is estimated at $913 (with a standard error of $106.86), while the mean earnings for Whites is estimated at $921 (with a standard error of $29.13)—these estimates are not statistically different. However, given the standard errors of these estimates, the upper bound of a 95 percent confidence interval would place Black earnings in excess of White earnings.

Our Oaxaca decomposition reveals that -$535 of the $3,610 Black-White earnings difference is accounted for by differences in the average characteristics of Black versus White educators. This negative value implies that White teachers generally reflect higher average values for the variables that are in our models than do Black teachers. The remaining component of the decomposition that is accounted for by other, unexplained, factors is valued at $4,145. This positive value implies that Blacks benefit positively from these unexplained factors. In the context of our analysis, the unexplained factors could include superior training received by Black teachers from HBCUs.

CONCLUSION

This chapter is unique in its use of the B&B data set to assess the White-Black earnings gap for teachers, and for its study of the affect of HBCU versus non-HBCU training on returns to education for teachers. Overall, the results may be interpreted to mean that HBCU attendance has no statistically significant effect on returns to education for Black or White teachers. This may be surprising to those who equate financial and other resources constraints that HBCUs face with an inability to produce educators with sufficient skills to perform effectively in the classroom and to elicit comparable earnings. The results presented in this chapter represent a different outcome; one that is supported by institutional advantages that

HBCUs have developed during their over 150-year history. This outcome is buttressed somewhat by CPS (2005) data on Black and White salaries in the "Educational services" industry. Note that the small sample of Black educators considered in Model 2.2 may contribute to the derivation of certain unexpected results.

We recommend that other scholars pursue further analysis of the rich B&B data set to sift out reasons for these interesting results; specifically, that efforts be undertaken to augment the explanatory variables that we use with variables that other scholars have incorporated into their models for explaining White-Black earning differences. These efforts may produce more complete explanations for White-Black earning differences for teachers. Finally, we plan to explore further the role of institutional advantages in the survival of HBCUs and other MSIs and hope that other scholars will do likewise.

REFERENCES

Allen, W., and Jewell, H. (2002). A backward glance forward: Past, present, and future perspectives on historically Black colleges and universities. *The Review of Higher Education, 25*(3), 241–61. Retrieved August 14, 2005, from http://muse.jhu.edu.ucfproxy.fcla.edu/journals/review_of_higher_education/v025/25.3allen.

Anderson, J. (1988). *The education of Blacks in the south, 1860–1935.* Chapel Hill, NC: The University of North Carolina Press.

Bahk, B., and Gort, M. (1993). Decomposing learning by doing in new plants. *The Journal of Political Economy, 101*(4), 561–83.

Bureau of Labor Statistics (2005). *Current population survey.* Usual weekly earnings of employed full-time wage and salary workers by class of worker (private versus public sector), intermediate industry, sex, race, and Hispanic or Latino ethnicity and Non-Hispanic ethnicity, annual average 2004. Washington, DC: U.S. Department of Labor. Unpublished tabulations from the *Current population survey.*

Bureau of Labor Statistics (2005). *Usual weekly earnings summary.* Washington, DC: U.S. Department of Labor. Retrieved August 13, 2005, from http://www.bls.gov/news.release/wkyeng.nro.htm.

Constantine, J. (1995). The effect of attending historically Black colleges and universities on future wages of Black students. *Industrial and Labor Relations Review, 48*(3), 531–46.

Ehrenberg, R., and Rothstein, D. (1994). Do historically Black institutions of higher education confer unique advantages on Black students? An initial analysis. In R. G. Ehrenberg (Ed.), *Choices and consequences: contemporary policy issues in education.* Ithaca, NY: ILR Press.

Feltovich, N., and Papageorgiou, C. (2004). An experimental study of statistical discrimination by employers. *Southern Economic Journal, 70*(4), 837–49.

Freedman, S. (2005). On education, little-noticed crisis at Black colleges. *New York Times.* Retrieved August 14, 2005, from http://query.nytimes.com/search/restricted/article?res=FA0E15F7355B0C708CDDA10894DD404482.

Griliches, Z. (1977). Estimating the returns to schooling: some econometric problems. *Econometrica, 45*(1), 1–22.

Hanushek, E. (1998). The evidence on class size. Occasional Paper 98–1. W. Allen Institute of Political Economy, University of Rochester, 1–40.

Heckman, J., Layne-Farrar, A., and Todd, P. (1996). Human capital pricing equations with an application to estimating the effect of schooling quality on earnings. *The Review of Economics and Statistics, 78*(4), 562–610.

Hirsch, B., and Schumacher, E. (1992). Labor earnings, discrimination, and the racial composition of jobs. *The Journal of Human Resources, 27*(4), 602–28.

Mason, P. (1997). Race, culture, and skill: Interracial wage differences among African Americans, Latinos, and Whites. *Review of Black Political Economy, 25*(3), 5–39.

Maxwell, N. (1994). The effect on Black-White wage differences of differences in the quantity of quality education. *Industrial and Labor Relations Review, 47*(2), 249–64.

National Center for Education Statistics. (2004). *Digest of education statistics, 2003*. Washington, DC: U.S. Department of Education.

National Center for Education Statistics. (2000). *Monitoring school quality: An indicators report*. Washington, DC: U.S. Department of Education, Office of Educational Research and Improvement.

National Center for Education Statistics, Baccalaureate and Beyond Dataset. http://nces.ed.gov/surveys/B&B/.

Neal, D., and Johnson, W. (1996). The role of premarket factors in Black-White wage differences. *Journal of Political Economy, 104*(5), 869–95.

Oaxaca, R. (1973). Male-female wage differentials in urban labor markets. *International Economic Review, 14*(3), 693–709.

Phillips, I. (2002). *Shared governance on Black college campuses.* Retrieved August 3, 2005, from http://web1.epnet.com.ucfproxy.fcla.edu/citation.asp?tb=1andug=sid+810C2FBC%2D7E14.

Ricardo, D. (1817). *Principles of political economy and taxation*. London: J. M. Dent. (A 1911 reprint.)

Rivkin, S., Hanushek, E., and Kain, J. (2002). Teachers, schools and academic achievement. *NBER Working Paper* 6691, revised July.

Roscoe, W. (2001). *What is a historically Black college or university (HBCU)?* Retrieved August 5, 2005, from http://www.thehighschoolgraduate.com/editorial/UShbcu.htm.

Smith, A. (1776). *An inquiry into the nature and causes of the wealth of nations.* Indianapolis, IN: Liberty Press. (A 1981 reprint.)

United Negro College Fund. (2005). *Historically Black colleges and universities (HBCUs)—an historical overview: Why are historically Black colleges and universities important?* Retrieved July 28, 2005, from http://www.uncf.org/aboutus/hbcus.asp.

U.S. Department of Education. (1991). Office for Civil Rights, Washington, DC (2001). Retrieved August 3, 2005, from http://www.ed.gov/about/offices/list/ocr/docs/hq9511.html.

PART III

Interconnections and Common Issues

CHAPTER 14

Social Justice at Historically Black and Hispanic-Serving Institutions

Mission Statements and Administrative Voices

Terrell L. Strayhorn and Joan B. Hirt

What is the role of education in social justice? This question has been revisited periodically over the ages. In ancient times, philosophers believed that education served a social function of preparing individuals for their "place" in society (Plato, 1945). Tracking individuals through schooling into their natural, proper position in society was just. This role of education persisted over centuries. Indeed, colonial colleges served as training schools or seminaries to prepare the elite as clergy and state political leaders (Lucas, 1994).

However, discussions since the mid-twentieth century suggest that allowing individuals to choose their position or place in society is more just and egalitarian (Bogotch, 2000; Gutmann, 1987). This democratic notion of education applies to higher learning as well. The social function of postsecondary education has expanded to include equal access and opportunity for all people including minorities. Education's function has become more closely aligned with notions of upward mobility, equality, equity, and justice (Chang, Whitt, Jones, and Hakuta, 2003). This is particularly true for African Americans and Hispanics.

American higher education traditionally has accommodated African Americans at historically Black colleges and universities (HBCUs) and more recently Latino/a students at Hispanic-Serving Institutions (HSIs). However, these colleges and universities have served a purpose that extends beyond merely educating large numbers of underrepresented students. They have in the past, and continue today, to fulfill a critical social-justice function in America.

Although different socioeconomic, political, and geographic forces shaped HBCUs and HSIs, their commitment to educating underrepresented students has led both types of institutions to play important social justice roles. This chapter addresses the social justice role of HBCUs and HSIs in two ways. First, we employ a blended model of social justice to examine how institutional mission statements of HBCUs and HSIs reflect issues of social justice. Second, we use the same model to examine the perceptions of administrators employed at such institutions to see if they reflect a social-justice perspective.

We address HBCUs and HSIs in this chapter, but it is important to explain why a third type of Minority-Serving Institution (MSI), tribal colleges, was not included. Our work focused on mission statements and administrators. Mission statements for all three types were available to us. We were also readily able to collect data from HBCU and HSI administrators. However, repeated attempts to collect information from tribal college administrators failed, thus, we included only HBCUs and HSIs in our analysis.

We use findings from a recent national study to explore the roles and mission of HBCUs and HSIs relative to social justice. Specifically, the results address the following questions: (*a*) How is social justice reflected in the mission statements of these two types of institutions? (*b*) How is social justice reflected in the comments of administrators who work at such institutions? We begin by describing the conceptual framework we employ and our data sets on HBCUs and HSIs. We then explore the relationship between social justice and the missions of HBCUs and HSIs and how administrators at these campuses embrace notions of social justice.

AN INTEGRATED SOCIAL JUSTICE FRAMEWORK

Social justice is one term with many meanings. The concept has eluded precise definition for centuries. To some, social justice is in obvious contrast with individual justice (Arrigo, 1999; Bedau, 1982; Miller, 1976; Szumski, Debner, O'Neill, Hall, and Jordan, 1984). To others, social justice is closely related to (re-)distributive justice (Hobhouse, 1922/1965; Hochschild, 1982) and the reallocation of scarce resources (Bedau, 1982). Still, a Platonic conception of justice is defined as giving to every person his or her due (Brighouse, 2000; Plato, 1945; Rawls, 1971).

Several models have been posited to conceptualize social justice. Though these models vary in their overall content and structure, a number of commonalities exist. For example, a significant proportion of the models are concerned with the role of power (Arrigo, 1999; Bogotch, 2000) and outcomes such as social change (Bourdieu and Passerson, 1977/1996; Hobhouse, 1922).

To develop an integrated social justice framework, we reviewed several models and identified the common elements among them. Six such elements were revealed. The first of these is power. "Social justice is about power" (Arrigo, 1999, p. 259). Bogotch (2000) argues that social justice requires the moral use of power. That is, social justice necessitates the proper use of power to bring about balance and fairness for all. To that end, social justice is about challenging the *powers that be* or *societal forces* (Terkel, 1977). By challenging the configuration and function (Bourdieu and Passerson, 1977/1996) of such forces, social justice reconceptualizes power so that imbalances are reduced or removed (Arrigo, 1999).

Social justice is also related to changing society. "Critical social justice seeks change" (Arrigo, 1999, p. 260). How this change occurs varies from theory to theory, but the notion that social change is an integral part of social justice is constant. Social justice is concerned with changing material conditions (Bogotch, 2000) and balancing out inequalities in society (Hobhouse, 1922/1965). Equality results from changing society's structure. Thus, social justice anticipates a more harmonious or equitable social organization (Hobhouse). Finally, the individual plays a significant role in social change as he or she is always part of a larger effort to affect change (Rawls, 1971).

Empowerment of the disempowered is a third construct of the model. One goal of social justice is to ensure that all voices are heard—the individual and collective, the empowered and disempowered (Arrigo, 1999). Bogotch (2000) and others point out that social justice is an ongoing struggle to promote individual agency in disempowered members. Justice of this sort aims to analyze systematic oppression, thwart repression, and promote liberty and freedom. Freire (1970) called attention to the fact that in education empowerment is often achieved through "a pedagogy of possibility" (McLaren, 1999, p. 49). That is, educators should empower disempowered students by teaching in ways that promote hope, possibility, self-esteem, and self-worth (Bogotch, 2000; Hobhouse, 1922/1965).

Cultural maintenance and critique is a fourth construct of our integrated model. This construct focuses on the preservation of culture and the maintenance of specific subgroups in society (Bourdieu and Passerson, 1977/1996). Social justice in an educational context emphasizes education as a vehicle for cultural conservation and critique.

Another component of the model is equality of opportunity. Rawls (1971) suggested that the basic idea underlying social justice is fairness. Others posit that social justice involves notions of "equality" (Braham, 1981; Levin, 1981). Equality refers to both equality of opportunity and equality of conditions.

Finally, the sixth construct of the model refers to democracy and citizenship. In many ways, these are the consummate goals of education in a democratic society (Gutmann, 1987; Hochschild, 1982; Dewey, 1916). The literature suggests that there is a relationship between social justice and notions of democracy and citizenship. Social justice is by definition societal and therefore concerned with principles of democracy and citizenship (Arrigo, 1999; Hobhouse, 1922/1965; Plato, 1945). Social justice is closely related to democratic mores, such as the common good, civility, and social responsibility (Bedau, 1982; Hobhouse, 1922). These are key concepts of this final construct.

In summary, borrowing from several models, we identified six constructs to develop an integrated conceptual framework of social justice: (*a*) power, (*b*) social change, (*c*) empowerment of the disempowered, (*d*) cultural maintenance and critique, (*e*) equality of opportunity, and (*f*) democracy and citizenship. This framework is used to examine the role and mission of two types of Minority-Serving Institutions relative to social justice and to highlight elements of social justice embedded in the comments of professionals who work at HBCUs and HSIs.

THE DATA SETS

To examine the relationship between social justice and two types of Minority-Serving Institutions (MSIs), we analyzed two data sets from a national study on the nature of professional life of administrators at various institutional types. The first consisted of institutional mission statements from a purposive sample of HBCUs and HSIs in the United States. The second data set included comments from administrators who work at such institutions. The procedures and sample for this study are described below.

First, we generated a list of all historically Black colleges and all Hispanic-Serving Institutions in the nation. The research team collected institutional mission statements using one of three methods: (*a*) via the internet using each institution's website; (*b*) through undergraduate and graduate catalogs for institutions that did not have mission statements posted on their website; or (*c*) directly from executive officers at the institution. The final data set consisted of missions from 55 HBCUs and 61 HSIs.

Comments from administrators who work at HBCUs and HSIs represented the second database. HBCU administrator data were collected using two procedures. First, we attended a national conference for student affairs professionals who worked at HBCUs. During the conference, we conducted a focus group and collected written responses to the *National Professional Worklife Survey* (NPWS) developed for the study. To add to the data collected at that national conference, the research team contacted the chief student affairs officers at over 25 other HBCUs and asked those institutional leaders if members of their staff would be willing to participate in this study. These administrators provided access to the participants for the researchers. Respondents completed the NPWS and participated in either a group or one-on-one interview. In the end, 70 HBCU administrators provided us with data. They were employed by institutions that represented over one-third of all HBCUs in the country and included officers who worked in residence life, career services, academic advising, admissions, and student activities, among other offices.

HSI administrator data were collected by contacting chief student affairs officers at HSIs and asking them to provide access to administrators on their campuses. Respondents completed the instrument and, if they volunteered, were interviewed by phone. In all, a total of 194 administrators from 61 HSIs provided data for the study. They represented a broad range of functional areas similar to their HBCU counterparts. In all cases, interviews were audiotaped and transcribed in order to facilitate the content analysis of data. This study used qualitative techniques as the primary method of analysis. Qualitative techniques are particularly useful at unpacking the depth of details and results in a wealth of rich, thick data. In fact, the term qualitative implies a focus on meanings and endogenous understandings. Content analysis is a form of naturalistic or qualitative research (Denzin and Lincoln, 2000).

Content analysis was conducted using the integrated social justice framework. The framework provided a useful tool for analyzing the intricate details of the statements and administrators' comments (Reichel and Ramey, 1987; Strayhorn, 2006). While the findings reveal some clear relationships between mission statements, administrators' comments, and social justice, two cautionary notes must be made. Mission statements are public proclamations of an institution's espoused values and may not reveal how committed an institution is to social justice in terms of its curriculum, programs, services, or actions. Second, many respondents were student affairs administrators. Student affairs practitioners are typically drawn to the profession because of their commitment to serve students. In that sense, it is possible they have a natural inclination to issues of social justice. The findings we report in this chapter should be interpreted in light of these qualifications.

SOCIAL JUSTICE AND THE MISSION OF HBCUS AND HSIS

Institutions of higher education exist to achieve certain goals and purposes. Each has its own mission (Lucas, 1994). Mission statements, then, can be viewed as declarations of predetermined institutional goals, roles, and purpose. To the extent that this is true, mission statements provide evidence to understand the relationship between social justice and institutions serving Blacks and Hispanics.

Power

The first construct of the social justice frame is power. Power refers to the authority, control, and influence of individuals and institutions. Evidence of power is revealed in the mission statements of HBCUs and HSIs:

> [Said university] is the premier public institution of higher education in [location], with a growing national and international reputation. Renowned as an institution of access and excellence at both the undergraduate and graduate levels, [said university] is committed to research and discovery, teaching and learning, and public service. [Said university] embraces the multicultural traditions of [location], serves as a center for intellectual and creative resources, and is a catalyst for the economic development of [state] [HSI mission statement].

> [Said university] is a premier historically Black university that nurtures students within a value-based environment focused on excellence in teaching and learning, research, and public service [HBCU mission statement].

Terms like "premier public institution," "premier historically Black university," and "growing national and international reputation" suggest power. Generally, power relates to the position and authority of MSIs in the broader hierarchy of higher education. The evidence suggests that HBCUs and HSIs recognize the role that power can play and may be seeking to establish power through their mission statements—their public pronouncements of status.

Social Change

Social change is related to addressing problems in society. It implies changing the material conditions of society (Bogotch, 2000) and balancing out inequalities (Hobhouse, 1922/1965). In other cases, social change refers to financial benefits such as economic development. Evidence of a desire to promote social change is prevalent in MSI mission statements:

> Students will leave [said institution] prepared for success in the world of work and further studies, possessing a greater appreciation of the history and culture of Africa and the African Diaspora, the struggles and accomplishments of women, and a realization of their own ability and the possibilities to help change the world [HBCU mission statement].

> [Said university] is an urban, multi-campus, research university serving [region], the state, the nation and the international community. It fulfills its mission by imparting knowledge through excellent teaching, promoting public service, discovering new knowledge, solving problems through research, and fostering creativity [HSI mission statement].

Social change is overtly reflected in phrases like "the possibilities to help change the world." Covertly, the mission statements refer to providing students at these institutions opportunities to overcome the inequalities they have faced in life. These overt and covert messages all reflect elements of social change.

Empowerment of the Disempowered

Another construct of the social justice frame is empowerment of the disempowered. That is, social justice seeks to ensure that all voices are heard—the individual and collective, the empowered and disempowered (Arrigo, 1999). Justice of this sort aims to analyze systemic oppression, thwart repression, and empower. Empowerment suggests promoting liberty, tolerance, and freedom. Mission statements reflect these notions:

> [Said] University seeks to instill in its students [a] vision of a world that celebrates God's dwelling within us and among us, where life is reverenced and nurtured, where hatred and injustice are eradicated and where the intellectual life is promoted and supported [HSI mission statement].

> [Said institution] promotes academic excellence in the liberal arts, and develops the intellectual, ethical, and leadership potential of its students. [It] seeks to empower the total person, who appreciates the many cultures of the world and commits to positive social change [HBCU mission statement].

While many postsecondary institutions claim to educate students for success, MSI mission statements specify the empowerment of students. This empowerment is aimed not only at promoting individual success, but also at making the world a place "where hatred and injustice are eradicated" for other disenfranchised groups.

Cultural Maintenance and Critique

Racial pride and identity are also important concepts at these two types of MSIs. These concepts are related to cultural maintenance and critique. Mission statements reflect this element of social justice as follows:

> [Said university] recognizes as a strength the multilingual, multicultural population of the region and state and accepts the responsibility to be particularly mindful and supportive of the unique opportunities afforded by this diversity. The University aspires to promote increased access to all levels of education and to help people better understand and appreciate diversity, tolerance and cooperation. The University is committed to help preserve and enhance the rich cultural heritage of the region it serves and to broaden its student diversity by reaching out to students from other states and nations [HSI mission statement].

> [Said university] embraces the uniqueness and contributions of the African Diaspora, celebrating the value of cultural and intellectual diversity [HBCU mission statement].

Promoting cultural appreciation may be a goal of many colleges and universities, but for MSIs it is a defining characteristic. These institutions have recognized the unique niche they fulfill in terms of elevating cultural awareness to a new level. Appreciating the cultural heritages of their students provides an avenue to supporting those heritages.

Equality of Opportunity

Minority-Serving Institutions are committed to educating traditionally underrepresented students, specifically Blacks and Hispanics. In this way, they seek to ensure access to higher education for such students and to provide equality of opportunity for education. Equality of opportunity is evident in the mission statements:

> [Said] University is a comprehensive, research-oriented, historically Black private university providing an educational experience of exceptional quality to students of high academic potential with particular emphasis upon the provision of educational opportunities to promising Black students [HBCU mission statement].

> The mission of [said university] is to provide a gifted and diverse group of students with a total educational experience of the highest quality—one that prepares them for leadership in an increasingly complex, interdependent and pluralistic world. The distinctive interdisciplinary and multicultural focus on the College's academic program seeks to foster both the fulfillment of individual aspirations and a deeply rooted commitment to the public good. Respect for and the practice of justice, fairness, and integrity—the belief that no attribute such as race, ethnicity, age, or physical ability should impair anyone's access to or enjoyment of any feature of [said university] [HSI mission statement].

Ensuring equal opportunity to higher education is a central goal of HBCUs and HSIs. In particular, these institutions are committed to providing equal access to "an educational experience . . . with particular emphasis upon" minority students. HBCUs and HSIs assert that "no attribute such as race, ethnicity, age, or physical ability should impair . . . access." This reflects their commitment to equality of opportunity.

Democracy and Citizenship

Democracy and citizenship represent the last construct of the social justice frame. In many ways, these are the consummate goals of education in a democratic society (Gutmann, 1987; Hochschild, 1982; Dewey, 1916). Social justice is closely related to democratic values such as the common good, civility, global citizenship, community service, and social responsibility. These are key concepts of this final construct and they are reflected in MSI mission statements.

> [Said] University is a comprehensive research university, unique and irreplaceable, defined by its core values, the excellence of all its activities in instruction, research and service, and by its enduring commitment to educating youth, African Americans and other people of color in particular, for leadership and service to our nation and the global community [HBCU mission statement].

> The University encourages the exchange of ideas; fosters the cultural, emotional, intellectual, physical, and social growth of students; nurtures a lasting appreciation of learning; encourages increased relationships with people of diverse backgrounds; and furthers an appreciation for the benefits and opportunities derived from community involvement. [Said University], through advanced technology and telecommunications, creates opportunities for its students, the faculty and staff, and the communities it serves to participate more fully in educational efforts which provide access to information and outreach to the global community [HSI mission statement].

Instilling values like "leadership and service to our nation and the global community" and "outreach to the global community" are keystones of education at these two types of institutions. Perhaps this focus on democracy and citizenship is driven by the fact that HBCU and HSI students are members of historically disenfranchised groups. Promoting responsible citizenship may be held in higher regard among such groups.

Overall, then, MSI mission statements, while filled with the lofty language endemic to most institutional mission statements also reflect some unique elements. The overt references to issues of empowerment, social change, and citizenship reflect a distinctive social justice orientation at these colleges and universities. Mission statements, however, are written communiqués of an organization's espoused values. Whether those values are enacted in the institution's culture depends in large measure on the professionals who work at those institutions.

SOCIAL JUSTICE AND MSI ADMINISTRATIVE PERSPECTIVES

One way to further explore the nature and role of an institution is to gather information from those who work there. Such comments illustrate not only what the institution *may* be about but also what those who work there *say* it is about. To this end, we interviewed and analyzed comments from student affairs administrators at HBCUs and HSIs. Administrators' comments reflected four social justice concepts: power, empowerment, cultural maintenance and critique, and equality of opportunity.

Power

Power is reflected in the comments from administrators in a number of ways. For example, they talked about the significance of power when comparing themselves to other elite institutions and other MSIs. Consider the following:

> Oh the lack of resources. Not getting our fair share of the pie has always been [a problem for HBCUs] . . . Between now and 2025 there's some HBCUs out of the 103—some of them are going to fail . . . They're just . . . Well you see [name of one troubled HBCU]. Some others are in trouble. [Name of another HBCU] down in [name of state] is already closed. And [name of first HBCU] is on the way [out]. They're not going to make it [HBCU administrator].

> When I look at . . . where my university is we're surrounded by other, I would say more competitive universities—maybe more, how do I say this . . . I think the best word is competitive. More competitive universities. And I always come back, you know . . . I might have a meeting down the street at one of these universities that has a lot more money than we'll ever have and just has so many more resources [HSI administrator].

Recall that power refers to authority in either the institutional or personal sense. In mission statements, HBCUs and HSIs seek to affirm the institutional power they hold in the hierarchy of higher education. In comments from administrators, however, it is the lack of power that is implicit. Administrators at MSIs are acutely aware that the most measurable form of power is resources and resources at these institutions are scarce.

Empowerment of the Disempowered

The notion of empowerment of the disempowered is another construct of the social justice frame reflected in the MSI administrators' comments. It refers to concepts such as liberation, overcoming odds, and amplifying the voices of the silent and disempowered. For example:

> Seeing a first-generation college student succeed and have their family learning right along with them. Even if they go through tough times, and stress times. And you have to understand—yes we are a predominantly Hispanic-Serving Institution, but our target is first-generation. So that's the perspective I'm coming from. It is seeing that student grow inside and outside the classroom, and seeing them succeeding. . . . And seeing that empowerment in a positive way, when all the odds were against them. Or so they thought when they first came. Seeing the multicultural aspect enhances everybody's learning at the institution. Seeing the Hispanic student who had one perspective on life and the world open up and accept, and be accepting, that traditional roles within cultures is not a prescribed mandate for their life. But instead seeing that they have options that they can marry successfully with their culture [HSI administrator].

> I have some of the sharpest students I have EVER seen in life come from an HBCU. And I have some of the students that were so very marginal. [They] come to a college campus like an HBCU and leave here with all the confidence in the world. That enables them to gain that job that makes them shine [HBCU administrator].

Empowerment is evident in the language of HBCU and HSI mission statements, and administrators at these colleges and universities embrace that opportunity to empower students. In fact, it was the most rewarding aspect of the job for many participants. It was often mentioned as an irreplaceable intrinsic reward they believe was unavailable to professionals at other (non-MSI) institutions.

Cultural Maintenance and Critique

The fourth construct of the social-justice frame, cultural maintenance and critique, was reflected in administrative comments. In addition, respondents reported that the reasons they chose to work at a MSI ranged from finding opportunities to fulfill the needs of minority students and minority communities, to meeting their own need of generosity—that is, a way of giving back. These are key concepts of cultural maintenance and critique.

> Yeah, that's the best part of the whole deal and that's why I, like many other people, that's the main reason I got involved in the first place. [I] was looking forward to the opportunity of working with students, to kind of repay the debt that I owe the people who worked with me when I was a student—helped me and my peers to develop, get some appreciation for ourselves and life and all the rest of it [HBCU administrator].

> I think [working at an HSI is] unique because it offers the opportunity to learn, interact, and create community support for our Hispanic population that will be very soon our predominant culture, or "minority group." They WILL become the majority-minority. And seeing good solid education with which our students that will be our leaders and our majority in the future, that will in many ways rule decisions we make—both community and state wide, as well as within our country [HSI administrator].

> I think the sense of accomplishment, and for me—and I've worked in this business for a long time—being really, really able to give back. And knowing that I'm in an area that I feel is MY purpose in life. And to be able to really give back and to be a part of molding and shaping another young person's life, especially young African Americans. And that is my greatest joy [HBCU administrator].

The overt commitment to promoting cultural interests of minority students cited in missions statements of MSIs is mirrored in comments from administrators at HBCUs and HSIs. Sentiments like these were repeated time and again by participants. Unequivocally they believe that working at a MSI enables them to maintain the cultural traditions of the students they serve. Often, these are their own cultural traditions, but nevertheless an allegiance to cultural awareness and maintenance is pervasive among administrative professionals at these institutions.

Equality of Opportunity

Equality of opportunity is reflected in administrators' comments in a number of ways. For example, they talked about their own opportunity to help underserved minority students as well as the opportunity given to minority students who attend MSIs:

> I think it's the opportunity to serve an underserved population. I think that's the most unique thing is that we have an opportunity to reach out to a group of students that have been underserved and ARE being underserved [HSI administrator].

> So I think that the HBCU still is the place . . . where first-generation students and parents [come]; that we are still the beacon of hope for students. We are still that land of opportunity. We are still that place that if I can make it, they're going to love me enough on that campus to enable me to make it [HBCU administrator].

> But I can tell you from my perspective that it is really very rewarding to know that I'm helping a group of people that need a break—because many of them are sons and daughters of migratory workers. They do not have the complete education that some of our more fortunate students have. So it's wonderful to see them come in and be able to counsel them and help them to develop the skills they need to be successful here and then to see them go on and graduate and do big things—become attorneys and city council people and take their places in business and industry as well. And that's very, very wonderful [HSI administrator].

Nearly all the administrators we interviewed talked about providing access to higher education for members of underserved populations. Indeed, equality of opportunity seemed at the heart of their work for many. In this regard, administrators have purposefully and willingly embraced the social justice notions engendered in the mission statements of their institutions.

CONCLUSION

In conclusion, it seems clear that MSIs are committed to serving traditionally underrepresented students and fulfilling roles related to social justice. Though such institutions developed out of different sociopolitical contexts, they serve strikingly similar roles in terms of social justice. Historically Black colleges were established to ensure access to higher education for Blacks at a time when few White colleges would even admit them. Hispanic-Serving Institutions, on the other hand, were recently added to the higher education landscape as a result of changing demographic trends. Despite these differences in origin, HBCUs and HSIs share a similar role relative to social justice.

This role is formally reflected in the mission statements of MSIs. These statements relate to external parties what the institutions are supposed to be about. The mission statements we analyzed encompass elements of social justice in overt and covert formats and make clear the commitment of these colleges and universities to principles like empowerment, social change, and democracy. What formalized statements say about a campus, however, are only meaningful if those sentiments are actualized in the campus culture. Comments from HBCU and HSI administrators suggest they are. There is a commitment to educating the disempowered and to sustaining and promoting the cultural heritages of students from underrepresented groups that is resoundingly clear in the perceptions of student affairs administrators on these campuses. The congruency between what the mission statements reveal and what administrators report suggest that social justice is an entrenched value at these colleges and universities. Indeed, social justice may serve as the guidepost for these institutions that fulfill a unique niche in the higher education hierarchy in America.

HBCUs and HSIs serve as instruments for social change and strive to educate leaders among targeted populations who will become responsible citizens, empower themselves and others, and work to effect social change. All of these are issues of social justice and speak to the important role that historically Black and Hispanic-Serving Institutions play in the American higher education arena.

REFERENCES

Anderson, J. D. (1988). *The education of Blacks in the south, 1865–1930.* Chapel Hill, NC: The University of North Carolina Press.

Arrigo, B. A. (1999). *Social justice, criminal justice: The maturation of critical theory in law, crime, and deviance.* Belmont, CA: West/Wadsworth.

Bedau, H. A. (1982). Social justice: What it is and why it matters. In Bowling Green State University (Ed.), *Social Justice* (pp. 85–98). Bowling Green, OH: The Applied Philosophy Program, Bowling Green State University.

Bogotch, I. E. (2000). Educational leadership and social justice: Theory into practice. Paper presented at the Annual meeting of the University Council for Educational Administration (UCEA), Albuquerque, New Mexico.

Bourdieu, P., and Passerson, J. C. (1977/1996). *Reproduction in education, society, and culture.* Thousand Oaks, CA: Sage Publications.

Braham, R. L. (Ed.). (1981). *Social Justice.* Boston, MA: Martinus Nijhoff Publishing.

Brighouse, H. (2000). *School choice and social justice.* New York: Oxford University Press.

Browning, J. E. S., and Williams, J. B. (1978). History and goals of Black institutions of higher learning. In C. V. Willie and R. R. Edmonds (Eds.), *Black colleges in America: Challenge, development, survival* (pp. 68–93). New York: Teachers College Press.

Chang, M. J., Whitt, D., Jones, J., and Hakuta, K. (2003). *Compelling interest: Examining the evidence on racial dynamics in colleges and universities.* Stanford, CA: Stanford University Press.

Denzin, N. K., and Lincoln, Y. S. (2000). *Handbook of qualitative research.* Thousand Oaks, CA: Sage.

Dewey, J. (1916). *Democracy and education.* New York: The MacMillan Company.

Friere, P. (1970). *Pedagogy of the oppressed.* New York: Continuum.

Gutmann, A. (1987). *Democratic education.* Princeton, NJ: Princeton University Press.

Hirt, J. B. (2006). *Where you work matters: Student affairs administration at different types of institutions.* Lanham, MD: University Press of America.

Hispanic yearbook. (2002). McLean, VA: TIYM Publishing Company.

Hobhouse, L. T. (1922/1965). *The elements of social justice.* London: George Allen and Unwin Ltd.

Hochschild, J. (1982). Justice, the poor and the redistribution of wealth. In Bowling Green State University (Ed.), *Social justice* (pp. 55–67). Bowling Green, OH: The Applied Philosophy Program, Bowling Green State University.

Laden, B. V. (2001). Hispanic-serving institutions: Myths and realities. *Peabody Journal of Education, 76,* 73–92.

Levin, M. (1981). Equality of opportunity. In R. L. Braham (Ed.), *Social justice* (pp. 55–78). Boston, MA: Martinus Nijhoff Publishing.

Lucas, C. (1994). *American higher education: A history.* New York: St. Martin's Griffin.

McLaren, P. (1999). A pedagogy of possibility: Reflecting upon Paulo Freire's politics of education. *Educational Researcher, 28*(2), 49–54.

Miller, D. (1976). *Social justice.* Oxford: Oxford University Press.

Plato. (1945). *The Republic of Plato* (F. M. Cornford, Trans.). New York: Oxford University Press. (Original work published 360 BCE.)

Rawls, J. (1971). *A theory of justice.* Cambridge, MA: Harvard University Press.

Reichel, M., and Ramey, M. A. (Eds.). (1987). *Conceptual frameworks for bibliographic education: Theory to practice.* Littleton, CO: Libraries Unlimited, Inc.

Strayhorn, T. L. (2006). *Frameworks for assessing learning and development outcomes.* Washington, DC: Council for the Advancement of Standards in Higher Education.

Szumski, B., Debner, C., O'Neill, T., Hall, L., and Jordan, P. (Eds.). (1984). *Social justice: Opposing viewpoints.* St. Paul, MN: Greenhaven Press.

Terkel, S. (1977). *Talking to myself: A memoir of my times.* New York: Pantheon Books.

U.S. Census Bureau. (2002). *Resident population estimates of the United States by sex, race, and Hispanic origin: April 1 to July 1, 1999, with short-term projection to June 1, 2001.* Washington, DC: Author.

U. S. Department of Education. (2005). *Enrollment in postsecondary institutions, Fall 2003; Graduation rates 1997 and 2000 cohorts; and financial statistics, fiscal year 2003.* Washington, DC: Author.

U. S. Department of Education. (1995). *Fall enrollment in colleges and universities; IPEDS Fall enrollment survey.* Washington, DC: Author.

Wallenstein, P. R. (2000, Fall). Colleges of 1862, Colleges of 1890, and HBCUs: A brief account of past and present. *Diversity News, 7,* 8–9, 11.

Wallenstein, P. R. (2004). Higher education and civil rights: South Carolina, 1860s–1960s. *History of Higher Education Annual, 23,* 1–22.

CHAPTER 15

Student Engagement and Student Success at Historically Black and Hispanic-Serving Institutions

Brian K. Bridges, Jillian Kinzie,
Thomas F. Nelson Laird, and George D. Kuh

The changing demographics of college students in the United States are well-documented. Less is known about the quality of undergraduate education and student experiences at Minority-Serving Institutions (MSIs)—Hispanic-Serving Institutions (HSIs), Historically Black Colleges and Universities (HBCUs), and Tribal Colleges and Universities (TCUs).

Significant progress has been made over the last 35 years in enrolling more students from groups historically underrepresented in U.S. colleges and universities (Bauman & Graf, 2003). This progress of minority student enrollment and the growth in importance of MSIs has been well-documented throughout this book. By all accounts, MSIs are important sources of educational opportunity for the growing proportion of underrepresented students. Although they have unique histories, purposes, and campus cultures, MSIs share a common goal in their commitment to educate underserved populations. Given the students they serve, it would be instructive for all postsecondary institutions to better understand the nature of the student experience at MSIs and the factors and conditions they create to help their students succeed.

PURPOSE AND OVERVIEW

Toward the end of helping institutions better understand their students, this chapter focuses on the experiences of baccalaureate degree-seeking students at HSIs and HBCUs. We rely on data from the National Survey of Student Engagement (NSSE)—a survey that annually measures the extent to which students at four-year colleges and universities engage in educational practices associated with high levels of learning and development. It would be worthwhile to also examine students' experiences at tribal colleges. However, only a small number of these institutions award baccalaureate degrees and, consequently, too few participate in NSSE to allow us to make meaningful statements about their students' experiences. We, therefore, concentrate on analyses that examine students' experiences at the other two types of MSIs.

More specifically, we explore three questions: (1) to what extent do students at HBCUs and HSIs engage in effective educational practices—activities empirically related to desired learning and personal development outcomes of college?; (2) Do the experiences of students at HBCUs and HSIs differ in distinctive ways from their counterparts attending Predominantly White Institutions (PWIs)?; (3) What can we learn from educationally effective HBCUs and HSIs, those that engage and graduate students at higher-than-predicted levels? What conditions do they create to facilitate student success and what can we learn from them that can be adapted by other colleges and universities to engage students at higher levels?

Our analyses draw for the most part on the survey data from NSSE. We also summarize key findings from the Documenting Effective Educational Practice (DEEP) project (Kuh, Kinzie, Schuh, Whitt & Associates, 2005), a study of twenty strong performing colleges and universities, that enable us to describe some distinguishing features of HBCUs and HSIs and the conditions they create to facilitate minority student success.

The chapter is divided into three parts. First, we briefly review the literature about student engagement and related aspects of the undergraduate experience at HBCUs and HSIs. In the second part, we examine engagement patterns of students at these institutions and look more closely at HBCUs and HSIs that appear to outperform other institutions of their type, seeking clues about what they do that makes them more educationally effective. We close with a discussion of student engagement and educational effectiveness at HBCUs and HSIs.

THE STUDENT EXPERIENCE AT HBCUS AND HSIS: A REVIEW

A substantial body of research indicates that students from all ethnic backgrounds benefit from participating in educationally effective activities, inside and outside the classroom. Among these desired outcomes are cognitive development (Anaya, 1996; Kuh, 1995); psychosocial development and positive images of self (Badura, Millard, Peluso, & Ortman, 2000; Chickering & Reisser,

1993); moral and ethical development (Jones & Watt, 1999; Liddell & Davis, 1996); and persistence (Berger & Milem, 1999; Swail, with Redd and Perna, 2003). At the same time, some studies show that minority students must contend with circumstances that may prevent them from taking full advantage of learning opportunities, especially at PWIs (Crosson, 1988; Feagin, Vera, & Imani, 1996; Swail et al., 2003; Turner, 1994). In large part, this is due to substandard pre-college educational preparation and higher proportions of students from low socioeconomic backgrounds and first-generation origins.

Hispanic populations are concentrated in urban centers that tend to contain severely segregated neighborhoods of lower socioeconomic status. Inadequate high school preparation often leads either to high drop-out rates or low college-going rates, which in turn affects the Hispanic baccalaureate pipeline (Garcia, 2001; O'Brien & Zudak, 1998). The average Hispanic student is less likely to pursue and complete a baccalaureate degree in comparison to White, Asian, and African American students (Benitez, 1998; Miller & Garcia, 2004; O'Brien & Zudak, 1998). In addition, Hispanic students—the vast majority of whom are the first in their families to go to college—face difficulties that include academic underpreparedness, racism, and disconcerting messages that create tensions between their culture of orientation, familial obligations, and educational aspirations (Dayton, Gonzalez-Vasquez, Martinez, & Plum, 2004; Ortiz, 2004).

Hoffman, Llagas, and Snyder (2003) reported that African American students were likely to attend public high schools with high minority concentrations from low socioeconomic communities, were less likely than White students to take advanced mathematics and science courses, and were less likely than White or Hispanic students to take advanced placement exams. According to O'Brien and Zudak (1998, p. 7), "African Americans and Hispanics are increasingly isolated in inferior schools" and that "both groups are far more likely than Whites to attend schools in areas of concentrated poverty" (see also Garcia, 2001; Orfield, 1997). O'Brien and Zudak (1998) concluded that segregated neighborhoods usually equate to inferior resources, which eventually results in inferior levels of education for minority groups. Collectively, the research on Hispanic and African American students suggests that these two groups face serious, although not identical, challenges when they attend PWIs.

MOVING THROUGH: WHAT STUDENTS EXPERIENCE AT HBCUS AND HSIS

African American students' experiences at HBCUs differ in some important ways from their counterparts attending PWIs. Generally, African American students at HBCUs tend to be more satisfied, more confident, and gain more in academic and personal development (Allen, 1986, 1992; Allen, Epps, & Haniff, 1991; DeSousa & Kuh, 1996; Fleming, 1984, 2001; Flowers & Pascarella, 1999; Watson & Kuh, 1996). Flowers and Pascarella (1999) found that African American students' openness to racial and cultural diversity is not hindered by the homogeneous environment of an HBCU, even though they tend not to report as many experiences with diversity (Kuh & Umbach, 2005). Another study indicates that African American HBCU students devote more effort to academic activities; report more significant gains in intellectual development, critical thinking, and cultural awareness; and enjoy greater personal and social benefits than African Americans at PWIs (DeSousa & Kuh, 1996).

The effects of attending PWIs and HBCUs for African American students are not always consistent across all outcomes, especially when pre-college academic preparation is taken into consideration. African American students' prior academic ability may play a more significant role in shaping cognitive outcomes than perceptions of discrimination and the academic performance for African American students at HBCUs and PWIs may be more of a function of pre-college differences in students' educational preparation than of institutional environments (Cabrera et al.,1999; Kim, 2002). However, the preponderance of evidence supports the notion that HBCU attendance has a significant positive effect on many African American student outcomes, especially graduation rates.

The relatively small amount of literature on Hispanic students at HSIs yields limited and mixed results (Abraham et al., 2002; Benitez, 1998; Dayton, et al., 2004; Laden, 1999, 2001, 2004). According to Laden (2004), "many HSIs offer a variety of academic and student support programs and holistic approaches that are specifically designed to raise Latino student aspirations and enhance their retention and completion rates" (p. 193). Dayton et al. (2004) and Laden (2001, 2004) suggest that faculty and administrators, particularly those who are Hispanic, can play a key role in facilitating academic and social integration as well as academic success. However, as Laden (2004) indicates, it is not clear how widespread these benefits are at HSIs.

UNIQUE MISSIONS: EDUCATIONAL PRACTICE AND CAMPUS CULTURES AT HBCUS AND HSIS

HBCUs and HSIs differ in significant ways, as illustrated by their varied institutional legacies and cultures (Raines, 1998). HBCUs were created specifically to educate African Americans and served primarily as their only postsecondary option until the mid-twentieth century. One legacy of this history is that the environments on these campuses are tailored to promote

African American collegiate success. In contrast, nearly all HSIs were founded first as PWIs, which have only in the last decade or two come to serve increasing numbers of Hispanic students. As a result, compared with HBCUs, HSIs do not have the same clarity of mission or developed policies and practices that are sensitive to the cultures from which their students originate (Dayton et al., 2004). Instead, HSIs are primarily the result of social, political, economic, and demographic shifts of the past 30 years (Laden, 2001).

Although some claim that HBCUs do not reflect the world in which students compete after graduation, there is evidence that these institutions provide a socially representative setting that fosters student engagement, retention, and success in college (Allen et al., 1991). Some research also suggests that a critical mass of Hispanic faculty, administrators, and programs at HSIs can have similarly positive effects on Hispanic students (Dayton et al., 2004; Swail et al., 2003). While HBCUs appear to be relatively effective in inducing student engagement and academic success among African American students, much less is known about the Hispanic student experience at HSIs compared with PWIs. In fact, given the differences in how HBCUs and HSIs developed, there is room to speculate that the impact of attending an HSI for Hispanic students is probably less than that for African American students attending HBCUs.

THEORETICAL PERSPECTIVES ON THE STUDENT EXPERIENCE AT HBCUS AND HSIS

Two perspectives inform our exploration of the student experience at institutions that serve large numbers of African American and Hispanic students: habitus and human capital theory. Bourdieu's central construct of habitus provides an understanding of what happens to many historically underserved students during college. Habitus is a system of enduring dispositions that incorporates previous experiences which can impose unconscious limits on an individual's educational and career aspirations (Bourdieu & Passeron, 1977). All aspects of a students' social condition, including race/ethnicity and gender, play a part in the development of habitus. Habitus also shapes individual actions, such as choosing a major field or their perceptions of whether certain opportunities are available to them, such as doing research with a faculty member or studying abroad. Because race and gender are embodied in the conception of habitus, it is an instructive lens through which we can deepen our understanding and appreciation for how students' background characteristics and pre-college experiences combine to shape what they do and the meaning they make of college life (Horvat, 2003).

The habitus perspective is also a heuristic for exploring the complex and deep-rooted patterns that have limited access of historically underserved students to postsecondary educational opportunities. The construct is especially useful for understanding individual behavior when grounded in a specific social or educational setting (Lareau & Horvat, 1998).

Although habitus can perpetuate self-conceptions of low status and may predispose students to use less productive educational strategies, it also has a dynamic component that accommodates the possibility that students can adopt new approaches to managing academic and social challenges. Developing new ways of responding can be triggered in different ways, such as encounters with new situations, exposure to the habitus of others, or interacting with people who originate from very different backgrounds, all of which occur with regularity in the college environment (Harker, 1984; Lamont & Lareau, 1988). Therefore, because students come to college with habitus that mediates their participation in and interpretation of various educational activities, understanding the background characteristics and precollege experiences of underserved students in the context of HBCUs and HSIs contrasted with that of their counterparts at PWIs will help us better understand their collegiate experiences and what they get from college.

Human capital theory also guides our work. Attending college can be a liberating, developmentally powerful experience with the potential to increase individual productivity and, to some degree, the quality of life of the larger society (Williams & Swail, 2005). According to a human capital model, the acquisition of knowledge and skills raises the value of individuals' human capital, resulting in their increased employability, productivity, and earnings potential (Becker, 1964). Colleges and universities can help create additional measures of human capital for their students by increasing their knowledge, developing their critical thinking abilities, and cultivating sensibilities and dispositions that support lifelong learning. In this view, postsecondary institutions are obliged to strengthen human capital by educating more students with varied backgrounds than ever before. McCabe (2000) estimates that as many as 85 percent of high school graduates in the coming decade will need postsecondary education to attain the level of knowledge and skills necessary to manage in an increasingly complex world. The demands for education require increased attention to insure that all students who enroll in some form of postsecondary education succeed.

Taken together, the habitus and human capital perspectives provide an accounting of some of the key factors that come into play to shape what historically underserved students are prepared to do when they get to college and influence the meanings they make of their experiences. Another key factor bearing on their chances for success in college is the degree to which they engage in activities that are associated with academic achievement and persistence. This concept is called "student engagement."

Student engagement represents two critical features. The first is the amount of time and effort students invest in their studies and other educationally purposeful activities. The second is how the institution allocates its resources and organizes curricula, other learning opportunities, and support services to encourage students to participate in activities consistent with persistence, satisfaction, learning and graduation (Kuh, 2001). The second aspect of student engagement represents the margin of educational quality that institutions contribute—a measure of value added—and something that a college or university can influence to some degree. By learning more about student engagement at HBCUs and HSIs, it is possible to identify the engagement practices that may mediate student background characteristics and predispositions, increase our understanding of how differences in students' backgrounds affect their experiences in college, and enhance the capacity of institutions to develop human capital of increasingly diverse student populations.

STUDENT ENGAGEMENT IN EFFECTIVE EDUCATIONAL PRACTICES AT HBCUS, HSIS, AND PWIS

To begin to answer the questions posed earlier in this chapter about the nature of student engagement at HBCUs, HSIs, and PWIs, we turn to data collected in 2004 and 2005 by the National Survey of Student Engagement. With about 500 four-year institutions participating each of these years, including about 70 HBCUs and HSIs, the database includes a substantial amount of information about the college experiences of Hispanic/Latino/a and African American students at institutions with different racial compositions. More specifically, the findings reported later are based on responses from about 16,000 Hispanic/Latino/a students from 36 HSIs (26 public, 10 private) and 639 PWIs (274 public, 365 private), as well as 23,000 African American students from 37 HBCUs (23 public, 14 private) and 650 PWIs (276 public, 374 private).

NSSE questions focus on the frequency with which students participate in what prior research has shown to be effective educational practices. For example, students are asked how often they participated in a community-based project as a part of a course, discussed ideas with faculty outside of class, and used an electronic medium for an assignment. In addition, students identify the degree to which their courses emphasize different mental processes (e.g., memorizing and analyzing), how many hours per week they spend studying, working, or participating in co-curricular activities, as well as how they would characterize their relationships with people on campus (the survey is available through the NSSE website, www.nsse.iub.edu).

Our analyses focused on the differences in background characteristics of students who attend HSIs, HBCUs, and PWIs and their engagement in effective educational practices in college. These student level characteristics provide insight about the habitus for these groups. On balance, it appears that background characteristics and previous experiences play a role in the type of institution a student chooses to attend, but the dynamic differs for African Americans and Hispanics, depending on the type of institution they attend.

African American students at HBCUs are more likely than African American students at PWIs to live on campus and be enrolled full-time. Seniors at HBCUs are also more likely to have mothers with higher levels of education. In addition, HBCU students are less likely to be older and be transfer students. First-year HBCU students are less likely to be female than their PWI counterparts.

In contrast, HSI students are more likely than their counterparts at PWIs to be older and transfer students. Senior students at HSIs are more likely to be female. At the same time, students at HSIs are less likely to have mothers with higher levels of education, be full-time students, be members of a fraternity or sorority, be an athlete, and live on campus.

Given these differences, our interest in comparing and understanding better the experiences of students at HSIs and HBCUs, and their counterparts at PWIs, takes on an additional level of complexity. If, indeed, Hispanic/Latino/a students at HSIs start with different dispositions and preferences rooted in habitus than Hispanic/Latino/a students at PWIs, we can speculate as to whether or not HSI attendance mediates this difference. For HBCUs, the question turns toward determining whether the differences between African American students at HBCUs and PWIs are a function of a difference in students' experiences and outcomes after controlling for their background characteristics.

Analyzing student engagement and educational gains of Hispanic/Latino/a students at HSIs and PWIs and African American students at HBCUs and PWIs reveals distinct patterns for the groups (tables 15.1 and 15.2). Except for a couple of areas, students attending HBCUs show positive effects consistent with previous research that show advantages for these institutions, such as African American HBCU students reporting greater intellectual gains than their counterparts at PWIs and more frequent interactions with faculty (Allen, 1992; Flowers, 2003). Our findings also corroborate the widespread perception that HBCUs provide more supportive learning environments for their students. For example, compared with their counterparts at PWIs, HBCU African American students report having more contact with faculty, a greater belief that their institutions contribute to their spiri-

Table 15.1 Differences Between Students at HBCUs and PWIs on Effective Educational Practices and Outcomes

	First-year students		Seniors	
Measure	ES no controls	ES with controls	ES no controls	ES with controls
Academic challenge	−0.01	−0.01	0.06**	0.03
Higher-order thinking	0.00	0.01	0.06**	0.04
Active & collaborative learning	0.25***	0.23***	0.42***	0.31***
Participation in community project	0.30***	0.28***	0.44***	0.38***
Student-faculty interaction	0.13***	0.08**	0.36***	0.25***
Discussion with faculty outside of class	0.17***	0.14***	0.34***	0.28***
Enriching educational experiences	−0.03	−0.01	0.20***	0.09**
Diverse interactions	−0.38***	−0.37***	−0.29***	−0.32***
Community service or volunteer	0.18***	0.17***	0.23***	0.15***
Used electronic medium for assignment	0.06**	0.07*	0.09***	0.04
Supportive campus environment	−0.06**	−0.09***	0.16***	0.09***
Relationships with others on campus	−0.12***	−0.15***	0.04	−0.02
Institution emphasizes academic support	−0.19***	−0.19***	−0.02	−0.07**
Satisfaction	−0.27***	−0.21***	−0.12***	−0.09***
Overall Gains	0.15***	0.12***	0.29***	0.23***
Working effectively with others	0.04*	−0.01	0.16***	0.08**
Voting in elections	0.36***	0.34***	0.56***	0.49***
Understanding yourself	0.18***	0.15***	0.27***	0.24***
Understanding people of other races/ethnicity	0.01	−0.01	0.17***	0.15***
Contributing to the welfare of the community	0.17***	0.18***	0.33***	0.31***
Sense of spirituality	0.32***	0.32***	0.48***	0.47***

* $p < .05$; ** $p < .01$; *** $p < .001$

Note: Control variables include student background and collegiate characteristics as well as institutional size and control.

tual growth, and a greater sense that their campus experience has contributed to their community involvement and civic engagement. Students at HBCUs also report greater increases in self-understanding and in the likelihood they will vote.

Consistent with Kuh and Umbach (2005), HBCU students report fewer experiences with diversity compared with students elsewhere, one of the negative effects associated with attending an HBCU. This is to be expected, given that HBCU enrollments are slightly over 80 percent African American on average (Provasnik & Shafer, 2004). Some other differences were mild surprises. For example, contrary to previous research, African American students at PWIs were more satisfied with their overall experience than African American HBCU students. In addition, first-year HBCU students did not

Table 15.2 Differences Between Students at HSIs and PWIs on Effective Educational Practices and Outcomes

	First-year students		Seniors	
Measure	ES no controls	ES with controls	ES no controls	ES with controls
Academic challenge	−0.08***	−0.02	0.01	0.07*
Higher-order thinking	−0.07**	−0.01	−0.01	0.06
Active & collaborative learning	−0.03	0.08**	0.09***	0.18***
Participation in community project	−0.06*	0.06*	0.07**	0.14***
Student-faculty interaction	−0.06*	0.04	−0.11***	0.04
Discussion with faculty outside of class	−0.05*	0.03	−0.06	0.04
Enriching educational experiences	−0.22***	−0.04	−0.31***	−0.05*
Diverse interactions	−0.30***	−0.13***	−0.27***	−0.11***
Community service or volunteer	−0.10***	0.03	−0.18***	−0.02
Used electronic medium for assignment	−0.08**	−0.04	0.05*	0.06*
Supportive campus environment	−0.03	0.07**	0.02	0.09***
Relationships with others on campus	0.03	0.10***	0.07**	0.08**
Institution emphasizes academic support	−0.08***	−0.00	−0.06*	0.02
Satisfaction	−0.10***	−0.04	−0.07**	−0.03
Overall Gains	0.01	0.07**	0.06*	0.12***
Working effectively with others	0.04	0.08**	0.05*	0.09***
Voting in elections	0.01	0.02	0.00	0.04
Understanding yourself	−0.00	0.05	−0.02	0.05*
Understanding people of other races/ethnicity	0.09***	0.11***	0.18***	0.20***
Contributing to the welfare of the community	−0.13***	0.00	−0.01	0.09***
Sense of spirituality	−0.05*	0.09**	0.01	0.13***

* $p < .05$; ** $p < .01$; *** $p < .001$

Note: Control variables include student background and collegiate characteristics as well as institutional size and control.

perceive their campus environment to be as supportive as their counterparts at PWIs, especially in terms of providing academic support.

The results of the HSI analyses do not distinguish between institutions and students to the same degree as the HBCU analyses, yet the results are potentially instructive. While the differences in student engagement for Hispanic students at HSIs and PWIs are generally quite small (effect sizes between -0.20 and 0.20), there appears to be a mitigating effect of attending an HSI. That is, without statistical controls for student background characteristics, the effects of Hispanic students attending HSIs tend to be unfavorable. However, when controls for gender, mother's education, enrollment status, and transfer status are entered, the HSI results improve slightly, suggesting a small compensatory effect for attending an HSI. In fact, controlling for student characteristics when they enter college—factors related to habitus perhaps—HSIs show a few, albeit very small, positive effects. For the most part, these effects stay small after controls are introduced. The results for seniors show the most sizable positive effects across the analyses (though relatively modest in size) on active and collaborative learning and gains in understanding people of other races/ethnicities.

To foreshadow our discussion of key findings from high performing HBCUs and HSIs in the next section, we examined the NSSE data to determine whether the presence of faculty members of the same ethnicity is a factor in student engagement. To do this, we compared NSSE scores of students at HSIs where at least 10 percent of the faculty are Hispanic with the scores of students at HSIs with a smaller percentage of Hispanic faculty members. At HSIs where Hispanics made up 10 percent or more of the faculty, students interacted more often with faculty and participated more frequently in active and collaborative learning activities and enriching educational experiences such as community service. This finding is consistent with other research showing that minority faculty members are more likely to use effective educational practices than White faculty members (Kuh, Nelson Laird, & Umbach, 2004).

CULTURES AND PRACTICES THAT FOSTER STUDENT SUCCESS AT HBCUS AND HSIS

NSSE data indicate that students of color at HBCUs and HSIs have educational experiences that differ in appreciable ways from their counterparts at PWIs. What are the programs, policies, practices and institutional cultures that might account for these differences? What can we learn about educational effectiveness from MSIs and their unique contributions that could be instructive for institutions interested in improving the conditions for underrepresented students in higher education? We can provide some answers to these questions from the Documenting Effective Educational Practice (DEEP) project.

Project DEEP was coordinated by the NSSE Institute for Effective Educational Practice at the Indiana University Center for Postsecondary Research with support from Lumina Foundation for Education and the Center of Inquiry in the Liberal Arts at Wabash College. A team of 24 researchers conducted in-depth case studies of 20 four-year colleges and universities that had both higher-than-predicted graduation rates and NSSE scores to discover what these strong performers do to promote high levels of student success (Kuh et al., 2005). Two HSIs—California State University, Monterey Bay (CSUMB) and the University of Texas at El Paso (UTEP); and two HBCUs—Fayetteville State University (FSU) and Winston-Salem State

University (WSSU) were in the study. Although the major findings from the study cut across the 20 institutions, HBCUs and HSIs enact distinct elements of effective practice.

The HBCUs and HSIs in the DEEP study had clearly articulated and unique educational missions that provided a rationale for the institutions' educational programs, policies, and practices. From its founding as an HSI in 1994, California State University, Monterey Bay (CSUMB) continued to evolve and distinguish itself as an innovative, learner-centered educational institution. The university integrates interdisciplinary academic programs, active and collaborative learning, and service learning throughout its curriculum. Its mission is clear and compelling, focusing squarely on "Vision Students," a reference to the population of students the institution is committed to serving—those who historically have been denied educational opportunity due to their socioeconomic or racial-ethnic backgrounds. The use of the term provides a constant reminder to faculty and staff of the institution's commitment to serving students whose life experiences and socioeconomic conditions have historically precluded their participation in higher education.

Winston-Salem State University's (WSSU) motto "Enter to learn, depart to serve," represents the university's educational philosophy and expectations—that those that enter its gates be open to learning and be willing to repay the debt they owe to society for the privilege of education. Toward that end, WSSU concentrates its efforts on helping students develop leadership skills based on a firm academic and social foundation. The widespread use of shared language and implicit terms ensures that the mission is understood by all members of the campus community.

The belief that all students can learn, regardless of their entering level preparation, and that the role of the institution is to do everything possible to ensure student success, is another salient feature that cuts across these four campuses. CSUMB's well-developed outcomes-based education approach provides a structure to clearly communicate educational expectations and outcomes to students. Moreover, CSUMB faculty adopted an assets-based philosophy of talent development, in which students' strengths, such as their ability to speak Spanish and their extensive work experience, are first assessed and then connected in meaningful ways to course and program-based learning objectives. FSU faculty and administrators manifest their commitment to student success by setting and holding students to high expectations. Challenging students with a "nobody fails here" attitude, faculty recognize, but do not lament, that their students may not be as well-prepared for college as they would like. Their motto is: "We work with the students we have, not those we wish we had" (Kuh et al., 2005, p. 117). These beliefs about human potential and the transformative power of higher education are deeply rooted in the institution's culture.

Community service tends to be another characteristic of effective educational practice at MSIs. Students attending WSSU, CSUMB, and UTEP participated in community service at particularly high levels, largely because such experiences were required through service learning and other mechanisms. For example, CSUMB requires all students to complete a lower and upper-level service learning experience and WSSU requires students in the freshmen seminar to complete 15 service hours during their first semester. These initiatives connect students to the local community and helps develop social responsibility by encouraging students to give back to their communities. Moreover, through service experiences, students at WSSU have the chance to build social connections with their peers.

HBCUs and HSIs in Project DEEP also employed engaging pedagogies to a high degree at all levels of the educational program. Faculty at FSU experimented with different instructional methods, including on-line discussion boards, games and contests, and assigning points to actively engage students. The College of Business, for example, requires upper division students to evaluate each other's group projects. Following the evaluations, students must list what they learned from the process. One faculty member summarized the importance of experimentation in the classroom when he stated: "If you don't engage students, you quickly lose them" (Kuh et al., 2005, p. 70).

Faculty at UTEP also frequently and skillfully use active and collaborative learning approaches in class. Most importantly, UTEP faculty members understand that many of their students must be taught how to get the most out of active and collaborative learning activities. All new students must complete an introduction to critical thinking course that emphasizes how to collaborate, work in teams, and participate actively in class. In addition, UTEP has facilitated its predominately first-generation, commuter students' connections to the institution and to their classmates via learning communities in which first-year students co-enroll in two or three courses. The structure of coordinated enrollment fosters study group development, in and out of class collaboration, and links students to peers who can help them focus on course requirements.

Faculty members and administrators at HBCUs and HSIs are committed to frequent, meaningful contacts with their students and to being good role models. Many HBCU faculty members described themselves as devoted to mentoring African American students as a way to give back to their community. These institutions also provide numerous well-designed opportunities for students and faculty to connect early in the educational process. Again, this was particularly true at the HBCUs where opportunities for students to interact with faculty in their major were common elements of the academic program. For example, freshman seminars at WSSU are discipline specific to facilitate early bonds with faculty in students' intended major. At FSU, every student is assigned a faculty advisor who also teaches their freshman seminar course, thus, students are in contact with their advisors several times a week. This regular contact presents ongoing opportunities to talk about academic, career, and personal matters that might affect the student's academic performance. Also, because advisors are seminar instructors, they have firsthand knowledge of what students are learning in class. These early experiences with influential adults help insure student success in all aspects of college life.

In sum, strong performing HBCUs and HSIs enact effective educational practices to a high degree and are intentional about creating conditions that support students academically and socially. They have in place policies and practices that connect students in meaningful ways to the campus, to faculty, and to peers. In addition, the use of active and collaborative learning approaches, particularly innovative pedagogical approaches, seems to have a positive impact on student success. In this regard, HSIs rely more on the use of collaborative learning activities, including learning communities, to connect Hispanic students, while HBCUs have taken greater advantage of the enriching educational opportunities provided to students and faculty through service learning. Equally important, the high performing HBCUs and HSIs not only offer a variety of educationally purposeful learning opportunities for their students, but also their student success programs and practices are of unusually high quality and often touch many students in meaningful ways.

STUDENT ENGAGEMENT AND EDUCATIONAL EFFECTIVENESS AT HBCUS AND HSIS

National data on student engagement combined with case studies of strong performing HBCUs and HSIs further our understanding and appreciation for the factors and conditions that distinguish them from PWIs and enable them to foster student success. At the outset of this examination, we theorized that HBCUs and HSIs provide opportunity structures for underrepresented students that might have a mediating effect on students' habitus, in that the institution provides both a shared habitus, a sense of belonging, and new opportunity structures. Although more students of color attending these schools have less advantaged backgrounds than many of their PWI counterparts, HBCUs and HSIs appear to offer students experiences in which their dispositions and tacit understandings fit with the culture of the institution. Moreover, these institutions successfully induce students to get involved in activities they might have otherwise not recognized as opportunities. African American and Hispanic students entering HBCUs, HSIs, and PWIs differ in terms of background characteristics, with those at PWIs tending to be more advantaged in terms of family educational background. Of course, White students, especially those from low-income backgrounds and families without college experience, also encounter some of these challenges.

We cannot precisely determine all the factors that contribute to what appear to be salutary effects of attending an HBCU or HSI. NSSE measures selected aspects of engagement in effective educational practices and only a handful of campus climate factors. The insights from the MSIs and other schools in the DEEP project are especially important to understanding what these institutions do and how they do it to foster student success. When we integrate NSSE data with DEEP findings, three patterns of findings distinguish HBCUs and HSIs from other institutions: high levels of student-faculty interaction, supportive campus environment, and a blanket of intrusive educationally effective policies and practices.

Students interact more frequently with faculty and staff at HBCUs and HSIs, especially when student background characteristics are controlled for the latter. This finding lends evidence to a popular belief that faculty and staff at MSIs are not only critical to student success, but also these faculty are more supportive of their students than PWI faculty and staff.

Students of color also report that the campus environment generally is more supportive of their academic and social needs. The lone exception was for first-year students at HBCUs who do not find the level of academic support as great as their counterparts at PWIs. Perhaps this is because at HBCUs the message is less about support and more about performing at high levels. Again for HSIs, when student background characteristics are controlled, the supportive campus environment measure has a small, positive effect.

Our judgment is that these two factors—student-faculty interaction and supportive campus climate—are critical to the third distinguishing feature which emerged from the DEEP study, a set of integrated policies and practices that induce students to take part in effective educational practices, sometimes even requiring students to do so. These programs and practices are not independent of, but exist and are effective *because,* they bring faculty and students into more frequent, meaningful contact, particularly around structured curricular components such as small freshman seminars linked to academic departments or to advising. Faculty members' willingness to be available and work with students through enriching educational experiences such as academic clubs, service learning, and community activities help engage students in tasks that lead to success, retention, and graduation.

This examination documents the engagement practices found among students at HBCUs and HSIs, and particularly those at strong-performing institutions, that may serve to mediate habitus in terms of student background characteristics and dispositions. In addition, after controlling for differences in student background characteristics, it appears that participating in effective educational practices at HBCUs and HSIs makes up for some of the student academic preparation and resource inequalities that exist between these campuses and PWIs that are amply documented (Benitez, 1998). One way they seem to compensate for the resource disadvantage is by cultivating a culture of affirmation, aspiration, and achievement. Stitching these attitudes and values together is a set of beliefs about human potential and talent development buttressed by a network of effective educational practices.

The habitus and human capital frameworks prompt us to ask questions about where institutions of higher education, particularly HBCUs and HSIs, should target their efforts. Should an institution try to attract the most prepared students who have the greatest potential for success and enhance their talents or human capital? Du Bois' (1969) notion of educating the "talented tenth" is a take on this form of talent development. Based on our analysis, HBCUs—whose students generally come from families with higher levels of education than those who attend HSIs—are more in the Du Boisian camp of talent development than HSIs. This is not to say that HBCUs do not educate a considerable percentage of African American students who are not admissible at some PWIs. This is another form of talent development in which HBCUs take great pride. HSIs more often deal with students who have less cultural capital and, therefore, must grapple with a different educational challenge in terms of human-capital development among Hispanics.

HBCUs and HSIs operate from a strong assets-based philosophy for student learning, and structure integrated and redundant opportunities for students to engage with their peers in important educational practices including active and collaborative learning and service learning experiences. In addition, HBCUs appear to connect students and faculty in ways that increase students' level of engagement and commitment to success, while HSIs effectively connect students to peers to promote success. This tapestry of tradition, clarity of mission (especially for many HBCUs), talent development philosophy, and supportive campus climate helps these institutions overcome substantial financial and physical plant inequalities to foster minority student success.

CONCLUSION

Human capital and habitus perspectives suggest that many historically underrepresented students may encounter challenges when they get to college that make it difficult for them to take advantage of their school's resources for learning and personal development. Although attending college does not by itself insure that a student will attain a social or economic status equivalent to others with similar levels of education, HBCUs and HSIs appear to provide compensatory effects, thereby adding value to the student experience. Indeed, the data summarized in this chapter suggest that HBCUs and HSIs generally help students overcome some of these challenges by engaging them at higher levels than their peers attending PWIs and that both first-year students and seniors at HBCUs and HSIs on balance report that they gain as much or more from college as do their peers at PWIs.

By making high-quality postsecondary educational experiences accessible and affordable, HBCUs and HSIs are positively influencing the meaning students make of their college experiences and expanding the human capital of students and families throughout America by providing first-generation college students with potentially life-changing opportunities. Other colleges and universities can learn some valuable lessons about promoting student success from HBCUs and HSIs, especially those that are demonstrably high performing.

REFERENCES

Abraham, J. P., Lujan, S. S., Lopez, E. E., and Walker, M. T. (2002). Graduating students'perceptions of outcomes of college experiences at a predominantly Hispanic university. *Journal of Hispanic Higher Education, 1*(3), 267–276.

American Indian Higher Education Consortium (AIHEC). (1999). *Tribal colleges: An introduction.* Alexandria, VA: American Indian Higher Education Consortium.

Allen, W. R. (1986). *Gender and campus differences in Black student academic performance, racial attitudes, and college satisfaction.* Atlanta, GA: Southern Education Foundation.

Allen, W. R. (1992). The color of success: African American college student outcomes at predominantly White and historically Black public colleges and universities. *Harvard Educational Review, 62*(1), 26–44.

Allen, W. R., Epps, E. G., and Haniff, N. Z. (Eds.). (1991). *College in Black and White: African American students in predominantly White and in historically Black public universities.* Albany, NY: State University of New York Press.

Anaya, G. (1996). College experiences and student learning: The influence of active learning, college environments, and cocurricular activities. *Journal of College Student Development, 37* (6), 611–622.

Badura, A. S., Millard, M., Peluso, E. A., and Ortman, N. (2000). Effects of peer education training on peer educators: Leadership, self-esteem, health knowledge, and health behaviors. *Journal of College Student Development, 41*(5), 471–478.

Bauman, K. J., and Graf, N. L. (2003). *Educational attainment: 2000. Census 2000 brief.* U.S. Department of Commerce. Washington, DC: Government Printing Office.

Becker, G. (1964). *Human capital: A theoretical and empirical analysis.* New York: Columbia University Press.

Benitez, M. (1998). Hispanic-serving institutions: Challenges and opportunities. *New Directions for Higher Education, 102,* 57–68.

Berger, J. B., and Milem, J. F. (1999). The role of student involvement and perceptions of integration in a causal model of student persistence. *Research in Higher Education, 40*(6), 641–664.

Bourdieu, P., and Passeron, J. C. (1977). *Reproduction in education, society, and culture.* London: Sage.

Boyer, P. (2002). Defying the odds. *Tribal College, 14*(2), 12.

Braxton, J. M., Milem, J. F., and Sullivan, A. S. (2000). The influence of active learning on the college departure process: Toward a revision of Tinto's theory. *The Journal of Higher Education, 71*(5), 569–590.

Cabrera, A. F., Nora, A., Terenzini, P. T., Pascarella, E. T., and Hagedorn, L. S. (1999). Campus racial climate and the adjustment of students to college: A comparison between White students and African American students. *Journal of Higher Education, 70*(2), 134–202.

Chickering, A. W., and Reisser, L. (1993). *Education and identity* (2nd ed.). San Francisco, CA: Jossey-Bass Inc., Publishers.

Crosson, P. H. (1988). Four-year college and university environments for minority degree achievement. *The Review of Higher Education, 11*(4), 365–382.

Dayton, B., Gonzalez-Vasquez, N., Martinez, C. R., and Plum, C. (2004). Hispanic-serving institutions through the eyes of students and administrators. In *New Directions for Student Services, #105.* San Francisco, CA: Jossey-Bass Inc., Publishers.

DeSousa, D. J., and Kuh, G. D. (1996). Does institutional racial composition make a difference in what Black students gain from college? *Journal of College Student Development, 37*(3), 257–267.

Du Bois, W. E. B. (1969 Ed.). *The souls of Black folk.* New York: New American Library.

Feagin, J., Vera, H., and Imani, N. (1996). *The agony of education: Black students at White colleges and universities.* New York: Routledge.

Fleming, J. (1984). *Blacks in college.* San Francisco, CA: Jossey-Bass Inc., Publishers.

Fleming, J. (2001). The impact of a historically Black college on African American students: The case of LeMoyne-Owen College. *Urban Education, 36*(5), 597–610.

Flowers, L. (2003). Effects of college racial composition on African American students' interactions with faculty. *College Student Affairs Journal, 23*(1), 54–63.

Flowers, L., and Pascarella, E. T. (1999). The effects of college racial composition on African American college students' orientations toward learning for self-understanding. *Professional Educator, 22*(1), 33–47.

Garcia, P. (2001). *Understanding obstacles and barriers to Hispanic baccalaureates.* Funded by the Hispanic Scholarship Fund, San Francisco; RAND Corporation, Arlington, VA. ERIC 477 485.

Harker, R. K. (1984). On reproduction, habitus and education. *British Journal of Sociology,* 5(2): 117–127.

Hoffman, K., Llagas, C., and Snyder, T. (2003). *Status and trends in the education of Blacks (Report No. NCES 2003–034).* Washington, DC: U.S. Department of Education, National Center for Education Statistics.

Horvat, E. M. (2003). The interactive effects of race and class in educational research: Theoretical insights from the work of Pierre Bourdieu. *Penn GSE Perspectives in Urban Education, 2*(1), 1–25.

Jones, C. E., and Watt, J. D. (1999). Psychosocial development and moral orientation among traditional-aged college students. *Journal of College Student Development, 40* (2), 125–132.

Kim, M. M. (2002). Historically Black vs. White institutions: Academic development among Black students. *The Review of Higher Education, 25*(4), 385–407.

Kuh, G. D. (1995). The other curriculum: Out-of-class experiences associated with student learning and personal development. *Journal of Higher Education, 66*(2), 123–155.

Kuh, G. D. (2001). Assessing what really matters to student learning: Inside the National Survey of Student Engagement. *Change, 33*(3), 10–17, 66.

Kuh, G. D., Kinzie, J., Schuh, J. H, Whitt, E. J., and Associates. (2005). *Student success in college: Creating conditions that matter.* San Francisco, CA: Jossey-Bass Inc., Publishers.

Kuh, G. D., Nelson Laird T. F., and Umbach, P. D. (2004). Aligning faculty and student behavior: Realizing the promise of greater expectations. *Liberal Education, 90*(4), 24–31.

Kuh, G. D., and Umbach, P. D. (2005). Experiencing diversity: What can we learn from liberal arts colleges? *Liberal Education, 91*(1), 14–21.

Laden, B. V. (1999). Two-year Hispanic-serving colleges. In B. Townsend (Ed.), *Two-year colleges for women and minorities* (pp. 151–194). New York: Falmer.

Laden, B. V. (2001). Hispanic-serving institutions: Myths and realities. *Peabody Journal of Education, 76*(1), 73–92.

Laden, B. V. (2004). Hispanic-serving institutions: What are they? Where are they? *Community College Journal of Research and Practice, 28*(3), 181–198.

Lamont, M., and Lareau, J. (1988). Cultural capital: Allusions, gaps and glissandos in recent theoretical developments. *Sociological Theory, 6,* 153–168.

Lareau, A., and Horvat, E. M. (1998). Moments of social inclusion and exclusion: Race, class and cultural capital in family school relationships. *Sociology of Education, 72(*1), 37–53.

Liddell, D. L., and Davis, T. L. (1996). The measure of moral orientation: Reliability and validity evidence. *Journal of College Student Development, 37* (5), 485–493.

Llagas, C. (2003). *Status and trends in the education of Hispanics.* (Report No. NCES 2003–008). Washington, DC: U.S. Department of Education, National Center for Education Statistics.

McCabe, R. H. (2000). *No One to Waste: A Report to Public Decision-Makers and Community College Leaders.* Washington, DC: Community College Press.

Miller, L. S., and Garcia, E. E. (2004). Better informing efforts to increase Latino student success in higher education. *Education and Urban Society, 36*(2), 189–204.

O'Brien, E. M., and Zudak, C. (1998). Minority-serving institutions: An overview. *New Directions for Higher Education, 102,* 5–15.

Orfield, G. (1997). *Deepening segregation in American public schools.* Civil Rights Project, Harvard Graduate School of Education, Cambridge, MA.

Ortiz, A. M. (2004). Promoting the success of Latino students: A call to action. *New Directions for Student Services, 105,* 89–97.

Ortiz, A. M., and Boyer, P. (2003). Student assessment in tribal colleges. In M. C. Brown and J. E. Lane (Eds.), *Studying Diverse Institutions: Contexts, Challenges, and Considerations.* New Directions for Institutional Research, no. 118. San Francisco, CA: Jossey-Bass Inc., Publishers.

Outcalt, C. L., and Skewes-Cox, T. E. (2002). Involvement, interaction, and satisfaction: The human environment at HBCUs. *The Review of Higher Education, 25*(3), 331–347.

Provasnik, S., and Shafer, L. L. (2004). *Historically Black colleges and universities, 1976 to 2001* (Report No. NCES 2004–062). Washington, DC: U.S. Department of Education, National Center for Education Statistics.

Raines, R. T. (1998). Collaboration and cooperation among Minority-Serving Institutions. In J. P. Merisotis and C. T. O'Brien (Eds.), Minority-serving institutions: Distinct purposes, common goals. *New Directions in Higher Education, No. 102* (pp. 69–80). San Francisco, CA: Jossey-Bass Inc., Publishers.

Swail, W.S., with Redd, K. E., and Perna, L. W. (2003). *Retaining minority students in higher education: A framework for success.* Washington, DC: ASHE-ERIC Higher Education Report, Vol 30(2).

Turner, C. S. V. (1994). Guests in someone else's house: Students of color. *The Review of Higher Education, 17*(4), 355–370.

Watson, L. W., and Kuh, G. D. (1996). The influence of dominant race environments on student involvement, perceptions, and educational gains: A look at historically Black and predominantly White liberal arts institutions. *Journal of College Student Development, 37*(4), 415–424.

Williams, A., and Swail, W. S. (2005). *Is more better? The impact of postsecondary education on the economic and social well-being of American society.* Washington, DC: Educational Policy Institute.

CHAPTER 16

Teaching Latino, African American, and Native American Undergraduates

Faculty Attitudes, Conditions, and Practices

Frances K. Stage and Steven Hubbard

In this chapter, we examined variations in faculty attitudes, opinions about students, and satisfaction with their profession, and additionally we explored differences in learning environments for students attending Minority-Serving Institutions (MSIs). Results may be of interest to administrators and faculty who seek to optimize the learning environment for college students of color. This chapter describes the characteristics, perceptions, practices, and attitudes of faculty at Minority-Serving Institutions. Using a large national data set, we compared instructors at the Minority-Serving Institutions with instructors from similar institutions that had majority White students. Highlighting these differences allows us to further understand how campus environments and faculty culture may differ between MSIs and other campuses with similar academic missions. We examined these factors under the framework of campus environments and institutional ethos. Brown and Lane (2003) cautioned against comparing all institutions within large groups when student populations, institutional mission, and educational goals differ. In this study, we attempted to address that issue by grouping institutions according to Carnegie Classification and examining differences across campuses of different population groupings.

Many MSIs also face financial difficulties and report understaffed and underfunded campuses. These challenges may impact the ability of MSIs to successfully serve their student populations. As funding for higher education grows tighter, we see increased emphases on measurement and accountability

(Brown & Lane, 2003; Ortiz & Boyer, 2003). As institutions turn their focus to document value added and achievement of students, we see scores of studies that assess student views of their learning and their college experiences. Relatively few studies examine the conditions and attitudes of the instructors who work with those students.

Faculty attitudes towards students and teaching significantly influence the campus environment. Faculty beliefs, practices, and values can diminish or enhance minority student outcomes (Bensimon, Peña, & Castillo, 2004; Dodd, Garcia et al, 1995; Rendon & Hope, 1996). Possible differences between predominantly White institutions and Minority-Serving Institutions raise several questions regarding whether discrepancies exist in the learning environment of undergraduates. Do faculty attitudes at predominantly White institutions differ from faculty attitudes at MSIs? Do faculty opinions about undergraduate students at predominantly White institutions differ from faculty at Minority-Serving Institutions? How do these attitudes affect the conditions of student learning?

Historically, many postsecondary institutions in the United States were established to improve society, empower citizens, and promote democratic values. The aim to educate citizens enhanced the diversity of American higher education (Lane & Brown, 2003). Understanding campus environments and faculty attitudes toward undergraduate education helps us examine whether institutions create environments and educational structures that encourage opportunity for future leaders in our society.

THE CAMPUS ENVIRONMENT AND INSTITUTIONAL ETHOS

Institutions and, in particular, faculty can serve to enhance or detract from students' views of themselves as scholars. Native American students are more likely to succeed at institutions where they find strong networks of faculty and staff (Ortiz & Boyer, 2003). Additional research shows that Black students at historically Black institutions are likely to experience more positive attitudes regarding their abilities than are Black students at predominantly White institutions (Brown, 1994; Trent & Hill, 1994). Even at elite colleges African American students achieve significantly lower GPAs than their White peers with similar SAT scores (Bauman et al., 2005; Bowen & Bok, 1998; Massey, Charles, Lundy, & Fischer, 2003). Negative attitudes on the part of faculty can diminish enthusiasm on the part of learners, at the least, and, at worst, embarrass or intimidate them. By providing classroom experiences that foster participation and encouragement for a broad array of students, faculty can enhance student learning (Ortiz & Boyer, 2003; Stage, Muller, Kinzie & Simmons, 1998; Taylor, 2001).

FACULTY ATTITUDES

Research on faculty tends to focus on single and selective institutions and ignores the context of the classroom and faculty relationships with students. Those few national studies that do exist examine research publication and career satisfaction and advancement. Recent articles on faculty studied job satisfaction, scholarly productivity, employment status (e.g., tenure), compensation, and attitudes toward their work environment (Blackburn & Lawrence, 1995; Colbeck, 2002; Fairweather, 2002). In general, most do not focus on differences across institutional type.

Additionally, to assess campus environments, many studies have looked at the college experience from the student viewpoint (Pascarella & Terenzini, 1991), but few have examined the conditions, practices, and attitudes of faculty as they relate to the college student experience.

Faculty attitudes towards students and teaching significantly influence the campus environment. Beliefs, practices, and values can diminish or enhance minority student outcomes (Bensimon, Peña, & Castillo, 2004). By examining variations in faculty attitudes, opinions about students, and satisfaction with their profession, we can explore differences in learning environments for students attending Minority-Serving Institutions. Results may be of interest to administrators and faculty who seek to optimize the learning environment for students of color.

This study explored the preferences, perceptions, opinions, and attitudes of faculty at Minority-Serving Institutions. We began by focusing on institutions with higher percentages of Latino/a, African American, and Native American enrollment. Using the 1999 National Study of Postsecondary Faculty restricted use data set (NSOPF–99), we compared the responses of instructors in Minority-Serving Institutions with instructors from similar predominantly White institutions. Describing these differences allowed us to further understand how campus environments and faculty culture may differ between MSIs and other campuses with similar academic missions. Specifically, we explored how faculty from MSIs differed from similar institutions based on: (1) satisfaction with academic career, (2) perception of teaching and undergraduate students, (3) satisfaction with instructional duties, and (4) opinion about the institutional environment. The NSOPF–99 data set includes information on faculty and instructional staff employed by 819 institutions in the United States (Abraham et al., 2000). NSOPF–99 included two questionnaires—the institutional survey and faculty survey. The institutional survey obtained information on the number of faculty employed, tenure policies, retirement benefits, and faculty hires/departures. This faculty survey had seven subsections, which included employment, career background, institutional workload, job satisfaction, compensation, sociodemographic characteristics, and opinions.

Public and private not-for-profit degree granting institutions receiving U.S. financial aid (N=960) were selected to participate in the NSOPF–99 data collection. Of these institutions, 819 participated by providing a list of faculty that produced a sample of 19,213 faculty members. We selected full-time faculty with instructional duties who indicated their principal activities as research and teaching. We limited our sample to faculty from Doctoral, Comprehensive, Liberal Arts, and Community Colleges. We did not include part-time faculty, administrators, noninstructional researchers, and faculty from Research I and II institutions. The final sample size for this study was 6,786 faculty respondents.

To measure the preferences, attitudes, opinions, and perceptions of faculty from these institutions, we selected 15 questions from NSOPF–99 that addressed attitudes toward work (four questions), perceptions of students and teaching (four questions), satisfaction with the instructional environment (three questions), and opinions about the institutional environment (four questions). Specific items used for this study included: four items measuring satisfaction with Academic Career (e.g., satisfaction with work load); four items measuring Perception of Teaching and Undergraduate Students (e.g., satisfaction with quality of undergraduate students); three items measuring satisfaction with Instructional Duties (e.g., satisfaction with authority to decide courses taught); and four items measuring opinion about Institutional Environment (e.g., opinion about choosing Academic Career again).

For comparison purposes, we decided to use 25 percent or more minority enrollment as our definition of Minority-Serving Institutions because it is frequently used as the criterion to identify HSIs (Benítez, 1998). We divided the sample for each of the three Carnegie classifications and minority enrollment percentages, resulting in six categories. We compared the means of the faculty responses from institutions with higher percentages of minority enrollment with those from lower percentages of minority enrollment. We combined faculty from the three classifications for our first comparison. Responses of faculty from institutions with less than 10 percent Latino/a enrollment with faculty from those same kinds of institutions with over 25 percent Latino/a enrollment. We made the same comparisons similar variations in enrollment of African American and Native American students. Table 16.1 provides the number of institutions represented for each Carnegie Classification by enrollment.

Given the small representation of institutions with more than 25 percent Native American enrollments, one Liberal Arts institution and one Comprehensive institution, we examined only the grouped comparison reported in

Table 16.1 Institution Sample Size for Each Carnegie Classification and Minority Enrollment Percentage

		Enrollment					
Carnegie Classification	Number of Institutions	African American		Latino		Native American	
		<10	>25	<10	>25	<10	>25
Doctoral & Comprehensive	277	199	23	235	11	275	1
Liberal Arts	76	52	12	76	0	75	1
Community Colleges	283	175	49	190	31	280	0

table 16.2 in the next section. Additionally, we combined the responses of faculty from Doctoral and Comprehensive institutions for comparisons based on Latino/a and African American enrollments. For the Liberal Arts institutions, we compared the differences based on African American enrollments only. (No Liberal Arts institutions in the data set had a Latino/a enrollment over 25 percent.) Finally, this study compared the differences of faculty from Community Colleges based on both Latino/a and African American enrollments.

COMPARISONS OF FACULTY RESPONSES

We compared preferences, perceptions, opinions, and attitudes of faculty from Minority-Serving Institutions with those from predominantly White intuitions on the fifteen items. Analysis of Variance (ANOVA) was used to examine the differences based on Latino, African American, and Native American enrollment (in the first comparison only) and to identify significant statistical differences between low enrollment and relatively high enrollment institutions. Table 16.2 presents the results for all faculty from Doctoral, Comprehensive, Liberal Arts, and Community College institutions.

The left column identifies items from NSOPF–99. The next two present the response means of faculty from institutions with less than 10 and greater than 25 percent Latino/a enrollment. The fourth column indicates the significance level of the ANOVA analysis. The next six columns present the same statistical information based on the institution's African American enrollment and then Native American enrollment.

A few differences existed between faculty from institutions with Latino/a enrollment of less than 10 percent and faculty from institutions with Latino/a enrollment of greater than 25 percent. Faculty from institutions with higher Latino/a enrollment preferred to spend more time teaching undergraduates.

In addition, faculty from institutions with high levels of Latino/a enrollments were significantly less satisfied with their authority to decide their course content than faculty from predominantly White institutions.

Differences based on African American enrollment produced several significant results. But more positive responses did not always favor similar institutions. Faculty from institutions with higher African American enrollment were significantly more satisfied with their work load, *more* satisfied with their time available for class preparation, and preferred to spend more time teaching undergraduate students. However, they also were significantly *less* satisfied with their authority to make job decisions, less satisfied with the quality of their undergraduate students, and less satisfied with their authority to decide course content.

Additionally, a few differences existed between faculty from institutions with Native American enrollment of less than 10 percent and faculty from institutions with Native American enrollment of greater than 25 percent. Faculty from institutions with higher Native American enrollment were more satisfied with authority to make job decisions. But, faculty from institutions with higher levels of Native American enrollments were significantly less satisfied with the atmosphere for expression of ideas than faculty from predominantly White institutions. However, with only two institutions included in the greater than 25 percent enrollment, this should be interpreted with caution.

Because institutional type and mission can impact the attitudes, perceptions, and preferences of faculty members (Boyer, 1987), we next compared the responses of faculty based on the 1994 Carnegie Classifications. Table 16.3 presents results comparing faculty from Doctoral and Comprehensive institutions with less than 10 percent Latino/a enrollment with faculty from Doctoral and Comprehensive institutions with greater than 25 percent Latino/a enrollment.

Faculty from doctoral and comprehensive institutions with higher percentages of Latino/a enrollment preferred to spend less time teaching undergraduates and were less satisfied with their authority to decide course content (see table 16.3). The results from the comparison based on African American enrollment identified only one significant difference. Faculty from institutions with higher percentages of African American enrollment were more likely to believe that minority faculty were treated unfairly.

The NSOPF–99 data set included no liberal arts institutions with a Latino/a enrollment over 25 percent. However, several liberal arts institutions had an African American enrollment over 25 percent. Table 16.4 presents the results comparing faculty responses from institutions with lower African American enrollment with faculty responses from institutions with higher

African American enrollment. The comparison produced several significant results. Faculty from liberal arts institutions with higher percentages of African American enrollment were less satisfied with advancement opportunities, their jobs overall, quality of undergraduate students, authority to decide course content, and their authority to decide courses taught.

Finally, we compared the differences in faculty responses based on the Community College classification (table 16.5). Results indicate that faculty from institutions with higher percentages of Latino/a enrollment are significantly more satisfied with their work load. However, they preferred to spend less time teaching undergraduate students. This teaching preference result differs from our first analysis which indicated that faculty from the grouping of all institutions in the study with higher percentages of Latino/a enrollment preferred to spend more time teaching undergraduates.

Since we did not control for the Carnegie Classification in the first analysis, this result demonstrates that institutional mission and type is important when comparing differences in faculty at Minority-Serving Institutions. The comparison of community colleges based on African American enrollment indicated that faculty from community colleges with higher percentages of African American enrollment were less satisfied with the quality of undergraduate students and more satisfied with the time available for class preparation.

DISCUSSION

This study examined variations in faculty attitudes, opinions about students, and satisfaction with their profession across Minority-Serving Institutions compared with similar predominantly White institutions. We explored differences that faculty might make in learning environments for those students. Questions explored came from four categories: (1) satisfaction with academic career, (2) perception of teaching and undergraduate students, (3) satisfaction with instructional duties, and (4) opinion about the institutional environment.

For this study NSOPF–99 was useful in providing information concerning faculty attitudes and opinions about undergraduates, academic work, and the institution. A major limitation was that faculty teaching Native American students were virtually invisible in this large national data set. Of the full-time faculty engaged in teaching activities, only 27 faculty taught at two institutions (one liberal arts and one comprehensive) with more than 25 percent Native American students. Because most tribal colleges are two-year, it is likely that none of the 37 tribal colleges and universities (TCUs) participated in the NSOPF data collection. Additionally, NSOPF–99 did

Table 16.2 Comparison of Faculty Responses from Doctoral, Comprehensive, Liberal Arts, and Community College Institutions

Doctoral, Comprehensive, Liberal Arts, and Community Colleges NSOPF–99 Item	Latino Enrollment			African American Enrollment			Native American Enrollment		
	<10% N=5590 Mean (SD)	>25% N=369 Mean (SD)	Sig.	<10% N=4,855 Mean (SD)	>25% N=735 Mean (SD)	Sig.	<10% N =6,701 Mean (SD)	>25% N=27 Mean (SD)	Sig.
Satisfaction with authority to make job decisions	2.96 (0.91)	2.98 (0.91)	0.563	2.98 (0.90)	2.91 (0.95)	0.032*	2.97 (0.91)	2.56 (0.97)	0.019*
Satisfaction with work load	2.81 (0.96)	2.90 (0.96)	0.082	2.80 (0.96)	2.89 (0.95)	0.017*	2.82 (0.96)	2.52 (1.12)	0.108
Satisfaction with advancement opportunity	2.93 (0.99)	2.88 (1.01)	0.310	2.96 (0.99)	2.89 (0.96)	0.065	2.94 (0.98)	2.78 (1.19)	0.388
Satisfaction with job overall	3.14 (0.77)	3.21 (0.76)	0.074	3.16 (0.77)	3.16 (0.75)	0.931	3.16 (0.77)	2.81 (0.88)	0.20
Satisfaction with time available to advise students	3.05 (0.83)	3.06 (0.82)	0.862	3.05 (0.83)	3.10 (0.84)	0.196	3.06 (0.83)	3.04 (0.94)	0.878
Satisfaction with quality of undergraduate students	2.80 (0.85	2.73 (0.93)	0.095	2.83 (0.85)	2.65 (0.89)	0.000***	2.79 (0.86)	2.69 (0.84)	0.579
Time preferred teaching undergraduates	51.60 (29.49)	55.11 (28.91)	0.027*	50.87 (29.41)	58.17 (28.36)	0.000***	51.71 (29.46)	60.44 (24.21)	0.124
Opinion of undergraduates education at institution	2.58 (0.82)	2.63 (0.83)	0.284	2.58 (0.81)	2.64 (0.85)	0.081	2.60 (0.82)	2.85 (0.72)	0.109

Table 16.2 Comparison of Faculty Responses from Doctoral, Comprehensive, Liberal Arts, and Community College Institutions *(continued)*

Doctoral, Comprehensive, Liberal Arts, and Community Colleges NSOPF–99 Item	Latino Enrollment			African American Enrollment			Native American Enrollment		
	<10% N=5590 Mean (SD)	>25% N=369 Mean (SD)	Sig.	<10% N=4,855 Mean (SD)	>25% N=735 Mean (SD)	Sig.	<10% N =6,701 Mean (SD)	>25% N=27 Mean (SD)	Sig.
Satisfaction with authority to decide course content	3.71 (0.62)	3.60 (0.75)	0.000***	3.72 (0.62)	3.64 (0.67)	0.001***	3.71 (0.63)	3.74 (0.53)	0.785
Satisfaction with authority to decide courses taught	3.33 (0.79)	3.27 (0.84)	0.150	3.34 (0.80)	3.30 (0.80)	0.181	3.34 (0.80)	3.41 (0.75)	0.643
Satisfaction with time available for class preparation	2.99 (0.85)	3.03 (0.86)	0.452	2.99 (0.86)	3.07 (0.87)	0.011*	3.00 (0.86)	2.81 (0.88	0.269
Opinion about treatment of female faculty	3.02 (0.77)	3.09 (0.79)	0.088	3.03 (0.77)	3.05 (0.78)	0.582	3.04 (0.77)	2.81 (0.74)	0.136
Opinion about treatment of minority faculty	3.04 (0.73)	3.08 (0.84)	0.377	3.05 (0.73)	3.00 (0.81)	0.081	3.04 (0.74)	3.04 (0.65)	0.957
Opinion about choosing academic career again	3.35 (0.76) N=5590	3.38 (0.79)	0.421	3.35 (0.76)	3.35 (0.79)	0.889	3.35 (0.76)	3.37 (0.69)	0.906
Opinion of atmosphere for expression of ideas	2.38 (0.79) N=5590	2.40 (0.83) N=369	0.625	2.37 (0.80) N=4855	2.39 (0.78) N=735	0.741	2.38 (0.80)	1.96 (0.65)	0.006**

* $p<.05$; ** $p<.01$; *** $p<.001$

Table 16.3 Comparison of Faculty Responses from Doctoral/Comprehensive Institutions

Doctoral and Comprehensive Institutions NSOPF–99 Item	Latino Enrollment			African American Enrollment		
	<10% Mean (SD) N=2,879	>25% Mean (SD) N=131	Sig.	<10% Mean (SD) N=2,503	>25% Mean (SD) N=246.	Sig.
Satisfaction with authority to make job decisions	2.91 (1.05)	2.80 (1.43)	0.235	2.94 (1.02)	2.81 (0.98)	0.057
Satisfaction with work load	2.75 (0.96)	2.60 (1.00)	0.085	2.72 (0.97)	2.74 (0.94)	0.840
Satisfaction with advancement opportunity	2.93 (1.00)	2.91 (1.03)	0.820	2.95 (0.99)	2.87 (0.97)	0.218
Satisfaction with job overall	3.07 (0.77)	3.04 (0.81)	0.634	3.08 (0.78)	3.00 (0.76)	0.142
Satisfaction with time available to advise students	3.01 (0.98)	2.94 (1.37)	0.428	3.00 (0.97)	3.12 (0.81)	0.064
Satisfaction with quality of undergraduate students	2.26 (2.11)	2.22 (2.23)	0.837	2.29 (2.10)	2.33 (1.56)	0.740
Time preferred teaching undergraduates	43.65 (27.35)	38.47 (25.92)	0.034*	43.75 (27.05)	43.90 (27.81)	0.931
Opinion of undergraduate education at institution	2.62 (0.83)	2.60 (0.86)	0.773	2.61 (0.82)	2.72 (0.95)	0.067

Table 16.3 Comparison of Faculty Responses from Doctoral/Comprehensive Institution *(continued)*

Doctoral and Comprehensive Institutions NSOPF–99 Item	Latino Enrollment <10% Mean (SD) N=2,879	Latino Enrollment >25% Mean (SD) N=131	Sig.	African American Enrollment <10% Mean (SD) N=2,503	African American Enrollment >25% Mean (SD) N=246.	Sig.
Satisfaction with authority to decide course content	3.69 (0.84)	3.48 (1.39)	0.007**	3.70 (0.82)	3.61 (0.73)	0.084
Satisfaction with authority to decide courses taught	3.26 (0.97)	3.11 (1.41)	0.096	3.28 (0.96)	3.24 (0.83)	0.611
Satisfaction with time available for class preparation	2.98 (0.98)	2.91 (1.40)	0.401	2.98 (0.98)	3.02 (0.82)	0.521
Opinion about treatment of female faculty	2.98 (0.77)	3.04 (0.82)	0.396	3.00 (0.77)	3.00 (0.79)	0.969
Opinion about treatment of minority faculty	3.00 (0.72)	3.01 (0.91)	0.932	3.02 (0.72)	2.88 (0.85)	0.004**
Opinion about choosing academic career again	3.31 (0.79)	3.43 (0.74)	0.095	3.31 (0.79)	3.35 (0.85)	0.397
Opinion of atmosphere for expression of ideas	2.39 (0.80)	2.35 (0.83)	0.573 0.573	2.39 (0.80)	2.33 (0.80)	0.248

* $p<.05$; ** $p<.01$; *** $p<.001$

Table 16.4 Comparison of Faculty Responses from Liberal Arts Institutions based on African American Enrollment

	African American Enrollment		
Liberal Arts Institutions NSOPF–99	<10% Mean (SD) N=693	>25% Mean (SD) N=123	Sig.
Satisfaction with authority to make job decisions	3.08 (0.86)	2.93 (0.88)	0.225
Satisfaction with work load	2.81 (0.96)	2.82 (0.98)	0.870
Satisfaction with advancement opportunity	3.09 (0.96)	2.89 (0.97)	0.030*
Satisfaction with job overall	3.23 (0.78)	3.07 (0.81)	0.035*
Satisfaction with time available to advise students	3.14 (0.78)	3.04 (0.90)	0.417
Satisfaction with quality of undergraduate students	2.98 (0.84)	2.68 (0.87)	0.000***
Time preferred teaching undergraduates	57.15 (23.88)	60.40 (24.07)	0.165
Opinion of undergraduate education at institution	2.40 (0.79)	2.50 (0.84)	0.189
Satisfaction with authority to decide course content	3.80 (0.55)	3.67 (0.65)	0.024*
Satisfaction with authority to decide courses taught	3.44 (0.76)	3.15 (0.87)	0.003**
Satisfaction with time available for class prep	3.03 (0.84)	3.04 (0.97)	0.722
Opinion about treatment of female faculty	3.03 (0.79)	3.01 (0.82)	0.763
Opinion about treatment of minority faculty	3.04 (0.75)	2.93 (0.86)	0.168
Opinion about choosing academic career again	3.43 (0.73)	3.33 (0.78)	0.167
Opinion of atmosphere for expression of ideas	2.29 (0.76)	2.39 (0.83)	0.182

* p<.05; ** p<.01; *** p<.001

not include data on faculty from Liberal Arts institutions with over 25 percent Latino/a enrollment. An interesting question is whether a Hispanic-serving liberal arts institution exists.

A second limitation was that the data set does not provide identifiers for HBCUs or tribal colleges. An institution with large numbers of students of color does not necessarily have faculty and administrators who consciously serves those students (Contreras, Malcom & Bensimon, 2005). Historically Black colleges and universities with missions and histories that focus on educating Black Americans likely differ from predominantly Black institutions that do not have a similar focus. Finally, because our study relied on previously recorded data, we could not provide opportunities for faculty to specify the reasons for their opinions and attitudes. Nevertheless, despite these limitations we learned of interesting differences between faculty serving students at these institutions

Results indicated that institutional type is an important factor when looking at differences between predominantly White institutions and Minority-Serving Institutions. Initially, we compared all institutions regardless of type (excluding research institutions). We found a few differences between Hispanic-Serving Institutions and those with fewer Latino/a students as well as institutions with large numbers and smaller numbers of Native American students. More differences emerged when comparing predominantly Black institutions and those with lower enrollments of Black students. A positive result was that faculty members at predominantly Black institutions, preferred teaching undergraduate students and were more satisfied with their work loads and time for class preparation. However, they were less satisfied with the quality of their students and authority to make course content and other job decisions.

In the analysis according to institutional type, more specific differences emerged. At doctoral and comprehensive institutions with large numbers of Latino/a students, faculty preferred to spend less time teaching undergraduates and were less satisfied with their authority to decide course content. We found the sharpest distinction at liberal arts institutions, where faculty teaching larger numbers of African American students were less satisfied with the quality of undergraduate students, with aspects of their academic career, and with their authority to make decisions about courses. Disparities between minority serving community colleges and other community colleges included satisfaction with the quality of students and conditions of faculty service.

Clearly HBCUs have an impact on the education of African American students. HBCUs provided diversity in the types of institutions that serve minority students. Several liberal arts institutions had African American enrollments over 25 percent (many of them probably HBCUs). By contrast, no liberal arts institutions enrolled more than 25 percent Latino/a students and only one more than 25 percent Native American student enrollment. While Liberal arts institutions, particularly HBCUs play a major role in the education of African American students, no counterpart exists for Latino/a and Native American students.

Table 16.5 Comparison of Faculty Responses from Community Colleges

Community College Institutions NSOPF–99 Item	Latino Enrollment <10% Mean (SD) N=1,440	Latino Enrollment >25% Mean (SD) N=238	Sig	African American Enrollment <10% Mean (SD) N=1,313	African American Enrollment >25% Mean (SD) N=329	Sig
Satisfaction with authority to make job decisions	2.93 (0.92)	3.01 (0.90)	0.246	2.98 (0.91)	2.95 (0.93)	0.657
Satisfaction with work load	2.90 (0.96)	3.06 (0.89)	0.018*	2.92 (0.95)	3.02 (0.94)	0.110***
Satisfaction with advancement opportunity	2.88 (0.98)	2.86 (1.00)	0.725	2.93 (0.98)	2.88 (0.96)	0.365
Satisfaction with job overall	3.27 (0.72)	3.31 (0.71)	0.371	3.29 (0.72)	3.30 (0.70)	0.822
Satisfaction with time available to advise students	3.05 (0.84)	3.05 (0.83)	0.994	3.06 (0.84)	3.10 (0.84)	0.414
Satisfaction with quality of undergraduate students	2.78 (0.81)	2.70 (0.91)	0.174	2.79 (0.84)	2.68 (0.84)	0.050*
Time preferred teaching undergraduates	70.49 (23.48)	64.27 (26.30)	0.000***	69.32 (23.76)	69.23 (23.78)	0.952
Opinion of undergraduate education at institution	2.59 (0.79)	2.65 (0.81)	0.244	2.59 (0.80)	2.630 (0.77)	0.342

Table 16.5 Comparison of Faculty Responses from Community Colleges *(continued)*

Community College Institutions NSOPF–99 Item	Latino Enrollment			African American Enrollment		
	<10% Mean (SD) N=1,440	>25% Mean (SD) N=238	Sig	<10% Mean (SD) N=1,313	>25% Mean (SD) N=329	Sig
Opinion of undergraduate education at institution	2.59 (0.79)	2.65 (0.81)	0.244	2.59 (0.80)	2.630 (0.77)	0.342
Satisfaction with authority to decide course content	3.68 (0.64)	3.59 (0.76)	0.057	3.70 (0.64)	3.64 (0.65)	0.121
Satisfaction with authority to decide courses taught	3.38 (0.79)	3.28 (0.85)	0.072	3.38 (0.80)	3.40 (0.76)	0.659
Satisfaction with time available for class preparation	2.95 (0.91)	3.02 (0.86)	0.258	2.92 (0.90)	3.10 (0.90)	0.001***
Opinion about treatment of female faculty	3.12 (0.74)	3.12 (0.78)	0.984	3.14 (0.74)	3.12 (0.75)	0.543
Opinion about treatment of minority faculty	3.14 (0.71)	3.11 (0.80)	0.604	3.14 (0.71)	3.11 (0.75)	0.438
Opinion about choosing academic career again	3.38 (0.72)	3.36 (0.81)	0.602	3.40 (0.73)	3.33 (0.75)	0.146
Opinion of atmosphere for expression of ideas	2.41 (0.79)	2.43 (0.83)	0.708	2.39 (0.81)	2.42 (0.75)	0.459

* $p<.05$; ** $p<.01$; *** $p<.001$

RECOMMENDATIONS

Some aspects of the results were disconcerting—faculty at primarily undergraduate serving institutions prefer not to teach undergraduates. The negative views of work conditions on the part of faculty at liberal arts institutions serving large numbers of Black students likely negatively affects teaching. What is the obligation of college and university administrations to provide leadership that promotes teaching and learning on campuses? In a study of faculty motivation using a national data set, Hubbard (2005) found that faculty were more likely to value and put effort into teaching when their administration established undergraduate instruction as an important value of the institution. Additionally, an instructor's positive perception of the institution's instructional environment enhanced the variety and creativity of instructional practices in the undergraduate classroom (Hubbard, 2005). To enhance undergraduate education for Minority-Serving Institutions, administrators should clarify the value of undergraduate instruction verbally (i.e., mission and vision statements, goals, values) and actively (i.e., promotional practices, tenure decisions, instructional resources).

What is the role of institutional mission and the education of the faculty regarding demographic shifts and changing needs of students? These institutions presumably recruit students, promise them an education, and willingly take their tuition dollars. Educating faculty about their role in this enterprise should be part of the bargain.

Faculty knowledge of student populations can improve instruction. Institutional administrators should provide demographic information about their student population, provide comparisons with other similar institutions, and announce the accomplishments of successful undergraduates and alumni. Disseminating this type of information will improve the instructors' perceptions of undergraduate students and enhance the quality of undergraduate instruction.

Research found that the graduate experiences of faculty can enhance the quality of instructional practices (Fairweather & Rhoads, 1995; Hubbard, 2005). To improve instruction at Minority-Serving Institutions, graduate students should become familiar with instructional practices and the importance of self-efficacy and other learning theories in the undergraduate classroom—especially when instructing minority students. Minority-Serving Institutions can be an excellent resource for future faculty because they provide opportunities for graduate students to learn instructional practices and gain experience teaching in classrooms that consists of large numbers of students of color.

In a recent study of institutional missions of Hispanic-Serving Institutions, Contreras, Malcom and Bensimon (2005) found that many Hispanic-Serving Institutions, which used that designation to seek federal funding, did not describe this special role in the higher education community on their web sites or in their mission statements. Lack of mission at best suggests lack of consciousness about these growing numbers of students—the large numbers of first generation students, their unique histories and cultures, and their needs for role models—all of which should guide decisions about faculty hires, teaching approaches, campus services, and even concerts and lecture series.

This research affirms Brown and Lane's (2003) recommendation that Minority-Serving Institutions—predominantly Black institutions, tribal colleges, and Hispanic-Serving Institutions—should not be grouped into one category for research. Many differences existed based on institutional type and mission, enrollments, faculty attitudes, behaviors, and practices. While we learned of differences in faculty across institutions based on the demographic profiles of students served, more issues could be explored using national data sets, particularly those that allow for identification of HBCUs, TCUs, and HSIs. Some further questions that could be answered through quantitative approaches include: Are there differences in faculty attitudes, behaviors, and practices between historically Black colleges and predominantly Black institutions of similar types? Are there differences in faculty attitudes, behaviors, and practices across predominantly Black institutions, and Hispanic-Serving Institutions of similar types?

Future study should include qualitative approaches that provide opportunities for researchers to develop a deep understanding of faculty attitudes and opinions regarding work, instructional duties, and students. Such work might include institution specific examinations of the role of faculty in the college student experience. Additionally, questionnaires and interviews with faculty at a small number of institutions exploring similarities and differences in faculty attitudes, behaviors, and practices across institutions with differing mission would be productive. Finally, comparisons of institutional ethos across institutions with explicit missions to serve minority students and those with no such missions might be informative.

The faculty role in college students' experiences has not been closely examined, even though faculty are the most consistent point of contact with students. Researchers have found that they form an important link to the success of students (Pascarella & Terenzini, 1991), but in studies of student access and success, students are typically asked only a few cursory questions regarding their relationships with faculty. As resources become tight and faculty experience greater demands on their time, it is important to understand the ways that conditions of faculty work can affect the campus environment and the student experience. Faculty attitudes, opinions about students, and satisfaction with their profession, form an important aspect of the conditions under which college students seek to learn. Administrators and faculty, who seek to optimize the learning environment for minority college students, can add this important source of information to their efforts to make campus environments more conducive to learning.

REFERENCES

Abraham, S. Y., Steiger, D. M., Tourangeau, R., Kuhr, B. D., Wells, B., and Yang, Y. (2000). *1999 National study of postsecondary faculty: Field test report* (Technical Report). Washington DC: National Center for Educational Statistics.

American Indian Higher Education Consortium. (1999). *Tribal Colleges: An Introduction.* Alexandria, VA: American Indian Higher Education Consortium.

American Indian Higher Education Consortium. (2005). *Tribal Colleges and Universities.* Retrieved November 30, 2005, from http://www.aihec.org/college.html

Bandura, A. (1986). *Social foundations of thought and action: A social cognitive theory.* Englewood Cliffs, NJ: Prentice-Hall.

Bandura, A. (1999). *Self-efficacy: The exercise of control.* New York: Freeman.

Bauman, G. L., Bustillos, L. T., Bensimon, E. M. Brown, M. C., and Bartee, R. D. (2005). Achieving Equitable Educational Outcomes with All Students: The Institution's Role and Responsibilities. Washington, DC: Association of American Colleges and Universities.

Benítez, M. (1998). Hispanic-Serving Institutions: Challenges and opportunities. In J. P. Merisotis and E. M. O'Brien (Eds.), *Minority-Serving institutions: Distinct purposes, common goals* (pp. 57–68). San Francisco, CA: Jossey-Bass Inc., Publishers.

Bensimon, E. M., Castillo, C., Contreras-McGavin, C., Joseph, J., Ozaki, C. and Vallejo, E. (2004). Lift every voice: A qualitative investigation of the relationship between institutional commitment to diversity and opportunities for interactions with diverse peers. Paper presented at the annual meeting of the Association for the Study of Higher Education.

Blackburn, R. T., and Lawrence, J. H. (1995). *Faculty at work: Motivation, expectation, satisfaction.* Baltimore, MD: Johns Hopkins University Press.

Bowen, W. G., and Bok, D. (1998). *The Shape of the River: Long-term Consequences of Considering Race in College and University Admissions.* Princeton, NJ: Princeton University Press.

Boyer, E. L. (1987). College: The undergraduate experience in America. New York: Harper.

Boyer, P. (1998). Many Colleges, One Vision: A History of the American Indian Higher Education Consortium. *Tribal College, 9*(4), 16–22.

Boyer, P. (2000). Learning Lodge Institute: Montana Colleges Empower Cultures To Save Languages. *Tribal College, 11*(3), 12–14.

Brown, O. G. (1994). *Debunking the myth: Stories of African American university students.* Bloomington, IN: PHI Delta Kappa Educational Foundation.

Brown, M. C. (2003). Emics and etics of researching Black colleges: Applying facts and avoiding fallacies. In M. C. Brown and J. E. Lane (Eds.), *Studying diverse institutions: Contexts, challenges, and considerations* (pp. 27–40). San Francisco, CA: Jossey-Bass Inc., Publishers.

Brown, M. C., and Lane, J. E. (Eds.). (2003). *Studying diverse institutions: Contexts, challenges, and considerations.* San Francisco, CA: Jossey-Bass Inc., Publishers.

Colbeck, C. L. (2002). *Balancing teaching with other responsibilities: Integrating roles or feeding alligators.* Paper presented at the Annual Meeting of the American Educational Research Association, New Orleans, LA.

Contreras, F. E. Malcom, L., and Bensimon, E. M. (2005). Hispanic-serving Institutions: Closeted Identity and the Production of Equitable Outcomes for Latino/a Students. Paper presented at the Annual Meeting of the Association for the Study of Higher Education, Philadelphia, PA.

Cunningham, A. F., and Parker, C. (Eds.). (1998). *Tribal colleges as Community Institutions and Resources* (Vol. 102). San Francisco, CA: Jossey-Bass Inc., Publishers.

Davis, C., Ginorio, A. B., Hollenshead, C. S., Lazarus, B. B., Rayman, P. M., and Associates. (1996). The equity equation: Fostering the advancement of women in the sciences, mathematics, and engineering. San Francisco, CA: Jossey-Bass Inc., Publishers.

Dodd, J. M., Garcia, F., Meccage, C., and Nelson, J. R. (1995). American Indian Student Retention. *NASPA Journal* (Online), *33*(1), 72–78.

Fairweather, J. S. (2002). The mythologies of faculty productivity: Implications for institutional policy and decision making. *The Journal of Higher Education, 73*(1), 26–48.

Fairweather, J. S., and Rhoads, R. A. (1995). Teaching and the faculty role: Enhancing the commitment to instruction in American colleges and universities. *Educational Evaluation and Policy Analysis, 17*(2), 179–194.

Hannan, A., English, S., and Silver, H. (1999). Why innovate? Some preliminary findings from a research project on "innovations in teaching and learning in higher education." *Studies in Higher Education, 24*(3), 279–289.

Hanson, S. L. (1996). *Lost talent: Women in the sciences.* Philadelphia, PA: Temple University Press.

Hubbard, S.M. (2005). Identifying factors that influence instructional alternatives in the undergraduate math and science disciplines. Paper presented at the Annual Meeting of the Association for the Study of Higher Education, Philadelphia, PA.

Lane, J. E., and Brown, M. C. (2003). Looking backward to see ahead: Implications for research, policy, and practice. In M. C. Brown and J. E. Lane (Eds.), *Studying diverse institutions: Contexts, challenges, and considerations* (pp. 27–40). San Francisco, CA: Jossey-Bass Inc., Publishers.

Levitan, S. A., and Miller, E. I. (1993). *The Equivocal Prospects for Indian Reservations. Occasional Paper 1993–2.* Washington, DC: George Washington University, Center for Social Policy Studies.

Massey, D. S., Charles, C. Z., Lundy, G. F., and Fischer, M. J. (2003). *The source of the river: The social origins of freshmen at America's selective colleges and universities.* New Jersey: Princeton University Press.

Merisotis, J. P., and O'Brien, C. T. (Eds.). (1998). *Minority-Serving institutions: Distinct purposes, common goals.* San Francisco, CA: Jossey-Bass Inc., Publishers.

National Science Foundation. (1996). *Shaping the future: New expectations for undergraduate education in science, mathematics, engineering, and technology.* Washington, DC: NSF Division of Undergraduate Education.

O'Brien, E. M., and Zudack, C. (1998). Minority-Serving institutions: An Overview. In J. P. Merisotis and C. T. O'Brien (Eds.), *Minority-Serving institutions: Distinct purposes, common goals* (pp. 5–16). San Francisco, CA: Jossey-Bass Inc., Publishers.

Office of Indian Education Programs. (2006). *Higher Education Directory.* Retrieved November 30, 2005 from http://www.oiep.bia.edu.

Ortiz, A., and Boyer, P. (2003). Student Assessment in tribal colleges. In M. C. Brown and J. E. Lane (Eds.), *Studying diverse institutions: Contexts, challenges, and considerations* (pp. 41–49). San Francisco, CA: Jossey-Bass Inc., Publishers.

Pascarella, E., and Terenzini, P. (1991). *How college affects students.* San Francisco, CA: Jossey-Bass Inc., Publishers.

Pavel, D. M., Inglebret, E., and Banks, S. R. (2001). Tribal Colleges and Universities in an Era of Dynamic Development. *Peabody Journal of Education, 76*(1), 50–72.

Pavel, D. M., Skinner, R. R., Farris, E., Cahalan, M., Tippeconnic, J., and Stein, W. (1998). *American Indians and Alaska Natives in Postsecondary Education. Technical Report* (No. NCES–98–291): Westat, Inc., Rockville, MD, Mathematica Policy Research, Inc.; Plainsboro, NJ, Washington State Univ.; Pullman, Pennsylvania State Univ. University Park; Montana State Univ. Bozeman.

Redd, K. E. (1998). Historically Black colleges and universities: Making a comeback. In J. P. Merisotis and E. M. O'Brien (Eds.), *Minority-Serving institutions: Distinct purposes, common goals* (pp. 33–44). San Francisco, CA: Jossey-Bass Inc., Publishers.

Reed, J. B., and Zelio, J. A. (1995). *States and Tribes: Building New Traditions. A Broad Examination of the Condition of State-Tribal Relations.* Denver, CO: National Conference of State Legislatures.

Rendon, L. I., and Hope, R. O. (1996). *Educating a new minority: Transformng America's educational system for diversity.* Francisco, CA: Jossey-Bass Inc., Publishers.

Rosser, S. V. (Ed.). (1995). *Teaching the majority: Breaking the gender barrier in science, mathematics, and engineering.* New York: Teachers College Press.

Selfa, L. A., Suter, N., Myers, S., et al. (1997). *1993 National study of postsecondary faculty: Methodology report* (Technical Report). Washington, DC: National Center for Educational Statistics.

Stage, F. K., and Kinzie J. (1999). Reform in Undergraduate Science, Mathematics, Engineering, and Technology: The Classroom Context. Association for the Study of Higher Education. San Antonio, TX.

Stage, F. K., Muller, P. A., Kinzie, J., and Simmons, A. (1998). *Creating learning centered classrooms: What does learning theory have to say? 26*(4) Ashe-Eric Higher Education Report. Washington, DC: The George Washington University Graduate School of Education and Human Development.

Taylor, J. S. (2001). Through a Critical Lens: Native American Alienation from Higher Education. Paper presented at the Annual Meeting of the American Educational Research Association, April, Seattle, WA.

Trent, W., and Hill, J. (1994) The Contributions of Historically Black Colleges and Universities to the Production of African American Scientists and Engineers. In *Who will do science? Educating the next generation,* W. Pearson and A. Fechter (Eds.) (pp. 68–80). Baltimore, MD: Johns Hopkins University Press.

CHAPTER 17

Considering the Federal Classification of Hispanic-Serving Institutions and Historically Black Colleges and Universities

Michelle M. Espino and John J. Cheslock

Educational attainment varies substantially by race and ethnicity. In 2003, only 17 percent of African Americans and 11 percent of Hispanics over the age of 25 had a bachelor's degree or higher, while the corresponding figures for Asian Americans (49 percent) and Whites (30 percent) were substantially higher (Stoops, 2004). A number of issues contribute to low graduation rates for African American and Hispanic college students, namely, substandard K-12 education, limited social and cultural capital necessary for entering and completing higher education, and a lack of role models at the faculty and administrative levels (McDonough, 1997; Valenzuela, 1999). In addition, African Americans and Hispanics disproportionately attend community colleges and less selective institutions, which face challenges in providing quality education due to resource constraints (Fry, 2004). In an effort to improve the educational quality of institutions that serve mostly students of color, the federal government provides a variety of programs and grants.

To determine which institutions are eligible for special funding, the federal government has developed several classifications. Institutions with large shares of particular racial groups can apply for recognition as an Hispanic-Serving Institution (HSI), Alaska-Native-Serving Institution

---

Authors Note: We wish to thank Deborah Anderson, Judy Marquez Kiyama, and Matthew Matera for helpful comments.

(ANSI), or Native Hawaiian-Serving Institution (NHSI). Meanwhile, historically Black colleges and universities (HBCU) and tribal colleges and universities (TCUs) are granted permanent designations due to their historical missions. Relatively little work has critically examined the classification policies that determine which Minority-Serving Institutions qualify for special funding, and we seek to fill this void in the literature. This chapter examines the federal policy used to determine which institutions are designated as Hispanic-Serving Institutions (HSIs) or historically Black colleges and universities, with particular attention to historical context and the policy making process. These designations allow institutions to qualify for funding to strengthen their physical and academic infrastructures through Title III and Title V of the Higher Education Act of 1965. Both classification and funding programs are valuable tools for addressing issues of inequity among HBCUs, HSIs, and predominately White institutions (PWIs) and determining which institutions that disproportionately serve African American and Hispanic students will have access to additional federal funding. Utilizing data from the 2003 Integrated Postsecondary Education Data System (IPEDS), we evaluate the current HBCU and HSI policy and discuss the major policy implications of our findings and several potential changes to classification policy that may occur in the future.

A COMPARISON OF HBCU AND HSI HISTORY AND CLASSIFICATION

The classification and funding programs for Hispanic-Serving Institutions (HSIs) and historically Black colleges and universities (HBCUs) evolved over multiple reauthorizations of the Higher Education Act, within the context of the existing political environment. The political processes and supporting rationale that produced the Title III-Section B and Title V classification and funding programs were quite different, which partially explains some differences between HBCU and HSI classification policy.

As noted previously by numerous researchers, the history of HBCUs covers 164 years of racial discrimination, segregation, and inequitable funding from state and federal governments, which left the infrastructures of many HBCUs floundering by the 1960s (Allen and Jewell, 2002). The disparities in educational funding were more evident after the passing of the Civil Rights Act of 1964, which "prohibited the distribution of federal funds to colleges and universities that discriminated on the basis of race, color, or national origin" (Lamb, 1999, p. 250). The language used in the Civil Rights Act was focused on the PWIs that were not adhering to the *Brown v. Board of Education* ruling against segregation, but also affected predominately

Black colleges whose enrollments were beginning to decrease due to desegregation (Cobb, 1977).

The dual postsecondary educational system in many states had already designated certain institutions as predominately serving Black students, which made the classification of HBCUs quite simple; the process of creating special funding for these institutions, however, lasted several years. Concurrent with the publication of an influential report by Earl J. McGrath (1965), urging the federal government to rectify the disparities in educational resources between HBCUs and PWIs, Congress was considering the Title III "Developing Institutions" program within the Higher Education Act of 1965, which would allocate special funding to HBCUs. From a political perspective, funding a program exclusively for Black colleges was too difficult to develop, especially considering the recent passing of the Civil Rights Act. In order to diversify this funding program, small, predominately White colleges and, eventually, community colleges, which also struggled with funding and limited resources, were included (Cobb, 1977). Efforts to separate HBCUs from other institutions in Title III eventually led to the creation of Title III-Section B during the 1986 reauthorization of the Higher Education Act, which made the original intention behind Title III a reality (Roebuck and Murty, 1993).

While past discriminatory funding of HBCUs played a major role in the creation of Title III, a desire to improve the educational experiences of African American students also motivated this legislation. Consequently, Title III set a precedent for other institutions to advocate for classification and funding. Most notably, substantial lobbying occurred to procure funding for institutions whose missions did not target the educational development of specific racial groups, but were serving large numbers of Hispanic students (DeLoughry, 1989). While the lobbying efforts were eventually successful, the progress was incremental.

An initial proposal for the 1984 reauthorization of the Higher Education Act to modify Title III funding by "provid[ing] direct aid to institutions with high concentrations of Hispanic students," was not approved, but the proposal gained momentum in later reauthorizations (McDonald and García, 2003, p. 36). Eight years later, the 1992 reauthorization of the Higher Education Act formally recognized institutions with high Hispanic enrollments as Hispanic-Serving Institutions, although special funding was not included. An HSI was defined as any institution that had at least a 25 percent Hispanic undergraduate enrollment share and an Hispanic undergraduate population in which 75 percent were low-income and the first generation in their families to attend college. In 1996, Title III-Section A included a limited amount of funding for HSIs, which was then increased through the creation of a separate Title V "Developing Hispanic-Serving Institutions Program" during the 1998 reauthorization. The 1998 reauthorization also eased the requirements for HSI status by only requiring institutions to have a 25 percent Hispanic undergraduate enrollment share and an Hispanic undergraduate population in which 50 percent were low-income (Devarics, 2000).

Because the history and political process that produced the HBCU designation is so different than that leading to the HSI designation, one should not be surprised by the very different classification policies actually used to identify HBCUs and HSIs. These policies differ in two fundamental ways. First, the HBCU designation is permanent while the HSI designation is contingent on the institution meeting several criteria upon each funding request. Furthermore, Title V is a competitive grant program that requires institutions to first apply for eligibility in accordance with the Title V requirements and then, once granted eligibility, submit funding proposals. In contrast, Title III-Section B grants are noncompetitive, which guarantees a minimum allotment to each of the 105 HBCUs currently designated by the U.S. Department of Education (IDUES, 2005b). The second major difference is that the HBCU policy results in funds mostly going to institutions whose Black share of enrollment is extremely large, while institutions where Hispanic students comprise less than 50 percent of enrollment receive substantial amounts of funding as HSIs.

EVALUATING HBCU AND HSI CLASSIFICATION POLICY

While the classification of HBCUs was a simple process, the identification of HSIs was more complicated because very few institutions were created with the explicit mission of educating Hispanic students. As just discussed, policy makers developed a specific set of criteria to identify HSIs as a result of this ambiguity. Do the chosen criteria improve the educational attainment and experiences of Hispanic students more effectively than other alternatives?

The most obvious alteration to current HSI classification policy would be to expand or reduce the required Hispanic share of enrollment. The argument for increasing the required share is straightforward. Because Title V funding is limited, the money should flow to those institutions where Hispanic students are most prevalent. A higher share requirement ensures that the dollars appropriated to Title V will have a larger impact on Hispanic students, because they will enjoy a larger share of the improvements in institutional quality.

Such an argument, however, does not consider how HSI classification policy can impact legislators' willingness to appropriate additional dollars to

Title V. If the required Hispanic enrollment share was substantially increased, fewer institutions would qualify, and fewer legislators would represent institutions that could qualify for Title V funding. As a result, political support for more generous levels of Title V funding would likely fall. Hence, policy makers face a trade-off. If they increase the required Hispanic enrollment share, they can concentrate more of their funding on those students for whom the HSI program was created, but such an increase could also reduce the total amount of funds to be distributed via Title V in the long run.

The HSI designation and Title V funding can also impact the educational attainment of Hispanics by providing incentives for higher education institutions to serve Hispanic students. Institutions with Hispanic enrollment shares in the low twenties percent currently have an incentive to increase Hispanic enrollment to meet the 25 percent requirement, while those in the upper twenties have an incentive to maintain their current levels of Hispanic enrollment. The prevalence and strength of these incentives will depend upon the number of institutions near the minimum required share and the desirability of HSI classification and funding. If policy makers were to increase the required Hispanic enrollment share, these incentives may be troublesome in that they could promote segregation within higher education. For example, if the required share was 50 percent, federal policy may promote the concentration of Hispanic students within a few institutions that primarily serve Hispanics.

Other aspects of HSI classification policy could also be altered. In addition to the minimum Hispanic enrollment share, current policy requires institutions, in order to qualify for Title V funding, to have lower expenditures than other institutions offering similar instruction, sufficient financial need among their student body, and an Hispanic undergraduate population in which 50 percent are low-income (IDUES, 2005a). While the extent to which these requirements are currently used to actually disqualify institutions from funding is unclear, their presence within the Higher Education Act allows them to be utilized at any point in the future.

These additional requirements would likely target funding to those institutions and students where they would have the largest impact. If institutional spending has diminishing returns, which is quite likely the case, a Title V grant would have the biggest impact on quality at those institutions with the least resources. Furthermore, low-income students, who suffer numerous educational disadvantages prior to postsecondary education, would likely benefit most from increased educational quality. On the other hand, some of the incentives created by these requirements may be problematic. For example, why solely encourage those institutions with fewer financial resources to increase or maintain their enrollment of Hispanic students?

Similar concerns regarding imbedded incentives are not relevant to current HBCU policy, because the enrollment decisions taken by individual HBCUs do not impact their eligibility for Title III-Section B funding. Furthermore, non-HBCUs cannot qualify for funding by increasing their enrollment of Black students. HBCU policy does appear to effectively target its funds on Black students because most HBCUs have extremely large Black enrollment shares within their undergraduate student population. This effective targeting, however, is simply a result of segregation.

To promote and support the enrollment of Black students at non-HBCUs, the federal government could provide special institutional grants to those non-HBCUs that serve Black students. Such a policy would provide an incentive for non-HBCUs to increase their enrollment of Black students and would improve the educational quality of institutions that enroll large numbers of Black students. The importance of this latter contribution, of course, depends heavily on the number of non-HBCUs with large Black enrollments.

ANALYSIS OF POTENTIAL CHANGES TO CLASSIFICATION POLICY

The previous section demonstrates that the desirability of current classification policy depends upon several empirical questions, and we attempt to answer two of these questions here. We first examine how the number of HSIs and their geographical diversity would change if policy makers increased the required Hispanic enrollment share above the current 25 percent level. We then investigate the impact of a policy that provides funding to non-HBCUs with large Black enrollment shares, by estimating the number and types of institutions that would qualify.

In our analysis, we use data from the 2003 Integrated Postsecondary Education Data System (IPEDS) Enrollment and Institutional Characteristics surveys. Our sample of institutions includes all schools listed in IPEDS except those in the following groups: schools that do not report offering a degree and do not report a Carnegie classification, schools that primarily serve graduate students and do not offer undergraduate degrees, schools not eligible for Title IV funds, schools with total enrollment below 100 students, schools missing enrollment data for the fall of 2003, proprietary schools, and tribal colleges. Our sample contains 2,966 institutions.

Table 17.1 contains a variety of undergraduate full-time equivalent (FTE) enrollment figures for Hispanic students (panel A) and Black students (panel B) for the institutions in our sample. To illustrate the information contained in this table, we discuss the statistics presented in the eighth row of panel A. These figures demonstrate that, in the fall of 2003, 66 institutions (or 2.2% of all institutions in our sample) had a Hispanic enrollment share between 75 percent and 100 percent. On average, these schools enrolled 2,998 Hispanic students and 3,108 total students, which means their combined Hispanic enrollment was 197,870 (18.5% of all Hispanic students at institutions in our sample) and their combined total enrollment was 205,127 (2.0% of all students at institutions in our sample).

How would the number of HSIs change if policy makers increased the required Hispanic share of enrollment? In 2003, 226 schools, who enroll approximately half of all Hispanic students, meet the 25 percent standard currently used. Raising the figure to 50 percent would reduce the number of HSIs to 103 schools that educate 30 percent of all Hispanic students, while raising the requirement further to 75 percent would result in only 66 HSIs serving merely 18.5 percent of all Hispanic students.

Does the geographical diversity of HSIs also fall as the required Hispanic enrollment share is increased? Table 17.2 lists the number of institutions in each state that would qualify for HSI status at the 25 percent, 50 percent, and 75 percent cut-off for percent Hispanic. The results demonstrate that as the Hispanic share requirement grows, the number of represented states decreases and the share of institutions from Puerto Rico drastically increases. Consequently, political support for Title V funding would likely diminish as the Hispanic enrollment share requirement rises.

How many non-HBCUs would qualify for a policy that would provide funding to schools with large Black enrollment shares? We first consider a minimum Black enrollment share of 25 percent. Three hundred thirty of the 421 institutions in table 17.1 with a Black enrollment share above 25 percent are not HBCUs. These 330 "Black-Serving Institutions" (BSIs) differ from HBCUs in both enrollment composition and institutional type. Eighty-three of the 95 HBCUs in our sample have Black enrollment shares above 75 percent, while only 79 of the 330 BSIs have Black enrollment shares above 50 percent. In terms of institutional type, only 15 percent of HBCUs are two-year schools, while 67 percent of BSIs are two-year schools; the latter figure is close to the 57 percent share of two-year institutions among HSIs.

Certainly, any comprehensive effort to ensure that Black undergraduates enroll at institutions with sufficient funding would need to consider the financial health of BSIs, which enroll large numbers of African Americans. For our sample, these schools enroll 320,477 Black full-time equivalent students, substantially more than the 201,209 Black FTE students enrolled by our 95 HBCUs. Interestingly, the combined Black FTE enrollment at BSIs and HBCUs is smaller than the 544,150 Hispanic FTE students enrolled at HSIs, even though far fewer HSIs exist. This result occurs because

Table 17.1 2003 FTE Enrollment Figures for Different Values of Percent Hispanic and Percent Black

			Hispanic (Panel A) or Black (Panel B) Students				All Students	
	Number of Institutions	Percent of All Institutions (%)	Mean Enrollment	Total Number of Students	Percent of All Students (%)	Mean Enrollment	Total Number of Students	Percent of All Students (%)
A. Percent Hispanic								
$0 \leq P < 10$	2369	79.9	94	223,305	20.8	3,107	7,361,426	70.6
$10 \leq P < 20$	309	10.4	736	227,295	21.2	5,380	1,662,358	15.9
$20 \leq P < 25$	62	2.1	1,232	76,381	7.1	5,461	338,591	3.2
$25 \leq P < 30$	39	1.3	1,807	70,484	6.6	6,582	256,693	2.5
$30 \leq P < 40$	51	1.7	1,852	94,446	8.8	5,297	270,135	2.6
$40 \leq P < 50$	33	1.1	2,034	67,116	6.3	4,485	148,016	1.4
$50 \leq P < 75$	37	1.3	3,087	114,234	10.7	5,133	189,918	1.8
$75 \leq P \leq 100$	66	2.2	2,998	197,870	18.5	3,108	205,127	2.0
Total	2966	100.0	361	1,071,131	100.0	3,517	10,432,264	100.0
$P \geq 25$	226	7.6	2,408	544,150	50.8	4,734	1,069,889	10.3
B. Percent Black								
$0 \leq P < 10$	1953	65.9	158	308,216	26.0	3,629	7,086,591	67.9
$10 \leq P < 20$	472	15.9	552	260,412	22.0	3,919	1,849,589	17.7
$20 \leq P < 25$	120	4.1	819	98,222	8.3	3,701	444,138	4.3
$25 \leq P < 30$	79	2.7	914	72,227	6.1	3,317	262,028	2.5
$30 \leq P < 40$	101	3.4	965	97,446	8.2	2,886	291,501	2.8
$40 \leq P < 50$	72	2.4	878	63,236	5.3	1,995	143,654	1.4
$50 \leq P < 75$	67	2.3	1,024	68,580	5.8	1,719	115,181	1.1
$75 \leq P \leq 100$	102	3.4	2,132	217,504	18.3	2,349	239,584	2.3
Total	2966	100.0	400	1,185,844	100.0	3,517	10,432,266	100.0
$P \geq 25$	421	14.2	1,233	518,993	43.8	2,499	1,051,948	10.1

Table 17.2 State HSI Totals for Various Hispanic Enrollment Share Requirements

State	P ≥ 25	P ≥ 50	P ≥ 75
Arizona	11	1	0
California	65	13	3
Colorado	6	0	0
Florida	10	6	2
Illinois	8	3	1
Kansas	1	0	0
Massachusetts	1	0	0
New Jersey	4	0	0
New Mexico	22	8	1
New York	12	3	1
Puerto Rico	50	50	50
Texas	34	18	8
Washington	2	1	0
Total	226	103	66

the average total FTE enrollment at an HSI is around 4,700 while the corresponding figure for HBCUs and BSIs is close to 2,500.

CONCLUSION

Based on our results, we find little reason for policy makers to alter the 25 percent Hispanic enrollment share requirement for HSI designation. Decreasing the required share seems unnecessary, because 226 schools that serve over 50 percent of Hispanic students already qualify. In addition, increasing the share would substantially limit the geographical diversity of Hispanic-Serving Institutions and consequently, likely decrease the political support for generous levels of Title V funding.

Our empirical results, however, do not provide insight into whether incentives are imbedded in current classification policy, and future work needs to examine this issue. For example, do specific higher education institutions increase or maintain their enrollment of Hispanic students in order to qualify for the HSI designation and its associated funding? Such information is vital to evaluating HSI policy, because if strong incentives are present, Title V funding would not only improve the educational quality at certain institutions but also would influence overall Hispanic enrollment as well as the specific institutions that Hispanic students disproportionately attend. Such enrollment shifts may not always be positive. Institutions with a Hispanic enrollment share between 20 and 30 percent face the largest incentive to maintain or increase Hispanic enrollment, and of the 101 schools in our sample within this range, 67 are Associates colleges. In contrast, only three are Doctoral/Research universities and three are Baccalaureate colleges These findings suggest that HSI policy could increase the concentration of Hispanic students at institutions with fewer resources, even after Title V funding is received.

An evaluation of HBCU policy is less complex; because the designation is permanent, institutions have no incentive to adjust behavior in order to qualify. In general, current HBCU policy appears to address two major policy goals: alleviation of infrastructure deficiencies at HBCUs, resulting from past discriminatory funding, and improvements in the educational quality enjoyed by Black students. The presence of this latter goal suggests that non-HBCUs that serve substantial numbers of Black students should be eligible, like HSIs, for federal funding. Recently introduced legislation in the House of Representatives partially addresses this issue, by making predominately Black institutions (PBIs), which are defined as schools with at least 1,000 students and a Black enrollment share above 50 percent, eligible for funding under Title III-Section B (Walters, 2005). The proposed legislation is opposed by HBCUs because it would allow PBIs to compete with HBCUs for Title III-Section B funding, as opposed to creating another section of the Higher Education Act specifically for PBIs (Walters, 2005). If such legislation passed, the negative effect on HBCUs could be moderated by increased support for Title III-Section B funding by legislators in northern states whose constituents would now qualify for funding.

As discussed throughout this chapter, the current classification system is the by-product of numerous changes in institutional eligibility and funding program structure that slowly occurred over time, and the future will likely bring additional alterations. Proprietary, or for-profit institutions, which currently are eligible only for Title IV funding, are aggressively lobbying for a change in eligibility rules that would allow them to qualify for Titles III and V funding (Burd, 2003). Such a change would drastically increase the number of HSIs. One hundred forty-four of the 731 relevant proprietary schools listed in IPEDS have Hispanic enrollment shares above 25 percent. These 144 schools, however, only educate 53,773 FTE Hispanic students, far less than the 544,150 FTE Hispanic students enrolled at the 226 nonproprietary HSIs in our sample. Because a commensurate increase in Title V funding is unlikely to accompany the relaxed eligibility rules, the current HSIs strongly oppose this change.

Even if no alterations are made to the existing eligibility rules, increased competition for Title V funding should naturally occur over time as the expected increase in Hispanic students materializes. The number of schools with an Hispanic enrollment share above 25 percent should rise rapidly, as has been the case over the last 25 years. Among the 2,435 institutions in our sample that have consistently reported enrollment data since 1980, the number of institutions above 25 percent more than doubled between 1980 and 2003. Future growth at a similar pace may prompt legislators who wish to limit Title V expenditures to increase the Hispanic enrollment share required for eligibility.

With each reauthorization of the Higher Education Act of 1965, maintaining institutional aid to Minority-Serving Institutions (MSIs) is questioned. Will there ever be an end to this policy? Most policy makers say that the federal classification policies for Minority-Serving Institutions should continue, although reaching broad consensus regarding racial and ethnic issues in higher education policy is difficult (Williams, 1984). In the words of Henry Cobb (1977), the federal classification policies for historically Black colleges and universities and Hispanic-Serving Institutions should continue "until the job is done, until the societal traumas that keep these institutions underdeveloped have been removed, and until the national goal of providing equality of access has been achieved" (p. 117).

REFERENCES

Alliance for Equity in Higher Education. (2003). *Policy priorities for the higher education act reauthorization.* Retrieved December 1, 2003, from http://www.msi-alliance.org/.

Allen, W. R., and Jewell, J. O. (2002). A backward glance forward: Past, present, and future perspectives on historically Black colleges and universities. *The Review of Higher Education, 25*(3), 241–261.

Burd, S. (2003, September 5). For profit colleges want a little respect. *The Chronicle of Higher Education,* p. 23.

Cobb, H. E. (1977). *Report on the examination of the developing institutions program.* Washington, DC: U.S. Department of Health, Education, and Welfare/Office of Education.

DeLoughry, T. J. (1989, December 13). President directs secretary Cavazos to propose remedies for 'crisis' in Hispanics' education. *The Chronicle of Higher Education,* p. A1.

DeLoughry, T.J. (1990, May 30). Bush administration may be facing a new round of contention over how to improve educational opportunities for Hispanics. *The Chronicle of Higher Education,* p. A17.

Devarics, C. (1997). Can a rift be avoided? Changes in title III program. *Black Issues in Higher Education, 4,* 21–25.

Devarics, C. (2000). Hispanic-serving institutions make impressive strides. *Black Issues in Higher Education, 17*(16), 32–35.

Fry, R. (2004). *Latino youth finishing college: The role of selective pathways.* Washington, DC: Pew Hispanic Center.

Institutional Development and Undergraduate Education Service. (2005a). *Developing Hispanic-serving institutions program—Title V.* Retrieved June 23, 2005, from http://www.ed.gov/programs/idueshsi/index.html.

Institutional Development and Undergraduate Education Service. (2005b). *Title III part*

B, strengthening historically Black colleges and universities program. Retrieved June 23, 2005, from http://www.ed.gov/programs/iduestitle3b/index.html.

Lamb, V. L. (1999). Institutional and period determinants of baccalaureate degrees from historically Black colleges and universities: A research note. *Sociological Spectrum, 19*, 249–263.

McDonald, V., and García, T. (2003). Historical perspectives on Latino access to higher education: 1848–1990. In J. Castellanos and L. Jones (Eds.), *The majority in the minority: Expanding the representation of Latina/o faculty, administrators, and students in higher education* (pp. 15–43). Sterling: Stylus Publishing.

McDonough, P. (1997). *Choosing colleges: How social class and schools structure opportunity.* Albany: State University of New York Press.

McGrath, E. J. (1965). *The predominately Negro colleges and universities in transition*. New York: Columbia University Bureau of Publications.

Roebuck, J. B. and Murty, K. S. (1993). *Historically Black colleges and universities: Their place in American higher education*. Westport, CT: Praeger Publishers.

Stoops, N. (2004). *Educational attainment in the United States: 2003: Population characteristics.* Washington, DC: U.S. Census Bureau.

Valenzuela, A. (1999). *Subtractive schooling: U.S.-Mexican youth and the politics of caring.* Albany: State University of New York Press.

Walters, A. K. (2005, September 30). Predominately Black and historically Black colleges spar over federal funds. *The Chronicle of Higher Education*, p. A28.

Williams, J.B. (1984). Public policy and Black college development: An agenda for research. In A. Garibaldi (Ed.), *Black colleges and universities: Challenges for the future* (pp. 178–198). New York: Praeger Publishers.

CHAPTER 18

Coalition Formation among Minority-Serving Institutions

Deirdre Martinez

Before the 1998 reauthorization of the Higher Education Act (HEA), advocacy groups representing historically Black colleges and universities (HBCUs) and Hispanic-Serving Institutions (HSIs) were locked in a battle for funding. Lobbying leading up to the reauthorization "pitted Hispanic and Black advocacy groups against one another in the type of tense competition that in the past has divided them in debates over education outreach programs that Hispanics complain touch relatively few of their students" (Fletcher, 1998). HBCUs argued that they were entitled to more money because discrimination experienced by Hispanics in no way approached the discrimination that has historically been experienced by African Americans (Fletcher, 1998). Advocates for HSIs argued that the large and growing Hispanic population had been consistently underserved and the educational needs of this group had been all but ignored by the federal government (Benitez, 1998). In the end, the reauthorization made more money available to HSIs and tribal colleges and universities, without cutting into funding for HBCUs (Laden, 2001). Despite fears that the growing number of HSIs would siphon money away from HBCUs (Dervarics, 1997), HBCUs continue to receive significantly more funding than HSIs or tribal colleges. In fiscal year 2005, the 105 HBCUs were funded at $239 million under Title III of the HEA, compared to $95 million for the 242 HSIs and $24 million for 34 tribal colleges.

Yet shortly after the reauthorization battle, a surprising coalition was created. The Alliance for Equity in Higher Education formed in 1999 as a means of promoting greater collaboration and cooperation among colleges and universities that serve large numbers of students of color (Merisotis and

Goulian, 2004). The formation of the Alliance raises two sets of questions. The first concerns the motivation for the more powerful actor to join in coalition with the less powerful. How did the National Association for Equal Opportunity in Higher Education (NAFEO), a long-established and politically connected presence representing HBCUs in Washington, overcome their concern that HSIs would threaten their funding? What motivated them to form a coalition with the Hispanic Association of Colleges and Universities (HACU), which represents HSIs, and the American Indian Higher Education Consortium (AIHEC), which represents the tribal colleges? The primary motivational assumption in the study of coalition formation is that actors will behave in such a way as to maximize their expected utility (Reisinger, 1986). How does this rational actor model explain NAFEO's decision to join the coalition? How do we explain the formation of a coalition among groups who had been competing for limited resources? In particular, what does NAFEO gain by joining? What advantage does the coalition offer them over acting alone (Hojnacki, 1997)? A second set of questions centers on the mechanics of the creation of the coalition. How did the coalition actually emerge? Does this case confirm the importance of brokers in the formation of coalitions (Loomis, 1986)?

METHODOLOGY

Data collection began with a document review in order to identify existing explanations for the formation of a coalition among these groups. The bulk of the data for this chapter was obtained from document analysis and formal interviews with key organizational leaders at the Alliance, HACU, AIHEC, and NAFEO.

This chapter first reviews the literature on coalition formation and identifies relevant research that can be tested with this case: Kevin Hula's typology of motivational sources (1999), Marie Hojnacki's model of coalition formation (1997), and Burdett Loomis's coalition broker (1986). The next section describes historical relations among minority groups, and profiles the organizations under study. Building on this foundation, the subsequent section describes the events leading up to and following the 1998 reauthorization of the HEA, including the formation of the Alliance. Theoretical explanations are applied to the case, and conclusions are drawn.

LITERATURE REVIEW AND THEORETICAL FRAMEWORK

Explaining group coalition formation is at a relatively primitive stage compared to other areas of interest group research (Hojnacki, 1997; Hula, 1999).

As a result, little is known about the strategic choices groups make and how they make them as they attempt to achieve their policy goals in coalition or acting alone. As space constraints prohibit a thorough review of the literature, this section addresses the most recent literature that is most applicable to this case.

There is a difference of opinion about the reasons weaker and stronger organizations might join together. Foraging theory suggests that the stronger organization has less to gain from an alliance than the weaker (i.e., newer, fewer resources) organization (Gray and Lowery, 1998). Wilson (1973) suggests new (weak) organizations might prefer to lobby alone in order to develop their own identity.

According to Hula (1999), there are three main reasons for an organization to join a coalition, and the motivation for joining affects the role they play in the coalition. First, the decision could be entirely strategic; membership in a coalition helps an organization shape a public policy outcome. Coalition membership enables sharing of the workload as well as sharing of contacts and expertise. Second, organizations may perceive that selective benefits can be gained from joining. For example, they would have access to information they might not otherwise have. Third, organizations may join for symbolic reasons. Participation in a coalition may convince an organization's own membership that they are active on an issue; it may also demonstrate solidarity with another organization. In this case, "Cultivating an appearance rather than actually obtaining specific policy outcomes is the primary goal" (Hula, 1999, p. 241). Organizations joining coalitions for symbolic reasons are less likely to expend their resources on coalition goals. "Although they support the goal in principle, coalition membership is an end in itself, and they will remain on the periphery of the coalition, welcome all the same" (Hula, 1999, p. 256).

In a similar vein, Hojnacki (1997) identifies the variables that impact coalition formation. Assuming organizations are rational actors who will choose to join a coalition if membership maximizes their chances of success, Hojnacki identifies four variables that impact coalition participation: context, allies, autonomy, and character. First, by context, Hojnacki means the nature of the policy or the issue: whether or not it is highly contested, the likelihood of support from decision makers, and the scope of the issue. Second, an organization that perceives considerable opposition may find it advantageous to join with other like-minded organizations. Groups with experience as allies are more likely to join coalitions and are more likely to be perceived as valuable coalition members. Other groups considering joining a coalition will respond positively to the presence of a critical or "pivotal" ally on the coalition. Third, regarding autonomy, Hojnacki suggests that groups facing greater competition for resources are less likely to join coalitions, for fear of losing their identity and therefore their competitive edge. Finally, group character has implications for its decision to join a coalition. Corporations, for example, are more likely to be focused on outcomes that benefit their exclusive client base, while public interest organizations may have more reason to coalesce with like-minded groups. Based on these variables, Hojnacki predicts that group leaders are more likely to join a coalition when they have broad interest in an issue, perceive strong opposition to their goals, and believe that groups pivotal to their success will participate in the coalition.

Regarding the mechanics of coalition formation, it has been suggested that coalitions do not just emerge but are actively organized by brokers (Loomis, 1986). Brokers, typically representatives of law and public relations firms in Washington, D.C. bring organizations with common interests together. These brokers maintain the coalition by providing organization and structure. Brokers appear to be similar to the notion of policy entrepreneurs, defined as people who seek to initiate dynamic policy change (Mintrom, 1997). Their activities include identifying problems, networking, shaping the terms of policy debates, and building coalitions. Mintrom found that policy entrepreneurs play an important role in shaping policy debates. There is evidence that policy makers may also encourage coalition formation. From the perspective of policy makers, groups are encouraged to work out their differences outside the legislative process, rather than requiring Congress or the executive branch to resolve differences of opinion between groups. Members of Congress and their staffs, as well as agency staff, may initiate coalitions themselves in order to encourage groups to work out solutions and thereby avoid congressional paralysis on an issue (Hula, 1999).

BLACK—BROWN RELATIONS

Despite a number of shared experiences, including discrimination and lack of success in education, relations between Blacks and Hispanics in the United States have historically been difficult, and conflict has led to riots in Miami, Los Angeles, and Washington (Patchen, 1999; Piatt, 1997). At the federal level, Blacks and Hispanics have often been at odds in policy debates (Piatt, 1997).

In the African American community, some feel that other minority groups such as Hispanics benefit from the protesting and lobbying done by African Americans, and that Hispanics are free riding on African American policy wins (Rich, 1996). They are also concerned that Hispanic demands will displace or interfere with African American policy priorities. For example, bilingual education became a divisive issue when Blacks became concerned that the issue would shift resources from desegregation efforts (Falcon, 1988). There is also concern that Hispanics will displace Blacks in affirmative action programs (Piatt, 1997). Immigration policy has been another arena of conflict, as Blacks resisted increases in Hispanic immigration that might displace African American low-wage workers.

From their perspective, Latinos/as have perceived that African Americans have benefited more from affirmative action than Latinos/as. Latinos/as have noted Black support of the English Only movement and Black opposition to the extension of coverage to Latinos in amendments to the Voting Rights Act (Vaca, 2004). Hispanics argue that race relations have historically been viewed through a Black/White paradigm, which has relegated the concerns of other minority groups to the background (Mindiola, Niemann, and Rodriguez, 2002). The invisibility of Hispanics in policy making, some feel, has led to inequitable resource distribution, with African Americans receiving considerably more in federal program funds than Hispanics. Hispanic advocates regularly point out that Hispanics are underrepresented in federal programs and spending. Analysis by the Hispanic Association of Colleges and Universities finds that HBCUs receive $3,900 per student on average from federal grants, contracts, and appropriations, compared to $1,100 per student at HSIs (HACU, 2005). Raul Yzaguirre, former president of National Council of La Raza, argues forcefully that Hispanics do not have influence in policy making at the federal level. "Hispanics are not and have never been beneficiaries of the federal civil rights enforcement programs. With the exception of the Bilingual Education Act, Hispanics have never been specifically targeted by any federal education initiative" (Yzaguirre, 1991, p.179).

Evidence from each community reveals that "a divide exists between Blacks and Latinos/as that no amount of camouflage can hide." (Vaca, 2004, p.186). Hispanics feel that their needs are ignored at the expense of addressing African American policy priorities. African Americans perceive Hispanics as less deserving of government spending, given the absence of slavery from their history and the racial diversity within the Hispanic community. There is, however, an increasing awareness of the need to work together on issues that affect both communities (Shepard, 1998). The Alliance that is the focus of this chapter appears to one of these efforts.

MINORITY-SERVING INSTITUTIONS AND ADVOCACY ORGANIZATIONS

The term Minority-Serving Institution (MSI) was developed only in the last decade to describe those institutions serving large numbers of minority students (O'Brien and Zudak, 1998). These include those designated by the government as serving particular groups who have been historically discriminated against and who therefore are eligible for additional government funding. This section provides an overview of those institutions that have been formally designated as serving a particular group.

The leadership within each of these communities recognized the need to form an organization that could speak collectively for their institutions and could advocate on their behalf in Washington. The organizations that were created, NAFEO, HACU, and AIHEC, are recognized leaders within their issue niche and play important roles in legislative debates pertaining to Minority-Serving Institutions.

NATIONAL ASSOCIATION FOR EQUAL OPPORTUNITY

Several years after the designation of HBCUs in the Higher Education Act of 1965, a group of HBCU presidents organized a professional association that would pursue federal, foundation, and private funding opportunities on behalf of HBCUs. NAFEO member institutions are public and private, two- and four-year, community, regional, national and international comprehensive research institutions.

Like many nonprofit organizations, NAFEO has had periods in which the organization has floundered (Fields, 2002). According to past President Frederick S. Humphries, who served between 2001 and 2004, by 2001 the organization was near bankruptcy, with a $384,000 deficit, one million dollars in overdrafts in federal accounts, and internal financial irregularities (Basinger, 2004). There have also been divisions among the represented institutions; at the beginning of the decade only a third of the institutions were dues paying, and one of the criticisms had been that only the stronger and larger colleges and universities have benefited from their relationship with NAFEO (Fields, 2002). Humphries, who restored financial balance and increased the dues paying members to 80 percent, was ousted by the board of directors in 2004 apparently on the grounds that he was not sufficiently consultative (Basinger, 2004).

As of mid-2005, the organization continued to be on the road to recovery. The staff has been reduced, from 50 in 2004 to 35 in 2005. According to Leslie Baskerville, the current president and CEO, the staff reduction was intended to "make sure that we have an effective yet modest staff so that we can ensure we are transferring most of our resources to our members" (personal communication, April 14, 2005). They are also in the process of relocating their headquarters from Silver Spring, Maryland to Washington, D.C. in order to be closer to their allies and funders. While there does not appear to be an available annual report for 2004, the annual report for 2005 is in the final stages of development. The organization has multiple projects underway, both in coalition with other groups and on their own in service to their membership. Their Katrina hurricane relief effort reflects their ability to address a crisis quickly. NAFEO had three member institutions that were seriously damaged by Katrina and four that were also affected. NAFEO immediately started working with corporations, foundations, and the Congress to assist with a student and faculty evacuation program:

> We got money to create faculty fellowships so that they can remain engaged in research and perhaps even increase their research ability during this period while getting paid and staying connected with a higher education institution. We also sought money for the institutions to keep their leadership teams together and working on a recovery plan. (Leslie Baskerville, personal communication, November 14, 2005)

According to Baskerville, NAFEO also regularly participates in higher education legal cases:

> We also do things on a legal front. Recently NAFEO weighed in on the [*Gratz v.*] *Bollinger* decision. We're very concerned about diversity and want to be sure that students can go to the schools of their choice that best fits their needs. NAFEO has submitted amicus briefs on a number of recent higher education cases. (Leslie Baskerville, personal communication, November 14, 2005)

In addition to ramping up their capacity to serve as an information clearinghouse on Black issues in higher education and participating in leadership development programs with the United Negro College Fund and with the Alliance, NAFEO also is hoping to establish a legal definition for predominantly Black institutions (PBIs). Similar to HSIs, PBIs have arisen due to demographic changes. Baskerville explains NAFEO's position, and makes clear the difference between historically and predominately Black institutions:

> There is currently no legal definition of "predominantly Black" but we're seeking to get one in the Higher Education Act this cycle. Congressman Major Owens is interested in that. However, "historically" and "predominantly" are not interchangeable. The historically Black colleges have nothing to do with race but rather a historic need and the nation's sorry history of slavery and discrimination. It was the nation's way of acknowledging that these institutions that grew out of the dual system of education. . . . Predominantly Black colleges have cropped up for a number of reasons. and they are meeting a vital need in terms of expanding educational access to an underserved population. They are serving upwards of 200,000 students, but they are not interchangeable with HBCUs. We think the predominantly Black colleges should be defined based on [not only] the percentage of the student body that is African American, but also on income and generational status. (Leslie Baskerville, personal communication, November 14, 2005)

Baskerville does not agree with one congressman's bill that would include predominantly Black institutions in the HBCU title. She states: "We don't think it should be there; maybe it should be in 3(a). We don't think Historically Black and Predominantly Black are fungible and we feel that HBCUs already pass constitutional muster and we wouldn't want to complicate that." NAFEO currently represents 105 HBCUs and 20 Predominantly Black Colleges, and their approximate net assets for 2004 were $12 million.

HACU

In 1986, three educators in Texas saw a need to form an umbrella group for the colleges and universities serving large numbers of first-generation Hispanic college students. Initial funding came from Pew Charitable Trusts and the Ford Foundation (Flores, 2001). Since then, HACU has become an important voice for Hispanic higher education, and is the lead voice for Hispanic-Serving Institutions. In fact, without HACU, there would likely be no HSIs. Their efforts to organize two- and four-year colleges serving large numbers of Hispanics culminated in increased attention from policy makers, and, as a result, the creation of HSIs and access to considerable new federal funding (Laden, 2001).

By 2004, HACU's membership had grown to 395 member colleges, including 201 of the 242 HSIs and a large number of institutions with large or growing Hispanic populations but which do not yet meet the most stringent definition of HSI as defined by the 1998 HEA. In addition to continuing to lobby for a less onerous definition of HSI and increases in appropriations through Title V of HEA, HACU has obtained public and private funding for programs improving faculty capacity, increasing student participation in science and health, and promoting outreach to high school students. It also sponsors an internship program for Hispanic college students that by 2005 had served 5,000 participants and a scholarship program that disbursed $242,000 in 2005. In 2004 HACU had net assets of $2.6 million, with 65 percent of the revenues coming from government sources and 17 percent from corporations and foundations.

AMERICAN INDIAN HIGHER EDUCATION COUNCIL

AIHEC was founded in 1972 by the presidents of the nation's first six tribal colleges, as an informal collaboration among member colleges. Today, AIHEC has grown to represent 34 colleges in the United States and one Canadian institution. AIHEC's mission is to support the work of these colleges and the national movement for tribal self-determination. Its mission statement, adopted in 1973, identifies four objectives: (1) maintain commonly held standards of quality in American Indian education; (2) support the development of newly tribally controlled colleges; (3) promote and assist in the development of legislation to support American higher education; and (4) encourage greater participation by Native Americans in the development of higher education policy.

A major role played by AIHEC is to coordinate the efforts of various federal agencies to support tribal colleges. Rather than requiring individual colleges to apply for funds, agencies rely on AIHEC to develop applications and ensure accurate reporting. Currently AIHEC provides oversight of funds from a range of agencies, including the Department of Education, Health and Human Services, NASA and the National Science Foundation. In 2004, this pass-through funding amounted to approximately $20 million dollars.

AIHEC's other major focus is to increase the visibility of tribal colleges at the national level. Executive Director of AIHEC, Gerald Gipp, suggests several factors that make raising awareness of tribal colleges at the national level difficult: "We've been almost invisible as Native Americans for decades and we're not a big voting block. Federal agency people haven't recognized our needs and that's part of our job, to help them see our needs"(G. Gipp, personal communication, November 14, 2005). AIHEC has a staff of 16, with net assets of 1 million dollars in 2004.

THE 1998 REAUTHORIZATION

The 1998 reauthorization of the HEA was an opportunity for the growing numbers of Hispanics in Congress to capitalize on their increasing visibility and build on the progress made in the 1992 reauthorization. In 1992, HSIs were defined and funding was authorized. The 1998 reauthorization was an opportunity to raise the visibility of HSIs and increase authorization levels. As in 1992, HACU was expected to take the lead in early negotiations. Hispanic advocates had the additional advantage of a new Hispanic member of Congress who served on the Education and Labor Committee and who made clear his interest in higher education and funding for HSIs, Texas Congressman Ruben E. Hinojosa (Texas—D).

Like NAFEO, HACU has had moments in its history that were difficult. According to a key legislative staff person, one such moment was in 1997, when the leadership of the Washington staff was dismissed, leaving a void in the Hispanic higher education advocacy community on the eve of the 1998 HEA reauthorization (Anonymous legislative assistant who staffed the 1998 reauthorization for a member of the Education and Labor Committee, personal communication, June 5, 2005). Hinojosa, a member of the

Education and Labor Committee and the Congressional Hispanic Caucus, developed an ambitious HSI proposal and led the charge to elevate the status of HSIs by giving them their own section within Title III of the HEA, similar to the HBCU section.

NAFEO and the United Negro College Fund were adamantly opposed to the creation of a separate section for HSIs in Title III, and made public its opposition to the move (Mealer, 1998). It was supported by key congressional members. The ranking Democrat on the Education and Labor Committee at the time was Congressman Clay Shaw, a member of the Congressional Black Caucus and supporter of HBCUs. His lead staff person on higher education was Marshall Grigsby, who was a former HBCU president.

With the organizations divided, Congress was also paralyzed. According to a lead staff person during the HEA, it was the intervention of the American Council of Education (ACE), a leading higher education association that broke the logjam. According to my anonymous source,

> the higher ed [*sic*] groups were getting torn apart, the Administration was caught in the middle, and the Black members were under pressure to support the HBCU position. ACE finally stepped in and tried to negotiate. They sat down with the groups and said that HSIs can't have their own part of Title III but they could have their own Title. (anonymous, personal communication, June 5, 2005)

That became Title V of the HEA, which was eventually included in the bill that passed.

THE ALLIANCE

Few would have predicted that a coalition would emerge after the bruising 1998 debate. Wilbur C. Rich (1996) advances four possible reasons minorities avoid coalitions. First, groups are ethnocentric and therefore insular. Second, there is an established distrust among groups. Third, groups feel some are more able to assimilate than others. Fourth, groups have alliances with the White majority group. As of 1996, when Rich's book was published, the author found no formal coalitions among minorities.

However, as in other debates in which divisions exist, in this case there were also individuals situated further from the field of battle who suggested that working together would benefit all of the groups (Raines, 1998). Referring to HBCUs, Walter R. Allen and Joseph O. Jewell (2002) suggested that "HBCUs must continue to evolve and change to reflect America's new reality . . . best exemplified by the increasing number of racially, culturally, and economically diverse student bodies that they will be called upon to educate" (p. 258). Jamie P. Merisotis, president of the Institute for Higher Education

Policy, suggests that "the alliance was born of conflict and yet it really has been a vehicle for overcoming that" (J. P. Merisotis, personal communication, May 11, 2005). Merisotis recalls the first efforts to reconcile the groups:

> Coming out of that reauthorization a group of presidents along with the Kellogg Foundation decided that there should be a forum for discussing what happened here, why did we do this, and what can we learn from this, and so the sort of level heads said, what went wrong here. (J. P. Merisotis, personal communication, May 11, 2005)

After several difficult meetings of organization and institution leaders, it was decided that a formal coalition should be formed in order to enable the groups to work together. As J. P. Merisotis recalls, "as [then President of NAFEO] Henry Ponder said, 'why don't we stop fighting over crumbs and figure out how to get a bigger piece of the pie for all of us.' And so that was the motivation to create it" (J. P. Merisotis, personal communication, May 11, 2005).

All of the organization leaders interviewed recognized that increasing their visibility with congressional leadership would help them pursue more funding than they were currently receiving. Leslie Baskerville of NAFEO suggests that the inadequate level of funding for MSIs is the result of the lack of success MSIs have had in getting their message across combined with a resistance to providing funding that would largely benefit minorities:

> We as a community have probably not done as good a job as we could in educating policy makers about the importance of our institutions. Research is showing that the flagship institutions are disengaging from serving minority populations, and our institutions are really focusing on serving that population and our institutions are more cost effective and produce good outcomes. Those are the things that should resonate with policy makers. But we have not made that case. (Leslie Baskerville, personal communication, November 14, 2005)

Memos summarizing the early meetings reflect this sentiment (Overton-Adkins, 1999). Participants recognized a need to work together whenever possible and build trust between the groups so that inevitable differences could be managed constructively. They also felt that working together would strengthen their voice in negotiating with Congress. This was particularly the case for HACU, according to its president and CEO, Dr. Antonio Flores. Flores, who came to HACU just before the reauthorization, noted the limited understanding of HSIs in Washington:

> As a new CEO to HACU, I was surprised by the level of unfamiliarity on the part of Members of Congress about HSIs and HACU. The level of understanding was just not there for the cause of HSIs. HBCUs, obviously being around since 1890s were quite well known across government. (personal communication, August 4, 2005)

Membership in the Alliance, in addition to other efforts to reach out to policy makers, has raised the name recognition of HSIs and HACU dramatically. According to Flores: "We (HSIs) had not developed the infrastructure to make sure that our message got across. We weren't even in the ball game. Now not only are we in the ball game but we are scoring big points" (Flores, personal communication, August 4, 2005)

From the perspective of NAFEO, another factor in the decision to join together was that the fear HBCUs had going in to the 1998 reauthorization that their funding would be affected had not in fact materialized. As a congressional staff member recalls: "HBCUs were very afraid of a zero-sum game. When you look at what happened, nothing could be further from the truth. And since they were starting from a larger base, their numbers got bigger with every appropriation" (anonymous, personal communication, May 18, 2005).

Reflecting on the success of the Alliance in its first five years, Merisotis says, "One of the things we've overcome in five years is this zero-sum philosophy that if they gain, we lose, and we've realized that that wasn't going to happen" (J. P. Merisotis, personal communication, May 11, 2005). By 2003, House Republicans announced that increasing funding for Minority-Serving Institutions was one of their top ten education goals for the new Congress (Black Issues in Higher Education, 2003). Also in 2003, reflecting a willingness to support coalition members, even in instances which may not provide a direct benefit to all coalition members, the Alliance sent a letter to President Bush requesting that he issue an Executive Order establishing a President's Board of Advisors on Hispanic-Serving Institutions, similar to the two Executive Orders the President had signed for HBCUs and tribal colleges.

The technology gap was identified early on in the Alliance's development as an issue that was critical to all of its institutions and has been a focus of several jointly produced reports. In 2006, MSIs were anticipating the passage of the Minority-Serving Institution Digital and Wireless Technology Opportunity Act, which would authorize $1.2 billion over five years for technology upgrades and instruction at MSIs. In 2003, the Alliance received a four-year, $6 million grant from the W. K. Kellogg Foundation for a leadership development program designed to support and develop MSI leaders. The major goal of the MSI Leadership Fellows Program is that at least half of the individuals who participate in the program will have served or will be serving as a president, provost, or other high-level senior leader at an MSI by the end of the decade.

In addition to funding and programmatic successes, interview participants emphasized that the importance of the coalition went well beyond a greater capacity to raise funds. Leaders recognized the need for institutions of higher education to reflect the growing diversity of the nation and saw the Alliance as an important vehicle for building cross-cultural awareness. Baskerville makes this point:

> Certainly strengthening our ability to access dollars is important but it also created important opportunities for cultural exchange and the reach it gives us into other communities . . . we want our students to be able to compete anywhere, and the growing diversity of the nation means students need to be exposed to different languages and cultures. So we really want to work on building a multicultural curriculum so that we can compete nationally and internationally. So while it may be that there are financial advantages to the coalition, I think the advantages are broader, and I wouldn't want to overlook the value of better positioning ourselves to lead in a richly diverse, globally interdependent nation. (Leslie Baskerville, personal communication, November 14, 2005)

In fact, Baskerville reports that the congressional Black leadership has encouraged NAFEO to work independently of the Alliance on issues of funding. This is not surprising, given NAFEO's longer history and stronger ties to congressional leadership:

> The other thing is on the economic piece, there are times when the Alliance is not necessarily to NAFEO's economic benefit. For example, we are working with Alliance members on the Digital and Wireless Technology Act. There are members of Congress who are encouraging us to separate in order to bring more additional support to our institutions. But our commitment is to the whole and moving forward so that all of our institutions benefit. So while many times it's helpful, there are times when it would be better to go it alone. But if you're committed to the overall benefit to being part of a united team on those things where we share a common interest—technology is one but there are certainly others—you go it as a team. (Leslie Baskerville, personal communication, November 14, 2005)

The coalition members report a high level of satisfaction with the coalition initiatives. According to HACU President Flores,

> We're beyond where we expected to be. Originally we were thinking only about policy and legislation. We also now have the Kellogg fellows program, which we are very proud of because originally we were not thinking of going into the programmatic area, but we have been very successful with that program. . . . We are moving in the right direction, and we are doing it with mutual respect and collaboration. It's really a testament of the tremendous good will that has emerged from all of the leaders in the institutions that participate in this. (personal communication, August 4, 2005)

Gerald Gipp, Executive Director of AIHEC, agrees:

> Too often in the past different groups have tried to wage their own battles. This is a real opportunity for the three organizations to work together and ultimately to have greater impact, greater clout. From the American Indian standpoint, it is

> very important for us . . . we don't have a large population so every opportunity for access is critical. (G. Gipp, personal communication, June 7, 2005)

Gipp suggests that AIHEC has clearly benefited from the Alliance, and has gained as much or more from common grant initiatives as their larger alliance partners:

> Common grant initiatives have provided a direct benefit. For example, the Alliance obtained funding for leadership development. Each association gets ten fellows a year for three years. That says a lot about the leadership; even though they have more schools they are willing to divide the benefits from the program equally. (G. Gipp, personal communication, June 7, 2005)

While joint projects have been successful, the Alliance's future is far from certain. As college campuses continue to see increasing diversity, Alliance members will have to resolve some difficult questions. In the next section, I highlight some of these questions.

THE FUTURE OF THE ALLIANCE

NAFEO and the HBCUs were understandably concerned when Hispanics began to call for inclusion in what had previously been their exclusive funding source. Not only were there a large number of HSIs, but they also were likely to increase in number over time. The definition of HSIs has been recognized as problematic on all sides of the debate. Merisotis recognizes this as a challenge the Alliance will soon have to face:

> That's another issue that's going to come to a head at some point is, we need to look at the definition of HSI; what does it mean to be "serving" Hispanics? I think there's growing sentiment that the 25 percent standard is not right. The problem is, whether or not you have 25 percent or more Hispanic students has nothing to do with whether or how you serve them. So the question is, how do you measure "serving Hispanics." And that's the more complicated issue because there are a lot of institutions now that are new HSIs that just happened to have hit the trigger, but I wouldn't say they're serving Hispanics. On the other hand, there's great examples like University of Texas at Austin that are not HSIs but are huge servers of Hispanics. UT Austin graduates the highest percentage of Hispanics with graduate degrees than any institution in the country, and so of course they are a Hispanic-Serving Institution, but they don't fall under the current definition, so there's got to be a better way to do this. (J. P. Merisotis, personal communication, May 11, 2005)

As increasing numbers of schools are identified as Hispanic-Serving, it should also be noted that many of these schools are also serving large numbers of African Americans. According to HACU, of the 242 HSIs identified in 2002, 24 percent (59) had student bodies that were at least 18 percent Black; 6 were more than half Black. Of the 116 emerging HSIs that HACU identified in 2002 (institutions with Hispanic enrollment between 18% and 24.9%), almost half (51) had Black student populations over 18 percent, with the average of the 51 being 34 percent Black. Finally, while HBCUs may have historically served Blacks, they are increasingly serving other groups. Several HBCUs are now majority White, and one HBCU is also formally recognized as an HSI. St. Philips College in Texas, which is 50 percent Hispanic, 18.4 percent Black and 28.7 percent White. As colleges become more racially mixed, deciding how to distribute federal funds will undoubtedly become more complicated, and how these definitions are revised may pose a considerable challenge to HBCU and HSI advocates.

HACU's President Flores recognizes the blurring of the lines between HBCUs and HSIs and suggests this is an excellent reason for the continued success of the Alliance:

> All politics is local . . . when you go to the local level, guess what, Hispanics are populating all parts of the country—many HBCUs are now home to Latino students. . . . Essentially, if HBCUs benefit greatly from the coalition, that's good because they are going to be enrolling lots more Hispanic students. (A. Flores, personal communication, August 4, 2005)

For the time being, NAFEO and HACU represent particular institutions. NAFEO represents 118 institutions, mostly HBCUs, and HACU represents 395 institutions, half of which are HSIs. While they may find issues, such as technology and teacher training, that profit from coalition action, they exist to represent their particular members. In 2001, Congressman James Watts, a high-profile African American Republican, was the catalyst for a series of hearings in the 107th Congress entitled, "Responding to the Needs of historically Black colleges and universities in the 21st Century." Four hearings were held, and testimony was provided by a number of HBCU presidents and by then-President of NAFEO, Henry Ponder. Reflecting his priority to serve HBCUs first and the coalition second, Dr. Ponder made no reference to NAFEO's participation in the Alliance or to other Minority-Serving Institutions. There were no similar series of hearings for Hispanic-Serving Institutions or tribal colleges and universities, providing further evidence of the greater political strength of HBCUs compared to the other MSIs.

The coalition allows the groups to present a united front to Congress when necessary but also provides the freedom for the organizations to use their political capital exclusively. This is clearly an advantageous position for a group with better political connections. NAFEO might also have another reason to maintain its separate identity while at the same time working in coalition. NAFEO is aware that HBCUs are safer from constitutional challenge than institutions which are not defined historically but by the race/ethnicity of their student body:

> The trouble is MSIs may run into constitutional challenge and may die, whereas an HBCU has nothing to do with race/ethnicity and so could withstand constitutional muster. But we're trying to advance as a community, so we try to talk more about the things that we share. (Leslie Baskerville, personal communication, November 14, 2005)

For a group with less access, a united front that avoids congressional paralysis may be helpful, but it may also place that group in the position of "second fiddle," expected to be satisfied with regular but small funding increases. HACU's moderate approach, sensitive to the fact that HBCUs had been instrumental in establishing the funding pots that HSIs are now trying to access, is reflected in comments by Gumecindo Salas, current vice president of government relations at HACU:

> Now HBCUs might have had very good reason to be concerned. There was only so much money being put into Title III: African American, HBCUs' money. And then they started to see Native Americans coming in and taking their chunk, and then they see this massive group of Hispanics coming in—you know 150 more. They became alarmed because they said, "if we let that big mob in, there's going to be no more money for us because the pot wasn't growing," so there was a real reason to be antagonistic. And we have to recognize that. And recognize too that they've been around longer; they were very diligent in getting that money established, especially Title III in the HEA. Anybody else would have done the same thing. (G. Salas, personal communication, May 11, 2005)

THEORETICAL EXPLANATIONS

This chapter responds to three major theories of coalition formation. First, this study confirms the importance of a broker in the formation of a coalition. Second, while Kevin W. Hula's (1999) typology is useful when parsing out the motivations for joining coalitions, this study finds that the categories overlap considerably. Third, several revisions are made to Marie Hojnacki's (1997) findings regarding the decision to join a coalition.

THE BROKER

All accounts of the creation of the Alliance, while varying somewhat in the details, confirm the importance of a broker. Betty Overton-Atkins of the

Kellogg Foundation was instrumental in bringing together the leaders. According to Salas:

> It just happened that these people were together at the conference. They were talking about it and Betty from Kellogg said, "you people really need to work together." She was the higher education director, [and] she said, "if I could get a grant, would you be willing to work together?" And they said yes. (G. Salas, personal communication, May 11, 2005)

Jaime P. Merisotis, who was asked to facilitate the early conversations among the groups and whose organization manages the Alliance funding and projects, suggests that the nature of the broker was critical: "Betty Overton Atkins at Kellogg absolutely was the key to making this happen. And frankly it was because it was a funder that people agreed to come to the meeting" (J. P. Merisotis, personal communication, May 11, 2005).

Despite the clear advantages to NAFEO of joining a coalition, and the somewhat more limited but nevertheless real advantages to HACU and AIHEC, it is very unlikely that any one of the groups could have spearheaded the coalition independently. An outside, neutral source was necessary in order to bring the groups together.

MOTIVATION TO JOIN

Just as Lowi's (1999) three domains have been found to overlap, this paper finds that while Hula's three categories of incentives to which groups respond are useful factors to consider when analyzing group motivations, they are not distinct categories within which particular groups fall. Hula suggests there are three main reasons organizations join coalitions: to pursue strategic goals at reduced costs, to gather information, or to receive symbolic benefits. This chapter can identify strategic, selective, and symbolic reasons that motivated all three of the organizations to join the Alliance.

Joining with the other groups was both strategic and symbolic in that it allowed NAFEO to present a united front to legislators, and, in effect, neutralizes the threat from an adversarial relationship with the HSIs. Congressional testimony suggests that NAFEO continues to see higher education funding issues through a Black-White paradigm. Looking forward, however, supporting funding for HSIs is potentially also in the self-interest of NAFEO. As HBCUs increasingly become eligible for funding as HSIs, it is in the interest of NAFEO to support increased funding for HSIs. In addition, seeking funding for predominantly Black institutions is made easier by the precedent set by HSIs. NAFEO also obtained selective benefits by joining the coalition and gaining access to funding from the Kellogg Foundation in order to pursue joint funding opportunities.

From HACU's perspective, there were also clear strategic advantages to being part of the Alliance. Through the Alliance, HACU has gained access to NAFEO's political connections at least in some instances and has participated in the development of legislation that will fund a technology program for all MSIs equally. The real test will be the long-awaited reauthorization of the Higher Education Act; the Alliance has developed joint recommendations, but the organizations have also made individual requests on behalf of their respective constituencies. The funding of these individual requests will reveal the extent to which the Alliance has elevated the bargaining power of HSIs.

Regarding AIHEC, the smallest of the three groups, it also derives strategic, selective, and symbolic benefits from participation in the coalition. The coalition provides it with opportunities to be included in legislative proposals. It is provided with information for which it would not otherwise have had the resources to collect themselves; and it is able to announce legislative victories to its constituency without great expenditure of its own resources. Executive Director of AIHEC, Gerald Gipp, is very positive about their participation in the Alliance, and cites instances in which the leadership of the two larger organizations supported AIHEC on issues that were of exclusive concern to tribal colleges. AIHEC does not pose a threat to the other two groups because its population is small and not growing significantly. Its importance to the coalition is symbolic.

Another advantage each of the organizations may derive from the coalition not only falls under the category of symbolic, but also can be described as strategic: coalition membership can disguise moments when the organization is in disarray or lacking in political connections. Victories by the Alliance can be evidence to individual memberships that their organizations are providing valuable services. The Alliance also brings legislative victories to its organizations with limited expenditure of resources.

This case study also offers an opposing view to foraging theory, which suggests that a stronger organization has less to gain from an alliance than a weaker organization (Gray and Lowery, 1998). In this case, given the need to present a united front to legislators, the stronger organization (NAFEO) had as much to gain from allying with HACU and AIHEC as did the less established organizations. In fact, NAFEO arguably had more to gain as its base of funding was considerably higher than the other groups, a flat percentage increase across the groups results in more actual dollars authorized for HBCUs than for HSIs or tribal colleges. On the other hand, NAFEO's participation is not neatly defined as that of a rational actor if, as Baskerville reports, its allies in Congress have suggested that it would have had more to gain by going it alone.

With regard to Hojnacki's (1997) variables, this study provides an alternative perspective on one variable and confirms the other two. First, Hojnacki suggests that groups facing strong organized opposition are more likely to join together than those groups facing weak or unorganized opposition. In this case, the coalition members were each other's opposition, and joining together gave the groups an opportunity to work out their differences before approaching a largely receptive Congress with their requests. Second, this study confirms Hojnacki's findings with regard to allies and invitations to join a coalition. Hojnacki found that an organization that is invited to join a coalition is predisposed not to join. It is not likely in this case that any one of the groups would have been able to bring a coalition together, given the competitive relationship they had developed. This again confirms the importance of a broker, as Loomis (1986) found. Third, similar to Hojnacki's study, this study did not confirm the importance of autonomy. Those organizations competing for resources were actually more likely to join alliances. This study confirms Schlozman's and Tierney's (1986) findings that organizations are more likely to be successful if they present a united front to Congress, thereby reducing the level of conflict to which legislators are exposed and making it more likely that Congress will respond favorably to their requests.

CONCLUSION

The Alliance has clearly provided benefits to all of the participants. First, there are clear financial incentives for the Alliance members to work together. The technology bill and the leadership program are two significant developments that would not likely have come to pass without the Alliance. In addition to financial incentives, the coalition has improved the visibility of the two "junior" members of the coalition on the Hill and with the Administration. This allows them not only better access to federal funding, but also an improved ability to influence policy making. Finally, all coalition members point to the value of the Alliance as a way to improve cultural understanding across the groups.

While the Alliance appears to be the first formal effort at coalition building across racial and ethnic lines among Washington advocacy organizations, others may soon follow. At the National Council of La Raza's (NCLR) 2005 convention, Janet Murguia, their new president, announced it was time to "open a new book of collaboration between this nation's African American and Hispanic communities," and she spoke of her interest in connecting Urban League affiliates with La Raza affiliates across the country (Remarks at the National Affiliate Luncheon, July 16, 2005, Pennsylvania Convention Center). Murguia also announced that she will be the first NCLR president to address a plenary session of the Urban League's national conference. Murguia's perspective, and her influence with other organizational leadership, may be rooted in her background as a senior White House policy advisor under President Clinton. As the theoretical work on brokers finds, presidential administration staff see the advantages of minority groups working in coalition. Murguia may come to NCLR with this perspective, rather than a more territorial perspective one might find at the grassroots level. This tension between the more traditional activist role and the more recent tendency to compromise and coalesce can be difficult to overcome and will continue to pose a challenge to efforts to work together (Sierra, 1991).

As the often junior member of coalitions, Latinos must balance their need to be team players with their need to push for a more equal role. Caplow's model of coalitions assumed that one stronger member would control the internal dynamics of the coalition, which creates conditions for instability (Caplow, 1956). The extent to which NAFEO shares its political influence in a way that is more than symbolic, and the degree to which HACU pushes for a more equal standing, will determine the stability of this promising effort at coalition building among minority interest groups.

REFERENCES

Allen, W. R., and Jewell, J. O. (2002). A backward glance forward: Past, present and future perspectives on historically Black colleges and universities. *The Review of Higher Education, 25*(3), 241–261.

Basinger, J. (2004, May 14, 2004). National group of Black colleges ousts its president. *The Chronicle of Higher Education,* p. 31.

Baumgartner, F. R., and Jones, B. D. (1993). *Agendas and Instability in American Politics.* Chicago, IL: The University of Chicago Press.

Baumgartner, F. R., and Leech, B. L. (1998). *Basic interests: The importance of groups in politics and political science.* Princeton, NJ: Princeton University Press.

Benitez, M. (1998). Hispanic-serving institutions: Challenges and opportunities. *New Directions for Higher Education, 102,* 57–68.

Berry, J. M. (1997). *The Interest Group Society.* New York: Longman.

Black Issues in Higher Education. (2003). HBCUs, HSIs on House Agenda (Brief article). *Black Issues in Higher Education, 19*(25), 7.

Browne, W. P. (1990). Organized interests and their issue niches: A search for pluralism in a policy domain. *The Journal of Politics, 52*(2).

Caplow, T. (1956). A theory of coalitions in the triad. *American Sociological Review, 19,* 23–29.

Cobb, R. W., and Elder, C. D. (1972). *Participation in American politics: The dynamics of agenda-building.* Boston, MA: Allyn and Bacon.

Constantine, J. M. (1995). The effect of attending historically Black colleges and universities on future wages of Black students. *Industrial and Labor Relations Review, 48*(3), 531–546.

Cunningham, A. F., and Parker, C. (1998). Tribal Colleges as community institutions and resources. *New Directions for Higher Education (102)*, 45–55.

Dervarics, C. (1997). Can a rift be avoided? *Black Issues in Higher Education, 14*(19), 20–28.

Falcon, A. (1988). Black and Latino politics in New York City. In F. C. García (Ed.), *Latinos in the Political System*. South Bend, IN: Notre Dame University Press.

Fields, C. D. (2002). A renewed spirit: as NAFEO's new president, Dr. Frederick Humphries vows to make the organization the 'lead voice' for all historically Black colleges and universities. *Black Issues in Higher Education, 19*(12), 14.

Fletcher, M. A. (1998, February). White House Backs Plan to Aid Hispanic-Serving Colleges. *The Washington Post,* p. 10.

Flores, A. (2001, August 11). Hispanic college group celebrates its 15th year. *San Antonio Express-News,* p. 3B.

Gray, V., and Lowery, D. (1998). To lobby alone or in a flock. *American Politics Quarterly, 26*(1), 5–34.

HACU. (2004). *Emerging Hispanic-serving institutions.* Washington, DC: Hispanic Association of Colleges and Universities.

HACU. (2005). *2005 Legislative Agenda.* Washington, DC: Hispanic Association of Colleges and Universities.

Heinz, J. P. (1993). *The hollow core : private interests in national policy making.* Cambridge, MA: Harvard University Press.

Hojnacki, M. (1997). Interest groups' decisions to join alliances or work alone. *American Journal of Political Science, 41*(1), 61–87.

Hula, K. W. (1999). *Lobbying together : interest group coalitions in legislative politics.* Washington, DC: Georgetown University Press.

Laden, B. V. (1999). Celebratory socialization of culturally diverse students through academic programs and services. In K. M. Shaw, J. R. Valadez, and R. A. Rhoads (Eds.), *Community Colleges as Cultural Contexts.* New York: State University of New York.

Laden, B. V. (2001). Hispanic-serving institutions: Myths and realities. *Peabody Journal of Education, 76*(1), 73–92.

Loomis, B. A. (1986). Coalitions of Interests: Building bridges in a Balkanized state. In A. J. Cigler and B. A. Loomis (Eds.), *Interest Group Politics* (2nd ed.). Washington, DC: CQ Press.

Lowi, T. J. (1964). American business, public policy, case studies, and political theory. *World Politics, 16,* 677–715.

McKinnon, J. (2003). *The Black Population in the United States: March 2002.* Washington, DC: U.S. Census Bureau.

Mealer, B. (1998, January 16, 1998). Hispanic-serving institutions Seek More Federal Funds, Angering Black Colleges. *Chronicle of Higher Education,* p. A31.

Merisotis, J. P., and Goulian, K. A. (2004). The Alliance for Equity in Higher Education. *New Directions for Community Colleges* (127), 89–96.

Mindiola, T., Niemann, Y. F., and Rodriguez, N. (2002). *Black-brown relations and stereotypes* (1st ed.). Austin, TX: University of Texas Press.

Mintrom, M. (1997). Policy Entrepreneurs and the Diffusion of Innovation. *American Journal of Political Science, 41*(3), 738–770.

O'Brien, E. M., and Zudak, C. (1998). Minority-Serving Institutions: An overview. *New Directions for Higher Education, 102,* 5–15.

Overton-Adkins, B. J. (1999). HBCU, Tribal College, HSI meeting memo.

Patchen, M. (1999). *Diversity and Unity: Relations between racial and ethnic groups.* Chicago, IL: Nelson-Hall Publishers.

Piatt, B. (1997). *Black and Brown in America: The case for cooperation.* New York: New York University Press.

Raines, R. T. (1998). Collaboration and cooperation among Minority-Serving Institutions. *New Directions for Higher Education* (102), 69–80.

Ramirez, R. R., and de la Cruz, G. P. (2003). *The Hispanic Population in the United States: March 2002* (No. P20–545). Washington, DC: U.S. Census Bureau.

Redd, K. E. (1998). Historically Black colleges and universities: Making a comeback. *New Directions for Higher Education* (102), 33–43.

Reisinger, W. M. (1986). Situational and motivational assumptions in theories of coalition formation. *Legislative Studies Quarterly, XI*(4), 551–563.

Rich, W. C. (1996). *The politics of minority coalitions : race, ethnicity, and shared uncertainties.* Westport, CT: Praeger.

Salisbury, R. H. (1990). The paradox of interest groups in Washington—More groups, less clout. In A. King (Ed.), *The New American Political System.* Washington, DC: The AEI Press.

Schlozman, K. L., and Tierney, J. T. (1986). *Organized interests and American democracy.* New York: Harper and Row.

Shepard, S. (1998, April 21, 1988). Civil rights conference stresses bridge-building between groups. *The Atlanta Journal and Constitution,* p. 9A.

Sierra, C. M. (1991). Latino organizational strategies on immigration reform: Success and limits in public policymaking. In R. E. Villarreal and N. G. Hernandez (Eds.), *Latinos and Political Coalitions.* New York: Greenwood Press.

Stearns, C., and Watanabi, S. (2002). *Hispanic-serving institutions: Statistical trends from 1990 to 1999.* Washington, DC: National Center for Education Statistics.

Stoops, N. (2004). *Educational Attainment in the United States: 2003.* Washington, DC: U.S. Census Bureau.

Tierney, J. (1994). Interest group research: Questions and approaches. In W. J. Crotty, M. A. Schwartz and J. C. Green (Eds.), *Representing interests and interest group representation.* Lanham: University Press of America.

U.S. Census Bureau. (2003). *2000 Census of Population and Housing, Characteristics of American Indians and Alaska Natives by Tribe and Language: 2000.* Washington, DC: Department of Commerce.

U.S. Census Bureau. (2004). *Annual Estimates of the Population by Sex, Race and Hispanic or Latino Origin for the United States: April 1, 2000 to July 1, 2003, Table 3 (NC–EST2003–03).* Washington DC: Department of Commerce, Population Division.

Vaca, N. C. (2004). *The Presumed Alliance: the unspoken conflict between Latinos and Blacks and what it means for America.* New York: HarperCollins.

Villarreal, R. E., and Hernandez, N. G. (1991). Coalitional politics as a strategy for Latino empowerment: A developmental approach. In R. E. Villarreal and N. G. Hernandez (Eds.), *Latinos and Political Coalitions.* New York: Greenwood Press.

Wilson, J. Q. (1973). *Political organizations.* New York: Basic Books.

Wolanin, T. R. (1998). The federal investment in Minority-Serving Institutions. *New Directions for Higher Education* (102), 17–32.

Yin, R. K. (2003). *Case study research: design and methods* (3rd ed.). Thousand Oaks, CA: Sage Publications.

Yzaguirre, R. (1991). Keys to Hispanic empowerment. In R. E. Villarreal and N. G. Hernandez (Eds.), *Latinos and Political Coalitions.* New York: Greenwood Press.

CHAPTER 19

The Adversity of Diversity

Regional Associations and the Accreditation of Minority-Serving Institutions

Saran Donahoo and Wynetta Y. Lee

According to its legal structure, accreditation is a voluntary process in which colleges and universities participate in order to maintain federal aid eligibility and illustrate to others the quality of education provided to their students. However, the basic definition of accreditation fails to convey the full impact accreditation reviews, outcomes, and approvals have for many postsecondary schools. For Black colleges and other Minority-Serving Institutions, accreditation status often determines whether or not these schools have the opportunity to function at all. Given the importance of institutional accreditation and the less than positive history many postsecondary schools share with one southern accreditor, which has jurisdiction over most of these institutions, it is necessary to determine (*a*) how the regional associations address accreditation compliance and sanctions at the schools; (*b*) identify and compare trends in their review process at types of institutions; and (*c*) assess the overall equity of their penalty procedures.

Utilizing reports featured in *The Chronicle of Higher Education,* this chapter examines accreditation decisions issued by the regional associations, the impact these decisions have on individual institutions and institution types, and the influence accreditation has on the higher education arena. The text begins with a brief overview of the history of postsecondary accreditation in the United States, with special attention given to the Southern Association of Colleges and Schools (SACS) and its relationship with Black colleges and universities. The chapter also includes a description of the structure and approach employed, the presentation and analysis of data, and implications and conclusions regarding the current state of institutional accreditation for minority-serving schools, along with a discussion of the impact proposed changes might have on the accreditation process on these campuses.

REGIONAL ASSOCIATIONS AND THE VALUE OF ACCREDITATION

Accreditation is part of the evaluation process used to measure the quality of institutions and programs. In the United States, accreditation is primarily a voluntary self-regulation process maintained by nongovernmental agencies and associations. The foundation for the modern accreditation system developed in 1847 when the American Medical Association (AMA) became the first nonprofit association established to set and maintain professional standards. Following the AMA, four of the current regional education accreditation agencies also developed during the nineteenth century: the New England Association of Schools and Colleges (NEASC) in 1885; the Middle States Association of Schools and Colleges (MSA) in 1887; and in 1895 both the North Central Association of Colleges and Schools (NCACS) and the Southern Association of Colleges and Schools (SACS). The two remaining regional associations, the Northwest Association of Schools and Colleges (NWASC) and the Western Association of Schools and Colleges (WASC) developed in 1917 and 1962, respectively (Alstete, 2004; Bemis, 1983; Harcleroad, 1980).

Regional accreditation agencies concentrate on measuring the quality of higher education at the institutional level. Supported by membership fees from accredited schools, these associations establish standards that institutions must satisfy in order to gain and maintain institutional accreditation. The uses of accreditation include helping to preserve the academic value of higher education, providing a buffer against political influence over postsecondary institutions, and serving as both a marker of, and stimulus for, operating high-quality colleges and universities (Eaton, 2003). Since the early 1950s, accreditation has also served as a gatekeeper to financial aid and support. First established under the Veterans Readjustment Assistance Act of 1952, only accredited postsecondary institutions have the authority to award and accept federal and state student aid such as veterans' educational benefits, grants, and student loans. Likewise, many private employers also consider the accreditation status of an institution when making hiring decisions, supporting the educational pursuits of their employees, and disbursing charitable gifts (Alstete, 2004; Eaton, 2003; Harcleroad, 1980).

ACCREDITATION AND BLACK COLLEGES

Historically Black colleges and universities (HBCUs) have always faced an uphill battle in obtaining and retaining regional accreditation. Established primarily in the South, many of these institutions predate the establishment of any of the regional associations. Even so, the SACS maintained both written and unwritten policies denying membership to all HBCUs until 1930 (Trent, 1959). Supported by a grant from the General Education Board, SACS began to provide limited accreditation and approval to some HBCUs without allowing any of these institutions to become full members of the association (Clement, 1966). Even though neither the MSA nor the NCACS utilized the policy or practice of racially segregating their institutional members, more than 80 percent of HBCUs were and remain under the geographic jurisdiction of the SACS, and thus could not take advantage of membership opportunities provided by the other regional associations (Clement, 1966; Trent, 1959; Wright, 1958).[1]

Faced with limited access to regional accreditation, many HBCUs came together to form their own organization. Developed in 1933, the Association of Colleges and Secondary Schools for Negroes (ACSSN) permitted HBCUs across the country to attain full membership (Clement, 1966; Trent, 1959). However, the ACSSN chose not to act as an independent accrediting body, and instead required that perspective member institutions obtain approval from the SACS or another regional association (Rogers, 1989). Even so, the ACSSN did play a crucial role in getting HBCUs better access to and treatment from the SACS by working with that regional accreditor to establish standards and procedures for extending equal membership to these institutions. The ACSSN concluded business in 1964 following successful desegregation efforts of the 1950s and early 1960s including the SACS' decision to extend full membership to HBCUs in 1956 (Clement, 1966; Trent, 1959).

PROBLEM STATEMENT

Although the SACS no longer maintains membership restrictions specifically targeted at HBCUs, that regional accreditor continues to treat Black colleges as second-class institutions. Compared to the other regional associations, the SACS is more active and much more likely to publicly sanction and punish colleges and universities. Evidenced by stories reported in *The Chronicle of Higher Education* (*Chronicle*), the SACS and the other regional associations fail to treat all colleges and universities equally by punishing HBCUs and other Minority-Serving Institutions more harshly, and more frequently so, than their other member institutions.

Using the *Chronicle,* this chapter examines reported accreditation decisions made by the six regional associations. We focus on the regional associations because of the financial implications surrounding institution-level accreditation. By employing accreditation as an eligibility requirement to disburse financial aid and receive financial support, the federal government has transformed institutional accreditation from a "voluntary" review process to a fiscal necessity, which significantly influences institutional function, structure, and survival.

METHODS

This study uses articles published in the *Chronicle* from 1996 through (May) 2005 to monitor media coverage of regional accreditation decisions. This project focuses on the *Chronicle* because it serves as a key publication in higher education (Stepp, 2003a; Stepp, 2003b). Just under one million administrators, faculty members, libraries, and postsecondary institutions around the world subscribe to the *Chronicle* to stay informed about political, financial, and organizational changes impacting colleges and universities (Stepp, 2003b). While other publications such as *Diverse Issues in Higher Education* or even reports from the regional associations themselves also report on accreditation, this study focuses exclusively on accreditation information reported in the *Chronicle* because of its large number of subscribers and high level of usage, frequent electronic news alerts and updates, and high degree of availability and accessibility within the higher education arena. Using the *Chronicle* insures that each of the decisions included in the data set abided by a similar structure and received relatively equal attention within higher education and from the general public.

This analysis focuses primarily on regional association decisions, with special attention to those that impact HBCUs and other Minority-Serving Institutions (MSIs). However, the data set and analysis presented in this chapter do account for and examine regional accreditation decisions that influence predominantly White institutions (PWIs) in the United States as way of judging the overall actions of the regional associations and constructing a comparison group for analyzing the treatment received by MSIs.

The data set for this study contained 126 articles, accreditation updates, and news briefs published in the *Chronicle* from 1996 through May 2005. The research period allows us to examine the impact of changes to the accreditation landscape, such as the founding of the Council for Higher Education Accreditation in 1996, to monitor fluctuations in accreditation status for individual colleges and universities, and to construct a reasonable sample size in which to make comparisons between regional associations and institution types.

Even so, drawing on data from the *Chronicle* has limitations. Functioning under spatial and editorial restrictions, the *Chronicle* does not fully report accreditation rulings by all of the regional associations. Instead, the SACS generally gathers the most attention regardless of the level of activity displayed by the other regional associations. Furthermore, the articles provided by the *Chronicle* are often abridged either by the institutions listed (not all of those facing accreditation changes), or the descriptions of infractions committed (focus on the penalty rather than how institutions earned punitive outcomes).

Finally and most importantly, a significant limitation to the data is that the *Chronicle* and other media sources, which commonly report on postsecondary schools, continue to function under and help to perpetuate a biased system. This system manifests itself in two important ways. First, most of the stories reported by the media discuss crises and promote a negative view of colleges and universities (Holmes, 1996; Stepp, 2003b; Stewart, 2001). Second, the media continues to function under and feed into public perceptions of HBCUs and other MSIs as poorly administered, academically inferior institutions (Jones, 2004; Stewart, 2001). As a result, the *Chronicle* and mainstream media sources are more likely to report on penalties and other accreditation problems institutions experience than positive or favorable agency reviews.

DATA AND ANALYSIS

The 126 *Chronicle* articles in the data set reported on 284 accreditation decisions and changes made by the six regional associations. The data set includes 143 different institutions, many of which received repeated attention from the *Chronicle* as changes in their accreditation status occurred. Among the regional associations, the decisions of SACS were more often reported than those of other agencies, accounting for 220 (77.46%) of the accreditation decisions and status changes reported between 1996 and May 2005. The regional association with next highest reported level was the WASC, which had 27 (9.51%) accreditation changes during the same period. Among institution types, PWIs received the most attention from the regional associations. More than 60 percent or 173 of the reported accreditation decisions in the data set involved PWIs. The reporting of regional associations also paid disproportionate attention to HBCUs, which received 25.00 percent (71 decisions) of the reported decisions while comprising a much smaller percentage of the total number of American higher education institutions.

REGIONAL ASSOCIATION ASSESSMENTS

In addition to addressing all types of institutions, the report of the regional associations included a range of decisions and sanctions. Listed from the most favorable assessment to the harshest penalty, the spectrum of accreditation decisions reported in the data set collected from the *Chronicle* was as follows:

- *Accredited/Reaffirmed*—earned initial accreditation or had accreditation status renewed for additional period;
- *Reinstated/Regained*—regained full accreditation status after agency removed prior sanction;
- *Notice*—institution's accreditation status in jeopardy, at risk of receiving a sanction;
- *Warning*—failure to comply with policies established by accreditation agency, which often comes with a limited time to address the issues;
- *Probation*—failure to correct or make progress toward correcting compliance problems;
- *Show Cause*—institution required to explain and provide evidence as to why the agency should not revoke accreditation;
- *Lost*—agency revoked accreditation, often the result of long-term noncompliance.

Within the data the SACS issued the highest number of penalties (decisions ranging from *Warning* to *Lost*) at 132 or 60 percent and the highest number of favorable reviews (decisions resulting in outcomes of either *Accredited/Reaffirmed* or *Reinstated/Regained*) at 61 or approximately 28 percent of its actions. While far fewer in number, penalties made up a greater proportion of the reported determinations handed out by the WASC, accounting for approximately 63 percent of all that association's decisions between 1996 and 2005. Conversely, the NEASC reported the smallest number of accreditation changes of which 50 percent (2 institutions) received favorable outcomes, while 25 percent (1 institution) received a negative result.

ASSESSMENT AND INSTITUTIONAL RACIAL IDENTITY

Analysis of regional association decisions according to institution type categorized by student racial population indicates that the *Chronicle* overwhelmingly provides more information on those evaluations that result in an institutional penalty. One hundred and sixty-six (58%) of the decisions reported by the

Chronicle during the research period assessed a negative outcome against an institution. On the other hand, only 79 (28%) of these evaluations produced favorable conclusions for the institutions.

Disaggregating the articles by institution type indicates that colleges and universities, which serve large numbers of minority students tend to be overrepresented among those receiving negative reviews from the regional associations. Although only a small number appear within the overall sample, 75 percent (3 institutions) of Hispanic-Serving Institutions (HSIs) received negative accreditation reviews from a regional association. Similarly, accreditation evaluations for approximately 67 percent of MSIs, 63 percent of HBCUs, and 54 percent of tribal colleges and universities (TCUs) also resulted in penalties. As a group, predominantly Black institutions (PBIs) obtained the lowest percentage of negative results, as only 29 percent of those institutions in the sample garnered penalties.

Even so, student population alone did not improve the reported accreditation outcomes for colleges and universities during the period. Much like the institutions with large numbers of minority students, PWIs also tended to receive more negative rather than positive outcomes from the regional associations, as 57 percent of those decisions led to penalties. However, it is important to note that the SACS issued 59 percent of these reported sanctions. Along the same lines, all of the penalized HBCUs and HSIs fell under the jurisdiction of the SACS. While most PBIs generally received favorable accreditation reviews, half of the reviews handled by the SACS (two reports within the data set) also resulted in penalties for that category of institutions. None of the TCUs in the sample came under the jurisdiction of the SACS. The one MSI examined by the SACS did not receive a penalty from the association.[2]

CAUSES FOR ACTION

As reflected in the *Chronicle,* the activities monitored by the six regional associations fall under four general categories: academic, administrative, financial, and procedural. The *academic* grouping includes issues such as curriculum, graduation requirements, and admissions standards. *Administrative* refers to planning, governance, and leadership matters. Institutional debt, revenues, and endowments fall under the *financial* category. The *procedural* classification covers integrity, methods, and other matters directly related to the accreditation review process. While all six of the regional associations assess institutional quality by focusing on similar characteristics, these accreditors do not evenly evaluate or penalize postsecondary schools. Comparisons of the outcomes from accreditation reviews indicate that institutions sometimes endure harsher criticism and reprimands simply because of their geography and the number of minority students served.

ACADEMIC MATTERS

Of the accreditation reviews reported in the *Chronicle* between 1996 and 2005, academic matters served as the primary focus in 16 (5.6%) of the decisions publicized by the regional associations. Academic issues included too few or unqualified faculty, problematic online programs, inadequate library resources, and poor academics. Although only six of these decisions applied to Minority-Serving Institutions, these institutions received harsher penalties than PWIs. For example, Lenoir-Rhyne College (PWI) received twelve months of probation from the SACS after the review team questioned the communication and writing skills acquired by its students, the support established to maintain the library, and the use of computer labs on that campus. Yet, in another decision from the same association, Odessa College (HSI) received probation for six months because the review committee felt that two of its faculty members were teaching courses for which they were not academically qualified. While the HSI received a less severe penalty than the PWI, SACS applied different standards to these colleges by moving more swiftly in penalizing the MSI. Although the SACS did eventually choose to give Lenoir-Rhyne College a full year of probation, the agency actually identified the infraction committed by that institution three years before the college received any punishment. The MSI, however, received its penalty from the SACS almost immediately after the review committee issued its findings ("Accreditation update," 2005). In doing so, the SACS provided Lenoir-Rhyne College with a special advantage, since its perpetual noncompliance went unpunished for an extended period of time.

ADMINISTRATIVE MATTERS

The regional associations concentrated on administrative problems in 48 (17%) of the accreditation reviews reported in the *Chronicle*. Administrative concerns included outside interference with board authority, leadership controversies, and general conflicts with institutional governing boards. Often faced with meddling tribal leaders, the majority of the assessments conducted at TCUs (54%) fell under this category. The saga of administrative problems at Little Big Horn College (TCU) illustrates the impact strong tribal involvement has on regional accreditation status. A member of the NWCCU, Little Big Horn received a show cause order in 2001 after the board fired the institution's president at the behest of other members of the Crow tribe. The association later downgraded this sanction in June 2001 to one-year probation after the college named an interim president and external tribal members ended their involvement, officially restoring authority to the board (Basinger, 2000; McMurtrie, 2001a).

As part of another ongoing debate and power struggle, the Board of Trustees [Board] at Auburn University (PWI) was repeatedly accused of excessive involvement and interference by its regional association. Even though the conflict began in 1998, the *Chronicle* did not mention until October 2001 when the SACS announced its intention to launch a special review of the Board and the Board accused the association of violating its own accreditation and review policies (Dainow, 2001). Although a court ordered special investigator found no evidence to support the allegations made against the Board, SACS placed Auburn on one-year probation in December 2003 for trustee meddling (Bollag, 2003; Pulley, 2003). Specifically, SACS based its probation sanction on the Board's use of a special athletic committee to micromanage the men's basketball program (Brainard, 2004; Carnevale, 2004). While the faculty members who filed the initial complaint maintain that the Board's activities did not change, SACS did reinstate Auburn to fully accredited status in December 2004 (Bollag, 2004c).

Despite the punishment eventually leveled against Auburn, it does appear that the SACS made some attempt to diminish the conflict by delaying its involvement for three years. However, the regional association neglected to offer this same leniency when faced with a complaint involving Barber-Scotia College (an HBCU). Upon receiving a complaint in January 2004 that accused the college of awarding 28 degrees to students who had some questionable life-experience credits, the SACS completely revoked Barber-Scotia of its accreditation in June (Karlin-Resnick, 2004). To date, Barber-Scotia is operating without the benefit of regional accreditation, the eligibility to distribute federal financial aid, or the support the United Negro College Fund.[3]

The contrasting experiences of Little Big Horn College, Auburn University, and Barber-Scotia College demonstrate that the regional associations do not evaluate administrative matters or sanction institutions similarly. The NWCCU was unduly harsh on Little Big Horn by threatening to punish the institution *before* perceived wrongdoings on the part of the governing board had even taken place (Basinger, 2000). For its part, SACS failed to establish or apply clear policies regarding the amount of time between an institution's infraction and its effect on accreditation status even within its own jurisdiction. As such, the regional associations disadvantage minority-serving postsecondary schools because the likelihood that these institutions will receive a swift penalty only adds to, rather than resolves, the problems that disrupt institutional function. Without a doubt, restricting Barber-Scotia's access to financial resources has only further hindered that college's efforts to address its academic and administrative problems.

FINANCIAL RESOURCES

Budget deficits, high-debt levels, declining revenues, low or no endowment, improper distribution of federal financial aid, unpaid expenses, bounced checks, and bankruptcy are just some of the financial issues that garnered attention from the regional associations between 1996 and 2005. Accounting for 36 percent (101 items) of the overall sample, these financial topics proved to be chief among the stated reasons discussed in *Chronicle* accreditation reports and updates. These problems were reported as affecting a relatively equal number of minority-serving campuses (52 items) and PWIs (49 items), as well as one university that primarily serves nonresident aliens.

Among the regional associations, WASC proved to be the accreditor most interested in financial matters. Finances served as the primary concern in 41 percent of the decisions issued by the WASC. As with the other associations, the WASC did not approach the financial problems at Bethany College of the Assemblies of God (PWI) and D-Q University (TCU) in the same manner.

Bethany College has a tumultuous history, replete with many near accreditation disasters including a show cause order in 1971, warning status in 1979 and 1990, and probation in 1997 with an extension from the WASC in 1999 (McMurtrie, 2001b). Many of these accreditation changes revolved around finances such as Bethany College receiving probation after its debt increased to $10.5 million. Although the institution was still $8.5 million in debt, WASC chose to restore Bethany College to full accreditation status in 2001 under the conditions that the institution increase enrollment, develop a long-term plan, and improve fiscal management to maintain this standing (McMurtrie, 2001a; McMurtrie, 2001b).

Contrary to the patience WASC exhibited in dealing with Bethany College, the regional association was swift and relatively unforgiving in evaluating financial problems at D-Q University. Opened in 1971 as the only tribal college in California, WASC put D-Q University on show cause status during the summer of 2004. This decision came after the Bureau of Indian Affairs cut $277,000 from the University's $1.6 million budget. Unlike the generous time allotted to Bethany College, WASC gave D-Q fewer than six months to develop a plan and balance its budget following this loss ("Accreditation update," 2004). In response to D-Q's inability to satisfy the association within the time provided, WASC chose to rescind institutional accreditation at that university in January 2005, which led to the closure of D-Q University two months later (Read, 2005). Given the final result and impact of its accreditation penalty, D-Q University did not enjoy any of the generosity and patience WASC afforded to Bethany College. Indeed, the leniency received by Bethany College allowed that school to stay open just as the strict reproach directed at D-Q University helped to stimulate the latter school's closure. Essentially, the sanctions applied by WASC contributed as much to each institution's survival as the actual decisions made by individuals on either campus.

Although located in a different part of the country, PWIs and Minority-Serving Institutions under the jurisdiction of SACS experience similar financial assessments and outcomes as those colleges and universities subject to approval by WASC. Much like Bethany College, the SACS placed St. Andrews Presbyterian College (PWI) on probation in 1993 for having a debt in excess of $3 million and declining student enrollment. When the SACS lifted the probation and restored full accreditation in 1997, St. Andrews' debt remained over $3 million, having been only reduced by a total of $300,000 during the institution's four years of probation (Haworth, 1997). Unfortunately, the SACS was not as supportive of Knoxville College (HBCU). In December 1996, after 18 months of probation and amassing a debt of $3.2 million, SACS revoked the accreditation given to Knoxville for the second time in 11 years (Nicklin, 1997). Although Knoxville ended the 1995–1996 fiscal year with a $200,000 surplus, SACS refused to reinstate its accreditation status or apply a less severe penalty (Waller, 1997). Functioning without access to federal student aid or funds from the United Negro College Fund, Knoxville College has explored the possibility of becoming a work-college where students cover their tuition by completing various tasks at the institution. Despite these setbacks, Knoxville College has decreased its debt to $1.5 million (Mercer, 1998a). Even so, SACS still refuses to restore Knoxville to accredited status due to poor finances, improper administrative procedures, and lack of a recovery plan (Mercer, 1998a; Mercer, 1998b). Although Knoxville College remains open, the financial pressure of operating without the ability to award and accept federal student aid continues to influence the financial state of the institution (June, 2002).

Faced with financially troubled colleges and universities, the SACS and the WASC utilized the same basic approach. Both of these regional associations offered lesser sanctions, more time to fix problems, and easier access to redemption to PWIs under financial stress, but offered virtually irrecoverable harm and abandonment to Minority-Serving Institutions. Even though Knoxville College managed to make similar progress in addressing its financial problems in six months, while it took St. Andrews four years to accomplish the same thing, SACS still refused to offer Knoxville a reduced sanction. By refusing to evaluate the financial condition at all institutions similarly, the regional associations have weighted more heavily the accreditation process against minority-serving colleges and universities, denying these schools the reasonable time needed to address their funding concerns.

PROCEDURAL SHORTCOMINGS

Of the six regional associations, the SACS was the only one that chose to censure institutions for missteps in completing the institutional accreditation review process. Involving two postsecondary schools, the *Chronicle* featured six reports of procedural errors that led to sanctions by the southern accreditor. In both cases, the SACS penalized the institutions for failing to complete the accreditation review paperwork according to regulations established by the association. In December 2003, the SACS placed the University of Texas at Arlington on six months probation after that institution neglected to include a copy of its revised mission statement as part of its review submission (Bollag, 2003, Bollag, 2004a). A year later, Edward Waters College completely lost its regional accreditation after the SACS accused the college of breaching the integrity of the process by plagiarizing part of its accreditation report from one drafted by Alabama A and M University (Bollag, 2004b, Bollag, 2005a, Bollag, 2005b, and Bollag, 2005c). While neither institution agreed with the association's decisions, Edward Waters College challenged the SACS by taking the accreditor to court. In its lawsuit filed in March 2005, Edward Waters College alleged that the SACS denied due process to the college and violated accreditation policies established by the association (Bollag, 2005a and Bollag, 2005b). Rather than risk a court order overriding its decision, the SACS chose to settle the case with Edward Waters College by restoring accreditation to the institution in exchange for having the lawsuit dropped (Bollag, 2005d; Field, 2005).

The impact procedural errors had on the accreditation of these institutions clearly indicates the punitive nature of the SACS. Although the accusations brought against these institutions involve important elements of the accreditation review process, the violations themselves did not merit the harsh sanctions imposed upon each school. The denial of accreditation by itself does not help to improve institutional quality, structure, or compliance. Moreover, the successful opposition exhibited by Edward Waters College suggests that the SACS may have to revise its policies in order to provide better due process to institutions facing sanctions (Bollag, 2005d). Nevertheless, the mere fact that Edward Waters College had to go through the courts to regain its institutional accreditation further illustrates the disparate treatment the SACS and the other regional associations afford to postsecondary schools with high concentrations of minority students. For these colleges and universities, accreditation has been and continues to be an uphill battle for respect and recognition as valuable contributors to the higher education landscape. The frequent sanctions levied against Minority-Serving Institutions suggest that the regional associations simply do not value or evaluate postsecondary schools similarly.

IMPLICATIONS AND CONCLUSION

As reported in the *Chronicle,* institutional accreditation decisions are neither consistent nor impartial. To be certain, the regional accreditors repeatedly apply abrasive and severe penalties to institutions even for seemingly minor and easily correctable missteps. Without a doubt, the evaluation process utilized by the regional associations is so unpredictable that institutions experiencing similar compliance problems often receive very different accreditation results even from the same agency during the same time period.

Evidenced by reports published in the *Chronicle,* Minority-Serving Institutions disproportionately experience harsher sanctions from regional associations than other institutions. The inconsistencies perpetrated by the regional accreditation upon these colleges and universities not only punish them for their infractions, but also often jeopardize their ability to function and survive. Indeed, the penalties assessed against postsecondary schools with high concentrations of minority students make compliance matters under each of the four categories more difficult, if not impossible, to address by denying these institutions access to funding and other forms of support required to correct the problems cited by the accreditation agencies. Essentially, denying or withdrawing accreditation from Minority-Serving Institutions helps to exacerbate educational quality and other issues impacting the operation of these schools. At the same time, the frequent publication of negative accreditation reviews also helps to reinforce stereotypes about HBCUs and other MSIs, which generate image problems for all of these colleges and universities regardless of their accreditation status.

Originally scheduled for 2005, many hoped that the Reauthorization of the Higher Education Act of 1965 would lead to some improvements in regional accreditation. However, drafts of the legislation pay very little attention to the disparate treatment suffered by MSIs in the accreditation process. Rather, the proposed bill, H.R. 609, addresses accreditation by giving institutions the right to issue an official statement when an agency denies or revokes its approval, dictates the publication of evaluation team members without revealing which institutions each assessed, and prohibits members from the original evaluation team from serving on appeal panels (Burd, 2005). Even so, these measures do little to improve the accreditation process for MSIs because they make no attempt to address the equity of assessments or outcomes.

Beyond the equity issues that influence the accreditation process, the perspective of accreditation offered in H.R. 609 also fails MSIs and other institutions by neglecting to update its view and definition of accreditation. Despite the legal and political definition, accreditation is no longer a voluntary stamp of educational quality. The structure of federal financial aid and college costs, partially caused by pressure from a variety of sources, including regional accreditors, to expand and improve academic programs, prevents the vast majority of postsecondary schools from operating successfully without institutional accreditation. Likewise, the absence of institutional accreditation also complicates student and faculty recruitment for postsecondary schools as the lack of federal funding and questions of educational quality destroy the image and threaten the missions of unaccredited institutions. Essentially, it is erroneous to define accreditation as voluntary when the absence of these certifications of postsecondary school quality diminishes and even destroys sanctioned institutions.

NOTES

1. Institutions located in Delaware, Maryland, Pennsylvania, and the District of Columbia fall under the MSA, while the NCACS provides accreditation for those in Arkansas, Michigan, Missouri, Ohio, Oklahoma, and West Virginia; see the Higher Learning Commission (2003) and Middle States Commission on Higher Education (2005).

2. As with HBCUs and other MSIs, the SACS also appears to inequitably assess religious institutions, as 62 percent of that association's reviews resulted in penalties for those schools. While media and perceptions do have some influence on this overrepresentation, the SACS evaluations of these institutions pay greater attention to church involvement in academic affairs, thus requiring additional study.

3. As of January 4, 2006, Barber-Scotia was not part of the CHEA database of accredited postsecondary institutions and programs or the Commission on Colleges Database of the SACS Members and Candidates; see the CHEA (2006) and the Commission on Colleges (2005).

REFERENCES

About the chronicle of higher education. (2005). *The Chronicle of Higher Education*. Retrieved June 8, 2005, from http://chronicle.com/help/about.htm

Accreditation update. (2004, September 3). *The Chronicle of Higher Education, 51*(2) [Online]. Retrieved May 13, 2005, from http://chronicle.com/prm/weekly/v51/i02/02a03201.htm

Accreditation update. (2005, February 4). *The Chronicle of Higher Education, 51*(22) [Online]. Retrieved May 13, 2005, from http://chronicle.com/prm/weekly/v51/i22/22a02701.htm

Alstete, J. W. (2004). *Accreditation matters: Achieving academic recognition and renewal.* San Francisco, CA: ASHE-ERIC Higher Education Report, 30(4), Wiley Periodicals, Inc.

Basinger, J. (2000, December 15). Battle at Little Big Horn puts college at risk: Trustees' attempt to oust president threatens institutions accreditation and expansion. *The Chronicle of Higher Education, 47*(16) [On-line]. Retrieved May 13, 2005, from http://chronicle.com/prm/weekly/v47/i16/16a04301.htm

Bemis, J. F. (1983). Regional accreditation. In K. E. Young, C. M. Chambers, and H. R. Kells (Eds.), *Understanding accreditation: Contemporary perspectives on issues and practices in evaluating educational quality* (pp. 167–186). San Francisco, CA: Jossey-Bass Inc., Publishers.

Bollag, B. (2003, December 19). Grambling regains its accreditation; Auburn put on probation for trustee meddling. *The Chronicle of Higher Education, 50*(17) [On-line]. Retrieved May 16, 2005, from http://chronicle.com/prm/weekly/v50/i17/17a02901.htm

Bollag, B. (2004a, January 9). Regional accreditors penalize 13 institutions in New England and the South. *The Chronicle of Higher Education, 50*(18) [On-line]. Retrieved May 13, 2005, from http://chronicle.com/prm/weekly/v50/i18/18a03001.htm

Bollag, B. (2004b, December 9). Edward Waters College loses accreditation following plagiarism scandal. *The Chronicle of Higher Education* [On-line]. Retrieved June 18, 2005, from http://chronicle.com/prm/daily/2004/12/2004120904n.htm

Bollag, B. (2004c, December 17). Accreditor ends Auburn U.'s probation. *The Chronicle of Higher Education, 51*(17) [On-line]. Retrieved May 16, 2005, from http://chronicle.com/prm/weekly/v51/i17/17a03403.htm

Bollag, B. (2005a, March 11). College in Florida sues its accreditor. *The Chronicle of Higher Education, 51*(27) [On-line]. Retrieved May 16, 2005, from http://chronicle.com/prm/weekly/v51/i27/27a03101.htm

Bollag, B. (2005b, April 1). Another college sues southern accreditor. *The Chronicle of Higher Education, 51*(30) [On-line]. Retrieved May 16, 2005, from http://chronicle.com/prm/weekly/v51/i30/30a03903.htm

Bollag, B. (2005c, April 8). Court injunctions against accreditor's decisions arouse fears about the process. *The Chronicle of Higher Education, 51*(31) [On-line]. Retrieved May 13, 2005, from http://chronicle.com/prm/weekly/v51/i31/31a02501.htm

Bollag, B. (2005d, Jul 1). Settlement of college's accreditation lawsuit could spur changes in the process. *The Chronicle of Higher Education, 51*(43) [On-line]. Retrieved July 11, 2005, from http://chronicle.com/prm/weekly/v51/i43/43a02303.htm

Brainard, J. (2004, January 30). Auburn U. Chief resigns; Trustees quickly name one of their own as interim president. *The Chronicle of Higher Education, 50*(21) [On-line]. Retrieved May 16, 2005, from http://chronicle.com/prm/weekly/v50/i21/21a02401.htm

Brown, M. C., II, Donahoo, S., and Bertrand, R. D. (2001, November). The Black college and the quest for educational opportunity. *Urban Education, 36*(5), 553–571.

Burd, S. (2005, July 29). Huge education bill moves closer to passage in U.S. House. *The Chronicle of Higher Education, 51*(47) [On-line]. Retrieved August 2, 2005, from http://chronicle.com/prm/weekly/v51/i47/47a02301.htm

Carnevale, D. (2004, May 21). Auburn U. Trustees punt on athletics. *The Chronicle of Higher Education, 50*(37) [On-line]. Retrieved May 16, 2005, from http://chronicle.com/prm/weekly/v50/i37/37a02901.htm

Clement, R. E. (1966, Autumn). The historical development of higher education for Negro Americans. *The Journal of Negro Education, 35*(4), 299–305.

Commission on Colleges. (2005, July 11). *COC database for all member, candidate, and applicant colleges and universities.* Retrieved July 29, 2005, from http://www.sacscoc.org/search.asp

Council for Higher Education Accreditation. (2006, January 4). *Database of institutions and programs.* Retrieved October 2, 2006, from http://www.chea.org/search/search.asp

Dainow, S. (2001, August 17). Auburn U., facing a review of its actions, sues its accreditor. *The Chronicle of Higher Education, 47*(49) [On-line]. Retrieved May 13, 2005, from http://chronicle.com/prm/weekly/v47/i49/49a02502.htm

Eaton, J. S. (2003, May). *The value of accreditation: Four pivotal roles.* Washington, DC: Council for Higher Education Accreditation.

Field, K. (2005, June 17). Fla. college reaches tentative settlement. *The Chronicle of Higher Education, 51*(41) [On-line]. Retrieved July 11, 2005, from http://chronicle.com/prm/weekly/v51/i41/41a02102.htm

Harcleroad, F. F. (1980). *Accreditation: History, process, and problems.* Washington, DC: ERIC Clearinghouse on Higher Education, The George Washington University and American Association for Higher Education.

Haworth, K. (1997, July 11). Accreditor puts Mobile on probation, takes St. Andrews off. *The Chronicle of Higher Education, 43*(44) [On-line]. Retrieved May 28, 2005, from http://chronicle.com/prm/che-data/articles.dir/art-43.dir/issue-44.dir/44a03102.htm

Higher Education Amendments of 1998, Title I, Pub. L. No. 105–244, § 101, 112 Stat. 1581 (1998).

The Higher Learning Commission. (2003). *About the higher learning commission.* Retrieved June 7, 2005, from http://www.ncahigherlearningcommission.org/commission/

Holmes, B. J. (1996, July 25). The American press: Tainted by arrogance. *Black Issues in Higher Education, 13,* 52.

Jones, B. A. (2004). Toward strategic planning: Issues and status of Black colleges. In M. C. Brown, II, and K. Freeman (Eds.), *Black colleges: New perspectives on policy and practice* (pp. 149–159). Westport, CT: Praeger.

June, A. W. (2002, December 13). Knoxville College skipped payroll. *The Chronicle of Higher Education, 49*(16) [On-line]. Retrieved May 16, 2005, from http://chronicle.com/prm/weekly/v49/i16/16a03402.htm

Kaplin, W. A. (1975). *Respective roles of federal government, state governments, and private accrediting agencies in the governance of postsecondary education.* Washington, DC: Council on Postsecondary Education. (ERIC Document Reproduction Service No. ED 175359).

Karlin-Resnick, J. (2004, July 9). Historically-Black Barber-Scotia College loses its accreditation. *The Chronicle of Higher Education, 50*(44) [On-line]. Retrieved May 16, 2005, from http://chronicle.com/prm/weekly/v50/i44/44a02701.htm

Laden, B. V. (2001). Hispanic-serving institutions: Myths and realities. *Peabody Journal of Education, 76*(1), 73–92.

Lowery, C. (2002, July 5). Life U. loses key accreditation. *The Chronicle of Higher Education, 48*(43) [On-line]. Retrieved May 16, 2005, from http://chronicle.com/prm/weekly/v48/i43/43a02702.htm

McMurtrie, B. (2001a, August 3). Regional accreditors remove 3 colleges from probation. *The Chronicle of Higher Education, 47*(47) [On-line]. Retrieved May 13, 2005, from http://chronicle.com/prm/weekly/v47/i47/47a02902.htm

McMurtrie, B. (2001b, September 28). A college emerges from accrediting limbo: Bethany survived 'tough love' stance from western association, and now has a future.

The Chronicle of Higher Education, 48(5) [On-line]. Retrieved May 24, 2005, from http://chronicle.com/prm/weekly/v48/i05/05a04101.htm

McMurtrie, B. (2003, February 28). Regional accreditors penalize 16 colleges. *The Chronicle of Higher Education, 49*(25) [On-line]. Retrieved May 13, 2005, from http://chronicle.com/prm/weekly/v49/i25/25a03101.htm

Mercer, J. (1998a, June 5). With few students and no accreditation, a small Black college tries to rebound: Knoxville's recovery plans hinge on links to the community and ending its reliance on federal aid. *The Chronicle of Higher Education, 44*(39) [On-line]. Retrieved May 13, 2005, from http://chronicle.com/prm/che-data/articles.dir/art-44.dir/issue-39.dir/39a04401.htm

Mercer, J. (1998b, July 10). Knoxville College loses bid to regain accreditation. *The Chronicle of Higher Education, 44*(44) [On-line]. Retrieved May 13, 2005, from http://chronicle.com/prm/che-data/articles.dir/art-44.dir/issue-44.dir/44a02902.htm

Middle States Commission on Higher Education. (2005). *Institution directory* [On-line]. Retrieved June 7, 2005, from http://www.msche.org/institutions_directory.asp

National Center for Education Statistics. (2004). *The integrated postsecondary education data system (IPEDS) peer analysis system*. Retrieved June 9, 2005, from http://nces.ed.gov/ipedspas/

Nicklin, J. L. (1997, January 24). Accreditor rules on Knoxville and Barber-Scotia Colleges. *The Chronicle of Higher Education, 43*(20) [On-line]. Retrieved May 24, 2005, from http://chronicle.com/prm/che-data/articles.dir/art-43.dir/issue-20.dir/20a02901.htm

Pavel, D. M., Inglebret, E., and Banks, S. R. (2001). Tribal colleges and universities in an era of dynamic development. *Peabody Journal of Education, 76*(1), 50–72.

Pulley, J. L. (2003, January 10). Auburn Board cleared of wrongdoing. *The Chronicle of Higher Education, 49*(18) [On-line]. Retrieved May 16, 2005, from http://chronicle.com/prm/weekly/v49/i18/18a02602.htm

Read, B. (2005, March 4). California's only tribal college shuts its doors. *The Chronicle of Higher Education, 51*(26) [On-line]. Retrieved May 16, 2005, from http://chronicle.com/prm/weekly/v51/i26/26a02602.htm

Rogers, J. (1987/1989). Accreditation: Its national and regional value in 1987. In W. J. Roscoe (Ed.), *Accreditation of historically and predominantly Black colleges and universities* (pp. 1–11). Lanham, MD: NAFEO Research Institute.

Stepp, C. S. (2003a, January/February). Chronicling higher ed. *American Journalism Review, 25*(1), 24–25.

Stepp, C. S. (2003b, January/February). Higher examination. *American Journalism Review, 25*(1), 18–25.

Stewart, D. (2001, August 16). Advice to HBCUs: Use the media to your advantage. *Black Issues in Higher Education, 18*(13), 31.

Thompson, C. H. (1960, Summer). The present status of the Negro private and church-related college. *The Journal of Negro Education, 29*(3), 227–244.

Trenholm, H. C. (1932, Apr.). The accreditation of the Negro high school. *The Journal of Negro Education, 1*(1), 34–43.

Trent, W. J., Jr. (1959, Feb.). Private Negro colleges since the Gaines decision. *Journal of Educational Sociology, 32*(6), 267–274.

Waller, M. (1997, April 25). Knoxville College loses battle to retain its accreditation. *The Chronicle of Higher Education, 43*(33) [On-line]. Retrieved May 28, 2005, from http://chronicle.com/prm/che-data/articles.dir/art-43.dir/issue-33.dir/33a03602.htm

Wright, S. J. (1958, Summer). The future of the Negro private college: Philosophy and program. *The Journal of Negro Education, 27*(3), 406–413.

Young, K. E. (1983). Prologue: The changing scope of accreditation. In K. E. Young, C. M. Chambers, and H. R. Kells (Eds.), *Understanding accreditation: Contemporary perspectives on issues and practices in evaluating educational quality* (pp. 1–15). San Francisco, CA: Jossey-Bass Inc., Publishers.

CONTRIBUTORS

Angela R. Albert has 17 years to her credit in higher education. Currently, she is the Director of Grants Development at Seminole Community College in Sanford, Florida. She received a bachelor's degree from Southern Illinois University, a master's degree from Webster University, St. Louis, Missouri, and a doctoral degree from the University of Central Florida, Orlando, Florida. She is a member of the Florida Association of Women in Education, the American Association for Higher Education, and the National Consortium for Continuous Improvement. In 2001, she was inducted into the Omicron Lambda Chapter of Kappa Delta Pi, the International Honor Society for Education.

Walter R. Allen is a professor of education and the holder of the Allan Murray Carter Chair in Higher Education at the Graduate School of Education and Information Studies at the University of California, Los Angeles. He is also Professor of Sociology at UCLA and co-director of CHOICES, a longitudinal study of college access and attendance among African Americans and Latinos in California. Dr. Allen's research and teaching focus on comparative race, ethnicity and inequality; diversity in higher education; social inequality; and family studies. His degrees in the field of sociology are from Beloit College (B.A., 1971) and the University of Chicago (M.A., 1973; Ph.D., 1975). Dr. Allen has also worked as a consultant to courts, communities, foundations, business and government. Dr. Allen's publications include: *The Color Line and the Quality of Life in America* (1987); *Enacting Diverse Learning Environments: Improving the Climate for Racial/Ethnic Diversity in Higher Education Institutions* (1999); *College in Black and White* (1991); *Black American Families, 1965–84* (1986); *Beginnings: The Social and Affective Development of Black Children* (1985); *Stony the Road: The Black*

Struggle for Higher Education in California (2002); and *African American Education: Race, Community, Inequality and Achievement* (2002).

Andrea L. Beach is an assistant professor in the department of Educational Leadership, Research, and Technology at Western Michigan University, where she teaches in the Higher Education Leadership doctoral program. Her research centers on issues of organizational climate in universities, support of innovation in teaching and learning, and faculty development as an organizational change lever. She is co-author on *Creating the Future of Faculty Development: Learning from the Past, Understanding the Present* and has published on the variation of faculty work, characteristics of the faculty development community, faculty development priorities at historically Black colleges and universities, and faculty learning communities.

Benjamin Baez is associate professor in the Department of Educational Leadership and Policy Studies at Florida International University. His research interests include legal issues in education, diversity in higher education, and privatization of public education. He is the author of *Affirmative Action, Hate Speech, and Tenure: Narratives About Race, Law, and the Academy* (Routledge Falmer, 2002) and "The Study of Diversity: The 'Knowledge of Difference' and the Limits of Science" in the *Journal of Higher Education*.

Estela Mara Bensimon is a professor of higher education in the division of Educational Policy and Administration and director of the Center for Urban Education. She served as associate dean for the Rossier School of Education from 1996–2000. Dr. Bensimon's research interests include academic leadership, organizational change, urban colleges and universities and women and minority faculty in higher education. A sampling of her publications include: with Kelly Ward and Karla Sanders, "Working with Junior Faculty: The Role of Department Chairs" (Anker Publishers, 2000); with Harold O'Neil, Jr., Michael Diamond and Michael Moore, "The Academic Scorecard" (Dec., 1999); With Marta Soto, "Can we rebuild civic life without a multiracial university?" (1997) with William G. Tierney, "Promotion and Tenure: Community and Socialization in Academe" (SUNY Press, 1996); with Anna Neumann and Robert Birnbaum, "Making Sense of Administrative Leadership: The "L" Word in Higher Education" (in ASHE-ERIC High Education Report, 1989). Dr. Bensimon was the editor of "Multicultural Teaching and Learning: Strategies for Organizational Change" (National Center on Postsecondary Teaching, Learning and Assessment, 1994).

Brian K. Bridges is associate director for the Center for Advancement of Racial and Ethnic Equity at the American Council on Education and assistant professorial lecturer of Higher Education Administration at The George Washington University. Dr. Bridges previously served as associate director of the Indiana University Center for Postsecondary Research where he coordinated the Building Engagement and Attainment of Minority Students Project (BEAMS) for the National Survey of Student Engagement (NSSE) and coordinated the annual NSSE survey administration.

John J. Cheslock is an assistant professor in the Center for the Study of Higher Education at the University of Arizona. His research focuses on the economics of higher education with a special interest in tuition and financial aid policy, faculty labor markets, the role of Title IX in intercollegiate athletics, and revenue stratification across institutions. His work has been published in the *American Economic Review*, *Economics of Education Review*, *Journal of Higher Education*, and *Review of Higher Education*.

Frances E. Contreras is an assistant professor at the University of Washington in the College of Education in Leadership and Policy Studies. Dr. Contreras presently researches issues of equity and access for underrepresented students in the education pipeline. She addresses transitions between K–12 and higher education, community college transfer, faculty diversity, affirmative action in higher education, and the role of the public policy arena in higher education access for underserved students of color. Dr. Contreras has conducted research using the College Board data on Latino high achievers in the United States and is currently completing a manuscript with Patricia Gandara entitled, "Understanding the Latino Education Gap: Why Latinos Don't Go to College."

Phyllis Worthy Dawkins is the Director of the Faculty Development Program, the Dean of the College of Professional Studies, and Professor Physical Education at Johnson C. Smith University. She directs a comprehensive campus-based faculty development program around six strands: Learning Communities, Learning Across the Curriculum, Instructional Technology, Pedagogy, New Faculty Orientation and Discussion Series. She is one of the co-directors of the Historically Black Colleges and Universities (HBCU) Faculty Development Network and serves as a faculty development consultant, evaluator and presenter.

Saran Donahoo is an assistant professor in the Department of Educational Administration and Higher Education at Southern Illinois University-Carbondale. She earned both her doctorate in higher education administration and her M.A. in history at the University of Illinois at Urbana-Champaign. She completed her B.A. in secondary education at the University of Arizona. Her research interests include legal issues affecting education, educational policy, international/comparative education, and educational diversity and equity for both K-12 and post-secondary education. Her published works include articles in *Equity & Excellence in Education*, *Urban Education*, and *Education and Urban Society* as well as an array of book chapters.

Noah D. Drezner is a Ph.D. candidate in higher education at the University of Pennsylvania. His research interests include philanthropy and fundraising as it pertains to higher education. Additionally, Drezner's work focuses on the ways in which minority and special serving institutions add to the civic literacy of the nation. Recently, Mr. Drezner published "Advancing Gallaudet: Alumni Support for the Nation's University for the Deaf and Hard-of-Hearing and its Similarities to Black Colleges and Universities" (2005) and "Recessions & Tax-Cuts: The Impact of Economic Cycles on Individual Giving, Philanthropy, and Higher Education" in the *International Journal of Educational Advancement* (2007).

Michelle M. Espino is a doctoral candidate in the Center for the Study of Higher Education at the University of Arizona. She is also a 2007–2008 Ford Foundation Dissertation Fellowship recipient. Her research interests include Latina/o educational pathways, public policy in relation to underrepresented populations and Minority-Serving Institutions, member experiences in culture-based fraternities and sororities, and service-learning. Currently, she is completing her dissertation, which focuses on the educational pathways of Chicana and Chicano scholars.

Stella M. Flores is an assistant professor of Public Policy and Higher Education at Vanderbilt University. Her research focuses on college access policies for Latino and other underrepresented minority students. She is co-author of *Percent Plans in College Admissions: A Comparative Analysis of Three States' Experiences* published in 2003 by The Civil Rights Project at Harvard University, co-editor of *Legacies of Brown: Multiracial Equity in American Education* published in 2004 by the *Harvard Education Review*, and co-editor of *Latino Educational Opportunity* published in 2006 by Jossey Bass.

Marybeth Gasman is an assistant professor of Higher Education at the University of Pennsylvania. Her work explores issues pertaining to the history of philanthropy and historically black colleges, black leadership, contemporary fundraising issues at black colleges, and African-American giving. Dr. Gasman has published several books, including: *Supporting Alma Mater: Successful Strategies for Securing Funds from Black College Alumni* (CASE Books, 2003), which won the

H.S. Warwick Prize for Outstanding Research on Philanthropy in 2004. She also edited *Uplifting a People: African American Philanthropy and Education* (Peter Lang Publishers, 2005), which won the Association of Fundraising Professional's Skytone Ryan Research Prize in 2006. In addition to these works, Dr. Gasman just finished: *Envisioning Black Colleges: A History of the United Negro College Fund* (Johns Hopkins University Press, 2007). Dr. Gasman has published many peer-reviewed articles in journals such as *Teachers College Record*, the *Journal of Higher Education*, the *American Educational Research Journal*, *Educational Researcher*, and the *History of Education Quarterly*. She was awarded the 2006 Promising Scholar/Early Career Award from the Association for the Study of Higher Education (ASHE).

Jessie L. Grant is currently the interim director of campus life at St. Thomas University in Miami Florida. He has held student affairs positions at numerous colleges and universities, and was one the first participants in the Donna M. Bourassa Mid-Level Management Institute sponsored by ACPA. A recent Ph.D. from Western Michigan University, his dissertation was a job satisfaction study of mid-level administrators in student affairs.

Justin P. Guillory is a doctoral candidate pursuing a Ph.D. in higher education Administration. He was raised on the Nez Perce reservation in Lapwai, Idaho. Justin and his wife are proud parents of two young sons. Justin's mixed-blood heritage includes African American, Native American (Nez Perce descendant) and Hispanic ancestry. His previous professional experience includes working as a tribal college administrator for over three years. He is currently in his third year serving as the graduate assistant for the Native American Student Center within the Office of Multicultural Student Services. His research interests include but are not limited to access and equity in higher education, minority student retention and achievement, and community building.

Linda Serra Hagedorn is professor and chair of the Educational Administration and Policy Department at the College of Education at the University of Florida as well as the Director of the Institute of Higher Education. She is the Project Director of the Transfer and Retention of Urban Community College Students Project (TRUCCS) and a partner in Lumina's Achieving the Dream Initiative. Dr. Hagedorn's research focuses on community college issues, college retention of underrepresented student groups, and equity. Her most recent publications include: *An Investigation of Critical Mass: The Role of Latino Representation in the Retention of Urban Community College Students*; and *Transitions within the Community College: Pathways to Access and Inclusion.*

Joan B. Hirt is associate professor of Educational Leadership and Policy Studies at Virginia Tech. Her research focuses on professionalization issues among administrators with particular attention to student affairs administrators. She is author of *Where You Work Matters: Student Affairs Administration at Different Types of Institutions,* and co-author of both *Supervising New Professionals in Student Affairs* and *Learning through Supervised Practice in Student Affairs.* She has an abiding interest in professional issues at minority-serving institutions and her work has appeared in some of the most prestigious refereed sources including the *Journal of College Student Development*, the *NASPA Journal*, and the *Review of Higher Education.*

Steven Hubbard is clinical assistant professor in Administration, Leadership and Technology at New York University. His research focus is in student learning, assessment, faculty development, and research on GLBT college students. He is currently working on several projects on faculty attitudes at minority serving institutions and the development of minority scientists. Before coming to NYU, Hubbard worked for ten years as a student affairs administrator at The University of Iowa and Hamline University. He is coordinator of the Steinhardt master's degree program in higher education, and he earned his Ph.D. in higher education from New York University in 2006.

Philo A. Hutcheson is associate professor of educational policy studies at Georgia State University. His publications include a co-authored article, "National Higher Education Policy Commissions in the Post-World War II Era: Issues of Representation"; *The Sophist's Bane* (Fall 2003); *A Professional Professoriate: Unionization, Bureaucratization, and the AAUP* (Vanderbilt University Press, 2000); and two co-authored chapters, "Re-Considering the Washington-Du Bois Debate: Two Black Colleges in 1910–1911," in *Southern Education in the 20th Century* (1999) and "The Church-Affiliated Two-Year College and Issues of Access," in *Community Colleges for Women and Minorities* (1999). He is currently working on a book on the 1947 President's Commission on Higher Education for publication in 2007.

Jillian Kinzie is associate director of the NSSE Institute for Effective Educational Practice and the Indiana University Center for Postsecondary Research. She earned her Ph.D. in higher education with a minor in Women's Studies at Indiana University Bloomington. Prior to this, she held a visiting faculty appointment in the Higher Education and Student Affairs department at Indiana University, and worked as an administrator in academic and student affairs at Miami University (OH) for several years. She is co-author of *Student Success in College: Creating Conditions that Matter* (Jossey-Bass, 2005); *One Size Does Not Fit All: Traditional and Innovative Models of Student Affairs Practice* (Routledge, 2006).

George D. Kuh is chancellor's professor of higher education at Indiana University Bloomington where he directs the Center for Postsecondary Research, home to the National Survey of Student Engagement (NSSE) and related initiatives. A past president of the Association for the Study of Higher Education (ASHE), Kuh has written extensively about student engagement, assessment, institutional improvement, and college and university cultures and has consulted with more than 175 educational institutions and agencies in the United States and abroad.

Berta Vigil Laden was an associate professor in higher education in the Department of Theory and Policy Studies at the Ontario Institute for Studies in Education of the University of Toronto (OISE/UT) where she also served as the coordinator of the Community College Leadership Doctoral Program. Her research focused on policy issues of access, equity, race, class, and gender, and educational and career transition for underrepresented students and faculty of color. Although her research encompassed higher education issues, her special interests were Latino students and Hispanic-Serving Institutions, comparative research on American and Canadian community colleges, and transfer issues related to college/university collaboration and partnerships.

Thomas F. Nelson Laird is an assistant professor of higher education at Indiana University Bloomington. He also directs the Faculty Survey of Student Engagement, a project run through the Center for Postsecondary Research. Tom received his Ph.D. in higher education from the University of Michigan in 2003. His work focuses on improving teaching and learning at colleges and universities, particularly how to effectively promote learning and development through student experiences with diversity. His research has appeared in publications, including the *Journal of Higher Education*, the *Journal of College Student Development*, *Liberal Education*, and *Research in Higher Education.*

Wynetta Y. Lee is associate vice president for Academic Planning, Research & Graduate Studies at California State University—Monterey Bay. Dr. Lee has extensive experience in program development, implementation and assessment in higher education. Her primary research focuses on educational equity and academic success of micro-student populations in higher education (including minorities, women, academically under prepared students and community college transfer students). Her secondary research interests include impact assessments of higher education policies and programs (e. g., diversity initiatives and curriculum reform).

Lindsey E. Malcom is a Ph.D. candidate in the Rossier School of Education at the University of Southern California. She also serves as a research assistant in the Center for Urban Education. Her research focuses on minority students in science-related fields with an emphasis on the role of community colleges, Hispanic Serving Institutions, and financial aid in providing access to these students.

Deirdre Martinez is director of the Fels Public Policy Internship Program and a lecturer at the University of Pennsylvania. Prior to earning her doctorate with distinction in education policy at the University of Pennsylvania in 2006, she worked as an advocate and policy analyst in the nonprofit sector and served as Legislative Director to Congressman Xavier Becerra (D-CA). Her dissertation, which won the Politics of Education Association's Outstanding Dissertation Award, adapts John Kindgon's multiple streams model to decision-making within interest groups. Dr. Martinez teaches on the policy process, and her manuscript, "Who Speaks for Hispanics: A Profile of National Hispanic Interest Groups" has been accepted for publication by SUNY Press.

Charmaine Jackson Mercer is an analyst in Social Legislation at the Congressional Research Service (CRS). She has worked in the Domestic Social Policy Division of CRS since 2002, focusing on the federal Pell Grant program, the federal student aid need analysis formula and minority-serving institutions of higher education, among other things. Charmaine was also a Presidential Management Intern from 2002–2004. Prior to coming to CRS, she served as the director of the Ronald McNair Scholars Program, one of the federal TRIO programs, at Claremont Graduate University (Claremont) in southern California. Charmaine received her doctorate in political science from Claremont, with a focus on politics and higher education policy. Her dissertation examined the federal government's movement toward electronic delivery of services and the digital divide. She earned her master's degree in political science from Claremont and her bachelor's degree in political science from San Diego State University. Charmaine is also a member of Delta Sigma Theta Sorority, Inc. She enjoys running and is an avid reader of fiction. Charmaine is a native of Pasadena, California and currently resides in Baltimore, MD with her husband.

James T. Minor is assistant professor of higher education in the Department of Educational Administration in the College of Education at Michigan State University (MSU). Prior to joining the MSU faculty he completed a three year post as a research associate at the University of Southern California, in the Center for Higher Education Policy Analysis. Dr. Minor earned his Ph.D. from University of Wisconsin-Madison in the Department of Educational Leadership and Policy Analysis. His research interests include institutional governance and decision-making and higher education policy. His current work involves an examination of selection/appointment processes of public trustees and the relationship to the performance of public higher education systems. He also directs a funded project that examines the contemporary role of public HBCUs.

Otoniel Jiménez Morfín is a Ph.D. Candidate in the department of Educational Policy Studies at the University of Illinois at Urbana-Champaign. His research specialization is on social stratification, program evaluation, social capital, and diversity issues in higher education for African American and Latino students. He is also co-author of "Hiding the Politically Obvious: A Critical Race Theory Preview of Diversity as Racial Neutrality in Higher Education" published in *Educational Policy* in 2006. Otoniel Jiménez Morfín also teaches on social foundations of community colleges and on the educational pipeline for marginalized communities.

Julie S. Park is a Ph.D. student in the Higher Education and Organizational Change division of the UCLA Graduate School of Education and Information Studies. Her research interests include the campus racial climate, spirituality in higher education, and the experiences of Asian American students. She has been the recipient of fellowships from the Spencer Foundation, Harvard Civil Rights Project, Leadership Conference on Civil Rights, U.S. Department of Education, and National Association of Student Personnel Administrators. Before coming to UCLA, she earned B.A. degrees in Sociology, Women Studies, and English at Vanderbilt University.

Athena Perrakis is assistant professor of leadership studies and chair of the higher education program at the University of San Diego. Her current research focuses on senior executive academic administration. She has completed data collection for a regional study of college and university presidents and will begin data collection in spring 2007 for a regional study of provosts and CIOs. She has also written about and researched the history, development, and missions of Hispanic-serving institutions. Her next study on HSIs will explore the satisfaction of senior administrators of color on HSI-designated campuses.

Brooks B. Robinson is a senior professor of economics and management at the Keller Graduate School of Management, Arlington, Virginia. He obtained a bachelor's degree from the University of Wisconsin-Madison, and master's and doctoral degrees from George Mason University, Fairfax, Virginia. Selected articles include: "Disparity in Present Value Net Social Security Wealth" in *Black Scholar* (1994, spring; 19–29); and "Bureaucratic Inefficiency: Failure to Capture the Efficiencies of Outsourcing," in *Public Choice* (2001, Vol. 107, Nos. 3–4; 253–70). A member of the National Center for Public Policy Research's Project 21, he prepares frequent "New Vision Commentaries" for U.S. newspapers.

Stephen L. Rozman is professor of political science and director of the Center for Civic Engagement & Social Responsibility at Tougaloo College. He is also founder and co-director of the HBCU Faculty Development Network, the leading faculty development network for historically black colleges and universities. He has directed many faculty development projects at Tougaloo College and is currently the director of grants related to community-based research and a global issues honors consortium. He is active in building partnerships with community-based organizations to facilitate service-learning and community-based research.

Frances K. Stage is professor of Administration, Leadership, and Technology at New York University and a former Senior Fellow at the National Science Foundation. Her research specialization includes college student learning, especially for math and science courses and student participation in math and science majors. Stage is author or co-author of several books, articles, and chapters focusing on college students and the methods used to study them. She is lead author of the book, *Creating Learning Centered Classrooms: What Does Theory Have to Say?* Stage was awarded the 2006 Research Achievement Award from the Association for the Study of Higher Education (ASHE).

James B. Stedman recently retired from the Congressional Research Service where he was a Specialist in Social Legislation. His areas of responsibility included higher education policy analysis. He has earned a B.A. in history, an M.A. in history, and an M.A.T. in elementary education.

Terrell L. Strayhorn is assistant professor of higher education and special assistant to the provost at The University of Tennessee, Knoxville. His research centers on the experiences of racial/ethnic minorities in higher education with a particular emphasis on disparities in achievement and persistence. He is author of *Frameworks for Assessing Learning and Development Outcomes* and *Money Matters: Financial Aid and Graduate Student Persistence.* He has authored over 30 peer-reviewed journal articles, book chapters and other scholarly works. His work has been accepted for publication in some of the most prestigious refereed journals including the *Journal of Higher Education, Journal of College Student Development,* and the *NASPA Journal.*

Robert T. Teranishi is assistant professor of higher education at New York University and co-director for The National Commission on Asian American and Pacific Islander Research in Education. Teranishi is also a faculty affiliate with The Steinhardt Institute for Higher Education Policy and the Alliance for International Higher Education Policy Studies. His research interests include the study of access, equity, and diversity in higher education.

Caroline Sotello Viernes Turner is a professor in the division of Educational Leadership and Policy Studies at Arizona State University. Her research and teaching interests include access and equity in higher education, faculty development, and organizational change. Her publications include a book entitled *Diversifying the Faculty: A Guidebook for Search Committees* and a co-authored book entitled *Faculty of Color in Academe: Bittersweet Success*. In 2001–2002, she was selected as an American Council on Education Fellow. Professor Turner's present research includes a Spencer Foundation funded study of the faculty search committee process and hiring of faculty of color, a PEW Foundation funded study of Latino faculty in theological education, a Ford Foundation funded study of Diversity in Academe Post-Grutter, and a study of Women of Color Pioneer Presidents in Higher Education. Turner received her doctorate in Administration and Policy Analysis from the Stanford University School of Education.

Kelly Ward is associate professor department of Educational Leadership and Counseling Psychology at the Washington State University. She is interested in faculty issues including integration of teaching, research, and service; work and family concerns for faculty; and new faculty development. Ward is also interested in the service role of higher education including faculty outreach and engagement.

Index